RICHARD G. KRAUS, Ed.D.

Recreation Division
Herbert H. Lehman College
City University of New York
Bronx, New York

BARBARA J. BATES, Ed.D.

Recreation Division
Herbert H. Lehman College
City University of New York
Bronx, New York

RECREATION LEADERSHIP AND SUPERVISION:
Guidelines for Professional Development

W. B. SAUNDERS COMPANY
Philadelphia, London, Toronto

W. B. Saunders Company: West Washington Square
Philadelphia, PA 19105

1 St. Anne's Road
Eastbourne, East Sussex BN21 3UN, England

1 Goldthorne Avenue
Toronto, Ontario M8Z 5T9, Canada

Library of Congress Cataloging in Publication Data

Kraus, Richard G.

Recreation leadership and supervision.

Includes index.

1. Recreation leadership.   I. Bates, Barbara J.,
   joint author.   II. Title.

GV14.5.K69   790'.023   74-12915

ISBN 0-7216-5509-2

Recreation Leadership and Supervision:
Guidelines for Professional Development   ISBN   0-7216-5509-2

Last digit is the print number: 9   8   7   6   5

about the authors

Dr. Barbara Bates has had a number of years of experience as a Recreation Leader and District and Special Services Supervisor for the city of Richmond, California, and as a camping program director for the Girl Scouts. She obtained her master's degree from San Francisco State College, and her doctorate from the University of Oregon. She has been on the faculty of the Department of Recreation and Park Management of the University of Oregon, where she was also Administrative Director of Project Extend-ed, a federally funded research project in therapeutic camping. At present she is in charge of the undergraduate recreation curriculum at Herbert H. Lehman College of the City University of New York.

Dr. Richard Kraus has held positions as a playground specialist and workshop director for the Westchester County, New York, Recreation Commission, and for numerous other public and voluntary agencies. He holds a master's degree and doctorate from Teachers College, Columbia University. He has served as a consultant on programs and personnel for Job Corps, the New York City Parks, Recreation and Cultural Affairs Administration, the Y.W.C.A., and the New York State Department of Social Services. He has carried out several research studies and has written several textbooks on recreation leadership, programming, and administration. At present he is coordinator of the Recreation Division and advisor to the graduate recreation curriculum at Herbert H. Lehman College.

This book has been designed to serve as a basic text in college and university courses in recreation leadership and supervision, and to provide a useful resource for professional workers in this field.

Recreation Leadership and Supervision: Guidelines for Professional Development presents a practical, theoretically sound overview of practices, methods, and the processes of staff development in leisure service. It combines a detailed analysis of the qualities and roles of leaders and supervisors, with descriptions of professional preparation, orientation, in-service training, and the supervision and evaluation of personnel.

How does this book differ from others that have been published in the past on the same subject?

First, it covers the broad range of public, voluntary, therapeutic, commercial, and other types of recreation agencies more thoroughly than previous texts, which have tended to focus on public and voluntary organizations alone. Second, instead of providing descriptions of activities, which are available in many other sources, it offers an analysis of varied leadership functions and methods, including many of the innovative techniques being used today.

Recreation Leadership and Supervision should lend itself to use on a number of levels of professional preparation. In community colleges, emphasis should be given to those chapters providing a general orientation to the field and basic leadership methods. In senior colleges, sections dealing with group dynamics, professional development, and more specialized leadership roles and methods should receive emphasis. In graduate programs, where supervision is a key concern, staff development practices, supervisory principles and methods, problem-solving, and case studies should be stressed. On all levels, both faculty members and students should find the sections on professional preparation and field work and internship helpful.

Several themes of the text should be called to the prospective reader's attention. Throughout, the position is taken that recreation professionals must strive to make recreation a more significant community service by dealing with important social problems and issues. This means that leisure agencies must provide meaningful services for populations of all kinds—the poor, the physically or emotionally disabled, the aging, racial minorities, and girls and women—that have in the past been discriminated against in many programs. In addition, it is essential that such groups be given greater opportunity than in the past for employment and advancement in the recreation field.

At the same time, recreation leaders and supervisors must come to grips frankly with rapidly changing attitudes, patterns of behavior, and life styles in our society as they affect leisure activities participation. They must seek to build a total awareness of the significance of leisure in modern life, and to promote constructive values of participation — particularly in an era in which so many forms of play have been corrupted for commercial gain, and in which passive "spectatoritis" and the exploitation of sport on all levels have become increasingly evident.

Recreation professionals must confront the pressing problems of environmental protection, both in the design of new facilities and programs, and in planning for use of the natural environment. Professionals in park-related activities, in particular, are in a key position to promote fuller community awareness of ecological challenges and workable responses to them, including conservation education and antipollution programs and projects. The continuing energy crisis must be perceived both as a challenge and as an opportunity, in that it emphasizes the need to meet the leisure demands of vast population groups close to home in energy-conserving rather than in wasteful ways.

The nature of employment in recreation and park service has changed markedly and will continue to change. Instead of being simply leaders, supervisors, or administrators, many new professionals are likely to become therapists, researchers, planners, consultants, or community organizers. It seems probable that as we move toward the four-day or three-day work week, the 12-month school year, and similar changes, the very nature of work assignments in recreation will shift markedly. Shared jobs, the greater use of "session" workers, or the use of "flex-time" (in which individual work schedules become highly flexible, in order to meet both job demands and personal inclinations) are some of the probable changes which may be anticipated.

Particularly as young people throughout our society indicate that they find their work boring and monotonous, and as work values in general decline, it will be more and more essential that leisure values be reaffirmed and strengthened. To accomplish this, the range of recreational opportunities made available to all must grow in richness, diversity, and depth. This must be the fundamental goal of all recreation and park professionals, today and tomorrow.

The authors wish to stress that, although they have used the pronoun "he" throughout much of the text to refer to the individual recreation professional, this was simply as a convenience in order to avoid the cumbersome "he or she." Members of both sexes are and should be employed at all levels of recreation service, and the discrimination that has in the past prevented many capable women from reaching the highest administrative positions in this field must be eliminated. The reader should also recognize that the many photographs throughout the text have not been assigned to chapters based on their subject matter. Instead, they have been randomly placed in order to give a diverse picture of the range of recreation leadership and supervisory roles.

The authors acknowledge the assistance of hundreds of fellow educators, professional practitioners, and students. While it is not possible to name all of these individuals in this preface, special thanks are given to the following:

Among the college professors who have contributed to the book, either by providing requested information or through their writings, are: Elliott Avedon, Joseph Bannon, Geoff Godbey, David Gray, Fred Martin, Clair Jean Mundy, James Murphy, John Nesbitt, David Parker, Richard Ramsay, Harve Rawson, Leslie Reid, H. Douglas Sessoms, Thomas Stein, Ed Storey, and Louis Twardzik.

Hundreds of community or agency administrators submitted such materials as departmental brochures, leadership manuals, job descriptions, supervisory guidelines, and photographs. Among these were the following: Gertrude Blanchard, of Richmond, California; Kevin Donnelly, of Walt Disney World; Richard Endres, of Camp Confidence, Brainerd, Minnesota; Joanna Gould, of Alexandria, Virginia; Creighton Hale and James Butler of Little League, Inc.; Richard Jordan, of Boys' Clubs of America; Janet Pomeroy, of the Recreation Center for the Handicapped, San Francisco, California; Richard Stracke, of the Kansas City, Missouri, Veteran's Administration Hospital; and many other professionals in the United States and Canada.

Finally, a considerable number of graduate students — chiefly at Herbert H. Lehman College — contributed materials in the form of case studies or staff development guidelines. These students, most of whom are recreation supervisors or administrators at present, include: Fred Cintron, Thomas De Carlo, Thomas Doherty, Helen Kramer, Frank Magaletta, Bonnie McCarthy, Robert McCullough, Daniel Miller, Gregory Murphy, John Pringle, Jeff Raelson, Georgia Silverstein, Leona Wegert, and Nancy Widrewitz.

To them, and to all others who contributed to the text in one form or another, wholehearted appreciation is expressed.

RICHARD G. KRAUS
BARBARA J. BATES

contents

FOUR — Principles and Problems in Recreation Supervision

one

foundations of
recreation leadership

recreation leadership and supervision: the social context

Who is the Recreation Leader or Supervisor?

He or she may be a program supervisor for an urban park system, a drama specialist in a large recreation center, a physical activities director in a Young Women's Christian Association, a leader in a summer play street operated by the Police Athletic League, or a volunteer worker in a Golden Age center. He may also be a recreation therapist in a psychiatric hospital, a roving worker assigned to youth gangs in a big-city slum, a naturalist for the National Park Service, or any of a thousand other persons.

What is the Background of the Recreation Leader or Supervisor?

He may be a college graduate, with a bachelor's degree in recreation and park leadership or administration. He might also have a degree in physical education, psychology, art or music, with years of professional experience in the recreation field. He might have a doctorate in the psychology of play or the sociology of leisure — or he might be a recreation aide who is planning to attend a local community college as a first step on the work-study career ladder that will lead to full professional status.

What is the Professional Commitment of the Recreation Leader or Supervisor?

He may be an active member of the National Recreation and Park Association or the Canadian Parks and Recreation Association. He reads its professional publications regularly, attends national, state, or provincial conferences, and is active in professional development activities within his department. Or — he may have no idea that such organizations exist. He

3

may work in a private nursing home as an activity aide, and not realize that he, the recreation therapist in a nearby Veterans Administration Hospital, and the superintendent of the town recreation and park department are all part of the same professional movement.

How Does the Recreation Leader or Supervisor View His Job?

He may often be troubled by the lack of public understanding of his work and its purpose. Yet, as he welcomes an elderly couple to his Senior Center and sees them develop new hobbies and make new friends, as he helps the members of a youth gang begin to move into more constructive agency programs, as he plans the construction of a new park, or as he watches people of every age gliding around a skating rink, playing in a community symphony orchestra, or picnicking on a grassy lawn, he has the powerful conviction that the task of recreation leadership and supervision is an important one. It may be demanding and difficult, it may take long hours, and it may mix much frustration with an occasional triumph, but it is a significant and rewarding endeavor!

This, then, is the background of the recreation leader or supervisor in the United States and Canada today. In what social context does this professional person work? Play, once seen as sinful or at best as peripheral to the major purposes of life, has emerged as an important preoccupation of society on every level. Recreation has become a vital concern of government, social agencies, and modern industry. We identify ourselves today through our play. We enrich our personalities, find personal fulfillment, and express our national character and values through sport, outdoor recreation, hobbies, cultural interests, and a host of similar leisure pursuits.

THE MEANING OF RECREATION

The term *recreation* has become increasingly familiar to all in our society. For most of us, it means what we do for fun — our hobbies, amusements, pastimes — the activities that provide pleasure, relaxation, and amusement in our free time.

Recreation: Early Definitions

For centuries, such activities were regarded as significant only because they were thought to "re-create" individuals, restoring their energies and enabling them to take part again in work. They were not seen as having a significant purpose of their own. Thus, the medieval theologian, St.

Thomas Aquinas, wrote in the 13th century:

> Playful actions . . . are not directed to an end; but the pleasure derived from such actions is directed to the recreation and rest of the soul.[1]

In the first professional textbooks on the theory of recreation that appeared in the United States during the 1930's and 1940's, this view of recreation as a form of human activity that had no extrinsic purpose and was engaged in only for its own sake, was reaffirmed. Play and recreation were regarded as activities carried on within free time, voluntarily chosen, pleasurable — and *not* concerned with meeting important personal or social goals.

However, this view of recreation did not last long. As more and more public and voluntary agencies began to sponsor leisure programs, the conviction grew that recreation should be designed to make a significant contribution to society. It should be goal-oriented and should conform to prevailing standards of morality.

Recreation: Contemporary Definitions

A modern definition of recreation, embodying the key elements that are generally accepted by authorities in this field, can be stated as follows: Recreation consists of activities or experiences which are carried on voluntarily in leisure time. They are chosen by the participants, either for pleasure or to satisfy certain personal needs. When provided as part of organized community programs, recreation must be designed to achieve constructive and socially desirable goals.

This definition emphasizes the idea of participation in activity; it stresses the need to provide programs in playgrounds, community centers, parks, and a host of other settings, so people may engage in recreation. A somewhat different view of recreation — not as activity but as an emotional experience or condition — has been proposed by Gray and Greben:

> Recreation is an emotional condition within an individual human being that flows from a feeling of well-being and self-satisfaction. It is characterized by feelings of mastery, achievement, exhilaration, acceptance, success, personal worth, and pleasure. It reinforces a positive self-image. Recreation is a response to aesthetic experience, achievement of personal goals, or positive feedback from others. It is independent of activity, leisure, or social acceptance.[2]

Similarly, Stein suggests that recreation can best be defined as a feeling, a product of human behavior through which man becomes re-created,

---

[1] St. Thomas Aquinas, cited in John W. Churchill: *Recreation: A Conceptual Analysis.* Ann Arbor, Michigan, Doctoral thesis, 1968, p. 14.

[2] David E. Gray and Seymour Greben, "Future Perspectives." In *Parks and Recreation,* July, 1974, p. 49.

refreshed, and renewed. He writes that the activities which yield this effect are as varied as life itself, and he concludes:

> Recreation is, thus, an end product; i.e., what happens to a person as the result of an activity, rather than the activity itself.[3]

Recreation may thus be regarded as an activity, an experience, or an emotional condition brought about in an individual as a result of engaging in leisure pursuits within a certain framework of personal motivation and expectation. It may involve a tremendously broad set of possible interests, that range from sports, hobbies, and social or cultural interests, to mathematical, scientific, or exploratory involvements. It may consist of a superficial, momentary episode, or it may demand a lifetime of serious commitment.

Even the simplest recreation experience may involve a complex set of events. Thus, as casual an activity as a family trip to a baseball game may include: making the decision to go, checking the schedule, getting the family together, driving the car, parking at a distance from the stadium, waiting in line for tickets, climbing to seats, watching the game (being aroused, excited, amused, or irritated, and booing or cheering the outcome), and finally making the trip home, children sunburned and sleepy, or possibly with stomachaches from too many hot dogs. The game might be forgotten almost immediately or, on the other hand, might be remembered for 30 or 40 years in family conversations which begin, "Do you remember the time we all drove to Three Rivers Stadium and saw the Dodgers play? . . ."

Most definitions of recreation view it primarily as a *personal* phenomenon. However, it must also be understood as an important element in our societal life and as a key aspect of our modern economy. For the past several decades, it has been accepted as a significant responsibility of government on all levels in the United States and Canada — similar to such functions as education, law enforcement, sanitation, or welfare services.

Finally, recreation must be perceived as a *movement*. It embraces the interests of hundreds of colleges and universities which provide professional preparation in it, thousands of different government agencies, tens of thousands of voluntary or private organizations, hundreds of thousands of professional workers, millions of volunteers and participants, and, finally, billions of dollars spent each year. It ranges from informal, free, and self-directed activity in the home or neighborhood, to the establishment of multimillion dollar business enterprises like Disneyland, or huge municipal stadiums. It may involve a single person playing a game of solitaire, or millions of families, swarming like lemmings, traveling the highways each summer in search of vacation play.

---

[3] Thomas A. Stein: *Some Affective Outcomes Accompanying a Camping Experience of Physically Handicapped Adults.* Madison, Wisconsin, University of Wisconsin, Unpublished Doctoral Thesis, 1962, p. 11.

GROWTH OF ORGANIZED RECREATION SERVICE

In its varied forms, recreation has become a major aspect of modern life. Beginning with the establishment of a few playgrounds for young children in large cities, it has expanded rapidly as a form of governmental service. In the United States, this growth was most dramatic during the middle decades of the 20th century.

Government Recreation Agencies

During the 20-year period between 1946 and 1966, the total number of community recreation and park departments in cities and counties throughout the United States almost doubled, from 1,743 to 3,142. The number of full- and part-time paid leaders more than doubled, from 41,149 to 119,515. In 1950, city and county recreation agencies reported 17,142 recreation and park areas, with a total of 644,067 acres. By 1966, the number of areas was reported to have increased to 50,509, and the acreage more than doubled, to 1,496,378 acres.

An example of the growth of municipal spending on recreation and parks in the United States during the decade of the 1960's may be found in Table 1–1. Even allowing for an inflationary trend during this period, it gives dramatic evidence of sharply increased governmental support.

Recreation and park services offered by other governmental agencies in the United States also expanded rapidly during this period. During the late 1960's alone, state park and recreation spending rose from $279.3 million to $386.8 million per year, with attendance growing from 391 million to 482.4 million visitors to state sites per year.

Similarly, in Canada, there has been a major expansion of recreation

TABLE 1–1   Per Capita Operating Expenses for Recreation and Parks in Eleven Cities, 1960–1970*

City	1960	1965	1970
New York	$4.22	$6.48	$6.92
Chicago	7.57	8.97	13.79
Los Angeles	4.78	5.67	8.72
San Antonio	1.72	2.56	4.98
St. Louis	4.82	5.57	8.44
Atlanta	3.67	4.76	9.85
Minneapolis	7.14	6.17	14.70
Nashville	5.09	4.50	5.95
Oakland	8.59	9.87	16.73
Dayton	5.70	7.15	12.73
Peoria	8.63	10.63	17.78
11-city average	5.63	6.58	10.96

* From National Recreation and Park Association Department of Research, 1971.

TABLE 1-2   Annual Expenditures for Recreation and Parks in Vancouver, Canada, 1962-1972*

Area of Spending	1962	1972
Maintenance and operation of parks, including supervision of playgrounds, community centers, and beaches.	$1,976,250	$3,825,450
Income operations, including boat rentals, indoor pools, rinks, refreshment booths, etc.	1,136,450	2,205,250
City-wide capital funds for purchasing and developing parks and recreation facilities.	941,236	2,801,600
Yearly cost of community centers and recreation projects per resident.	45¢	$1.83

* From 1972 Annual Report, Vancouver Department of Parks and Public Recreation.

and park programs offered by local municipalities, provincial authorities, and the national government. In 1970 alone, four new Canadian national parks were established, bringing to 24 the total number of parks stretching from Newfoundland to Vancouver Island. In addition, hundreds of new historic parks or designated sites have been established by the Canadian government in recent years, accompanying a boom of interest in outdoor recreation and vacation travel. The increased support of municipal recreation and parks in Canada is illustrated in Table 1-2, which shows expenditure growth in a single city.

In a variety of other ways, organized recreation service has expanded. Throughout the United States and Canada, thousands of voluntary agencies—such as the Boy and Girl Scouts, Campfire Girls, Boys' Clubs, Police Athletic League, Young Men's and Young Women's Christian Associations, Young Men's and Young Women's Hebrew Associations, Catholic Youth Organization, and many others—provide social, cultural, and recreational programs. Hundreds of school systems offer recreation, and it has become an increasing trend for two- and four-year colleges to provide evening session programs of continuing education for adults, often on a nondegree basis, that meet their needs for creative leisure involvement and personal enrichment.

Commercial Recreation Programs

Commercial recreation of every type has rapidly become one of America's largest and most successful businesses. Leading economic analysts have estimated that between $150 and $200 billion per year is spent in the United States on all forms of recreation. According to *U.S. News and World Report:*

The money Americans are now spending on spare-time activities exceeds national-defense funds. It is more than the outlay for construction of new homes. It surpasses the total of corporate profits. It is far larger than the aggregate income of this country's exports. And estimates are that the dollar value of leisure-time expenditures will more than double during the decade of the 1970's.[4]

Similarly, the Economic Council of Canada estimated, in its Sixth Annual Review, that expenditures on recreation "durables" (such products as radios, television sets, record players, sports and camping equipment, pleasure boats, cameras, and craft equipment) would increase from $32 per capita in 1967, to $50 per capita in 1975, stated in constant dollar terms.

Therapeutic Recreation Service

Another area of rapid growth in the field of recreation has been therapeutic recreation service — the provision of special programs for those with disability, either to promote the rehabilitative process or to enrich their leisure lives and help them become more fully integrated into community life. Such programs, designed to assist the mentally retarded, physically disabled, mentally ill, or the dependent aging person, have been established in thousands of institutions and community agencies throughout the United States and Canada. In a 1971 study of large metropolitan regions throughout the United States, Berryman, Logan, and Lander found that an extremely high percentage of organizations of various types offered recreation programs for disabled children and youth (Table 1–3).

TABLE 1–3   Agencies Providing Recreation for Disabled Children and Youth*

Types of Agencies	Percentage Providing Service
Commercial and proprietary businesses	81
Churches, libraries and museums	82
County and municipal recreation and park departments	94
Fraternal, service, and miscellaneous organizations	87
Hospitals and residential schools	100
Private and parochial school districts	96
U.S. Department of Agriculture, County Extension Service and 4-H Clubs	92

* From Berryman, Logan, and Lander: *Enhancement of Recreation Service to Disabled Children.* New York, New York University School of Education, Report of Children's Bureau Project, 1971, p. 6.

These examples demonstrate the rapid growth of organized recreation programs which are now sponsored by government, voluntary, commercial, therapeutic, and other types of agencies throughout the United States and Canada.

[4] "Leisure Boom: Biggest Ever and Still Growing." *U.S. News and World Report,* April 17, 1972, p. 42.

With social scientists predicting the continued expansion of leisure, it seems inescapable that recreation will continue to be an ever more important aspect of American life. As workers become increasingly bored with stereotyped and regimented jobs in industry, or as we move to new, postindustrial patterns of employment, it is also probable that we will seek more and more creative outlets and satisfactions in our leisure that are not available in our occupations.

Within this total framework, the role of professional leadership is of crucial importance. Only if the personnel employed in a given field — those who provide its programs, determine its policies, and plan and maintain its facilities — are highly capable both in the direct performance of their duties, and in interpreting them to the public, can the field expect to flourish. Thus, this text focuses on recreation leadership and supervision as a key aspect in the development of leisure-time activity delivery systems.

THE MEANING OF LEADERSHIP

Leadership: Definitions

The term *leadership* is familiar to most people. One tends to think of a leader as a person who possesses certain qualities: a man or woman who is forceful and has confidence, good ideas, and an aura of authority; a person whom others are willing to trust and follow. However, leadership has been defined more precisely by authorities in the fields of group dynamics, social psychology, business, and public administration.

A typical dictionary definition of the term *leader* is:

> One who or that which leads; as: (1) A person or animal that goes before to guide or show the way, or one who precedes or directs in some action, opinion or movement; esp.: (a) A guide; conductor. (b) One having authority to precede and direct . . .[5]

This definition suggests that leaders guide, direct, or even command. However, the contemporary literature in this field stresses the role of the leader as a persuader or enabler, rather than as a director. Davis describes leadership as:

> . . . the ability to persuade others to seek defined objectives enthusiastically. It is the human factor which binds a group together and motivates it toward goals.[6]

Pfiffner and Presthus assert that leadership is

> the art of coordinating and motivating individuals and groups to achieve desired ends.[7]

---

[5] Webster's New International Dictionary. Cambridge, Massachusetts, G. and C. Merriam Co., 1954.

[6] Keith Davis: *Human Relations at Work*. New York, McGraw-Hill Book Co., 1967, pp. 96–97.

[7] John M. Pfiffner and Robert V. Presthus: *Public Administration*. New York, Ronald Press, 1968, p. 92.

Slavson describes it as involving: (a) the ability to understand and to respond to the desires and needs of a group; (b) the capacity to help the group express these desires constructively and progressively; and (c) the power to focus the attention of a group upon one's self.[8] Tannenbaum and Massarik describe leadership as:

> . . . interpersonal influence . . . directed through the communication process, toward the attainment of a specified goal or goals.[9]

Recognizing that leadership has been defined in a wide variety of ways, how should it be regarded in the field of recreation?

Within the field of recreation service, leaders operate in a variety of group relationships. In some cases, they work with highly structured and stable clubs and groups. In others, they may supervise programs in which large numbers of individuals take part without developing group ties or continuing affiliations. Leaders may be responsible for organizing playground programs, sports leagues and tournaments, and classes in the performing arts, or they may supervise pool complexes or sportsman's centers and the like, working with single individuals or with hundreds or thousands of participants. Therefore, depending on the circumstances, their functions may vary widely.

Another important factor influencing the nature of recreation leadership involves the level of employment. Four such levels are as follows:

DIRECT PROGRAM LEADERSHIP.   Here, individuals are directly involved in the face-to-face leadership of groups of participants in recreation activities or programs.

TEAM LEADERSHIP.   Here, the leader is part of a team of other recreation workers on the same level; he must cooperate with them in shared professional assignments.

SUPERVISORY LEADERSHIP.   On this level, the leader is in charge of a number of subordinate workers, and it is his responsibility to supervise them in their varied professional tasks.

ADMINISTRATIVE LEADERSHIP.   Here, the individual must oversee, direct, and mobilize the efforts of an entire staff; he must also work cooperatively with other agency or department administrators and provide general direction for his program within the community.

This text is primarily concerned with the first and third levels of leadership just described: *direct program leadership* and *supervisory leadership*. In examining the nature of leadership in recreation service, it will be helpful first to define it, and next to identify its roles and functions.

Recreation Leadership Defined

Within this text, recreation leadership is defined as: *the process of working effectively with groups of participants or co-workers, in order to encourage,*

---

[8] S. R. Slavson: *Creative Group Education.* New York, Association Press, 1948, p. 24.

[9] Robert Tannenbaum and Fred Massarik: "Leadership: A Frame of Reference." *Management Science,* October, 1957, p. 3.

mobilize, and direct their fullest efforts in carrying on successful recreation programs. It must be emphasized that successful leadership involves a relationship both with participants and with other professionals in a team effort.

In the concluding section of this chapter, recreation leadership is examined as: (a) a formal professional role; (b) a set of functions or tasks; (c) a set of behaviors which come into play during the performance of assigned functions; and (d) a group of personal qualities which make for success in leadership roles.

RECREATION LEADERSHIP: ROLES, FUNCTIONS, BEHAVIORS, AND QUALITIES

Just as those who work in education in a direct service role are called "teachers," or those who provide medical service are called "doctors" or "nurses," those who lead and direct recreation activities are usually called "leaders."

Recreation Leadership as a Professional Role

Typically, the title of "leader" is applied to individuals who are responsible for conducting activities in playgrounds, parks, community centers, or similar recreation settings. The majority of Civil Service classification systems refer to the line job of providing face-to-face recreation programs as the "leadership" level. Positions include such titles as: *Recreation Leader, Assistant Recreation Leader,* or *Senior Recreation Leader.* Sometimes levels of seniority or responsibility are designated by titles such as *Leader I, Leader II,* and *Leader III.* In some departments, leaders may be designated as *Recreation Group Worker,* or *Recreation Director,* but such titles are in the minority. In other settings devoted to rehabilitation, the title *Recreation Therapist* or *Activities Therapist* is likely to be used.

Recreation Leadership as a Set of Functions or Tasks

A second way of perceiving recreation leadership is as a set of job responsibilities. For example, a playground leader might have such functions as: (a) planning a daily and weekly program schedule; (b) directing games of low organization, sports, arts and crafts, or music activity; (c) ordering and maintaining needed equipment and supplies; and (d) controlling the behavior of children on the playground and maintaining effective safety standards. Similarly, a recreation therapist in a psychiatric hospital might be expected to: (a) develop program activities for patients; (b) work closely with doctors, nurses, and other adjunctive therapists; (c) counsel patients

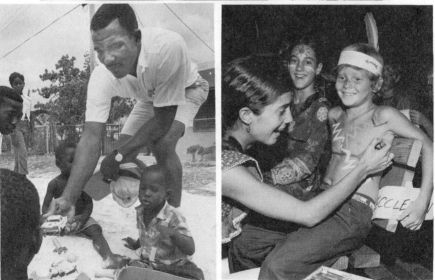

Playground Activities. Recreation leaders play many roles. Austin, Texas, leaders teach children to bake cookies (*A*) and take part in informal dramatics (*B*). A Hollywood, Florida, leader helps children engage in creative sandbox play (*C*), while an Orlando, Florida, youngster has his chest painted—"Indian-style" (*D*).

on their leisure needs and interests; (d) supervise volunteer workers in his department; (e) keep clinical notes on the progress of various patients; and (f) take part in regular team evaluation meetings which review individual patients.

Such functions and tasks comprise the act of leadership within any specific area of recreation service. Technical competence in carrying them out is essential for the effective leader.

Recreation Leadership as a Set of Interpersonal Behaviors

Obviously, the leader's behavioral style may contribute to, or detract from, his effectiveness in carrying out the functions that have just been described. How *do* leaders behave, in order to achieve successful programs? Certain behavioral approaches can be identified that may be clearly linked to successful performance with participants or co-workers.

For example, a recreation supervisor, in addition to such *technical* acts as filling out reports, preparing schedules, or assigning personnel to job stations, must also engage in a set of *interpersonal* behaviors. These will involve such interactions as communicating, assisting, rebuking, clarifying, giving support, praising, criticizing, guiding, inspiring, or motivating group members. Such behaviors should be as positive, constructive, and consistent as possible.

In general, "democratic" leadership behavior is believed to be more effective than "autocratic" or "laissez-faire" leadership, based on findings of research studies which are described in Chapter Three. Similarly, "participative" supervisors, who display consideration for the attitudes, feelings, and needs of those working under their direction, and who strive to improve their sense of autonomy and responsibility and strengthen their degree of motivation, are believed to be more successful than other types of supervisors.

Recreation Leadership as a Set of Personal Qualities

Finally, successful recreation leadership may be conceived of in terms of the specific personal qualities of the leader. The professional literature and leadership manuals published by municipal departments or voluntary agencies identify the following personal qualities or abilities as essential to high-level leadership performance.

The successful recreation leader should have:

1. A basic conviction that all human beings have worth and dignity, and a determination to help them improve the quality of their lives.

2. A strong belief in the importance of leisure in modern life, and in

the contribution to be made by recreation both as a personal experience and as a form of social service.

3. The ability to work effectively with others, drawing forth their best efforts as a catalyst or enabler, rather than as an authoritarian director.

4. The ability to think clearly and logically, to understand and analyze problem situations, and to arrive at intelligent conclusions.

5. Skill in communicating effectively with others, both verbally and in written form.

6. Such personal qualities as warmth, patience, empathy for the needs and feelings of others, and a sense of humor—all of which contribute to the ability to get along well with others.

7. A sound knowledge of human nature, both in an abstract sense (understanding individual or group psychology as described in the theoretical literature), and in terms of having a practical understanding of human behavior.

8. Good judgment, a strong sense of personal responsibility, and high moral standards in all areas of human relationships.

9. Specific knowledge of and interest in the field of recreation, including personal enthusiasm for varied forms of personal participation, as well as having leadership skills in some areas of activity.

10. Awareness of the community and the varied factions that comprise it, as well as awareness of the interplay of different organizations, agencies, and social groups in community life.

11. Emotional and psychological maturity. The successful leader should understand himself and others, should be as free from irrational prejudice as possible, and should be able to manage disagreement or opposition constructively.

12. A high level of motivation, and the ability to work hard; personal ambition, initiative, energy, confidence, and "stick-to-it-iveness."

13. The quality of being a "self-starter"—being able to clearly identify goals and move forcefully and directly toward them.

14. The ability to learn from defeats or mistakes, not rationalizing them, but facing them squarely and turning them into positive assets.

15. Integrity, honesty, and loyalty to the organization one works for, and to its goals and philosophy.

16. The capacity for making difficult decisions and then standing by them, without stalling or equivocating.

17. The ability to be both visionary and practical; having high ideals and visions of what might be possible in the future, and at the same time maintaining a realistic sense of practical problems that must be overcome in the present.

18. Flexibility, in the sense that the individual is ready to grow and change over a period of time, rather than cling to outmoded views or professional attitudes.

19. A point of view that sees cooperation, rather than competition and jealousy as a way of life.

20. The ability to trust others, and to delegate power and responsibility to them.

These qualities would obviously be important to anyone seeking advancement in any field of professional endeavor which involves working closely with other human beings. For the professional recreation leader or supervisor they are essential. They must be coupled, however, with a clear understanding of the goals and philosophy of the recreation field and with effective principles of recreation leadership, topics which are explored at length in Chapter Two.

Suggested Examination Questions or Topics for Student Reports

1. Summarize and compare the traditional and contemporary definitions of recreation which are presented in this text. Develop and justify your own definition of recreation.

2. What evidence is cited in the text to show the growth and acceptance of recreation as an important public concern and area of governmental responsibility? What evidence can be cited to show that it is not yet fully accepted and supported?

3. What are the implications of viewing recreation in terms of its emotional impact on the participant rather than as activity or experience (see Gray, Greben, and Stein statements)? What are the implications of this approach for recreation leaders?

4. Define leadership as a concept, and show how recreation leadership may be regarded as a role, set of functions, set of behaviors, or set of personal qualities.

Suggested Action Assignments for Students

1. Using interviews or questionnaires, survey a group of participants in a recreation program as to their understanding of the term "recreation," or their motives for participating.

2. Do a study of leadership in action—either of yourself or another leader—and identify and tally the functions and behaviors observed.

principles of recreation leadership

Any attempt to develop a meaningful set of principles of recreation leadership in American society must be based on an understanding of the role of the recreation movement, both past and present, the meaning of play and recreation in human life, and the specific philosophy and goals of recreation service in communities or in voluntary organizations.

THE RECREATION MOVEMENT: HISTORICAL PERSPECTIVES

The organized recreation movement had many roots in the 19th century. These included the development of state, federal, and city parks, the establishment of settlement houses and other youth-serving organizations, and the growth of public interest in sports and other recreational pastimes. However, the most important of these roots was the establishment of playgrounds for children in crowded city slums. This was carried out by groups of public spirited citizens before it became the responsibility of public school systems or municipal government.

The purpose of these early playgrounds was to provide safe, healthy, supervised settings in which children of poor families might play. It was recognized that the teeming city streets offered few constructive opportunities—but many dangerous or antisocial ones—for play. Too often children were tempted into gambling, drinking, theft, vice, or other delinquent pastimes. Thus, recreation was thought of primarily as a social service geared to protect both children and the community around them.

Playground leaders stressed the positive values of constructive play. Carefully organized and directed programs were seen not only as a means of preventing juvenile delinquency but also as a way of exposing young children—many of them from newly arrived immigrant families—to desirable social values by supplementing their education, providing cultural opportunities, and by teaching skills throughout life. In addition, many

17

voluntary youth-serving agencies which were established in the late 1800's and early 1900's, such as the Boy Scouts or Girl Scouts, the Y.M.C.A. and the Y.W.C.A., or the Boys' Clubs, had similar objectives. They were considered to be "character-building" agencies which taught respect for law and patriotic and religious values considered to be part of the American "way of life."

This, then, was the traditional heritage of the recreation movement. However, during the early and middle decades of the 20th century, its scope broadened markedly in both the United States and Canada. Instead of being primarily for the children of the poor, recreational programs were extended to meet the needs of all age groups and social classes. The merger of recreation and park departments marked the beginning of growing networks of athletic facilities, such as golf courses, tennis courts, skating rinks, swimming pools, and other elaborate and attractive facilities, which appealed to the middle and upper classes. Gradually, as many municipal recreation agencies shifted their efforts in this direction, they began to charge substantial fees for the use of public recreation and park facilities and programs. Typically, many provided public marinas, sportsman's centers, performing arts programs, or even country club facilities that were used only by the wealthier segments of the community. As this trend continued, in many communities the facilities and programs provided for poorer residents tended to deteriorate or to provide only minimal services.

In the mid 1960's, a new emphasis was given to programs designed specifically to meet the needs of the disadvantaged. With substantial help provided by the federal government in the United States, antipoverty agencies developed exciting new programs in urban ghettoes, many of them linking recreation with other vital social services and providing cultural and educational enrichment as well as job opportunities for teenagers and young adults. New emphasis was given to involving neighborhood residents in planning to meet local recreation and park needs through local councils, task forces, or specially funded organizations. As a consequence, in many urban recreation and park departments today, there are essentially two distinct kinds of goals.

First, there are goals which emphasize the value of recreation in meeting general personal and community needs for healthy and constructive leisure activities that provide enjoyment—without other social purposes or outcomes.

Second, there is the view of recreation as a form of social service geared specifically to meeting the needs of the socially or economically disadvantaged or to providing rehabilitation for the physically and mentally disabled. The goals of recreation, when seen in this light, would clearly be to overcome social pathology, to provide cultural and educational enrichment, serve as a vehicle for counseling and employment of youth, or to help integrate discharged mental patients or physically handicapped persons into community life.

During the past several years, there has been disagreement among many recreation professionals as to whether the essential purpose of this field is to provide pleasure and personal enrichment or significant social services. Some have warned that to give recreation the task of attempting to overcome all the social evils in our society makes it a "welfare" operation, and that this is a burden it should not attempt to take on. Others argue that the problems of modern urban life are such that recreation cannot possibly function effectively, unless it deals with social issues and attempts to meet head-on the critical problems of our communities.

The authors of this text believe that recreation and park professionals must work toward goals that encompass *both* viewpoints. This can best be done if they are buttressed by a sound philosophy of government responsibility for recreation and park services, and a full awareness of the meaning of play in human life.

Government's Role in Recreation

Throughout the world, all industrialized and urbanized nations have accepted the principle that government has an important responsibility for providing or assisting recreation programs to meet the leisure needs of its citizenry. However, the way this is done may vary widely according to each nation's values and political system.

For example, in the Soviet Union leisure was at first valued chiefly as a means of restoring workers to full energy and efficiency. During the Stakhanovite years, in which every effort was made to increase industrial and agricultural output, many workers were sent on subsidized leaves to special vacation resorts where they were encouraged to do little but rest, in order that they could return to their lathes and tractors with renewed vigor. Gradually, Soviet authorities came to recognize the potential of recreation for morale-building and youth indoctrination. Like Fascist Italy and Nazi Germany, they established a wide network of youth organizations that promoted unquestioning patriotism through the medium of clubs, cultural activities, games, and outdoor recreation. Since the 1950's, the Soviet Union has poured its energies into promoting national strength, morale, and prestige through the medium of competitive sports.

In the United States, we have had a much less structured and controlled view of leisure. We have accepted the view that government has a responsibility to meet the significant social needs of all citizens in areas in which they cannot provide adequately for themselves. However, we tend to distrust the power of the federal government, and to assign the actual responsibility for organizing and supporting leisure programs to municipal governments or voluntary agencies. Similarly, in Canada the primary responsibility for developing or assisting recreation services is found on the provincial or municipal level, although departments of education also play an important role. In neither the United States nor Canada does the government attempt to control the uses of leisure, or to use recreation as a medium for social control or indoctrination.

A

B

C

Sports Leadership. Sports for all age groups are a major leadership concern in community recreation. Montreal, Canada, leaders organize a track meet for girls (*A*), while Hollywood, Florida, leaders do the same for younger boys (*B*). Canoe racing is an exciting event in Ft. Lauderdale, Florida (*C*). Tennis is a popular activity in Washington, D.C. (*D*), and a guest instructor teaches judo in Hollywood, Florida (*E*).

D

E

Significance of Play

A second crucial area of understanding has to do with the meaning of *play* itself. Too often, this term is poorly understood or demeaned. It suffers in part from the historical effect of the work ethic, which glorified work and condemned play as either sinful or a waste of time. During the period of colonial settlement in America, religious and civil authorities condemned play and severely punished those who were found gambling, playing sports, dancing, or engaging in similar pursuits.

Even today, although we spend billions of dollars a year on recreation, and although condemnation of play has subsided, we tend still to think of it as a trivial or childish aspect of human life. Often the recreation student or beginning recreation worker finds that his friends and family have little understanding of his professional commitment. Recreation and park budgets tend to be placed at the bottom of the fiscal totem pole in a period of financial crisis, and medical and nursing staffs in hospitals too often fail to understand and support recreation as an important medium of rehabilitation.

Such attitudes stem from a lack of understanding of the value of play in human life. It is essential, in coming to grips with the task of the recreation leader and in developing principles of recreation leadership, that we examine past attempts to define the role of play.

THEORIES OF PLAY. During the 19th century, in both Europe and America, a number of major theories of play were developed. These included: (a) the *surplus-energy* theory, which saw play as essentially purposeless and motivated by the need to burn up excess energy; (b) the *recreation* theory, which held that play served chiefly as a means of conserving or restoring energy after a period of work; (c) the *instinct-practice* theory, which argued that play was intended to help the young of the species (both human and animal) practice the skills that would be needed in adult life; (d) the *catharsis* theory, which regarded play as a safety-valve for the release of bottled-up emotions or drives; (e) the *recapitulation* theory, which theorized that play represented a re-living of the past eras of man's existence; and (f) the *relaxation* theory, which saw play as an essential in restoring balance and emotional well-being after the stress and tension of modern life.

While none of these theories provides a total explanation for human play, each of them has some meaning and helps us understand the function of play in our lives today. More recent writers have presented somewhat more plausible or contemporary theories of play. For example, Bowen and Mitchell, in one of the pioneering recreation textbooks, offered a *self-expression* theory, which held that play was caused by man's natural urge for self-expression, and his need to fulfill such basic drives as the urge for acceptance by others, a sense of accomplishment, aesthetic urges, and the like.[1]

---

[1] The original source of this theory was W. P. Bowen and Elmer D. Mitchell: *The Theory of Organized Play.* New York, A. S. Barnes, 1923. Now see Allen V. Sapora and Elmer D. Mitchell: *The Theory of Play and Recreation.* New York, Ronald Press, 1961.

A Dutch historian of culture, Huizinga, defined play as "voluntary activity which takes place within fixed limits of time and place according to rules freely accepted but absolutely binding, having its aim in itself, and accompanied by a feeling of tension, joy, and the consciousness that it is different from ordinary life."[2] Huizinga's unique contribution was to portray play as a fundamental human drive influencing many social institutions, such as religion, the practice of law, or even warfare.

Contemporary investigators have suggested two additional theories of play, the *competence-effectance* and *stimulus-arousal* approaches. The first of these argues that play is motivated by a need to produce effects on the environment—both physical and social—and to test one's competence in handling challenges or meeting competition successfully. The stimulus-arousal theory represents a sharp break from the traditional view that organisms generally seek to *reduce* the level of stimulation created by such survival-related needs as hunger, thirst, or danger. The basic argument of the arousal theory is that play results from the need to generate interactions with the environment that *increase* stimulation. Simply stated, it suggests that people constantly seek excitement, discovery, challenge, or new experience, and that this general drive accounts for much exploratory play behavior.[3]

Whatever theory of play one accepts, it is obvious that experts in developmental psychology regard play as a vital aspect of human development. Two leading psychologists of the 1940's and 1950's, Gesell and Ilg, wrote, "Deeply absorbing play seems to be essential for full mental growth. Children who are capable of such intense play are most likely to give a good account of themselves when they grow up."[4] Frank writes:

> Play, as we are beginning to understand, is the way the child learns what no one can teach him. It is the way he explores and orients himself to the actual world of space and time, of things, animals, structures and people. . . .
>
> Through play the child practices and rehearses endlessly the complicated and subtle patterns of human living and communication which he must master if he is to become a participating adult in our social life.[5]

Play provides a means through which children explore their environment, develop manipulative skills, establish social relationships, express themselves creatively, and gain a sense of security. Edward Zigler, Director of the Office of Child Development of the United States Department of Health, Education, and Welfare, comments that his agency is thoroughly

---

[2] Johan Huizinga, *Homo Ludens: A Study of the Play Element in Culture.* Boston, Beacon Press, 1944, 1960.

[3] See M. J. Ellis: "Play and Its Theories Re-Examined." *Parks and Recreation,* August, 1971, pp. 51–55, 89.

[4] Arnold Gesell and Frances Ilg: *The Child From Five to Ten.* New York, Harper and Bros., 1946, p. 360.

[5] Lawrence K. Frank: "Mental Health and Outdoor Recreation." *Outdoor Recreation Resources Review Commission Report,* Vol. No. 22. U.S. Government Printing Office, Washington, D.C., 1962, p. 218.

committed to the support of play in child development programs such as
Head Start, day care, or other community youth projects. Zigler writes:

> All children need to be active. They need opportunities to hike, to
> explore, to discover things. They need a chance to create and achieve success
> through their own efforts. They also need to share common interests with
> other children of different ages and backgrounds. Play and recreation serve
> all these needs. I feel strongly that every child in this nation should have an
> opportunity to participate in meaningful play and recreation.[6]

PLAY AS A SOCIAL INSTITUTION.   Play and recreation must also be understood as important elements in the daily life and cultural practices of
various human societies. Such leading ethologists as Lorenz, Ardrey, and
Morris have formulated theories of human social behavior that underline
the powerful tendency toward aggression and warfare, the drives responsible for establishment of a "pecking order," or hierarchy of power, and the
concept of territoriality, in which all humans and animals seem to have a
built-in compulsion to defend their own geographical "turf." Some authors
have speculated that these dominant drives account for much human play,
particularly sports and games.

In the modern world, sports have become a major source of national
prestige and personal power. Athletes have become admired heroes of society and universities compete more vigorously in the sports world than
they do in the pursuit of scholarship or academic excellence. A strong case
can be made that the competitive forms of play in our modern society represent both a vestigial replay of earlier forms of religious practice or
modified warfare, and a direct expression of such drives as aggression and
territoriality. The parallel between war and play may be shown in that both
are clearly struggles for territory. In such games as football and hockey, the
object is to invade the opponent's terrain and finally cross over into his ultimate stronghold. Many of our sports today rely on the use of weapons of
the past, only slightly modified, such as the javelin, discus, or fencing foil.

Browne sums up the parallel between war and sports:

> . . . play at all levels and for all participants consists of practice in an arti-
> ficial but deadly serious arena, for entrance into an adult world which re-
> flects its ancient origins through the quest for territory, status, and weap-
> onry, all of which exist in many forms in our world today . . .[7]

In a broader sense, games, dance, music, folk drama, and literature
may all be seen as playlike forms of social expression which depict fundamental human values and institutions. Far from representing a trivial
aspect of society, anthropologists place great weight on the symbolic value
of such activities. Play is found within the entire class of mammals, al-

---

[6] Edward Zigler: "Play and Child Development." *Journal of Health, Physical Education and Recreation*, September, 1968, p. 36.

[7] Evelyn Browne: "An Ethological Theory of Play." *Journal of Health, Physical Education and Recreation*, September, 1968, p. 36.

though only man appears to play throughout his entire life span. It has also been learned that the more advanced a species is on the evolutionary scale, the more diverse and frequent are its play activities. Norbeck writes:

> For all forms of life, play may be defined as voluntary, pleasurable behavior that is separated in time from other activities and that has a quality of make-believe. Play thus transcends ordinary behavior. Human play differs uniquely from that of other species, however, because it is molded by culture, consciously and unconsciously. That is, human play is conditioned by learned attitudes and values that have no counterpart among nonhuman species.[8]

From an anthropological perspective, Norbeck writes that since play is universally found human behavior, it is therefore presumably vital to human life. He urges that play must not be regarded simply as a form of diversion, a rest from more serious activities, or as childish behavior. Instead, play "is both a biological and a sociocultural phenomenon that has significance in many ways . . ."[9]

While it is helpful for those who are professional workers in the field of recreation to have a basic understanding of the meaning of play in human life and its significance as a social phenomenon, it is of even greater importance for them to have a full and accurate understanding of the goals of community recreation. Only with this background is it possible to establish meaningful principles of recreation leadership.

GOALS OF COMMUNITY RECREATION

Community recreation is the term commonly applied to the programs provided by all public and voluntary recreation agencies within a given community. Through these programs a total spectrum of leisure opportunities of a socially constructive nature should be offered to community residents.

While each such agency may have somewhat distinct emphases or objectives, these goals may readily be grouped under the following eight headings: (1) improving the quality of life through the creative and constructive use of leisure; (2) contributing to the physical and mental health of the population; (3) strengthening community life by improving and enriching democratic values and increasing participation in civic activities; (4) providing a positive reinforcement to prevent antisocial forms of play, such as juvenile delinquency; (5) enriching the cultural and creative life of the community and supplementing the formal process of education for all ages; (6) improving safety standards by offering organized play programs in safe, supervised surroundings; (7) offering special services needed by the poor, or the physically, mentally, or socially disabled, who have unique leisure needs; and (8) protecting and beautifying the physical environment.

---

[8] Edward Norbeck: "Man at Play: A Natural History Magazine Special Supplement." December, 1971, p. 48.
[9] *Ibid.*

Each of these goals is discussed in fuller detail in the pages that follow. Examples are then given of the stated objectives of actual departments of community recreation and parks, or of voluntary or therapeutic agencies in the United States and Canada.

1. Improving the Quality of Life Through Enriched Leisure

The fact of increased leisure has become a fundamental aspect of modern life. The former Secretary of Labor of the United States, J. D. Hodgson, has stated:

> Tremendous shifts in the work life of the average man or woman have occurred during the past century, with the result that the time free of the necessity of earning a living has increased spectacularly. The "sunup to sundown" working day, which was generally standard in the early 1800's, is now as rare as the horse-drawn buggy. . . .
> The American worker sees in leisure time the opportunity for a fuller life — an opportunity that his forebears were denied. Now that it is within his reach, he fully intends to make the most of it.[10]

Today, leisure offers human beings an important choice between using the growing bulk of their uncommitted time in ways that are creative, constructive and socially desirable, or in ways that are boring, empty of purpose, or even self-destructive. Far from being a narrow concern, this problem is recognized throughout the world. In 1970, in Geneva, Switzerland, representatives of 16 international organizations, operating under the leadership of the International Recreation Association, developed the following statement, which has been widely published.

Charter for Leisure

Preface

Leisure time is that period of time at the complete disposal of an individual, after he has completed his work and fulfilled his other obligations. The uses of this time are of vital importance.

Leisure and recreation create a basis for compensating for many of the demands placed upon man by today's way of life. More important, they present the possibility of enriching life through participation in physical relaxation and sports, through an enjoyment of art, science, and nature. Leisure is important in all spheres of life, both urban and rural. Leisure pursuits offer man . . . a period of freedom, when man is able to enhance his value as a human being and as a productive member of his society. . . .

---

[10] J. D. Hodgson: "Leisure and the American Worker." *Journal of Health, Physical Education and Recreation,* March, 1972, pp. 38–39.

Article 1. Every man has a right to leisure time. This right comprises reasonable working hours, regular paid holidays, favorable traveling conditions and suitable social planning, including reasonable access to leisure facilities, areas and equipment, in order to enhance the advantages of leisure time.

Article 2. The right to enjoy leisure time with complete freedom is absolute. The prerequisites for undertaking individual leisure pursuits should be safeguarded to the same extent as those for collective enjoyment of leisure time.

Article 3. Every man has a right to easy access to recreational facilities open to the public, and to nature reserves by lakes, seas, wooded areas, in the mountains and to open spaces in general. These areas, their fauna and flora, must be protected and conserved.

Article 4. Every man has a right to participate in and be introduced to all types of recreation during leisure time, such as sports and games, open-air living, travel, theatre, dancing, pictorial art, music, science and handicrafts, irrespective of age, sex, or level of education.

Article 5. Leisure time should be unorganized in the sense that official authorities, urban planners, architects and private groups of individuals do not decide how others are to use their leisure time. The above-mentioned should create or assist in the planning of the leisure opportunities, aesthetic environments and recreation facilities required to enable man to exercise individual choice in the use of his leisure, according to his personal tastes and under his own responsibility.

Article 6. Every man has the right to the opportunity for learning how to enjoy his leisure time. Family, school, and community should instruct him in the art of exploiting his leisure time in the most sensible fashion. In schools, classes, and courses of instruction, children, adolescents, and adults must be given the opportunity to develop the skills, attitudes, and understandings essential for leisure literacy. . . .[11]

These high-sounding principles will only be meaningful if they are implemented on the local level. Thus, the provision of rich opportunities for leisure becomes a major goal of all community recreation departments and agencies.

2. Contributing to Physical and Mental Health

It has become widely accepted that engaging in a wide range of recreational pursuits will make a positive contribution to physical development and organic health, and to emotional well-being. Through games, sports, dance, and other forms of physical play, children and youth gain neuromuscular skill and generally improve their strength, fitness, agility, and endurance. For adults, particularly those in their middle years and beyond, regular exercise is a vital factor in preventing obesity, maintaining muscular tone, and promoting cardiovascular fitness.

However, comparatively few individuals — other than school, college,

---

[11] "Charter for Leisure." *Journal of Health, Physical Education and Recreation,* March, 1972, pp. 38–39.

or professional athletes—are willing to commit themselves to a strict regimen of physical conditioning exercise. Although Americans are sports lovers, they tend to be spectators rather than participants. Only three out of every hundred Americans participate in organized physical fitness programs, and fewer than twenty out of every hundred take part regularly in the two most popular sports, swimming and bowling. A recent survey on adult fitness, conducted for the President's Council on Physical Fitness and Sports, reveals that even the small fraction of American adults who take part in physical activity do so on such an irregular, low level of participation that little is accomplished to meet their basic health needs.[12] Therefore, there is a crucial need to provide active recreational sports programs to serve all age levels, with emphasis on activities such as tennis, golf, handball, swimming, skiing, or bicycling, that may be enjoyed throughout one's lifetime.

The linkage of recreation to emotional well-being is less widely understood and accepted. Such leading psychiatrists as William Menninger, Paul Haun, and Alexander Reid Martin have commented on the direct relationship between having a wide range of satisfying leisure involvements and good mental health. Robert H. Felix, formerly Director of the National Institute of Mental Health, has pointed out that recreation is an extremely valuable therapeutic medium in the treatment of the mentally ill and serves as a "great healing force" in molding leisure to promote physical and psychological well-being.

Recreation, however, is not useful only in treating the mentally ill. It is important for all persons to have a healthy balance between work and play. Recreation offers the opportunity for relaxation, a change of pace, and time to pursue creative interests and develop meaningful and supportive social relationships with others. Particularly in an era in which so many persons lead isolated, alienated lives in an urban society, the value of recreation in self-discovery and as a form of personal release is crucial. Gray has written of recreation as a form of "exploring inner space," by commenting:

> Tension, boredom, feelings of impotence, monotony, and frustration are common in contemporary society. Unsatisfactory patterns of human relationships combined with . . . isolation from a natural environment lead to emotional disorders which show up as anxiety, insecurity, depression, alienation, lack of confidence, and a poor self-image.[13]

While recreation obviously would not be a panacea for all such problems, for many persons it would offer personal satisfactions, meaningful involvement, and an opportunity for getting more pleasure out of life that would be extremely beneficial. Thus, a powerful case can be built for the value of recreation in improving both physical and mental health in the community.

---

[12] Charles A. Bucher: "National Adult Physical Fitness Survey: Some Implications." *Journal of Health, Physical Education and Recreation,* January, 1974, p. 25.

[13] David E. Gray: "Exploring Inner Space." *Parks and Recreation,* December, 1972, p. 18.

3. Strengthening Community Life and Democratic Values

In all societies in the past, people have established a common way of life by sharing recreational pursuits, celebrations, and festivities. In colonial America, rural residents typically joined together in cooperative work projects, such as barn raising or sheep shearing, and also in communal parties, picnics, or ceremonial balls, to celebrate the completion of work or important national holidays.

More recently, in communities in the United States and Canada, recreation has provided a common concern around which citizens of various socioeconomic classes or racial or religious backgrounds might join in mutual efforts. Hundreds of thousands of citizens contribute their services each year on the boards of voluntary youth organizations, or as nonpaid leaders in such programs. Thousands of adults act as volunteer coaches or officials in such youth sports programs as Little League Baseball, Biddy Basketball, or junior hockey leagues in Canada. Great numbers of others contribute their services on public recreation and park boards, or on community center recreation councils.

Often, community residents join together to promote the need for new parks and playgrounds, or innovative recreation programs. The experience of working together to plan and carry out such programs helps to promote a sense of belonging, a feeling of democratic participation in community processes, and of having a voice in one's own destiny. It was for this reason that the Office of Economic Opportunity in the United States sought to guarantee "maximum feasible participation" by local residents in community action programs rather than have all the authority reside in the hands of federal government employees.

4. Preventing Juvenile Delinquency

Since the beginning of the playground movement, one of the primary goals of community recreation has been to help prevent or control juvenile delinquency. During the first few decades of the 20th century, uncritical support was given to this function of public recreation. As an example, the chairman of the National Commission on Law Enforcement wrote in 1932:

> Children need wholesome outlets for their natural animal spirits. Youth is normally fond of adventure, delights in physical exercise and in taking risks. Deny the child innocent scope for these urges and it will find vent in criminal tendencies.[14]

The famous Warden Lawes of Sing Sing Prison wrote that it was a well-established fact that supervised recreation in city slums aided in crime

---

[14] George W. Wickersham, quoted in *Recreation: A Major Community Problem*. New York, National Recreation Association, 1936, p. 11.

prevention. Numerous observers at the time agreed that juvenile gangs often took part in criminal activities as a form of thrill-seeking behavior and that providing recreational opportunities was an effective means of attacking this problem. More recently, many sociologists and criminologists have concluded that delinquency stems from a variety of psychological or social causes, including weak or unstable family backgrounds and the general effects of social pathology in impoverished neighborhoods.

Any realistic program today which seeks to reduce or prevent juvenile delinquency must include improved family services, schools, and housing, and youth counseling, job training, and employment projects. However, youth authorities agree that recreation should be a vital component in such programs. First, it provides a medium through which children and youth who are *not* prone to delinquent behavior can be involved in enjoyable and challenging activities that reinforce their positive social values and goals. Second, as far as those children who are already showing signs of delinquent behavior or criminal gang affiliation are concerned, special programs must be designed. Some agencies seek to reach and involve children at an early point, before their antisocial tendencies are strongly established. Other communities provide teams of "roving leaders" or street gang workers to make contact with unaffiliated youth who resist formal contact with established programs (see Chapter Eleven). The goal of helping to prevent juvenile delinquency will continue to represent a major purpose of many communities in organizing recreational programs for youth.

5. Enriching Cultural Development

In the past, many community recreation programs have been narrowly conceived, consisting primarily of sports, games, and other outdoor recreation activities for children in after-school or vacation play settings. However, the basic concept of recreation today includes a full range of artistic, creative, and cultural pursuits. Thus, reading, creative writing, sculpture, painting, ceramics, dancing, singing, or playing in an orchestra or band should all be viewed as recreational acts.

Almost all community recreation departments offer arts and crafts, music, and similar activities as part of playground or community center programs. In addition, many departments also sponsor art or music centers with more advanced levels of instruction. Other departments formally sponsor or assist museums, libraries, dance companies, opera, symphony orchestras or choruses. Thus, recreation agencies make an important contribution to the development of the cultural life of the community.

In addition, such departments also frequently sponsor programs which supplement educational services. Typically, they may provide adult education classes, remedial education programs for youth, special science enrichment classes, and a host of other educationally-oriented activities.

6. Improving Safety Standards

Another significant purpose of community recreation and park programs is to contribute to community safety. In the early days of the recreation movement, the concern was chiefly about protecting children at play. For example, in the early 1930's, it was learned that over 4,000 children a year were killed by automobiles—many while playing ball or other street games. A National Conference on Street and Highway Safety called by President Hoover issued the following recommendation:

> Adequate playgrounds throughout the community should be provided and particularly there should be a playground for every school as a safety measure to keep children off the streets . . .[15]

Supervised community recreation programs promote desirable safety practices and help to prevent accidents. Many forms of play tend to be hazardous and, without regulations regarding the nature and use of equipment, rules of competition, or careful supervision, the number of injuries would be great. With the growth of aquatic play, the number of drownings each year has increased steadily.

Most drownings involve young people who are swimming or boating during the summer months; about two thirds of all drowning victims do not know how to swim. The fact that organized recreation programs provide qualified lifeguards who supervise swimming at lakes, beaches, or public pools undoubtedly helps to reduce the number of drownings that might otherwise occur. Similarly, the fact that millions of young people learn to swim through organized swimming instruction programs provided by public recreation departments helps to cut the drowning toll still further. In many other ways, organized recreation is a positive force for community safety, particularly in disadvantaged urban areas where children may not have adequate parental supervision.

7. Offering Special Services for the Poor or Disabled

Earlier in this chapter it was pointed out that urban slums—particularly those in which racial minority groups live—have tended to have the least adequate recreation programs and facilities. Research has shown that such neighborhoods have generally had far more limited and run-down parks and playgrounds than those in more affluent neighborhoods.

During the 1960's, however, partly as a consequence of the Civil Rights movement and partly because of the "war against poverty," many cities began to provide new and elaborate recreation facilities and programs in inner-city neighborhoods, often with Federal funding assistance. It was

---

[15] *Ibid.*, p. 10.

recognized that recreation provided an invaluable means of reaching disadvantaged children and youth with programs that combined varied forms of athletic, social, or cultural activities with other educational, vocational, or social services. In many cases, local residents were involved in planning such programs or in operating antipoverty organizations that provided valuable education in self-government or that initiated useful dialogues between the poor and the power structure. In some cities, many disadvantaged people — particularly members of racial minorities — were given paraprofessional jobs in recreation and the opportunity to continue their education and climb the Civil Service career ladder.

Similarly, recreation has increasingly become recognized as a vital community service for the physically or mentally disabled. Within the past decade, both public and voluntary recreation agencies have developed new programs to serve the orthopedically disabled, the blind, those with cerebral palsy, and numerous other groups with serious impairments. A number of public recreation and park departments, including federal and state agencies, have designed special parks and playgrounds for this purpose; all such departments today stress the need to design facilities that will not bar the disabled in wheelchairs or with other limitations.

The shifting emphasis in mental health care has led to the establishment of day clinics, after-care centers, and half-way houses to aid discharged mental patients or those who are receiving out-patient services. It would be overly optimistic to say that such needs are now being fully met. However, it has become increasingly clear that an important goal of public recreation and park departments and their voluntary agency counterparts is to provide specially designed programs and services that meet the unique needs of the disabled in society.

8. Protecting and Beautifying the Physical Environment

A profound shift in public thinking and national policy with respect to the environment came about in the 1960's and 1970's, with the realization that the industrialized nations of the world have been criminally careless in using up or despoiling their rich natural resources. We have covered huge areas of the United States and Canada with unrestricted residential or industrial development, or laid them waste with ruthless strip mining, unplanned lumbering, or other destructive practices. We have slaughtered and poisoned wildlife, and have permitted our great lakes and rivers and oceanfront areas to become so polluted that in many cases they can hardly sustain life.

Through federal legislation and local action, new programs of waste disposal, open space development, and more careful allocation of our resources, an effort has been made to reverse this trend. Many states have embarked on vigorous programs of open space acquisition and protection, and cities have done the same—often with assistance from the Land and Water Conservation Fund. The recreation and park profession has a vital stake in this total effort. Intelligent planning of land and water resources must insure that wildlife is protected, that primitive or natural areas are not disturbed, and that recreation itself—through the careless use of boating, snowmobiles, or similar equipment—does not further pollute the environment.

Many community recreation and park departments today sponsor programs of environmental education. Some have established natural preserves or wildlife museums. Others have spearheaded antipollution programs, waste collection or clean-up drives, or similar campaigns. Thus, it has become an increasingly important function of community recreation agencies to protect and beautify the natural environment.

Examples of Agency Goals

These eight areas of purpose outline the major contributions to be made by recreation which serves community needs. It is generally accepted today that each public or voluntary agency should have a written statement of its own philosophy and specific goals for recreation service. In a recently published manual for the evaluation and self-study of public recreation and park agencies, the National Recreation and Park Association defined these elements in the following terms.

Philosophy. A philosophy is a theoretical or conceptual framework of basic beliefs held by an individual, upon which principles may be established, goals developed, and from which methods and techniques are an outgrowth.

Goals. Goals are statements of general purpose or aim, what the department seeks to accomplish by its total operation. Whereas philosophy says, "This we believe," the goals say, "This we seek to accomplish." The goals must be within the stated legal purpose for which the department was created.[16]

Such statements should be developed by the professional staff and the advisory board or commission, and should be reviewed by the community at large. They should be compatible with the aims and objectives of the total recreation field, as defined by professional organizations. Since recreation should be responsive to changing community needs, long-range goals should be reviewed every few years, or whenever the top administrator of a department is changed. Short-term goals should be reviewed more frequently.

Goals may be presented in unitary form, or as a general philosophical statement. As an example of the first, the city of Phoenix, Arizona, has outlined a set of primary and secondary purposes for its Department of

---

[16] Betty van der Smissen: *Evaluation and Self-Study of Public Recreation and Parks Agencies.* Arlington, Virginia, National Recreation and Parks Association, 1972, pp. 10, 12.

Parks and Recreation that deal with community needs and with recreation as a profession.

Goals of Phoenix, Arizona, Department of Parks and Recreation

Primary Goals

1. To provide adequate physical facilities and . . . program opportunities to make it possible for the people of the community to become self-sustaining in their leisure.
2. Promote and further the organization, administration, financing and operation of community recreation.
3. To meet recreational needs with maximum effectiveness and with minimum expense.
4. To hold and preserve for the future, land, water and air spaces to assure essential freedom of choice in recreational experience.

Secondary Goals

1. Identify community recreational needs.
2. Identify goals and objectives and develop a master plan . . . to achieve them.
3. Develop and maintain high standards of professional leadership.
4. Instill confidence and a feeling of respect among employees at all levels.
5. Maintain effective communication within the department and between the department and the community.
6. Encourage inter-agency cooperation.
7. Provide activities which are recreational, educational, cultural, character-building, and which have carry-over value for all people . . .
8. Provide specialized leadership, information and advisory services on all phases of recreation and leisure activity.
9. Control, safeguard and maintain public recreation areas and facilities.

Goals for Recreation as a Profession

1. Unite forces of all agencies dealing with recreation.
2. Promote conservation of natural resources and personal resources.
3. Promote favorable recreation legislation.
4. Promote and maintain a high degree of professional ethics.
5. Create a favorable public image of the profession . . .[17]

---

[17] *Focus on the Recreation Division.* Phoenix, Arizona, Parks and Recreation Department, 1972.

An example of departmental goals presented in a general philosophical statement may be found in the following document, from Oakland, California.

Goals of Oakland, California, Parks and Recreation Commission

The Oakland Parks and Recreation Commission helps the citizens of Oakland discover and analyze needs and opportunities for worthy leisure-time pursuits for all. It seeks to provide public facilities, professional leadership, flexible programs and services, democratic planning and firm policies to help citizens meet these needs in order of greatest importance, according to sound principles of recreation planning and administration.

The Commission seeks to provide recreational experiences which are socially satisfying, physically healthy, mentally stimulating, aesthetically pleasing, and culturally creative. The Commission believes that equal opportunity should be available to all citizens for discovering and enjoying the skills and benefits of athletics, games, swimming, art, drama, dance, music, outdoor living and camping, social recreation, social and hobby clubs, public festivals, and many other facets of our great American culture.

The Commission recognizes that the recreation services and citizen contacts carried on daily by full-time professional staff in adequate neighborhood recreation centers are essential for serving the citizens in all areas of the city. Also recognized is the need for establishing certain programs and recreational services on a city-wide basis, when this is a more effective way to meet certain special needs.

The Commission recognizes a special obligation to serve children, youth, the aged, and individuals with special problems. It is particularly aware of the potential influence of recreation on character development and good citizenship. Because trained personnel are in daily contact with large numbers of citizens in the neighborhoods in which they reside, there is a special opportunity to influence the attitudes of citizens toward their city government as a whole.

The Commission recognizes its obligation to acquire, control, and safeguard for continued use of the general public those recreation facilities and services which should be publicly owned, controlled, or operated in the best interests of the total community.

The Commission recognizes the necessity for cooperating with, serving, and assisting community organizations and agencies, business concerns, public schools and other public departments which are providing large segments of the over-all leisure time and recreation program within the community. The Commission is aware of its obligations to know vividly what is happening in the community, and to help in establishing community cohesiveness and harmony through the total operation of an adequate and dynamic Parks and Recreation Department as a vital unit of municipal government.[18]

As another example, the Minister of Education for the Province of Ontario in Canada announced in 1968 the creation of a new Youth and Recreation Branch. It was the general function of this agency: (a) to provide a

---

[18] *Bulletin of Parks and Recreation Commission.* Oakland, California, 1972.

public information service to assist young people in Ontario with respect to education, recreation, employment, welfare, and other services; (b) to identify gaps in recreation and youth services; (c) to assist municipal council, school, and private agencies in offering recreation and adult education programs; and (d) to study amateur sport and develop a plan for a provincial sports federation in Ontario. In 1969, the Branch's specific responsibilities were defined as follows:

Goals of Ontario, Canada, Youth and Recreation Branch

1. To ensure that community leaders are trained and educated.

2. To identify or establish, and reinforce the agents in each community who can contribute to programs aimed at involving youth in community life and providing opportunities for the creative use of leisure.

3. To help in developing effective relationships and communication processes between the people in the communities and the institutions, agencies and organizations set up to serve them. . . .

4. To ensure the development of public information services concerning educational, developmental and employment opportunities for young people, and opportunities for leisure training and leisure education for everyone living in Ontario.

5. To foster public understanding and acceptance of the relationship between the wise and constructive use of leisure and the growth of the individual in society.

6. To seek, in cooperation with other groups, solutions to the problem of providing adequate physical resources and facilities for all the programs of recreation and cultural development needed by Ontario communities.

7. To institute and to encourage other groups to carry out programs of research into the developmental needs of the various groups contributing to the life of the community, programs to study leisure education, the special needs of youth, the development of services to meet needs that have been identified, and the means of achieving public acceptance of the significance of increasing leisure education.[19]

THE PROCESS OF ESTABLISHING GOALS

Each department that seeks to develop a statement of goals must be certain that these accurately represent the views of its sponsoring authority, its professional staff, and the population it seeks to serve. The process of establishing goals can be a difficult one. For example, the New York City Young Women's Christian Association recently examined its goals and reshaped them to meet crucial social needs. Like other traditional agen-

---

[19] *Youth and Recreation Branch.* Ontario, Canada, Department of Education, 1969.

cies, the Y.W.C.A. has sought to shift both its image and its fundamental philosophy to meet changing social problems and opportunities. In New York, the Y.W.C.A. was, in the late 1940's, an essentially white, middle-class organization serving 29,000 members. By the early 1970's it had embraced all races and ethnic groups, had initiated solutions to a variety of significant social problems that affected it, and was serving a membership of about 80,000 members in regular centers as well as in a number of store-front or other inner-city facilities throughout the city.

It undertook the task of redefining its purposes through a year-long series of meetings of various committees of staff workers, advisory groups, and members. In so doing, it developed the following criteria for goals: (a) goals will relate specifically to one or more Association objectives; (b) goals will be set for specific periods of time; (c) goals will serve as guidelines for evaluation of ongoing programs; (d) goals will serve as guidelines for development of new programs and allocation of resources; (e) goals will be measurable in concrete ways, such as numbers of participants, target groups, dollars, per cents, and/or time spans; (f) goals will make a substantial contribution to meeting community needs; and (g) goals will be attainable in terms of Y.W.C.A. potential. The final statement of agency goals included, among others, the following:

Goals of the Y.W.C.A. of the City of New York

Stimulate women and girls to develop and exercise their full potential as members of society.

Work toward equalizing life opportunities for all.

Promote involvement in social issues.

Serve as an advocate for young women and girls.

Create special opportunities for development of vocational and living skills.

Provide formal and informal physical education and recreation programs.

Promote the health of Y.W.C.A. members and the community at large.

Initiate a wide range of year-round camping opportunities.

Broaden membership to reflect the ethnic, cultural, and economic diversity of New York City.

Develop meaningful concept of "responsible membership" which strengthens the impact of the Y.W.C.A. movement.

Provide well-maintained facilities which enhance Y.W.C.A. programs and utilize them to their maximum potential.

Maintain flexible administrative and decision-making structures and processes built upon an effective volunteer-staff partnership.

Become an integral part of neighborhoods in which the Y.W.C.A. is located.

These goals are particularly interesting for two reasons. First, they demonstrate how recreation may only be *one* of the goals of an organization such as the Y.W.C.A., which also has multifold social purposes. Second, they represent two types of goals: (a) goals which are actual objectives of the Y.W.C.A. (purposes which it seeks to accomplish); and (b) operational guidelines related to such elements as membership participation or financial support which will help the organization reach its goals. Not uncommonly, both types of goals are stated together in a single listing of purpose. Obviously, each type of agency providing recreation service is likely to have its own unique set of goals, and to derive these in a special way.

Thus far, this chapter has presented an analysis of the background of professional recreation service, a statement of the government's role in recreation and of the significance of play, a listing of the general purposes of community recreation in the United States and Canada, and several examples of the goals of specific agencies or departments. In conclusion, it offers a set of basic principles of recreation leadership. These are derived from the literature, departmental manuals on leadership, and from the expressed views of many professional workers in the field.

PRINCIPLES OF RECREATION LEADERSHIP

1. The leader must operate on the basis of a sound philosophy of recreation and leisure. He must regard recreation as a significant aspect of human life, with a high potential for enhancing human growth and development and improving the total quality of community life.

2. The leader must have a sound knowledge of the basic theories of play, both past and present. He should also have a basic understanding of human development and of psychological principles that will help him work constructively with various individuals in improving motivation, dealing with individual or group behavior problems, and promoting healthy values.

3. The leader should be sensitive to the process of group dynamics, and should make use of whatever approach is likely to be most effective within a given situation or with a particular group—such as "democratic," "authoritarian," or "permissive" approaches. At the same time, he should move in the direction of democratic involvement, attempting to involve participants as fully as possible in the processes of active participation in group decision-making and self-management.

4. The leader should respect the needs of individuals within the groups he serves and must clearly recognize the differences among individuals in these groups. At the same time, he must balance these concerns with an awareness of the needs or rights of the groups themselves, of the agencies that sponsor them, or of the larger community.

5. The leader must regard recreation, not as an end in itself, but rather as a means to an end. Thus, a successful carnival, a tournament victory, or a high level of playground attendance are worthwhile only if they have helped to achieve the important purposes of community recreation.

6. The leader should strive for a reasonable balance between competition and cooperation, recognizing both as important forms of group activity. He must also strike a balance between other potentially conflicting goals

or emphases in program development, with the "greatest good for the greatest number" being his basic objective.

7. The leader should attempt to create an effective organization for planning and carrying out programs in order to realize as large a return as possible on all facilities, activities, and staff services.

8. The concerned leader should constantly evaluate the effectiveness and the specific outcomes of his programs as well as the quality of his own functioning. In so doing, he must measure outcomes against the stated goals of his agency or department, the expressed wishes of participants, and his own personal goals.

9. Leadership must constantly seek to promote desirable social values. The leader should consistently make his views or moral position known, and should set a constructive example for participants.

10. Successful leaders must be prepared to accept responsibilities and risks, to experiment and explore, to initiate, to pioneer. They cannot be satisfied with programs that just "get by," or with repeating the status quo. "Tired blood" is bad enough in an individual, but in a program concerned with promoting exciting and creative human involvement it is fatal. Therefore, the effective leader must constantly seek to innovate, to build his program, and to promote more meaningful services.

In applying these principles, the leader must recognize that there may be three different sets of values or expectations—those of the sponsoring agency, the participants, and his own.

As suggested earlier, the goals of sponsoring agencies may vary widely. For example, recreation programs for the *retarded* are likely to give heavy emphasis to the goal of helping individuals learn to live independently in the community and of reducing inappropriate behavior or appearance. Recreation in a *correctional* institution would be geared to promoting favorable morale in the penal setting and to developing constructive social values, as well as to introducing leisure interests and attitudes which will be helpful to residents after their return to the community. Recreation programs sponsored by *religious* organizations are likely to give emphasis to promoting special moral or spiritual values, to strengthening family-centered recreation activities, and to reinforcing the tie between young people and the religion itself.

It is essential that the leader be able to accept and work constructively with these agency goals if he is to be an effective staff member. Similarly, he must be able to understand and accept the needs and wishes of the participants he serves. However, this does not mean that he accepts these wishes in a completely noncritical way. Instead, it is his responsibility to interpose his own views and judgment, and to balance their desires—which may not be altogether desirable or constructive—with more mature or justifiable purposes.

Finally, the recreation leader must balance both agency and participant goals with his own personal needs, philosophy of recreation, and judgment of appropriate program goals and priorities. For example, the leader cannot function effectively in the service of an organization with which he seriously disagrees. Usually it is possible, through discussion and accommodation, to reconcile such possible conflicts.

In all such situations, it is important to recognize that, just as one's philosophy of recreation may be verbalized and discussed, so one's approach to leadership, like the behavior of group members, may be analyzed and interpreted. The truly effective leader must be sensitive both to his own attitudes and motivations as well as to the reasons why participants in recreation programs behave as they do.

For this reason, the study of group dynamics and the process of group leadership has become an extremely important element in the various disciplines of social service, including recreation. It underlies basic approaches to leadership training, staff development, program management, and problem-solving. It is dealt with in the chapter that follows.

Suggested Examination Questions or Topics for Student Reports

1. Two basic views of recreation service are presented in this chapter: one with a primary emphasis on its "fun" aspects, and the other regarding it as an important social service. How would the particular setting in which recreation is provided, or the population served, affect the emphasis stressed in recreation programs?

2. Carry out additional research regarding the contemporary or traditional concepts of play presented in this chapter, and present what you regard as a meaningful theory of play—i.e., why it is a universally found human activity, and what its purposes are.

3. Outline and discuss the major goals of community recreation, placing them in order of importance in modern life.

4. Summarize and discuss several of the key principles of recreation leadership that are presented at the conclusion of this chapter.

Suggested Action Assignments for Students

1. Select a public or voluntary agency that does *not* have an explicit set of goals or statement of its philosophy. Based on the literature and on interviews with the staff of this agency, develop such a written statement for it.

2. Select a public or voluntary agency that *has* such a statement. Based on careful observation of its structure and program, evaluate its effectiveness in achieving its goals or living up to its philosophy.

group dynamics in action

Group dynamics represents an important theoretical area of study within the field of social psychology. At the same time, it has been the subject of much applied research in such areas as business management, public administration, armed forces leadership, and social group work. It is therefore an important area of understanding for those concerned with recreation leadership and supervision.

UNDERSTANDING GROUP DYNAMICS

Group dynamics is essentially concerned with achieving an understanding of the nature and role of groups in modern life. It examines the way they are formed, the status and interrelationship of members, how different types of group structures affect the attitudes and productivity of members, how groups influence larger social institutions, and, finally, how different types of leadership affect group processes.

Knowledge about how groups operate may be derived either from empirical research, which observes natural groups in our society, or from research involving the controlled manipulation of groups. Such knowledge is directly useful to those working on any level of leadership, supervision, or administration, in that it helps a worker understand the behavior of others within the group, the overall influence of the group, and, finally, his or her own attitudes and responses to others. Reeves writes:

> Group dynamics is the study of the forces exerted by the group on the individual or by the individual on the group. We are thus concerned with group dynamics literally in almost every moment of our lives. . . .
>
> The study of group dynamics forces us into introspection. In striving to be a more effective member of the groups to which we belong, our first objective is to increase our sensitivity to the impact of our own personality on others. . . . The person who has a clear understanding of what makes him tick can, if he wishes, adjust more positively and more quickly to changes in a group situation. . . . Self-knowledge is closely related to intellectual and emotional maturity. The more a person studies group dynamics, the more easily he will increase his own self-knowledge. And this in turn will make quicker

41

and easier the necessary decisions about groups in which he wants to seek or maintain membership.[1]

Through a study of group dynamics one is able to understand such forms of behavior within groups as the aggression of some members toward others, the withdrawal of group members, or the particular psychological mechanisms or relationships which are developed. The nature of interaction among group members – their cohesiveness, their attitudes toward their leaders or the organization itself, the existence of cliques or factions, their ways of attacking problems or difficulties – all these are part of the study and practical uses of group dynamics.

IMPORTANCE OF GROUP DYNAMICS TO RECREATION PROFESSIONALS

Why is knowledge of group dynamics particularly important to recreation professionals? It should be extremely helpful in increasing personal awareness and sensitivity to the needs and behavior of others, and in helping them function more effectively with people in a variety of group relationships. Specifically, such knowledge and expertise may be helpful in the following types of situations.

SOCIALLY-ORIENTED GROUPS OF PARTICIPANTS. In working with groups where there is a primary emphasis on social involvement, and where the group process is an essential part of the experience for each participant, a knowledge of group dynamics can obviously be extremely important for the recreation leader. These might include social clubs for children and youth, membership groups in senior centers, therapeutic groups of patients in hospitals, after-care centers, or sheltered workshops.

ACTIVITY-ORIENTED GROUPS OF PARTICIPANTS. In many recreation situations the primary focus is on taking part in activities. Examples might be in highly structured team situations, as in sports, or in a much looser social framework, such as in an arts and crafts workshop. In such settings, the activity itself determines much of what happens in the group. However, even here there are many opportunities for meaningful social interaction, and for the behavior of group members or leaders to have a significant effect on group outcomes and successes.

WORKING WITH VOLUNTEERS OR ADVISORY GROUPS. Recreation leaders and supervisors are frequently called upon to work with groups of volunteers, committees of members, parents' groups, community center or neighborhood councils, or similar groups. In such situations, an understanding of the factors promoting successful group process is essential.

PROFESSIONAL TEAM RELATIONSHIPS. In all situations where a leader or supervisor must cooperate or work with other members of the profes-

---

[1] Elton T. Reeves: *The Dynamics of Group Behavior*. New York, American Management Association, 1970, pp. 12, 17.

sional team, a knowledge of human relationships is extremely helpful in promoting constructive teamwork.

ADMINISTRATIVE INTERACTION.   Within all public and voluntary agencies, high-level supervisors or administrators must work closely with other civic officials, officers of other departments or organizations, and municipal boards and commissions. While one might expect that by the time individuals had reached this level of authority they would be consistently effective in working with others, this is not necessarily the case. The same basic principles of group dynamics that are helpful in working with groups of participants or co-workers are likely to apply also in such high-level settings.

In all such situations, it is essential to recognize that groups of human beings have the capability for working or playing with each other in highly constructive, positive, and rewarding ways — or, conversely, in ways that involve conflict, tension, and destructive behavior. In part, this may stem from the psychological make-up of group members. However, it may also be heavily influenced by the nature of the group process and the leadership which is brought to bear upon it. As one approaches the study of group dynamics it is necessary first to understand the meaning and nature of groups as such.

A BASIC UNDERSTANDING OF GROUPS

There is no single, universally accepted definition of the term "group." Obviously, it is more than just a number of people. Reeves states:

> . . . a group consists of two or more people with common objectives. These objectives may be religious, philosophical, economic, recreational, or intellectual, or they may include all these areas.[2]

Muzafer and Carolyn Sherif emphasize the structure and influence of the group upon its members:

> A group is a social unit which consists of a number of individuals who stand in more or less status and role relationships to one another, and which possesses a set of values or norms of its own regulating the behavior of individual members, at least in matters of consequence to the group.[3]

Hartford defines group in the following terms:

> . . . at least two people — but usually more, gather with common purposes or like interests in a cognitive, affective and social interchange in single or repeated encounters sufficient for the participants to form impressions of each other, creating a set of norms . . . developing goals . . . evolving a sense of cohesion.[4]

---

[2] *Ibid.,* p. 11.

[3] Muzafer Sherif and Carolyn Sherif: *Groups in Harmony and Tension.* New York, Harper and Bros., 1953, p. 2.

[4] Margaret E. Hartford: *Groups in Social Work.* New York and London, Columbia University Press, 1972, p. 26.

Hinton and Reitz describe the term group in the following ways: (a) a group must consist of at least two or more people but with no upper limit on number, although realistically most functioning groups involve 20 members or less (if a group becomes larger, sub-groups are likely to appear); (b) groups are not merely random collections of individuals but involve behavioral interdependence in that members influence each others' behavior and perceive themselves psychologically as a group; (c) groups show memory for their past experience, although membership may change, and are capable of learning and responding as an entity; and (d) groups may meet the psychological and physical needs of members, such as the need for affiliation, security, social contact, or emotional support.[5]

Summing up this discussion, groups should be regarded as units of two or more people who have a meaningful relationship to each other in terms of sharing common goals, purposes, or needs. To the extent that their contact is a close and enduring one, they are likely to have common values and attitudes, and membership in the group will influence both the behavior of the group members and the overall setting in which the group exists.

Types of Groups

Obviously, there are many different kinds of groups in society. These might include family groups, youthful cliques or gangs, clubs, religious groups, neighborhood associations, political groups, union locals, service clubs or societies, groups of workers in an industrial plant, and many others. There are a number of ways of classifying, or categorizing, groups. Some sociologists have divided them into two broad categories: *primary groups,* which are important groups to which we have a deep and enduring affiliation and which affect our lives strongly; and *secondary groups,* which are more transitory, or less important and influential.

S. R. Slavson divided groups into three categories: (a) *compulsory groups,* in which membership is automatic or in which there is little choice about belonging, such as one's family, work team, or armed forces unit; (b) *motivated groups,* in which membership is voluntary but influenced by such motivations as the need for recognition, social acceptance, or approval, such as fraternal orders or clubs, church membership, honor societies, or service clubs; and (c) *voluntary groups,* in which one's chief reasons for joining are the need for social activity, friendship, or interest in a given type of activity, such as socially or culturally homogenous groups, activity-oriented groups, or hobby clubs.[6]

Other authorities have classified groups on the basis of their structure

---

[5] Bernard L. Hinton and H. Joseph Reitz: *Groups and Organizations.* Belmont, California, Wadsworth Publishing Co., Inc., 1971, pp. 31–32.

[6] S. R. Slavson: *Creative Group Education.* New York, Association Press, 1948, pp. 17–23.

and degree of official status: *formal,* those in which membership is enforced in some way, and has prescribed rules or obligations; *semi-formal,* in which there is a choice about membership but in which there are clear membership expectations and criteria; and *informal,* which represent fluid or casual associations or social contacts.

Approaches to the Study of Groups

Of the various types of groups that have been described, research in the field of group dynamics has tended to focus on work groups, special interest groups, and groups which have structured memberships, rather than on less formal groups. Early studies in the field of group behavior dealt with observations of groups in social welfare (such as children's groups in settlement houses), discussion groups in the adult education movement, and work groups in industry. A pioneer in the social group work movement, Grace Coyle, analyzed the process of group formation, membership selection, development of goals, and the establishment of common values, controls, and collective action. Schools of social work gradually emphasized the use of groups in social work programs and "small group process" became part of the basic competence of social workers.

During the 1930's, several strands of experimental research in group dynamics were developed. Some dealt with the effects of different types of leadership on group members in the armed forces, business and religious organizations, and in education. At this time, Moreno and Jennings developed an approach to the study of groups called "sociometry," which scientifically examined the nature of interaction patterns among group members.

During the 1940's and 1950's, emphasis was given to the use of small groups as the basis for theory building in social psychology, and for the improvement of training and administrative practices in a variety of institutions. In one study of the combat record of the American soldier in World War II, for example, it was found that small squads of soldiers who had developed a high degree of cohesion and friendship had higher levels of combat effectiveness and morale than other units, and that this process was more effective than Army indoctrination efforts in creating effective fighting units. Other studies, such as the famous Roethlisburger research at the Western Electric Company in Ohio, showed that small work groups had more effect on employee production than company policies or other corporate incentives. Another study, by Lazarsfeld, showed that voting tended to be influenced much more heavily by one's associates or family attitudes than by the mass media or political literature.[7]

During this period, a number of basic approaches to research in this field were developed. Cartwright and Zander identified a number of such

[7] See Hartford, *op. cit.,* pp. 10–26.

A

B   Carter L. Hamilton

   Nature Activities. Many recreation and park departments provide extensive nature- or ecology-oriented programs. An Austin, Texas, leader introduces children to a feathered friend (*A*), while Kansas City, Missouri, campers cautiously observe a giant snapping turtle (*B*). Children in Edmonton, Canada, visit an historic site (*C*), Washington, D.C. children care for their own garden plots (*D*), and a Rochester, Minnesota, nature specialist helps youngsters learn about plant life (*E*).

C

D

Sylvia Johnson

E

theoretical orientations:

FIELD THEORY.   This approach sees behavior as the result of a field of interdependent forces, with both individual and group behavior seen as part of a system of interrelated events.

SYSTEMS THEORY.   Somewhat similar to field theory. The group is perceived as a system of interlocking elements, such as the motivations and roles of members, with major emphasis given to group inputs and outputs.

SOCIOMETRIC ORIENTATION.   This approach to the study of groups relies heavily on the measurement of interpersonal choices among group members, in order to determine the status, power, and affiliations of each member.

PSYCHOANALYTIC ORIENTATION.   This is derived heavily from Freudian psychology and is concerned with motivational and defensive processes of individuals, as related to group life.

GENERAL PSYCHOLOGY ORIENTATION.   This approach applies basic concepts of general psychology that deal with such processes as learning, motivation, and perception directly to group dynamics.

EMPIRICAL-STATISTICAL ORIENTATION.   This approach relies heavily on empirical observation and on the application of statistical procedures to develop the basic concepts of group dynamics.

FORMAL MODELS APPROACH.   This method seeks to build rather abstract theoretical models of group structure and behavior, based on rigorous and complicated mathematical procedures.[8]

Throughout this period of systematic analysis of groups, certain elements of group behavior or structure were identified. These represent the characteristics that the group worker, leader, or supervisor must seek to understand if he is to work more effectively with groups. Examples of such characteristics, as identified and described by Hemphill and Westie, follow:

1. *Autonomy.*   The degree to which a group functions independently of other groups.

2. *Control.*   The degree to which a group controls or regulates the behavior of group members.

3. *Flexibility.*   The degree to which a group's activities are marked by informal procedures rather than by rigidly structured procedures.

4. *Hedonic Tone.*   The degree to which group participation is accompanied by a general feeling of pleasantness or agreeableness.

5. *Homogeneity.*   The degree to which members of a group possess similar characteristics.

6. *Intimacy.*   The degree to which members of a group are familiar with the personal details of one another's lives.

7. *Participation.*   The degree to which members of a group apply time and effort to group activities.

---

[8] Marvin E. Shaw: *Group Dynamics, The Psychology of Small Group Behavior.* New York, McGraw-Hill Book Co., 1971, pp. 15–17.

8. *Permeability.* The degree to which a group permits ready access to membership.

9. *Polarization.* The degree to which a group is oriented toward a single goal which is recognized and accepted by all members.

10. *Potency.* The degree to which a group has significance for its members.

11. *Stability.* The degree to which a group persists over a period of time with essentially the same characteristics.

12. *Stratification.* The degree to which a group orders its members into clearly defined status hierarchies.[9]

In addition to these characteristics of groups, researchers identified certain important group properties which became the focus of considerable study.

ESSENTIAL PROPERTIES OF GROUPS

These include the following: group cohesiveness, group morale, group norms, group structure, and group productivity.

GROUP COHESIVENESS. This may briefly be described as the force which tends to hold a group together. It varies widely since it is the result of many factors, such as the type and strength of the leadership, the nature of group objectives, and the degree of group homogeneity. It has been found that cohesiveness is directly proportional to the group's identification with its major objectives. Reeves writes:

> If the central objective of the group seems to its membership to be worthy of a considerable sacrifice in order to attain it, group solidarity will be high. . . .
>
> It is possible for a group's leaders to choose their actions with the express purpose of directly raising its cohesiveness. Group tasks can be assigned to teams made up of members who have interacted less frequently or less effectively than others. As these teams succeed in their tasks, new and stronger interpersonal relationships will be formed and cohesiveness will therefore increase.[10]

In general, it has been found that cooperation creates a higher degree of cohesiveness than competition does. If some members of a group are too dominating, or have other unpleasant characteristics, cohesiveness will be lowered. Highly cohesive groups are usually able to accept hostility from external sources and return it, without fighting internally. Such groups tend to be highly productive and able to work efficiently on assigned tasks.

GROUP MORALE. Group morale may be described as a positive and optimistic feeling about the group, and a conviction that it is a successful or important body worthy of support. It is heavily influenced by the nature of

---

[9] John K. Hemphill and Charles M. Westie, in Hinton and Reitz, *op. cit.,* pp. 5–6.
[10] Reeves, *op. cit.,* p. 108.

the group's goals; for example, the following factors tend to strengthen group morale:

1. Having positive, easily recognized and understood objectives which the group members themselves support fully.

2. Achievement of satisfactions, such as self-expression, recognition, or a sense of prestige, from group involvement.

3. A shared feeling of progress being made toward group goals.

4. Realistic levels of aspiration and achievement that are set beyond past accomplishments of the group — but not unrealistically so. There should be both immediate and long-range objectives.

5. Equality of sacrifice or gain within the group. No one member should either be called upon to give too much or to receive excessive rewards from the group's activities.

6. A high degree of self-identification with the group that may be achieved through such devices as special rituals, slogans, or uniforms.

GROUP NORMS. Group norms represent the values, traditions, and standards of behavior which are characteristic of a group. They are usually strongest when they have grown naturally over a period of time rather than when they are imposed on group members by higher authority. Most individuals tend to base their personal values on the views of those around them — originally from family contacts, then from play groups or other peers, and ultimately from the enduring group associations, or references groups, that persist throughout life. It seems to be a normal mode of behavior to act or react in ways that people one respects consider to be socially acceptable. Hare says:

> Some individuals are . . . relatively insensitive to pressures, but a person cannot remain a social being . . . and stand wholly apart from social pressure.[11]

Lewin makes a similar observation:

> When an individual tries to diverge too much from group standards he will be ridiculed, treated severely, and finally ousted from the group.[12]

Group sanctions is the term used to describe the way in which groups enforce their norms. Sanctions may range from mild censure to actual expulsion from a group. While some sanctions may involve a formal punishment by authority or an outside force, most group sanctions are imposed by the group members themselves, and thus they have considerable weight and influence. An example would be the process of putting a group member who has transgressed its rules into "Coventry," or social isolation. In order to minimize conflict and disorder, members of groups tend to reach implicit or explicit agreements about rights and obligations; when these are violated, sanctions are imposed.

---

[11] A. Paul Hare: *Handbook of Small Group Research.* New York, Free Press, 1962, p. 169.
[12] Kurt Lewin: *Field Theory in Social Science.* New York, Harper and Row, 1951.

However, many groups are able to enforce their norms without having to rely on sanctions. The success of such organizations as Alcoholics Anonymous, Synanon, or Weight Watchers seems to stem from the emotional identification of members with the total group, their desire to be approved by other members, and a sense of responsibility for the group that prevents them from letting down group expectations and standards.

GROUP STRUCTURE.   Instead of simply being collections of individuals who share uniform roles and levels of status, most groups tend to develop differentiated functions, identities, and degrees of prestige in their membership. Typically, some members are perceived as influential leaders, while others are followers. Some are identified with the "in-group" or power structure, while others are peripheral to group decisions and influence. There are also likely to be cliques or sub-groups of friends who relate closely to each other. This pattern of relationships and expected behaviors and roles is normally referred to by the term "group structure." Shaw writes:

> Each group member is more or less aware of this group structure and often can verbalize it quite clearly; yet there is no explicit statement concerning the organization of the group. Group structure may therefore be either formal or informal; it may be explicitly recognized and stated or merely implicit in the functioning of the group. In either case, the group structure exerts a pervasive influence upon the behavior of the members of the group.[13]

GROUP PRODUCTIVITY.   Group productivity refers to the overall effectiveness of group members in working together to achieve their goals. In general, it depends on three elements: task demands, resources, and process.

Task demands consist of the job to be done, and whether or not it is within an appropriate range of activities or responsibilities for the group. If task demands are excessively difficult, or are so simple that they do not represent a challenge, group productivity is likely to be low. Similarly, if goals are unclear, or if assigned tasks are not attractive to group members, they may not accept them fully, and this too will limit productivity.

The resources available to a group, in terms of accomplishing a given task, also limit its potential productivity. Resources include all the relevant knowledge, abilities, skills, or tools possessed by the members of the group; it is best if important capabilities are well distributed among group members rather than concentrated in a few individuals.

Process refers to the way in which people use their resources: the actual steps and individual or collective actions taken by group members in carrying out a task. Steiner writes:

> In a productive group, these actions will include the intellective and communicative behaviors by which members evaluate, pool, and assemble their resources; decide who shall do what, when; assign differential weights to one

---

[13] Shaw, *op. cit.,* p. 236.

another's contributions; and extoll each other to participate fully in the group's task-oriented activities.[14]

There has been considerable research in the area of group productivity. Much of it has concentrated on the effectiveness of groups in carrying out assigned tasks in comparison to the effectiveness of individuals. Based on a considerable bulk of experimental findings, Shaw reports that a number of plausible generalizations have been developed regarding the productivity of groups. These follow:

1. The mere presence of others increases the motivation level of a performing individual; individuals perform better in the presence of others than they do alone.

2. Group judgments are superior to individual judgments on tasks that involve random error.

3. Groups usually produce more and better solutions to problems than do individuals working alone.

4. Groups usually require more time to complete a task than do individuals working alone.

5. Groups learn faster than individuals.

6. More new and radical ideas are produced by both individuals and groups when critical evaluation of ideas is suspended during the production period.[15]

These findings suggest the extreme importance of groups throughout our lives. Hartford points out that,

"... not only do one's values, beliefs and behaviors seem to stem from his interactions with others, but one's very impression of himself or herself — one's identity, one's assessment of his own worth, also develop from associations with others."[16]

This is obviously extremely important in therapeutic groups, in group experiences which are designed to improve professional performance, or in helping members become more effective team workers.

In all investigations of group dynamics, it is appropriate to ask, "What is the effect of group leadership? Under what kinds of leadership are groups most likely to function effectively, to develop and maintain constructive interrelationships, and to be highly productive?"

THE STUDY OF GROUP LEADERSHIP

Within the field of group dynamics, leaders have been perceived as those group members who are the focus of group attention, who have

[14] Ivan D. Steiner: *Group Process and Productivity.* New York and London, Academic Press, 1972, p. 8.

[15] Shaw, *op. cit.,* pp. 79–83.

[16] Hartford, *op. cit.,* p. 34.

strong influence on group decisions, who can lead groups toward their goals and affect the level of group performance, and who help groups define their character. Steiner points out that group dynamics theorists and researchers have identified leaders in the following ways:

> Leaders are persons assigned to the leader role by an experimenter, either with or without the enumeration of special duties and functions.
>
> Leaders are persons identified as such by observers or by group members.
>
> Leaders are persons whose presence and/or behavior in the group strongly influence the group's activities or products.
>
> Leaders are persons who are highly chosen by other members as friends, confidants, or co-workers.
>
> Leaders are persons whose suggestions, commands, or example are regularly accepted and followed by other group members.
>
> Leaders are persons who occupy certain positions within an institutionalized role structure — foremen, lieutenants, company presidents.
>
> Leaders are persons with whom others identify, and who therefore inspire and channel the activities of group members.
>
> Leaders are persons who are observed to perform certain specified functions.[17]

It is apparent that these descriptions refer chiefly to leaders of an informal nature, that is, individuals who assume leadership roles within groups but who do not have an official or appointive status. It is possible to achieve leadership status in a variety of ways, including the following:

1. *Elected Leaders.* In political life and large membership organizations, it is customary for leaders to be selected by choice of the majority through formal voting procedures. Presumably, leadership candidates are widely known to their constituency and are chosen by virtue of their capability and past performance, although too often such choices may be determined by clever political manipulation or adroit marketing of the candidate's image.

2. *Appointed Leaders.* In business firms and many other types of organizations, it is customary for high-level administrators to appoint individuals to leadership positions. This is done customarily because the administrator is familiar with the personality and skills of his subordinates and is able to judge their capability for assuming leadership responsibilities.

3. *Career-Process Leaders.* This describes the type of leader who assumes a post of responsibility after having come up through the career ranks of an organization. It is necessary for him to meet the formal requirements of experience, personnel evaluations, examinations, or similar processes, in order to become eligible for a specific position. The most

---

[17] Steiner, *op. cit.,* p. 174.

obvious example is the individual who rises through the "merit system" of Civil Service advancement procedures.

4. *Inherited Leaders.* This is most obvious in those nations with royal families, where the post of ruler is passed from parent to child. It operates less formally in political life, when wives, brothers, or other close relatives may inherit the "mantle" of leadership and replace a key political figure who becomes ill or dies. It may also operate in other areas of public life, in which close associates of a key official may take over a post on his retirement or death, with popular consent.

5. *Emergent Leaders.* This describes the type of leader who emerges as the choice of a group because, in a given situation or over a sustained period of time, he displays the needed qualities for assuming leadership responsibilities and helping the group achieve its goals. Instead of being formally elected or appointed, the emergent leader takes on this role without official recognition or approval.

Within the field of recreation and parks, examples may be given of each category of leader. The *elected leader* is found in any recreation club or organization that elects its own officers, such as a Senior Citizens club or a neighborhood council. The *appointed leader* may be illustrated by the commissioner or superintendent of recreation and parks, who is appointed to his post by the mayor or city council. The *career-process leader* represents the majority of professionals who rise to supervisory or administrative positions by rising through the hierarchy of an organization and meeting formal requirements along the way. The *inherited leader* is less widely found, but an example might be in a situation where a husband may succeed his wife as chairman of a community recreation board or commission. Finally, the *emergent leader* is to be found in any kind of work team or group of recreation participants in which one individual emerges with leadership responsibilities because of his contributions to the group and his overall personality.

Exactly what constitutes the effective leader? Why are some individuals identified and accepted as leaders, while others who are apparently capable are never chosen?

THEORIES OF GROUP LEADERSHIP

Over the past several decades, several basic theories of group leadership have been presented. Four of these, the "trait," "situational," "functional," and "contingency" theories, are described here.

Trait Theory of Leadership

One of the earliest theories of leadership, this theory suggested that there were certain specific traits or qualities shared by all successful leaders. It stemmed from the philosophical orientation of the western world, which held that human beings could become whatever they wished, provided that they worked hard and persevered in their efforts. Thus, individuals became leaders because of their personal drive and attributes, and individual characteristics were seen as the major determinants of leadership. In public life, industrial, political, or military figures were widely adulated, and the view became accepted that there were one or more unique and innate traits which were shared by all great leaders.

However, scientific research on leadership revealed that there was no single set of traits or identifiable qualities that characterized all leaders. Certain qualities tended to appear frequently enough to permit some generalizations. Research by Stogdill and others showed that group leaders tended to have traits related to ability, sociability, and motivation to a higher degree than other group members. Group leaders rated high with respect to *ability* in such categories as intelligence, insight, verbal facility, and adaptability. Leaders exceed group members in *sociability* factors, such as responsibility, social participation, cooperativeness, and popularity. With respect to *motivation,* group leaders had a higher level of initiative and persistence than group members.

Other important factors may include the willingness to make decisions when needed, and to risk making incorrect decisions; charisma, defined as personal magnetism and appeal; the ability to project a "parent image" to members of the group; the quality of being fair and impartial; and the drive for power or influence over others.

However, it must be emphasized that no single trait has been identified as the *key* to being a leader. Gradually, the conviction has emerged that different leadership qualities are required in different situations, and indeed, that the trait positively related to leadership in one situation may be unrelated or even negatively associated in another.

Situational Theory of Leadership

This view suggests that leaders arise or emerge in situations where their personal qualities or capabilities will best serve group members.

In some situations, a group may require a leader who will be a forceful morale-builder, an external representative or negotiator, or an expert in human relations. The qualities called for in the leader of a military squad in a battle situation are likely to be bravery, a cool head, a knowledge of military tactics, sound judgment, and the ability to inspire men. On the other hand, a group of educators selecting a chairman to head up a team to carry out a study and issue a report might require an individual with knowledge of the subject, experience in the field, the ability to communicate in both written and verbal form, and a high level of scholarly ability. Thus, the situational theory has held that leadership selection is most likely to be affected by the demands and needs of a given situation rather than by possession of a particular leadership trait or a set of traits.

Functional Theory of Leadership

This theory suggests that leadership arises from the complex needs of the group for specific kinds of tasks to be performed. Many of these responsibilities may be undertaken by different members of the group, and so it is assumed that leadership is a shared process in which the functions to be performed determine who the leaders are at any given time.

For example, a work team in a large organization that has been assigned responsibility for a major project will require different kinds of leaders. Some individuals will be needed who are highly creative and who can generate exciting ideas. Others will be needed who are practical, who can sift through these proposals and follow through with careful planning. The team may need resource persons with specialized knowledge or skills (how to select equipment, how to set up a marketing plan, how to solve personnel problems), persons with public relations skills, evaluators, and others to fill a variety of different functions. It may also require one individual who has the special ability to coordinate others and get them to work together effectively, and who may serve as "program manager" or the nominal leader of the group.

Essentially, this theory argues that leadership is neither a single skill nor the responsibility of a single individual, but is instead a process in which all group members share in varying degrees as a group carries out its work.

Contingency Theory of Leadership

This theory is based on leadership research carried out by Fiedler during the 1960's. Two kinds of leadership are identified, based on responses to a sociometric questionnaire which asks respondents to rate their most preferred and least preferred co-workers on a set of behavioral characteristics. The two types are: *high "ASo-LPC" persons,* who seek self-esteem by gaining recognition from others and who derive their major satisfactions from successful interpersonal relationships; and *low "ASo-LPC" persons,* who derive major satisfaction from success in task performance, even at the risk of having poor interpersonal relationships with fellow workers.[18]

Fiedler determined that the relationship of one's leadership style to his effectiveness with a particular group could only be measured if three situational variables were considered: (a) the leader's *position power,* meaning the degree of legitimate authority and the ability to give rewards or punishment; (b) the *structure of the task,* meaning how clearly its goals and solutions are outlined in advance and made known to group members, with the implication being that the more structured the task is, the more favorable the situation is for the leader; and (c) the *personal relationship* between the

---

[18] Shaw, *op. cit.,* pp. 275–276.

leader and other group members, with emphasis on their mutual feeling tone, and the support and loyalty he is able to elicit from them.

Based on considerable experimentation, Shaw summarizes the conclusions reached by Fiedler:

> These patterns of behavior determine the relative effectiveness of leaders in various situations. The task-oriented leader tends to be more effective when the situation is either highly favorable or highly unfavorable for the leader, whereas the relationship-oriented leader tends to be more effective in situations that are only moderately favorable or moderately unfavorable.[19]

The contingency model of leadership is significant in that it demonstrates that the type of leadership behavior that is most likely to be effective depends on the situation and the task to be performed; in addition, it specifies ways of examining tasks to determine what leadership behaviors are likely to be most successful in carrying them out.

RESEARCH IN GROUP LEADERSHIP STYLES

For the past several decades, there have been numerous studies of group behavior and the effects of different styles of leadership. At a comparatively early point it was determined that the same group will behave in markedly different ways when operating under different leaders. Several studies of group leadership styles showed that:

> Leaders of more effective groups tended to play a more differentiated role than leaders of less effective groups; they spent more time in planning, providing materials and assistance, and discussing action to be taken.
>
> More effective leaders delegated authority to others more frequently than less effective leaders.
>
> More effective leaders checked up on subordinates less often, and were more supportive in manner than less effective ones.
>
> More effective leaders were able to develop cohesiveness among their group members to a fuller degree than less effective ones.
>
> In general, it was found that effective leaders placed stress on developing good working teams, with a friendly, cooperative group climate, high internal loyalty and broad involvement in decision-making and policy formulation.[20]

Other studies of small problem-solving groups found that different members assumed different leadership roles. Typically, one member in a group assumed the role of "social-emotional needs satisfier," while another became a "task-accomplishment specialist." It was commented that this seemed to parallel many family structures, in which mothers tended to as-

---

[19] *Ibid.*, p. 278.

[20] Dorwin Cartwright and Alvin Zander: *Group Dynamics: Research and Theory.* New York, Harper and Row, 1960, pp. 487–489.

sume the role of meeting social and emotional needs, while fathers emphasized task accomplishment.

Lewin Studies of Group Leadership

A pioneering series of studies of different leadership styles and their effects on participants was carried out in the late 1930's and early 1940's by Kurt Lewin and a number of associates.[21] Four comparable groups of ten-year-old boys were observed as they successively experienced *autocratic, democratic,* and *permissive* (laissez-faire) adult leadership. Each group met after school and engaged in varied hobby activities, such as arts and crafts, for three six-week periods. In each period they had a different adult leader who employed a different leadership style.

The *autocratic* leader assigned all responsibilities and made all decisions, without discussing his plans with group members or seeking their views. He dispensed rewards and punishments in an authoritarian fashion, remaining aloof from active participation with the group except when showing activities. The *democratic* leader shared in policy-making and in decisions about group activities with the participants. He helped them clarify the goals of the group and made his own standards and expectations known to the group. Rather than rigidly assign them to sub-groups, he gave group members the choice of working with their close friends. The *permissive* leader gave help when needed but otherwise remained aloof from the group. He permitted them to make all decisions and made no attempt to guide or evaluate the group's activities.

Using movies and observational records, extensive records were kept of each group's participation day by day. It was found that in autocratically run groups members tended to depend heavily on the adult leader and did not develop the capacity for taking independent action. When the autocratic leader absented himself, group members had difficulty in carrying on. By contrast, in democratic and permissive leadership groups there was considerably more friendly interaction and interdependence. When there were difficulties or sudden emergencies, members of the democratically led groups were best able to work together, express individual views, and come to group decisions. The expression of hostility was 30 times as great in the autocratic as in the democratic groups, and there was considerably more scapegoating in the autocratic groups than in the other two.

In general, group members tended to prefer the democratic and permissive leaders to those who were autocratic in style. While the studies did not prove that democratic leadership was the only effective form of leadership, they did demonstrate its value under the experimental conditions described. Realistically, many individuals are so accustomed to autocratic

---

[21] See Ralph K. White and Ronald Lippitt: *Autocracy and Democracy.* New York, Harper and Bros., 1960.

direction that they feel secure with it, and it takes a period of time for them to handle themselves in a mature way in a democratically led group. In fact, a number of studies in industrial and problem-solving situations that followed the Lewin experiments showed that autocratically directed groups tended to have a higher level of productivity, although personal satisfaction was generally greater in groups that were democratically led.

One might conclude that in recreation situations, where the satisfaction of group members and their development in terms of personal growth and maturity, and their ability to function well as members of society are key goals, democratic leadership is the most appropriate.

Sherif Studies of Manipulation

Another series of studies, carried out by Muzafer and Carolyn Sherif during the 1950's, dealt with the experimental production of group structures, norms, and hostile intergroup relationships.[22] These studies involved camping programs for boys in Connecticut and Oklahoma.

In the first experiment, 24 boys who were about 12 years old were divided into two evenly matched groups called the "Red Devils" and the "Blue Dogs." Each group developed a hierarchical structure, with status roles and power relations based on the members' size, their ability in games, intelligence, and personality characteristics. The group developed its own set of norms, methods of praise and punishment, secret hideouts, and the like. The "Red Devils" and "Blue Dogs" were exposed to a period of friction, which was deliberately caused through the use of competitive games and other devices intended to cause frustration. The experimenters succeeded in bringing about strongly hostile attitudes and behavior, in which each group held negative stereotypes and expressed considerable antagonism toward the members of the opposite group.

In the second series of experiments, known as the Robber's Cave Experiment, the experimenters again induced a series of mutually frustrating and competitive activities which resulted in highly negative behavior between the groups. There was physical violence, name-calling, sneak raids, insulting posters, and considerable bitterness and accusations.

Although staff members were instructed, after the period of intergroup friction, to do away with the hostility as much as possible, they found it extremely difficult to do this. The Sherifs write:

> Perhaps the most remarkable observation of this period was that, in spite of their efforts to break up the in-groups by bringing the boys all together in camp duties and activities, campfires, birthday parties, and athletic events emphasizing individual rather than group competition, the preferences of the boys tended, on the whole, to follow the in-group lines. The old songs,

---

[22] Muzafer Sherif and Carolyn Sherif: *An Outline of Social Psychology*. New York, Harper and Bros., 1956, pp. 192–202, 293–300.

names, and stereotypes derogatory to the out-group continued to crop up. Such observations indicate a strong tendency for attitudes toward in-group and out-group to persist even though the conditions which gave rise to them no longer exist.[23]

Various devices, such as involving members of both factions in a camp-wide softball team against a team of outsiders or calling on all the boys to cooperate in a major camp emergency, were used in trying to reduce the hostility and re-establish a state of cooperation and mutual acceptance. Ultimately, this was accomplished.

What were the implications of these experiments? First, they provided an excellent demonstration of the tendency of groups to coalesce and rapidly develop their own norms, loyalties, and internal group structure. Second, they showed how ready the group members were to engage in hostile, aggressive behavior against those whom they had recently regarded as their friends, but whom they now saw as enemies. The effect of aggression — as exemplified in competitive camp activities — was worthy of notice. Although it is generally assumed that by giving vent to aggression one can reduce one's level of hostility, these experiments showed that the more competition the campers engaged in the greater their antagonism grew.

The Sherif studies provide a graphic example of the *power* of group leadership to influence the attitude and behavior of group members, both for positive and negative goals. It is worth comment that the experimenters found it easier to promote negative and hostile values and behavior than to build constructive and desirable intergroup relationships.

There have been few recent research studies with direct relevance for recreation situations. Chapter Thirteen, however, describes the principles involved in the development of "T-groups," "encounter," or "sensitivity" groups. This movement represented the major thrust in group dynamics during the 1960's and early 1970's. It contains much potential for developing improved human relationships in both leader-participant and work-team group situations.

A final area of concern in this chapter is the examination of theory and practice in the field of social group work, a professional field with close ties to recreation, particularly in institutional programs or youth service settings.

BASIC CONCEPTS OF SOCIAL GROUP WORK

Social group work is a field of professional practice that has made sustained attempts to apply theoretical understandings of group process to actual programs of social service. It is important for recreation professionals to understand the basic concepts of this field for two reasons.

---

[23] *Ibid.,* p. 299.

1. In many situations recreation leaders work with problem groups, in which they must provide direct counseling, organize "rap" sessions, or work in other meaningful ways to assist group members. In such situations their function is closely related to the goals of social group work, and it is helpful for them to understand this field.

2. Recreation personnel often work side-by-side with social group workers in hospitals, rehabilitation centers, youth homes, or correctional institutions. It is important for them to be able to communicate and cooperate effectively with each other in such settings as well as in other agencies where recreation leaders may be employed by, or may themselves employ, a social group worker.

Social Group Work Defined

An early definition of social group work saw it as:

> . . . one way of giving service or help to individuals. . . . Primarily it is a specialized method of providing growth opportunities for individuals and groups in the functional settings of social work, recreation and education.[24]

At a later point, Konopka defined it in the following terms:

> Social group work is a method of social work which helps individuals enhance their social functioning through purposeful group experiences and to cope more effectively with their personal, group, or community problems.[25]

The two other major emphases within the social work field are *case work* and *community organization*. The *case worker* deals primarily with single individuals and their families, counseling them, helping them work out their problems, or referring them to other agencies for direct service. The *community organization specialist* attempts to help people organize themselves to bring about constructive social change—both to correct immediate problems and to attack the larger social situation that creates the problems. In contrast, the *social group worker* is primarily concerned with using groups as a medium through which people can become more effective in solving their own problems and developing in social maturity and human relationships. Many social group workers regard groups as a microcosm, or small replica, of the larger community; if participants can develop strengths, skills, and self-understanding within groups, it will help them function more effectively in the world at large.

---

[24] Harleigh Trecker, quoted in Gisela Konopka: *Group Work in the Institution.* New York, Association Press, 1970, p. 25.

[25] Gisela Konopka: *Social Group Work: A Helping Process.* Englewood Cliffs, New Jersey, Prentice-Hall, 1963, p. 20.

Qualities of Social Group Workers

In addition to developing a basic philosophy based on respect for all human beings and faith in their capacity to grow and change, the social group worker should have a deep sense of responsibility to use his profession ethically and skillfully to achieve important human outcomes. Through professional education, he should have capabilities in the following areas:

Knowledge. He should have knowledge of individual dynamics and group behavior (both normal and pathological); social policy; administrative principles; and community resources and community organization.

Skill. He should have skill in direct work with groups; supervision of lay staff and volunteers; diagnosis of individual and group behavior; recording, summarizing, and analyzing group process and individual behavior; referral to other agencies or professional workers; and a degree of skill in such areas as casework, counseling and community development.

Attitude. His attitude should reflect professional discipline and integrity; respect for and appreciation of the contribution of others within his agency or organization; an inquiring mind; flexibility in the use of principles and tools; freedom and creativity in the way he uses himself.[26]

Social workers are employed in a variety of settings, some of which involve groups which are comparatively normal in their level of adjustment and ability to function, while others are composed primarily of individuals who have emotional, social, or other disabilities. No matter what the situation, the social group worker generally seeks to achieve the following outcomes, in terms of the growth of participants, through the group process:

1. *Individualization.* The worker does not attempt to create conformity or "group thinking." Instead, his goal is to help participants develop sound and healthy self-concepts, to be better able to conform to group norms, and to interact meaningfully with other group members.

2. *Sense of Belonging.* In modern society, many individuals suffer from a deep sense of alienation; they have difficulty in feeling that they "belong." Healthy group experiences can be extremely effective in giving participants the feeling that they are important to others and are accepted by them.

3. *Capacity to Participate.* Successful group involvement can strengthen each member's ability to share in group activities and decision making and to take responsibility and assist others, thus becoming more effective as a citizen in the overall community.

4. *Increased Respect for Differences Among People.* By taking part in a group, which may include people of other races, creeds, ages, or personal characteristics, group members may learn to accept others more fully and, in so doing, to develop a greater sense of self-worth.

---

[26] Gisela Konopka: *Group Work in the Institution.* New York, Association Press, 1970, pp. 42–43.

5. *Warm and Accepting Social Climate.* Positive group experiences may help establish an atmosphere of warmth and respect for others and the willingness to have a free interplay of human personalities without being overly defensive or hostile.[27]

In order to achieve such outcomes the group worker must be highly sensitive to the interplay of personalities within the group. He should be able to recognize the psychological drives and mechanisms at work within the individual group members, the various natural leaders, the group structure (including both the "in-group" and the "peripheral" members), and the nature of group norms, values, and sanctions. In achieving this understanding he should be fully knowledgeable about theory and practice in group dynamics, as summarized earlier in this chapter.

Social Group Work Principles

While it is difficult to outline a single set of working principles or methods, the following guidelines apply generally to the work of social group workers.

1. The social group worker has a helping and enabling function rather than a directive one. It is his task to help group members move toward greater independence and autonomy; to do this group members must learn to take a full degree of responsibility for their own behavior and for the management of the group.

2. The worker should form a meaningful relationship with all group members and should attempt to understand their needs, both those which they express overtly and also their deeper, hidden needs and drives, which are likely to be revealed only with time and exploration.

3. The worker should make it clear that he accepts all group members, although he may not accept or approve of all their behavior, particularly when it is antisocial or self-destructive.

4. The worker must start at the point where the group is, without immediately imposing demanding goals, limitations, or models of how he wants members to behave. However, he must then seek to guide them in directions that they will find more satisfying and rewarding, and which ultimately will bring about constructive changes in their lives.

5. In order to understand the group better, the worker should study it consciously and analyze individual and group behavior as thoroughly and systematically as possible. He observes and records facts, he interprets statements and actions, and he diagnoses and evaluates. As a psychotherapist might, he makes full use of nonverbal material.

6. The worker should recognize each member of the group as a unique individual having his own qualities and needs. At the same time, he

---

[27] *Ibid.*, pp. 44–46.

must also perceive him as a participant within the total group structure, with a unique role or roles, status level, and affiliations with others.

7. He encourages each group member to participate according to his own capabilities and needs, and he helps him become a more effective group member.

8. He recognizes that group members must learn from the results of their own decisions and efforts. He therefore gives the group latitude to plan and carry out its own program activities and projects.

9. He encourages the group to review its values, norms, and sanctions, to understand its own behavior, and to move toward a more constructive and effective program.

10. He maintains regular records, such as narratives, anecdotes, and other reports, and regularly evaluates the progress of the group, the role played by individual members, and the role he is playing as its leader.

RELATIONSHIP BETWEEN RECREATION AND
SOCIAL GROUP WORK

Recreation and social group work have certain points of similarity, as mentioned earlier, and certain differences. They are both concerned with using recreation as a medium to meet human needs and to promote social growth and community well-being. Recreation leaders tend to work with large numbers of participants and usually do not become involved deeply with single individuals or small groups. Although many recreation leaders do develop intense bonds with participants, more commonly their role is primarily concerned with organizing, planning, scheduling, and directing activities.

In contrast, social group workers usually do not regard provision of activities as a primary focus of their work. Instead, recreation becomes an important medium through which to work. The group worker's primary goal is in the area of human relationships. Activities are a way of reaching and involving members of youth groups, gangs, groups in treatment, or adult groups, in order to deal with problems, strengthen the members' participation in community life, or bring about other constructive individual and social change.

Many group workers have a responsibility for supervising recreation activities in institutions. As an example, in large child-care homes, a social group worker might be in charge of all social service and activity programs, although actual group leadership might be carried out by recreation workers, house parents, or child-care workers. Often, in such settings, play activities are seen as having an important therapeutic purpose. Redl and Wineman have written:

> The recreational diet and its implementation are of utmost importance in the treatment of the ego-disturbed child. In their various aspects, they offer the child a chance for expressional discharge within organizational, sublima-

tional, and frustration-acceptance levels mainly circumscribed by the particular ego disabilities from which he suffers. . . .

The clinician recognizes that one of the most vital . . . experiential areas is that of gratifying play. Normal children seem to have an inner guiding hand, which helps them to find these outlets so necessary to their emotional health. With the ego-disturbed child, making up for this missing mental hygiene vitamin is one of the most important functions of the residential milieu.[28]

Group workers in institutions would tend, then, to offer play activities with a strong emphasis on providing such values as: (a) helping children gain satisfaction through the learning and mastery of skills; (b) helping children learn the art of sublimation through play; (c) teaching children to be able to release aggressive feelings in socially acceptable ways; and (d) helping them master relationships with others, including both children and adults. It is this emphasis on the use of recreation as a psychodynamic medium that distinguishes the social group worker from the typical recreation leader — although a recreation leader who worked in such a setting should gain, through observation and consultation, increasing competence in using recreation experience to achieve treatment goals.

Indeed, in all settings, those concerned with the direct provision of recreation services must realize that their ultimate purpose is *not* just to provide activities, facilities, or program services. Particularly in situations where they are working with youth groups and clubs, with patients in hospitals, or with aging people in senior centers or nursing homes, they must be fully aware of the important potential of recreational involvement and of the effect of constructive group experiences.

Recreation leaders, however, must not confuse themselves with social workers, or attempt to play the role of specialists in group dynamics. In the first place, they are not usually trained to do this sort of job, and while they may have a high degree of intuitive understanding or the ability to relate well to groups, this is not enough. More important, group dynamics is *not* the recreation leader's overriding concern. For example, many of the groups that recreation leaders supervise are temporary aggregates of people with shifting memberships rather than groups with continuity, stable memberships, and a meaningful set of common goals and needs.

For practical reasons the recreation leader cannot act as a democratic group leader would in the fullest sense. While he might wish to act as an enabler or catalyst, permitting group members to go through a painful process of trial-and-error and making their own decisions (even if they are wrong), often he cannot afford to let them do this. His job is to supervise effective and successful programs. Therefore, the playground leader, the tournament director, or the drama specialist who is arranging a theater festival must take vigorous leadership action. He cannot wait through the slow

---

[28] Fritz Redl and David Wineman: *Children Who Hate.* Glencoe, Illinois, Free Press, 1957, pp. 36–37.

and difficult process of group decision making if he is confronted with an immediate problem of safety, discipline, or an emergency.

Those who have worked with groups for a sustained period know that the development of democratic and self-governing processes is a frustrating and time-consuming process. It is axiomatic that the majority of members of many organizations are not willing to assume regular responsibilities, attend meetings, and undertake the hard work that must be done. In such situations the leader must be ready to work with the loyal few who can be counted on, to help them take responsibility to the greatest degree possible and to play a directive role when necessary.

With these limitations, the final message of this chapter is that recreation leaders and supervisors must be as aware as possible of the significance of group dynamics. They should understand how groups function, their values, and how they may be worked with to enrich program outcomes for all participants. In many cases recreation leaders and supervisors themselves can bring this kind of knowledge and awareness to bear, to improve group processes. In other, more difficult cases specialists in group dynamics may be brought in to diagnose and work with the situation. For example, in some recreation and park departments sensitivity training programs have been established to improve interpersonal relationships among staff members.

Thus, in both day-by-day program leadership and in more complicated problems involving participant or staff relations, the use of group dynamics principles and expertise is an important element in the broad field of recreation leadership and supervision.

Suggested Examination Questions or Topics for Student Reports

1. Define group dynamics and show why, in your view, it is essential that recreation leaders and supervisors be knowledgeable in this area.
2. Identify and discuss several of the key aspects of groups (such as their types, their properties or characteristics, or their effects on participants) that you believe can be illustrated in recreational groups.
3. What are the major implications for recreation leaders of the Lewin-Lippitt-White or Sherif studies in group leadership styles and methods? Go to original reports of these studies to document your response.
4. Present and summarize several of the basic principles of social group work that are presented in this chapter. To what extent would these apply to recreation leadership?

Suggested Action Assignments for Students

1. Carefully examine a recreation club or other fairly stable group of participants. Analyze its structure, the roles played by various members of the group, and their allegiances, cliques or friendships.
2. Examine an agency or institution in which social group work is practiced as the primary discipline. Determine the role of recreation in this setting.

career development
in recreation

professional preparation in recreation service

This chapter deals with professional preparation in recreation and park leadership, supervision, and administration. It briefly summarizes the history of this field, describes its recent growth, outlines its objectives, and gives examples of college and university curricula on community college, baccalaureate, and graduate levels. It concludes by assessing the present status of professional preparation in recreation and parks, and by discussing a number of important issues facing recreation educators today.

BACKGROUND OF PROFESSIONAL PREPARATION IN RECREATION AND PARKS

One of the most frequently heard comments about the field of recreation and park service is that it is an extremely new area of professional specialization. Indeed, college degree programs in recreation were not initiated until the 1930's, and were not widely accepted until the 1960's. Prior to this, many colleges had offered single courses in recreation leadership, usually in departments of physical education. To assist these departments, the Playground Association of America developed several suggested curricula in leadership, based on recommendations made at its first Congress in Chicago, in 1907. These curricula included: (a) *The Normal Course in Play*, a detailed manual which covered both the theory and practical conduct of recreation activities, and which was intended for those planning to become professional playground directors or for those planning to work in special institutions for the handicapped; (b) *The Course in Play for Grade Teachers*, a much shorter and less detailed curriculum designed to help elementary school teachers lead play activities; and (c) *The Institute Course in Play*, a training manual suggested for playground supervisors to use in preparing part-time or seasonal leaders to conduct programs.

In 1926, the National Recreation Association established a special one-year graduate training institute, known as the National Recreation School, to train recreation administrators who were already in the field. This institute helped prepare 300 practitioners for executive leadership in the recreation field. Also, special institutes directed by National Recreation Association consultants under the auspices of the Extension Service of the United States Department of Agriculture afforded training opportunities for thousands of participants from rural communities and organizations.

The first specialized college degree in recreation was approved at the University of Minnesota in 1937. Other colleges which had already developed a cluster of recreation courses in their physical education departments began to follow suit. However, by the end of World War II there were only a dozen or so colleges with recreation majors. In addition, other colleges provided specialized training for park administrators, often in connection with departments of forestry, conservation, or landscape architecture. By 1950, there were 37 colleges and universities with recreation and parks curricula, and by 1960, 64 senior colleges and universities and two community colleges offered such programs. Then, during the mid- and late 1960's, professional preparation in recreation and parks expanded at an accelerated rate. There were several reasons for this development.

Factors Promoting Higher Education in Recreation and Parks

1. During the 1960's, it became apparent that recreation had become a major economic force, and that employment in this field represented a major area of job opportunity for young people. The United States Department of Labor made the following statement:

    Employment opportunities for well qualified workers were excellent in early 1965. Shortages existed in all parts of the country for trained recreation workers, particularly in local government, hospitals, and youth-serving organizations.

    Opportunities for recreation workers are expected to increase rapidly at least through the mid-1970's. Thousands of recreation workers will be needed annually to allow for growth and to replace personnel who leave the field because of retirements, death, and transfers to other occupations. . . . Increased leisure time and rising levels of per capita income should foster growth in almost all recreational fields during the next ten years.[1]

    These projections were supported by a nationwide study of manpower needs that was carried out by the National Recreation and Park Association under a grant from the Federal Administration on Aging.

---

[1] *Employment Outlooks for Recreation Workers.* Washington, D.C., Occupational Outlook Report Series (Bulletin No. 1450–69), U.S. Department of Labor, 1966–1967, pp. 2–3.

This report predicted that there would be a need for hundreds of thousands of new recreation and park professionals in the years ahead.

2. The federal government made a major contribution to the field when, in 1962, it published the findings of the Outdoor Recreation Resources Review Commission. Based on an extensive inventory of the nation's park and outdoor recreation systems, and of public participation in outdoor recreation, the Commission's report resulted in the establishment of the Bureau of Outdoor Recreation, in the passage of the Land and Water Conservation Fund Act, and in extensive new programs of outdoor recreation throughout the United States.

3. A third significant factor in both the United States and Canada was the merging of recreation and park agencies and professional organizations. In the United States, the National Recreation and Park Association, and in Canada, the Canadian Parks/Recreation Association, lent considerable strength to professional development in recreation and parks. The formerly diffuse image of recreation and park practitioners became sharpened in the eyes of many young people. The Society of Park and Recreation Educators, a branch of the National Recreation and Park Association, became active in promoting research, special institutes, and higher standards in the growing number of college and university curricula.

4. The changing role of recreation in many communities also increased interest in the field. The inclusion of recreation as an important service of programs initiated as part of the "war on poverty" in the United States, such as the Community Action Programs of the Office of Economic Opportunity, the Job Corps, and Vista, gave financial support to recreation services in many inner-city areas. Therapeutic recreation also grew considerably during this period, opening up large new areas of potential employment.

5. Changes in colleges and universities themselves promoted the growth of recreation and parks in higher education. Great numbers of new community colleges — designed to meet the needs of students who would not normally attend four-year colleges and to provide qualified personnel to carry out vitally-needed human services — were established. Many colleges shifted away from a liberal arts focus toward more practical, job-oriented programs, with emphasis on human services. Finally, as the education profession became overpopulated with an abundance of qualified graduates — and a shortage of openings — many colleges began to consider other fields in which they might offer degrees. As a consequence, many college physical education departments established new recreation programs in order to assure more diversified job opportunities for their majors.

For all these reasons, enrollment in college recreation curricula began to grow steadily, and there was a rapid increase in the number of departments offering degrees in this field.

Growth of College and University Departments

In 1967, the American Association for Health, Physical Education and Recreation identified 103 colleges and universities with an undergraduate major in this field. The Society of Park and Recreation Educators reported in 1970 that there were 220 college curricula. In 1973, the total was 287 and the projection was that the number would be 350, by 1975.[2] The number of commmunity colleges with degree programs has expanded markedly. By 1973, there were 119.

Not only was there a much greater number of college programs, but the number of students majoring in recreation also climbed sharply. For example, the number of undergraduate majors per curriculum had averaged 55 in 1967; by 1973, it was 125. A number of departments, such as those at Kent State, Ohio, the University of Wisconsin at Lacrosse, and several California state colleges (including those at San Jose, San Diego, Sacramento, and Northridge), had well over 400 major students per department. The total number of students climbed during this period to almost 22,000.

CURRICULUM DEVELOPMENT IN RECREATION AND PARKS

Curriculum development in recreation and parks involved a process of gradual change rather than the sudden emergence of unique new programs. Most of the pioneering curricula were assigned to departments of health, physical education, and recreation, and had a comparatively small number of courses, with emphasis given to recreation leadership. Only gradually did the goals of these curricula shift to preparing supervisors and administrators and to meeting specialized needs in the field. Similarly, many key courses, such as those in principles, administration, facilities, and evaluation, tended to cover all three areas (health, physical education, and recreation). Often, faculty members had joint responsibilities in the three areas, with their own backgrounds being primarily in physical education.

However, as recreation curricula became established and expanded in size, several changes took place. An increasing number of curricula gained administrative independence by acquiring separate faculties with members who increasingly held advanced degrees in recreation. As enrollments grew, recreation majors no longer shared key courses with health and physical education majors. Instead, specialized courses in recreation and parks were offered, along with new degree options in important areas of professional specialization.

---

[2] Thomas A. Stein: "Recreation and Park Education in the United States and Canada — 1973." *Parks and Recreation,* January, 1974, pp. 32–35. See also: 1973 *Educational Resources Study* of Society of Park and Recreation Educators.

Role of Professional Conferences

Giving direction to these changes was a series of major conferences which developed recommendations for professional education in recreation and parks. These conferences included the following:

PERE MARQUETTE CONFERENCE. This national conference, held in 1950, dealt with graduate study in health, physical education, and recreation. It outlined the purposes of graduate education in the three fields and made specific recommendations with respect to programs, degree requirements, counseling, course options, and faculty qualifications.

CONFERENCE ON RECREATION FOR THE ILL AND HANDICAPPED. Sponsored by Comeback, Inc., this meeting was held in New York City in 1961. It brought together leading recreation educators and practitioners and sought to develop curriculum models to meet changing needs in therapeutic recreation. It concluded that well-qualified practitioners should have a general undergraduate major in recreation, which was to be followed by a carefully designed graduate program emphasizing medical and psychiatric nomenclature, the techniques of adapting program activities for the ill and disabled, and preparation of individuals for new roles in the field, such as training and consultation services.

NATIONAL RECREATION EDUCATION PROJECT. The Federation of National Professional Organizations for Recreation established a working committee whose purpose was to develop an accreditation plan for recreation and parks higher education. In 1965, the committee presented a comprehensive set of proposals, including guidelines for degree programs on undergraduate, master's, and doctoral levels. On the master's degree level, for example, it recommended six possible specialization options in: (1) recreation program supervision and administration; (2) recreation and park administration; (3) resource administration for agencies with land management functions; (4) camping administration; (5) college union administration; and (6) therapeutic recreation administration.

NATIONAL CONFERENCE ON PROFESSIONAL EDUCATION FOR OUTDOOR RECREATION. This 1964 meeting was co-sponsored by the Bureau of Outdoor Recreation and Syracuse University. It brought together leaders in government agencies, representatives of professional organizations, and university educators. Conference participants agreed that a much more thorough analysis of the task of preparing specialists in outdoor recreation was needed, including the development of new interdisciplinary courses and curricula.

GRADUATE EDUCATION CONFERENCE IN HEALTH, PHYSICAL EDUCATION AND RECREATION. This meeting, sponsored in 1967 by the American Association for Health, Physical Education and Recreation, dealt with the goals and organization of graduate education in the three fields. It outlined the special functions of a master's degree and a doctorate and urged the development of specialized programs dealing with therapeutic recreation, youth-serving agencies, and the needs of religious, industrial, Senior Center, armed forces, and outdoor interpretation organizations.

NATIONAL FORUM AND MODEL CITIES WORKSHOP. In May, 1970, in response to changing social needs, a national forum was held at Grambling College, Louisiana, that dealt with the role of black colleges and universities in recreation and parks education. Assisted by the National Recreation and Park Association and a number of federal agencies, it focused on the problem of getting larger numbers of minority group members into recreation departments and affording them the opportunity for career advancement. The forum also dealt with the need to support and strengthen the curricula of black colleges in recreation and parks.

Still other conferences and study groups developed reports and recommendations for professional education in recreation and parks during this period. Special conferences were held that dealt with the development of major programs in community colleges and the role of therapeutic recreation and adapted physical education personnel in serving the disabled. Recommendations developed at such meetings have been extremely helpful, both to colleges and universities that have initiated new curricula in recreation and parks and also to those seeking to upgrade existing programs.

EXAMPLES OF CURRICULA IN RECREATION AND PARKS

In the pages that follow, a number of examples of recreation and park curricula on community college, baccalaureate, and master's degree levels, and guidelines for developing such curricula, are provided.

Community College Programs

Community college programs in recreation and parks are intended to serve two kinds of needs: (a) direct preparation for employment on appropriate levels through *terminal* programs; and (b) preparation for *transfer* to a four-year college in order to complete a baccalaureate degree. Those completing the first option are generally equipped with a substantial number of practical, skills-oriented courses that help them to assume direct activity leadership responsibilities. Those electing the second option generally take fewer specialized courses in recreation and a greater number of courses in general education or liberal arts, which will assist them in transferring to four-year colleges.

A typical statement of the objectives of a community college follows.

Curriculum Objectives of the Greenfield,
Massachusetts, Community College

The Recreation Leadership Curriculum is designed to provide the student with the following knowledges or competencies:

1. An understanding of the theory of leisure and recreation.

2. Knowledge of the organizations or agencies (public, private, and commercial) providing recreation services.

3. Knowledge of comprehensive programming in relation to range, depth, continuity, balance, challenge, and interrelatedness.

4. An understanding of program development in relation to the maximum use of community resources—people and facilities.

5. Competency to instruct and/or lead individuals or groups in several major program areas: crafts, drama, music, lifetime sports, aquatics, outdoor recreation and social recreation.

6. Knowledge of human relations and personnel problems at the leadership and supervisory levels.

7. Knowledge of the supervisory responsibilities, including records, reports, and accountability.

8. Leadership experience with different age groups of varying degrees of health, in a variety of settings and situations.

9. An understanding of the characteristics and behavior of a "true" professional.

The course of study intended to achieve these objectives falls into two categories: *general education* courses, including work in the social and behavioral sciences, communication arts, sciences, and humanities; and specialized courses in *recreation,* including general theory courses, skills, or direct leadership courses, with four required semesters of field work.

Degree Options, Catonsville, Maryland, Community College

In many community colleges, students are permitted to elect a choice of specialized degree options. For example, at the Catonsville, Maryland, Community College, the Recreation Leadership Curriculum offers three majors: *Recreation Program Leadership, Therapeutic Recreation Leadership,* and *Outdoor Education Leadership.* Typically, students are required to take general education courses, "core" recreation courses, and special recreation courses assigned to the option. Examples of such courses follow.

General Education Courses. These include courses in English composition, speech, science, government, mathematics, social science, and humanities.

Required Recreation Courses. These include such "core" courses as: introduction to leisure services, program planning, and directed practice in recreation (field work).

Specialized Courses, Assigned to Options. In the general option, Recreation Program Leadership, students must take courses in games and social activities, music and drama, individual lifetime sports or physical education skills, and outdoor education and camping. In the other two options similar courses are required.

A

B

    Staff Development. An important supervisory responsibility is the provision of orientation and in-service training clinics and workshops. Summer leaders practice useful games in a pre-season training program in Orlando, Florida (*A*), discuss methods in Vancouver, Canada (*B*), and learn about pool filtration systems in Cleveland, Ohio (*C*). Supervisors and administrators plan together for a summer program in Abington Township, Pennsylvania (*D*) and for a basketball tournament in Nassau County, New York (*E*):

C

D

E

Programs in Four-Year Colleges

Obviously, senior colleges which offer bachelor's degree programs in recreation and parks demonstrate both greater diversity and depth in their curricula than community colleges do. Typically, their statements of objectives tend to be more ambitious and conceptual in nature. An example is drawn from the Recreation Education Department of the University of British Columbia, Canada:

Objectives of the Curriculum, Recreation
Education Department, University of British
Columbia, Canada

The objectives of the curriculum are to foster an educational experience which provides the student with:

1. A broad cultural background encompassing foundation study in the humanities and the social and natural sciences. The specific objective is to provide the student with a better understanding of himself and his relation to others in a constantly changing society.

2. A knowledge of studies closely related to recreation education, encompassing human growth and development, adult education, community planning, architecture, and the like. The specific objective is to provide the student with a knowledge of people and the use made of their environments, the diversity of opportunities often made available to them, and concepts of community, social, and physical planning.

3. A series of specific professional understandings encompassing the history, philosophy, and principles of leisure and recreation, the organization and administration of recreation and facilities for programming, the process of working with groups, the training and supervision of leaders, program media and methods of leadership, and the direct contact with agencies in the field. The specific objective is to develop the particular competencies required in the worker role and a knowledge of the tools and methodology of the professional practitioner.

4. A concept of appreciation of the reasons *why* as well as *how* a specific function is instituted, maintained, changed or discontinued. The specific objective is to produce a graduate who will be readily capable of assuming supervisory and administrative responsibilities after the initial professional experience is satisfactorily completed.

Degree Options in Four-Year Colleges

Although earlier curriculum conferences had recommended only a few specialized degree options as suitable for undergraduate curricula in recreation and parks, by the mid-1970's many colleges had developed a much greater variety of specializations. For example, the Society of Park and Recreation Educators identified the following degree options in colleges and universities in 1973 (Table 4–1).

A specific example of the kinds of options offered on the undergraduate level may be found in the Clemson University, South Carolina, curriculum.

Department of Recreation and Park Administration, Clemson University, South Carolina

This program is designed to provide a broad liberal arts education and to develop the basic knowledge and skills needed to administer leisure service programs in three areas of major emphasis: *Rehabilitative Recreation, Recreation and Park Administration,* and *Recreation Resource Management.* Within each of these areas, it is possible to concentrate further, as shown in this diagram:

GENERAL EDUCATION
(50 Hours)

Accounting, Biological Science, Composition, Economics, History, Literature, Mathematics, Physical Science, Political Science, Psychology, Sociology, Speech

Electives
(15 Hours)

RECREATION & PARK ADMINISTRATION
(44 Hours)
Core Curriculum

EMPHASIS AREAS
(26 Hours)

REHABILITATIVE RECREATION	RECREATION AND PARK ADMINISTRATION	RECREATION RESOURCE MANAGEMENT
Correctional Institutions	Public Agencies	Area and Facility Management
Aging	Semi-Public and Private Agencies	Resource Planning, Development, and Interpretation
Mental or Physical Disabilities	Outdoor Education and Recreation	
	Inner-City	

The Core Curriculum, typical of many college programs in general recreation and park administration, includes courses such as the following: Introduction to Community Recreation, History and Principles of Outdoor Recreation, Program Planning for Recreation, Camp Organization and Administration, Recreation Leadership, Recreation Administration, Facility and Site Planning, Recreation Research, and Field Training in Recreation.

TABLE 4–1   Curriculum Options in Degree Programs in United States and Canada

Recreation Program Management	98	Older Citizens and Aging	29
Recreation and Park Administration	98	Commercial/Tourism	26
Therapeutic Recreation	80	Research	23
Outdoor Recreation and Camping	75	Industrial Recreation	18
Park Management	67	Corrections	18
Voluntary and Youth Service	51	College Unions	15
School Recreation	40		

Other courses, including planning, environmental interpretation, and special programs for minority populations, totaled 21. Increased emphasis was found in the areas of park management, therapeutic recreation, outdoor recreation and camping.

Examples of Specialized Degree Programs

Two examples of specialized degree programs, drawn from the curricula of the University of Missouri and Waterloo University, follow below.

Department of Recreation and Park Administration,
University of Missouri at Columbia

A typical example of degree requirements which lead to a specialization in *Recreation and Park Administration* may be found in this curriculum. In addition to college liberal arts requirements, undergraduate majors are required to take a minimum of 39 credits distributed among three categories (A, B, and C) in the major field.

    A.   LEADERSHIP PROGRAM AREAS (ACTIVITY SKILLS)
          Group One   (minimum of three of the five areas and 10 credits must
                     be taken)
          1.   Music
          2.   Arts and Crafts
          3.   Dramatics
          4.   Games, Rhythms, Sports
          5.   Nature
          Group Two   (minimum of two of the three areas and four credits must
                     be taken)
          1.   Camping and Aquatics
          2.   Social Programs
          3.   Methods of Teaching or Coaching or Officiating
    B.   RECREATION THEORY COURSES (MINIMUM OF SEVEN COURSES)
          1.   Introduction to Recreation and Park Administration
          2.   Resources, Agencies, and Organizations in Recreation and Parks
          3.   Planning Recreation Areas and Facilities
          4.   Principles of Interpretive Outdoor Recreation
          5.   Community Recreation
          6.   Senior Seminar

     7. Problems
     8. Theory and Practice of Group Leadership
     9. Analysis of Leisure Recreation Services
   10. Introduction to Administration in Recreation and Parks
   11. Introduction to Therapeutic Recreation
   12. Operation of Therapeutic Recreation Services
   13. Outdoor Recreation-Education
   14. Park Management
   15. Recreation Land Management and Planning
C. PRACTICAL FIELD EXPERIENCES (FOUR CREDITS)
    1. Field Instruction

In addition, students are required to take approximately 16 credits of elective work from such fields as community health, economics, horticulture, education, management, physical education, psychology, regional and community affairs, sociology, social work, zoology, or other areas of special interest.

— University of Waterloo, Ontario, Canada

A number of colleges and universities have begun innovative programs intended to explore leisure as a scholarly discipline rather than as a narrowly conceived area of professional employment. For example, the Department of Recreation, in the School of Human Kinetics and Leisure Sciences at the University of Waterloo, has developed an undergraduate curriculum which focuses on the growing impact of increased leisure on industrial society and the effects of continuing technological change on patterns of leisure time use.

Recreation and leisure majors at the University of Waterloo may elect one of four areas of concentration: *Leisure Studies, Therapeutic Recreation, Recreation Administration,* or *Outdoor Recreation and Education.* The curriculum offers a range of courses with scholarly or theoretical orientations, such as:

Introduction to the Study of Leisure
Orientation to Communication Media and Technology
Seminar on Recreation and Leisure
Colloquium on Religion and Leisure
Comparative Recreation Systems
Statistical Techniques Applied to Leisure Studies

Philosophy of Leisure
Sociology of Leisure
Travel and Tourism
Sport in Society
Leisure and Psychopathology
Growth, Development and Aging
The Individual in Sport Situations

However, students are not restricted to such courses. A substantial number of other courses deal with more practical concerns, such as parks management, the operation of camping and outdoor education programs, or programs in therapeutic recreation. There is no requirement for activity courses aimed directly at developing leadership skills. Since many Canadian community colleges concentrate heavily in the area of training personnel for such responsibilities, it is apparently assumed that university programs should focus on higher levels of administration or scholarship.

Graduate Curricula in Recreation and Parks

In master's degree programs on the graduate level, one tends to find a heavier concentration on specialized degree programs which focus not only on different *areas* of program service but also on providing advanced professional preparation for different types of *roles* in recreation and park agencies. For example, at the Pennsylvania State University, graduate students are equipped in four areas of graduate specialization for roles as *practitioners* (professional workers in the field), *researchers*, or college and university *educators*.

Graduate Curricula at the Pennsylvania State University

1. *Recreation and Park Administration.* Emphasizes knowledge essential to administration of recreation and park systems, including the management and operation of outdoor recreation areas and facilities in state park systems and the National Park Service. It is concerned with the function of services in an urban society and relates directly to urban planning and public administration.

   Park Planning. Emphasis focuses on the knowledge and methodologies required for broad scale planning for park and recreation development. Park planners work on a design team within public agencies or private consulting firms with landscape architects, engineers, administrators, and interpretive planners in developing national or state parks, or other large recreation areas.

2. *Recreation Program Supervision and Administration.* Relates to the development and administration of programs in various settings, such as municipal departments, voluntary agencies, churches, armed forces, state and federal agencies, and so on. Emphasis may be placed on special groups, such as inner-city and poverty groups, the aged, children and youth, or upon the meaning of leisure, with study directed toward the historical, philosophical, and social bases of recreation and leisure. Urban social planning is a particular aspect of this area.

3. *Therapeutic Recreation* relates to the development and administration of programs serving the mentally retarded, physically disabled, emotionally disturbed, and aging in both institutional and community settings. The program is directed toward the conceptual understandings of recreation's role in a comprehensive rehabilitation process, including both clinical and community facets, and thus prepares the student

to work with a broad range of disability areas in either a medical setting or in the community . . .

4. *Camping, Outdoor Education, and Outdoor Interpretive Services* focus on the administration of resident camp programs; school-oriented outdoor education, including resident outdoor schools and the integration and utilization of the natural environment into the curriculum; and on public interpretive programs, especially in the nature center complex in its whole program, in coordination of community outdoor education programs, and in development of overall outdoor recreation programs under various auspices. Each of the three aspects represents a special emphasis within this area of specialization:

   a. Administration and supervision of resident camp operations.

   b. Administration and supervision of school-sponsored environmental education programs, including resident outdoor programs, field laboratories, and experiences.

   c. Administration and supervision of public environmental education programs.

Graduate offerings in many colleges and universities are tending to become increasingly sophisticated and scholarly in their approach to such options. Whereas a number of years ago they frequently included the same types of courses as undergraduate curricula, many graduate programs today exclude all courses directly concerned with leadership and program activities. Instead, the emphasis is on higher levels of administrative responsibility, research, and interdisciplinary or advanced adademic courses. This is particularly true in those colleges or universities that offer graduate studies related to natural resource management. One example is the Texas A and M University.

Texas A and M University

This institution's Department of Recreation and Parks (situated in the School of Natural Bio-Sciences, in the College of Agriculture) offers a Master of Arts degree, a Master of Science, and a doctorate in *Recreation and Resources Management.* It also offers an M.A. in *Natural Resources Development.* The rationale of the program, which places a strong emphasis on interdisciplinary scholarship, is stated in the following passage:

> Graduate course offerings . . . are designed to provide scientific solutions to problems encountered by administrators, educators, and professional practitioners. The focus is on the total leisure environment and its resource base. This encompasses . . . studies in comprehensive recreation resource planning, quality and carrying capacity, user preferences and demand, agency administration, and alternative methods for meeting leisure needs. These courses stress the study of spatial relationships between humans and the natural environment in various recreational settings in which the primary concern is managerial response to man's critical need of open space, and utilization of leisure through recreational pursuits.

Graduate courses include titles such as the following:

Recreation and Leisure Concepts	Analytical Techniques in Recreation
Conceptual Foundations of Recreation and Resources Development	Recreation Resource Communication
Recreation Organization and Policy	Travel and Tourism
Recreation and Park Design	Professional Internship
Socio-Economic Issues in Outdoor Recreation	Recreation Resource Development
Recreation Systems Planning	Problems
	Special Topics

The examples that have been given of curriculum and courses on the community college, four-year college, and graduate levels of higher education give a general picture of professional preparation in recreation and parks today. In reviewing these topics, there are several specific questions which should be asked:

What is the overall quality of these institutions, and how may they be improved?

What are some of the current problems and issues in professional preparation, and what steps are being taken to meet them?

What are some of the desirable directions for the future in this field?

APPRAISING THE QUALITY OF COLLEGE CURRICULA

Although many degree programs in colleges and universities throughout the United States and Canada are based on solidly conceived and supported curricula, too many others are inadequate. Among the catalogue descriptions reviewed for this text were a number of curricula that included no more than three or four courses in recreation. Others continued to require physical education courses related to principles, anatomy, kinesiology and physiology, sports skills, and tests and measurements—with only a limited number of courses in appropriate areas of recreation.

It is necessary therefore to ask a number of searching questions about recreation and park curricula today—particularly many of the newer programs which have recently proliferated throughout the United States and Canada. Among these questions should be the following:

Do they have appropriate specialized programs aimed at preparing students to meet legitimate professional needs within recognized content areas? Are the goals and content of each curriculum clearly organized and well thought out?

Are the courses diversified, geared to the appropriate level of professional needs and student capability, and staffed by a qualified group of faculty members? Do faculty members have acceptable degrees in or directly related to recreation and parks, or are they "retreads" from other academic disciplines with little knowledge of this field? Are faculty members in a reasonable ratio to students, and are their teaching loads fixed at a level which permits them to give attention to student needs and to carry on their own scholarly work or other professional commitments?

Are there adequate student services in areas such as counseling, career advisement, field supervision, and job placement? Are there needed resources available in terms of libraries, appropriate agencies for field work, and similar facilities?

Depending on the specific level of the program (community college, four-year college, or graduate level), are curricula geared to carry out appropriate functions? For example, are community colleges preparing students for entry-level, direct leadership positions as they *should* be doing, or are they preparing administrators? Are four-year colleges still training the majority of their students to serve as face-to-face leaders when their real need is for supervisory or administrative preparation? Have graduate programs defined their roles properly?

Is there an appropriate sequence and transition from one level to the next, or are students taking the same, repetitious courses with the same syllabi and textbooks as they move to higher levels of education?

Accreditation and Evaluation of College Programs

The screening of programs of higher education should normally be the responsibility of a national accrediting body closely associated with the major professional organization in any field of professional service. Since the early 1960's, there has been a continuing attempt to develop an independent accreditation process linked to the National Recreation and Park Association that would free recreation from its present affiliation with health and physical education.

While some professionals and educators resist the idea of accreditation, feeling that it might lead to fixed models of program content and the establishment of a *status quo* in a field that demands experimentation, creativity, and new techniques, most would welcome a meaningful accreditation process. Legitimate standards and evaluative criteria would help to insure the quality of professional education, to identify those college and university programs that are adequate, and to help to weed out those programs that are inferior. Storey describes a number of areas that might be used to examine departments in relation to admissions practices, student involvement, field work and internship, research activities, the quality of teaching, and the role of faculty members in providing field services and consultation to community agencies.[3]

---

[3] E. H. Storey: "Position Paper on Professional Education." Approved by Society of Park and Recreation Educators. *Communiqué*, May, 1972, pp. 17–18.

The National Recreation Education Project has not yet been successful in obtaining separate accreditation status and standards for the recreation and park field. It seems probable that if this is not achieved within the next several years, a system of voluntary registration and evaluation of degree programs, either with the Society of Park and Recreation Educators or with state recreation and park societies, will develop.

Guidelines for Curriculum Content

In 1973, the Society of Park and Recreation Educators issued a set of guidelines to assist colleges and universities in developing new curricula or in reviewing and revising existing programs in recreation and parks. It suggested that the following questions be asked:

Why is the initiation of a new program or revision of an existing curriculum desired?

What evidence suggests that there is a need for a new program?

Has an advisory committee that represents the local public and private agencies and political jurisdictions served by your institution been established to assist with curriculum development?

Have you assessed employment opportunities for your graduates?

Have channels of communication been opened with your college administration that identify the most appropriate administrative division/department/college that will support the program financially and philosophically?

Related disciplines are essential to the education of park and recreation students. Have these relationships been established and incorporated into the curriculum?

Have you sought guidance and advice from your state park and recreation society, state department of higher education, or similar agency?

Are those involved in the planning process familiar with past, present and future trends in parks, recreation, and leisure services?

Have you sought guidance from recognized park and recreation educators?

Have you identified and analyzed all other park and recreation curricula in your area and related this to your planning process? This analysis would include the number of curricula and students, degree levels, options, etc.

Are, or will, the resources at your college be sufficient to initiate or to revise your program (e.g., finances, classroom space, library facilities, computer center, etc.)?

Have you determined the availability of qualified full-time and adjunct faculty members to support your program? For example, many physical education teachers are not qualified by education or experience to teach recreation and/or park courses.

Have you identified the type of faculty expertise required, including those qualified in parks and recreation, as well as in other needed disciplines?

Do quality opportunities exist for students requiring field work/practicum experience?

Have you identified the unique resources in your college and surrounding area and applied this to your curriculum? For example, outstanding health services and facilities will strengthen a therapeutic recreation option.

CURRENT PROBLEMS AND ISSUES IN PROFESSIONAL PREPARATION

One of the key problems facing major college and university recreation and park departments today is the need to remain current. Our society is a dynamic and constantly changing one, and within each area of professional leisure service new needs, policies, and professional programs or methods tend to evolve rapidly. What this means is that college curricula— tied as they are to course descriptions, textbooks, fixed degree requirements which cannot easily be changed, and to the capabilities of faculty members—may have difficulty in responding to current needs.

Shifting Professional Needs

An excellent example of this problem may be found in the field of therapeutic recreation service. This area of professional service has changed markedly in recent years. For example, employment in therapeutic recreation previously was found chiefly in large hospitals, in special schools for the retarded or physically disabled, or in other long-term care facilities. The role of therapeutic recreation specialists was often confined to the development of recreation activity programs. Today, recreation workers are employed in nursing homes, in homes for dependent or disturbed youth, in correctional institutions, and in a host of other settings, including many community-based programs operated by public and voluntary agencies. The role has shifted from an exclusive concern with activity to responsibilities involving counseling, consultation, community organization, staff training, research, and similar functions.

Therapeutic recreation in many institutions has been influenced by such concepts as "milieu therapy," "therapeutic community," and the "continuum of care" approach. Increasingly, therapeutic recreation specialists are viewed as "social-systems specialists." In some settings, they have become members of departments of activity therapies, and their unique recreation functions have become blurred with those in other treatment services.

For all these reasons, it is essential to study present curricula, and to evolve new models and approaches to equipping professional personnel with skills and knowledge appropriate for changing needs in the field. In some cases, the development of new curricula in therapeutic recreation has been assisted by government grants. For example, 15 colleges were involved in the late 1960's and early 1970's in a special graduate curriculum development project in the field of therapeutic recreation and physical education for the disabled. These colleges, which included the universities of Oregon, North Carolina, Kentucky, Connecticut, and Indiana State University, San Jose State, and New York University, were assisted by a grant from the Bureau of Education for the Handicapped, a department of the United States Office of Education (Public Law 90-170), in identifying basic service needs and in developing graduate curricula for the specialized preparation of teachers, administrators, and researchers.

There is an obvious need to carry on similar projects to identify changing needs and construct new models of professional preparation in other areas of recreation and park service, such as community school programs, resource management, commercial recreation, or programs for the disadvantaged.

An Effective Role Within Institutions

In addition to meeting the needs of their own majors, college and university recreation and park departments must begin to play a larger role within their own institutions. Not long ago, recreation faculty members represented a little-known offshoot of physical education. Today, while they have gained independence and fuller recognition in many institutions, the field recreation majors represent is not yet fully understood and respected. Therefore, it is essential that they become more influential within the university family of scholars. Professors of recreation and parks should be active in presenting information and promoting awareness of leisure as a general concern and its specific relationship to ecology, child development, social problems, municipal planning, or other issues of public concern. Through articles, forums, lectures, symposiums, and other special programs, recreation and park educators should make their expertise and concerns known to the entire institution, and should recruit the assistance of faculty members from other departments in interdisciplinary programs.

Similarly, it is important that recreation and park faculty members become more active in working with community agencies. One important way in which this is done is through programs of field work and internship. In addition, skilled faculty members can use their expertise in the field by assisting communities or organizations through consultation, planning, or evaluation studies. Such efforts achieve the following: (a) they help to upgrade standards and practices in the field; (b) they provide college faculty members with a continuing, realistic exposure to professional practices and problems; (c) they help to maintain a healthy linkage between the educator and the practitioner and to bridge the gap between "town" and "gown"; and (d) they give students an opportunity for involvement in community-based projects.

Supply-Demand Balance

As described earlier in this chapter, the number of college and university recreation and park departments has expanded rapidly in recent years, and the trend seems likely to continue. This growth has been based heavily on the expectation that there would continue to be a shortage of qualified professionals in this field. However, it is apparent that the projections of need were somewhat exaggerated.

A number of factors were responsible for excessive employment predictions in this field. Among these were (a) the growth of leisure has not been as rapid as was predicted and, in particular, has not affected the workweek as much as it has vacations, holidays, and retirement; (b) while a tremendous amount of money continues to be spent on leisure, the bulk of it goes to commercial or private programs which do not normally employ professionally-qualified personnel; (c) the projections were based in part on social scientists' predictions regarding population, work patterns, the economy, and so on, which in many cases have not proved accurate; (d) budgetary problems in many cities and a number of states have resulted in fiscal cuts, job freezes or cutbacks, and a limited number of new recreation and park jobs; (e) while billions of dollars are spent by the federal and state governments to support recreation, much of this goes into land acquisition and resource development rather than to the support of actual recreation programs under professional leadership; and (f) many thousands of recreation jobs are not covered by Civil Service or other hiring qualification systems and, as a consequence, continue to be filled by unqualified persons rather than by professionally trained workers.

For all these reasons, the market for college-trained recreation and park personnel has not expanded in the 1970's to the extent predicted. At the same time, the number of degree programs and graduates in this field has grown markedly, creating a probable imbalance between supply and demand. While well-qualified and capable graduates are able to find positions, more marginal candidates are likely to have greater difficulty. There no longer is the "seller's market" for recreation personnel that existed during the 1950's and 1960's.

As a consequence, some educators have suggested that there should be limitations on the number of new degree programs. Apart from the question of how these steps might be taken, there are others who take the position that there should be no arbitrary restriction on programs, except for a positive accreditation process which would identify colleges with adequate curricula and faculty resources. Instead, these educators urge that the market for preparing recreation personnel should be open and competitive. Under such circumstances, the colleges which have the most effective programs and turn out the most highly-qualified graduates will prosper. Colleges with weaker programs probably will find their enrollments declining, and may in some cases phase out their curricula in this field.

The implications of this problem are two-fold: (a) colleges and universities should only initiate or continue majors in parks and recreation if they are thoroughly convinced that there is a realistic need for such programs in their region, based on careful documentation; and (b) they should then make every effort to equip their students with the needed skills and resources, to counsel them wisely, and to assist them throughout the entire process of professional development and placement.

Programs of Continuing Education

A final significant trend in professional preparation in recreation and parks is the growing reliance on programs of continuing education for recreation and park professionals who are already employed. Such programs are presently offered by industry, by professional planning or consulting organizations, and by recreation and parks organizations on the national or state levels, often in cooperation with colleges and universities.

INDUSTRY OR BUSINESS-SPONSORED PROGRAMS.   Many organizations in the recreation field provide extensive in-service training or orientation courses for personnel who have already been employed. These may serve to improve their current functioning, or to help prepare personnel to move up the career ladder to new opportunities. Such programs are described in Chapter Seven.

PROGRAMS OFFERED BY PROFESSIONAL CONSULTING FIRMS.   A number of consulting firms have moved into the field of advising firms in the area of commercial recreation by carrying out research, assisting in planning, or consulting on management problems. One such organization, the Leisure Industries Institute, has offered a series of management seminars geared to the needs of executive personnel in recreation, tourism, and related fields. Held in different locations across the United States, these seminars offer information and training to executives, potential investors, or government officials. Seminar topics in a recent year included these titles:

> RECREATION BUSINESS OVERVIEW: types, resources, policies, potential . . .
> PRACTICAL FINANCES OF RECREATION: costs, revenues, funding, accounting, purchasing, projections . . .
> PLANNING: feasibility studies, design, architecture, physical planning, markets, consulting and design services . . .
> SERVICE: food service, concessions, leasing, vending and franchising, contracting . . .
> ENTERTAINMENT AND SHOW: rides, live entertainment, costuming, preparation, costs, effectiveness . . .
> TRAVEL AND RESORTS: requirements, hotel facilities, recreation facilities, promotion, sales, costs, revenues . . .
> LEGAL: taxes, licensing, land management, legal services, contracts . . .
> PROMOTION AND SALES: promotion, advertising, public relations, salesmanship, group sales, techniques, media . . .
> OPERATIONS AND SEMINAR REVIEW: daily operations, maintenance, emergencies, theft, breakage; Seminar review and summary.

PROGRAMS OFFERED BY PROFESSIONAL
RECREATION AND PARK ORGANIZATIONS

As part of its general program of field service, the National Recreation and Park Association has organized a number of special workshops for recreation and park administrators. These workshops, designed to promote both general executive development and expertise within specific areas of professional concern, are based on the following conviction, as expressed by Donald Henkel, manager of the N.R.P.A. Office of Education and Professional Services:

> It is said that education should be a continuous and lifelong process—a process that requires not only the acquisition of basic skills and knowledge gained in the classroom, but practical application as well. Increasingly, the concept of formal education for youth and practical application for adults is blurring into a continuum of alternating experiences, especially for professionals.[4]

Several examples of such programs follow. Typically, they are organized in cooperation with a leading college or university, using its staff resources and facilities.

INDIANA UNIVERSITY EXECUTIVE DEVELOPMENT PROGRAM. This series of two one-week sessions, held a year apart, has been jointly sponsored by the University's Department of Recreation and Park Administration and the National Recreation and Park Association, in conjunction with the University's Graduate School of Business. The sessions have focused on improving management skills, with an emphasis on new techniques, philosophies, and technologies of management. Course content has included the following: "management by objectives," "decision-making processes," "planning and policy formulation," "organizational structures and trends," "environmental forecasting," and "motivation-behavior analysis."

NORTH CAROLINA STATE UNIVERSITY REVENUE SOURCES MANAGEMENT SCHOOL. This extremely popular course, directed by the University's Department of Recreation Resources Administration, also consists of two one-week sessions, held a year apart at Oglebay Park, West Virginia. Administrators attending the first year's course are given a broad introduction to new professional approaches in areas such as revenue sources management, basic skills and techniques, and methods of operation required in matters such as management principles, budgets, entrance and admission fees, rental fees, merchandising, and similar areas of fiscal concern. Those who attend the second year are exposed to other facets of administrative responsibility, such as the management of special service facilities, cash controls, contracts, work force costs, public relations, feasibility studies, and special services.

---

[4] Donald Henkel: "NRPA Continuing Education." *Parks and Recreation*, August, 1972, pp. 26–31.

MICHIGAN STATE UNIVERSITY PARK AND RECREATION LAW ENFORCE-
MENT INSTITUTE. This final example of a continuing education course,
co-sponsored by the American Park and Recreation Society, Michigan State
University's Department of Park and Recreation Resources, and the School
of Criminal Justice, has the basic objective of teaching the principles and
techniques of law enforcement to recreation and park administrators. It
deals with four basic elements:

> Philosophy of law enforcement, including human relations and com-
> munity relations concerns.
>
> Law enforcement operational techniques, including equipment selection,
> crowd control, traffic control, investigative procedures, emergency plans, and
> communication techniques.
>
> Constitution and criminal justice administration, including review of ar-
> rest, search, field interviews, civil rights and liability elements, and drafting of
> park rules and regulations.
>
> Organizational structure, personnel, chain of command, levels of law en-
> forcement, interagency cooperation, and insurance and bonding procedures.

It seems clear that this type of continuing education can be carried on
more meaningfully in national programs of workshops and courses that attract experienced professionals and are staffed by highly capable faculty
members from leading colleges or universities than could programs which
are part of the regular curriculum of smaller institutions scattered
throughout the United States and Canada.

DIRECTIONS FOR THE FUTURE IN
PROFESSIONAL PREPARATION

What directions are envisioned for the future development of professional preparation in recreation and parks?

First, it seems likely that the number of curricula and of students
majoring in this field will continue to grow steadily. With the increased
public awareness of leisure time and the opportunities in this field, many
new colleges and universities are considering the development of new recreation and park majors. Whether or not these departments thrive and
continue to serve the field will depend on two factors: (a) whether employment in public, voluntary, private, and commercial agencies continues to
grow; and (b) whether more rigorous standards of job selection, such as
certification, registration or licensing procedures, give priority to college-
trained personnel in filling the bulk of future recreation and park openings.

Next, it is probable that the focus of college programs will continue to
diversify, with more specialized curricula being devised for new areas of
recreation program leadership or administrative responsibility. As the
earlier analysis of degree options today has shown, there are at least 14 spe-

cialized options provided in today's curricula. It seems probable that a number of these, such as commercial recreation and tourism, will receive markedly increased attention in the years ahead, and that entirely new options will come into being.

Based on current social trends, it is likely that much greater numbers of women will be recruited into the field, and that they will be prepared for supervisory or administrative level positions which few women have held in the past. Similarly, efforts are being made to draw higher percentages of those who are socially disadvantaged or those of racial or ethnic minority groups into recreation and park service on professional levels. New and different kinds of professional roles are likely to be developed, and the role of higher education on each level will need to be clarified with respect to its unique functions.

Reid suggests that recreation and park education will undergo a drastic metamorphosis, with university and senior college programs facing an increasingly difficult dilemma. On the one hand, he suggests that administrative pressures will urge fuller concentration on upper division (junior/senior levels) and on graduate programs. On the other hand, he writes:

> . . . two-year community and junior colleges, and vocational and technical institutes, will compete vigorously — and successfully — to train a two-year graduate who will be eminently employable as an entry-level professional.
>
> As universities lose the battle for undergraduate students, programs will evolve into degree specialties that combine public service, political science, social psychology, law, government, health, and business administration. These new programs, under a variety of leisure and community service titles, are *not* in the future. They are already attracting national attention.[5]

How accurate are such predictions? This chapter has already shown how a number of colleges and universities have developed upper-level and graduate programs which are highly specialized and rooted in the social and behavioral sciences in their approach to the study of leisure. This development appears to be based on the assumption that four-year college graduates should not move into positions of direct leadership in recreation and park services, since community colleges have successfully assumed this responsibility.

However, it is not clear that two-year recreation program graduates are being widely accepted on professional levels of employment in recreation and park agencies. The majority of Civil Service departments and voluntary organizations appear to have maintained their basic baccalaureate degree requirement for professional positions. By the same token, most four-year college graduates, or even those completing master's degrees, appear to be finding employment in fairly traditional roles in recreation and park agencies. Although an increasing number of positions have become available for planners, researchers, consultants and educators, these posi-

---

[5] Leslie M. Reid: "The Role and Direction of Recreation Education in the 1970's." *Communiqué,* December, 1970, p. 30.

tions are few indeed when compared to the great majority of jobs requiring the familiar services of administrators, supervisors, leaders, and program specialists. And, despite Reid's discussion of interdisciplinary degree specialties as a major new direction in recreation and park education, such arrangements have been fully explored in only a few colleges and universities.

In conclusion, it would appear that within the foreseeable future the majority of graduates from professional recreation and park curricula will continue to seek employment in basically familiar programs and roles. In all likelihood there will be only limited changes in college and university curricula, although experimentation will be encouraged and some adventuresome institutions are likely to develop highly innovative programs. The greater "push," however, will be toward upgrading and improving existing programs so that graduates who seek to enter the field will be of the highest possible caliber.

Suggested Examination Questions or Topics for Student Reports

1. Based on information provided in this chapter, and on your own observation and experience, what were the key factors promoting the rapid growth in professional education in recreation and parks in the United States and Canada?
2. Select one of the three levels of higher education (two-year, four-year or graduate curricula). Develop several guidelines for recreation and park curricula on this level, including the types of program options that you believe should be offered.
3. What actions should the profession take to upgrade and strengthen professional preparation in recreation and parks?
4. Several examples of continuing professional education for those already in the field are described in this chapter. In what other areas of leadership, supervision or administration do you feel such programs should be offered?

Suggested Action Assignments for Students

1. Based on criteria found in the literature, evaluate the recreation and park curriculum found in your own institution (this might best be done as a team project).
2. Carry out a survey of recreation and park curricula in your region that might be used for guidance to high school students seeking to enter the field.

five

field work and internship

A key element in the professional preparation of recreation and park personnel today is field work or internship experience. Within such related fields as education or social work, field work is regarded as an essential part of the college curriculum. For example, in a publication of the Family Service Association of America, Oswald writes:

> Students, practitioners, and most educators hold field work to be the core of professional social work education. In field work, principles are identified and made usable in particular situations; theoretical understanding is increased and is translated into the specific actions designed to help people meet social needs.... The Council on Social Work Education requires schools to offer supervised practice in social work as a condition of accreditation ...[1]

Professional conferences have stressed the need for adequate field work experience in college and university recreation curricula. At a national professional preparation conference sponsored by the American Association for Health, Physical Education and Recreation, it was emphasized that professional competencies in recreation can best be developed through meaningful laboratory experiences. In 1968, a National Recreation Forum on "Educating for Tomorrow's Leaders" recommended that field experiences be made an integral part of the professional preparation of recreation personnel. It stated:

> Prerequisite to adequate preparation for a professional career is a proportionate amount of on-the-job experience under the supervision of competent and qualified personnel. The effectiveness of blending classroom course work with practical experience has been proved time and again.[2]

In a number of studies, students in recreation and park curricula have indicated that they regard field work as being the most important of all un-

---

[1] Ida Oswald: "Field Work Instruction: Facts and Outlook." In *Trends in Field Work Instruction*, New York, Family Service Association of America, 1966. p. 7.

[2] Peter Verhoven, Ed.: *Educating Tomorrow's Leaders*. Washington, D.C., National Recreation and Park Association, 1968, p. 35.

dergraduate courses. Micklewright, for example, found that graduates of recreation curricula rated field work experience as the most significant and valuable of all the courses they had taken.[3]

Terminology

There is a marked lack of uniformity with respect to field work practices in college and university recreation and park curricula around the United States and Canada. Even the terminology used to describe these courses varies considerably. A few of the varied titles used in different colleges are

"Practicum in Recreation" — University of Georgia
"Professional Laboratory Experience" — Western Illinois University
"Professional Integration" — Slippery Rock State College, Pennsylvania
"Cooperative Education Program" — Texas A and M University

The two most common titles appear to be "field work" and "internship." These terms are often used interchangeably, with the possible distinction that internship is used more frequently to describe full-time involvement and also to refer to one-year work-study programs for graduates of recreation and park departments. In this text, the terms "field work" and "internship" are defined as follows:

That phase of professional education in recreation and parks in which the student is placed in an off-campus field setting for an extended period of time under the supervision of both a practicing professional employed by a cooperating agency and a college representative. This experience serves as part of the student's formal academic preparation, and comprises a substantial part, or the entire course load, of the student for the academic semester during which the experience is scheduled.[4]

GENERAL NATURE OF FIELD WORK PROGRAMS

The most recent comprehensive study of field work programs in four-year recreation and park curricula was reported by Clair Jean Mundy in 1972. Mundy's analysis of 79 colleges throughout the United States contained detailed information on practices in field work supervision and administration in these colleges. A number of her key findings are summarized in the following pages, to provide an overview of field work practices today.

---

[3] See George Butler: "Research Reviews and Abstracts." *Recreation,* January, 1955, p. 30.

[4] Adapted from Clair Jean Mundy: *A Descriptive Study of Selected Practices in the Administration and Supervision of Field Work Programs in Selected Four-Year Recreation and Park Curricula.* New York, Teachers College, Columbia University, Ed.D. Thesis, 1972, p. 12.

Patterns of Field Work Placement

Mundy found that there were three distinct patterns of field work placement: (a) Part-time placement; (b) Full-time placement; and (c) Two- or three-term, part-time placement. Only about 16 per cent of the recreation and park departments she studied used the first method, while over 40 per cent used each of the other two patterns.

PART-TIME PLACEMENT. Under this method, the field work student is placed for one term or less at a cooperating agency, while at the same time taking other academic courses (as many as 9 or 12 semester hours) at the college. Students generally are scheduled for such placements in the second half of the junior year, or the first half of the senior year. Over the entire semester students typically spend between 140 and 200 clock hours at the agency and receive between two and four credits for the assignment. Since students are taking college courses at the same time, most part-time field work arrangements are made within an approximate 30-mile radius of the college, making it possible for college supervisors to maintain direct contact with field work students and agency supervisors.

FULL-TIME PLACEMENT. The full-time field work student is typically assigned to a community agency or institution for an entire term during his senior year. Since he has no academic commitment, he may be placed at a considerable distance (in some cases several hundred miles) from the college, living in the community where he is carrying out the assignment. The amount of academic credit granted for the term is normally between 9 and 12 semester hours. Since it is not feasible to hold seminars related to the field work experience during the semester, they are normally scheduled as orientation sessions prior to the assignments, and as post-seminars at the end of the semester.

TWO- OR THREE-TERM, PART-TIME PLACEMENT. Under this system students are placed in different agencies for two or more semesters, on a part-time basis. Students are usually assigned during the last half of the junior year and continue to do field work throughout the senior year. The total time given to field work may range from 400 to 500 clock hours. As in the first arrangement, students would normally attend classes at the college while doing field work.

While Mundy did not attempt to assess the comparative strengths and weaknesses of the three approaches, she did conclude that

> . . . it is logical that the pattern or patterns which offered a large number of clock hours of field placement, a great variety and depth of experiences, and a substantial degree of college and agency supervision would have a stronger field work program than the placement pattern which did not allow for these factors.[6]

Mundy also examined a number of administrative aspects of field work courses. She found that 81 per cent of the colleges which were surveyed

---

[6] *Ibid.,* p. 52.

TABLE 5-1 Major Experiences During the Field Work Program[7]

Experience	Percentage of Colleges Reporting
Organizing activities*	93.6
Leading activities*	92.4
Attending staff, board, and community meetings	91.1
Observing activities	84.8
Observing administrative procedures	83.5
Observing maintenance procedures	81.0
Supervising activities*	77.2
Participating in administrative procedures	65.8
Participating in maintenance procedures	64.5

* Activities in which field work students spent the largest portion of their time, according to college supervisors.

held seminars in conjunction with field work, while 19 per cent did not. In 77 per cent of the colleges, field work placement decisions were jointly made by the student, the college, and the field work agency. College supervisors most frequently visited students at cooperating agencies twice a semester. Certain standards were applied in the approval of agency supervisors responsible for field work students; many colleges indicated that such individuals were required to have a specified minimal amount of professional experience, to hold a master's degree, or to be certified by a national or state recreation organization.

The most common experiences in which students took part during field work were those listed in Table 5-1.

Because field work and internship are such vital aspects of the professional preparation of recreation and park personnel, and because they are of interest both to college educators and to agency administrators, this text examines the programs of a number of leading recreation and park curricula throughout the United States and Canada.

EXAMPLES OF COLLEGE FIELD WORK PROGRAMS

All college field work manuals (over 70 were examined to provide information for this text) include statements of goals as well as actual procedures and requirements. Field work was seen as having the following purposes:

GOALS OF FIELD WORK

1. It provides a practical experience in realistic situations, and thus serves as a link between classroom theory and actual professional practice.

[7] *Ibid.*, p. 78.

2. It offers a full-fledged orientation to the professional field, and therefore is an important educational experience for most students.

3. It provides an opportunity to develop leadership and supervisory skills and understandings in a realistic setting.

4. It helps students understand their own capability and select areas for specialization in future course work or for possible employment.

5. It gives faculty members helpful information to use in the counseling of students by providing a picture of their strengths and weaknesses.

6. It provides feedback about the effectiveness of the college curriculum, suggesting areas needing program expansion or revision to improve the professional preparation of students.

7. It serves to develop and maintain links of communication between college educators and field practitioners that are helpful in enriching both.

8. It is invaluable for students as far as obtaining future employment is concerned by providing experience, job contacts, personal references, and other forms of assistance.

These goals are summed up in the following passage from the field work manual of the Western Illinois University at Macomb:

> One of the most difficult and yet one of the most important adjustments for the graduating senior from a curriculum in recreation and park administration is the application of what he has studied at the college or university to the "live" situation in the "real world." The recreation and park laboratory field experience is designed to provide an opportunity for practical application of classroom theory in professional field work before graduation. The student should acquire experience in recreation and park planning, leadership, supervision, and program evaluation by working in a private or public recreation and/or park agency under highly trained personnel in the local department and university faculty supervision.

PROCESS OF PLANNING FIELD WORK ASSIGNMENTS

A number of elements must be considered in the selection of field work agencies and in enlisting students to work with specific agencies. These include the following: the preliminary course work or experience students must have before taking field work; the desired characteristics of field work agencies; the selection of field work agencies; the preparation of student resumés; and the step-by-step arrangements of making the actual placement.

Required Preparation for Field Work

Most colleges stipulate that field work may not be taken until the student's junior or senior year. In some cases, students must have taken certain basic courses as part of the prerequisite. This may involve courses in leadership, observation of agencies, brief field work involvements, or previous leadership in the field.

At the University of Utah, for example, students must complete 200 clock hours of practical experience in a paid or nonpaid recreation position before entering Leisure Studies 382, the major field work course. This requirement is strictly enforced; a full eight weeks of summer work, for example, is worth only 100 of the 200 required hours. Students are encouraged to work in a variety of settings to fulfill the prerequisite. The major field work course involves a minimum of 485 clock hours over a nine-week period.

At the University of Montana, students must take a course in guided observation of recreation programs and another in field experience, both without credit, before entering the major Recreation Practicum. The University of Colorado offers a preliminary course, titled Recreation 433, Field Work, in which students must observe at least three recreation agencies, each for a minimum of 45 hours, before taking Recreation 439, Internship in Recreation. Other colleges have similar requirements which are intended to insure that students will be knowledgeable before entering their major field work assignment.

Desired Characteristics of Field Work Agencies

Customarily, college recreation departments develop a list of expectations for field work agencies that must be met if the agencies are to be considered for field work placements. The following statement outlines the requirements set by the University of Louisville for selection of potential field work agencies.

AGENCY REQUIREMENTS

1. Field work training may be carried on in any recognized public, voluntary or private agencies. Such agencies might include public park and recreation departments, hospitals, industrial plants, Girl Scouts, Boy Scouts, YMCA's, Boys' Clubs, camps, private clubs, or similar agencies.

2. Field work agencies must be located within the Falls Cities area, or within close proximity (within 50 miles) to borders of the State.

3. Eligible agencies must:
   a. have a recognized standing in the state or community
   b. have adequate areas, facilities and equipment to conduct a broad recreation program
   c. employ adequate staff to supervise students during field work training (statement to staff qualifications is appended)

4. Agencies . . . approved by the University will be made known so that all students will be aware of the field work opportunities available to them in different types of agencies and throughout the state.

In addition, college field work manuals may outline certain other expectations of the agency. The following points might be considered: (a) the willingness of the agency to accept the student and give him sufficient supervision; (b) the potential contribution of the experience to the student's professional growth, and its relationship to his professional interests or goals; and (c) the feasibility of the experience, in terms of the time required, the distance from the college, the abilities and skills of the student, and similar factors.

Selection of Field Work Agencies

The actual selection of an appropriate field work agency is of crucial importance. If it is not done with care, this extremely important part of the student's professional education may prove to be a negative or frustrating experience. To assist students in their selection of agencies, some college departments of recreation and parks prepare detailed listings of cooperating agencies to which they have sent students in the past, or which have indicated interest in receiving field-work students.

The University of Quebec at Trois Rivières, in Canada, for example, prepares an extensive booklet listing 25 nearby agencies at which field work may be arranged. These include municipal recreation departments, regional recreation councils, school districts or colleges, hospitals, correctional institutions, outdoor recreation and camping agencies, tourist organizations, and similar facilities. A detailed description of each such agency is given, including its sponsorship, location, conditions and hours of work, planned responsibilities of field work students, desired qualifications of students, and the salaries that will be paid (in this case, it is expected that students will be paid during the field work assignment). Since much of the preliminary "leg-work" of developing arrangements for field work has been done jointly by the college and the community agency before the student applies, this booklet is extremely helpful in making field work choices.

The actual process of making contact with the field work agency is done in a variety of ways. Often, the student is expected to take responsibility at this point. For example, at the California State College at Hayward, students are asked to submit to their advisors a formal written proposal containing the following elements: (a) the discipline or specialty in which they are interested; (b) their first and second choices of agencies in which they wish to work; (c) their reasons for these selections; and (d) a summary of the student's past paid and volunteer experiences. Following this, an instructor will review each proposal and, if it is approved, the student is authorized to contact the desired agency to request an interview. The interview has a two-fold purpose: it helps the agency determine if the student will be acceptable to it, and it helps the student confirm that the agency will meet his or her needs.

An example of the actual steps carried out in this process may be found in the field work manual of Eastern Washington State College:

INTERNSHIP PLACEMENT

1. Complete the Internship Placement form. It is due on Internship Coordinator's desk five weeks before the end of the quarter prior to internship.

2. Read a number of internship notebooks from past years (Chairman's office).

3. The student makes an appointment with academic advisor to assess his strengths, limitations, needs, and to discuss possible internship placements.

4. Immediately after student has completed Step 1, the student makes an appointment with Internship Coordinator for that quarter. The purpose of this interview will be the review of the papers, personal resumés, discussion of preferences for placement, and contacts to be made.

5. Internship Coordinator or student will contact the agency . . . and ascertain if they are interested in accepting the student. It is recommended that the student contact more than one agency to be sure that he/she finds the experience he/she wants for internship.

6. When the student receives the "go-ahead" from the coordinator, he then will contact a designated individual at the agency and make an appointment for an interview.

7. The student dresses for the interview and conducts himself as though applying for a job. He prepares questions, takes personal data sheets, and should be knowledgeable about the agency and the local community.

8. Immediately after the interview, the student indicates to the Coordinator whether or not he/she would like to be placed in the agency.

9. The Internship Coordinator will check agency's willingness to accept the student; will notify student of confirmation of placement; and will write a letter to the agency, confirming assignment of the student.

Procedural guidelines of this type may also include detailed statements of the number of credits and clock hours assigned to the field work course, the point at which it is to be taken, required courses in the department that must be taken as prerequisites, specific elements relating to pay (some colleges permit or require this, while others do not), sick leave, student housing for distant assignments, and similar information.

Preparation of Student Résumés

Many colleges require that students prepare a detailed personal résumé before applying for a field work affiliation. This is helpful to the faculty advisor and potential agency supervisors in considering the student's background and skills. It is also useful practice for a later date, when students will need to make up résumés for a regular job application. The University of Maryland suggests the following *Sample Résumé* format for students. When a student has made up his own résumé, a copy of it is attached to his application for field work and sent to the cooperating agency before he is interviewed.

Sample Résumé

CAMPUS ADDRESS. Include zip code, local phone, and area code.
HOME ADDRESS. Include zip code, home phone, and area code.
BIRTH DATA. Include birthdate and place of birth.
MARITAL STATUS.
DRAFT STATUS (for men).
GENERAL HEALTH.
OCCUPATION.
EDUCATION.

    I. *University.* Include all colleges and various curricula, dates, major and minor(s).
   II. *High School(s).* Include dates of enrollment and date of graduation.

ACTIVITIES. Most recent first, interest groups, clubs, offices held, etc.
SCHOLARSHIPS.
HONORS.
CAMPUS AND COMMUNITY SERVICE.
PROFESSIONAL COURSES COMPLETED. Include professional courses and allied required professional courses.
PROFESSIONAL EXPERIENCE AND TRAINING. Include paid and volunteer professional work.
OTHER WORK EXPERIENCES.
SPECIAL APTITUDES OR TRAINING. Musical ability, art, etc.
UNUSUAL EXPERIENCES OR ACCOMPLISHMENTS.
REFERENCES. Include from three to five character and professional references, e.g., clergymen, employer, teacher, *no* relatives; list full addresses and telephone numbers, if available.

Field work manuals in other colleges may require additional areas of information. For example, the *Intern Inventory* used by the Department of Recreation and Parks of the University of Florida at Gainesville asks the following questions:

    "What subjects do you enjoy most in college?"
    "In what clubs and/or social groups do you take part or have taken part?"
    "What are the kinds of experiences you would like the internship to provide?"
    "What weaknesses do you have which you feel the internship can strengthen?"
    "What specific leadership skills do you have, in sports, music, crafts, hobbies, etc.?"
    "What strengths do you have which you feel the internship should utilize?"
    "Why did you choose recreation as a profession?"

ADMINISTRATIVE ARRANGEMENTS AND POLICIES

Once the field work placement has been made, it is necessary to have a number of policies and procedures which govern the student's performance, the supervisory responsibilities of the college and field agency supervisors, evaluation, and grading. It is desirable to define clearly the responsibilities of each of the parties to the agreement—the student, the college, and the field agency. The University of Missouri, for example, outlines the following detailed responsibilities of students (this excerpt has been taken from a full statement describing the role of each of the parties):

V.   Conduct and Responsibilities of the Student to the Agency in Relation to Field Work in Recreation and Park Assignments.

     A.   To familiarize himself with the regulations and philosophies pertaining to the agency and to modify his attitude and behavior accordingly.

     B.   To plan thoroughly and in advance for all assignments.

     C.   To report to an assignment at least fifteen minutes prior to the time when due.

     D.   To be well-groomed and appropriately dressed for all assignments.

     E.   To notify the Agency Supervisor well in advance of cases of absence.

     F.   To be tactful, courteous and respectful to all personnel involved.

     G.   To use discretion as to the people with whom he associates and the places he goes.

     H.   To consult with the Agency-Supervisor when confronted with problems.

VI.   Responsibility of the Student to the University in Relation to Field Work in Recreation and Park Administration.

     A.   To be the best example possible of a representative of the University.

     B.   To notify the Director of Field Work as soon as possible of starting date and address and telephone number of field work location.

     C.   To keep the Director of Field Work informed of all work conducted for the agency during field work.

         1.   Orientation or initial report to include: (a) statement of duties; (b) time schedule; (c) activities; (d) place of operation; (e) plan of action.

         2.   Weekly Reports to include: (a) narrative account of activities; (b) interpretation; (c) contact between meetings; (d) plans for remaining time.

         3.   Final Report to include: (a) Agency description—purposes, facilities, methods, leadership and finance; (b) community description; (c) objectives: agency, group, participants, and

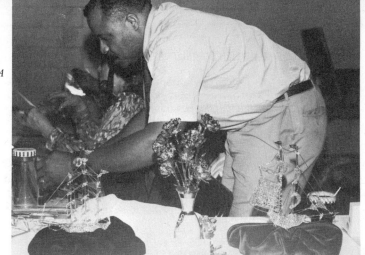

A

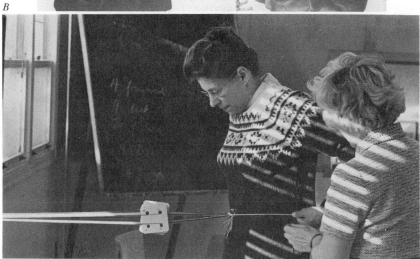

B

C

Emerich C. Gross

Arts and Crafts. Arts and crafts appeal to a wide range of participants. An arts specialist in Lincoln, Nebraska, demonstrates glass-blowing (*A*), and primitive weaving techniques are taught in Edmonton, Canada (*B*). Children enjoy an outdoor painting class sponsored by New York City's Police Athletic League (*C*).

student; (d) program planning; (e) student's evaluation of experience — methods, program leadership, supervisory practices; (f) self-analysis of shortcomings and strengths; (g) recommendation; (h) attach printed and mimeographed materials
used by agency and student during field practice.

The college department should also make completely explicit how
problems are to be dealt with, and where authority is to be placed at each
stage of the field work process. For example, the California State College at
Hayward has developed the following policies with respect to the supervision of field work students.

It is expected that the student will be supervised by a professionally-
qualified member of the agency staff, and that the student will take direction
from the agency supervisor. Should discrepancies arise between the requirements of the agency and the expectations of the college, the student should
follow the directions of the agency supervisor and should notify the university
supervisor so that differences may be reconciled. If the intern is not performing to the expectations of the agency then the agency supervisor *should immediately* notify the university supervisor. . . .

Upon placement, the student assumes responsibility for functioning as a
staff member, in terms of work productivity and his relationships with the
public and other staff members. Students are expected to conduct themselves
in the best interests of the agency and the university, and to recognize that the
quality of their appearance and behavior will influence the public's impression of the agency and the university. Confidential information entrusted to
the student, as a staff member, must be respected. In similar fashion, the
student must guard against publicly criticizing agency philosophy, techniques, etc.

The university supervisor will meet with the student and the agency
supervisor periodically during the experience. Additional contacts may be
made by phone. The purpose of such contacts and visitations will be to
evaluate student progress and to give attention to any problems that may
arise.

At the conclusion of the internship experience, the agency supervisor
shall write a statement evaluating the student's performance. This evaluation
will be discussed with the student by the agency supervisor and, following
this, will be filed with the student's university advisor. The final evaluation . . . should grow out of the evaluations made during the periodic meetings of the agency supervisor, the student, and the university supervisor.
Evaluation is intended to be a continuous process; the student will have the
greatest opportunity for growth if strengths and weaknesses are discussed as
they are observed.

The academic grade which the student shall receive is the responsibility
of the university supervisor only. The university supervisor will be guided by
the evaluation of the agency supervisor, but any question the student may
have concerning the academic grade should be discussed with the university
supervisor.

CONTENT OF THE FIELD WORK EXPERIENCE

Many college recreation and park departments outline in advance the
kinds of experiences that students should have in field work assignments.

For example, the University of Western Illinois stipulates that the experience should include: ". . . assignments with more than one age group; encompass at least four program fields; give an understanding of the scope of the agency operations; give opportunities to plan, organize, and lead program activities; and give opportunities to observe and participate in administrative and maintenance procedures."

Suggested Schedules of Field Work Involvements

Some colleges outline in detail the kinds of experiences they expect their field work students to have, and when they should be scheduled. The University of Maryland has prepared a suggested Field Work Calendar of assignments which students should complete during a 16-week practicum, in addition to regular tasks they may be given by the agency (see Table 5–2).

In some situations, the suggested schedule of field work experiences is developed not by the college but by the agency itself. For example, the Mendota, Wisconsin, State Hospital has developed the following outline of learning experiences for field work students accepted into its activity therapy program.

1. First Week

Student meets with Field Work Program Director, checks in, gets meal tickets, living quarters, etc. He is given an orientation to the Wisconsin Mental Health System, the Mendota Hospital organization, and the activity therapy program through meetings with the Student Program Director and Coordinators, and with Unit Activity Therapy Supervisors. At the end of the week, he begins primary treatment service assignment.

2. Second and Third Weeks

Student spends maximum time working directly with a Supervisor on treatment service assignment. Attention is focused on understanding the philosophy and goals of the treatment service, the role of the recreation therapist on the treatment service, the functions of other staff members and patients . . ., the organizational and communication patterns of the service, and the need to establish good working relationships with both staff and patients.

3. Fourth and Fifth Weeks

During this period, in addition to working in primary treatment service, students are involved in other learning experiences, such as: exposure to other treatment services and support services, meetings with Clinic Department heads, and participation in special hospital staff training programs.

4. Sixth Week Through End of Field Work

Student moves from assisting Student Supervisor to more autonomous leadership roles: planning, carrying out and evaluating program activities;

TABLE 5-2 University of Maryland—Field Work Calendar

Week	Objectives, Projects, Activities, Reports, Etc.	
1	Managing Authorities	—Get acquainted—meet staff, tour facilities. Make organization chart. Start Operational Manual. List objectives of agency. Initial Report due.
2	"Office Management"	—Determine short term and long term projects, telephone and office equipment, forms. Agency Supervisor's Progress Report due.
3	Legal Basis	—Collect data on legal authorization, City or County Council Meeting, written materials on Liability insurance. Start Notebook.
4	Community Organization	—Written material on History, Attend P.T.A. or Recreation Council Meeting.
5	Program—Services, Program Planning	—Observe neighborhood agency. List program objectives, collect general regulations.
6	Sources and Revenues	—Attend Budget Hearing, Short Term Project
7	Accounting and Budgeting	—Interview auditor. Discuss Mid-Semester Evaluation.
8	Personnel and In-Service Training	—Plan a training session. Mid-Semester Rating Sheet due.
9	Supervision—use of volunteers	—Write your philosophy as agency worker. Start Placement forms.
10	Records and Reports	—Registration and attendance. Start Final Report. Visit N.R.P.A.
11	Facilities, Standards, Planning	—Do facility analysis, summary contracts, bid forms. Attend State Society Workshop.
12	Maintenance, care of equipment	—Prepare maintenance schedule, Purchasing procedures, Attend State Society Meeting.
13	Executive Board Relations—Attend Board Meeting	—Complete Placement Forms. Interview Board member. Long Term Project.
14	Public Relations	—Prepare recruitment program. Evaluate or work on Annual Report.
15	Research and Evaluation	—List research needs of agency. Discuss Final Evaluation Rating Sheet. Submit Notebook.
16	Thank You's	—Final Rating Sheet due. Final report due.

determining supply needs and requisitioning necessary materials; writing patient progress reports and providing verbal feedback to the treatment team; and writing reports on special activity events. Throughout, the readiness of students for higher levels of responsibility is determined jointly by the student and the Student Supervisor, in coordination with the Student Coordinator and the Student Program Director.

Other Field Work Requirements

Most colleges hold special seminars to accompany and enrich the field work assignment. When the student is carrying out his field work in the college community itself, or is working close by, such seminars may be held regularly during the field work semester. When the assignment is being carried out at a distance from the college, the seminars may be arranged at the beginning and end of the semester, or at one or two key points during the semester. The purpose of such seminars is usually to help students discuss and analyze the experiences they are having in the field. Topics may be developed during the semester itself, based on the suggestions of the students, and may follow a problem-solving format. In some cases, seminars may follow a set routine, covering practical topics chosen by the faculty advisor. For example, at the American River College in Sacramento, California, a 17-week seminar series for field work students covers such topics as:

"Attitudes, Grooming, and Job Behavior"
"Public Relations and Publicity"
"Job Applications and Interviewing"
"Personnel Policies and Staff Relations"
"Experiences of Previous Field Work Students"
"Expectation of Cooperating Agencies"

In addition, colleges normally require regular conferences between students and both agency supervisors and college advisors during the course of the field work experience. These conferences, combined with student reports, provide the basis for evaluation of field work students. Typically, student reports include the following: (a) initial reports, giving details of the agency and the assignment; (b) weekly narrative reports, which may include work-time summaries; and (c) final reports, which sum up and analyze the field work experience.

Evaluation of Student Performance

At the end of the field work experience, the agency supervisor is usually requested to fill out a detailed evaluation of the student's performance and to hold a final review session with him. Customarily, grades are assigned by faculty advisors (see page 108).

OTHER FORMS OF INTERNSHIP

The first section of this chapter has dealt with field work courses offered by colleges and university recreation and park departments. In addition to such courses, a number of other forms of internship are available to students who are either at an advanced level in their professional study or who have graduated from college and are beginning their careers. In some cases, internships such as these are sponsored by municipal recreation and park departments in cooperation with the National Recreation and Park Association. In other cases, municipalities provide internships independently, or in association with nearby colleges and universities. The term *internship,* when used in such situations, usually refers to a period of full-time employment on a paid basis, in which the intern is not only assigned a substantial work load but is provided full experience in supervisory and administrative activities.

Example of N.R.P.A. Internship: Baltimore, Maryland

A number of major cities have provided internships in cooperation with the National Recreation and Park Association during the past few years. A good example is Baltimore, Maryland, where the municipal recreation bureau has organized a carefully structured year-long internship experience which includes the following elements:

1. ORIENTATION AND FIRST FIVE WEEKS ASSIGNMENTS. This includes meeting with the department superintendent, assignment to a district supervisor for exposure to a geographic section of the city, one-day visits or tours with special supervisors, and assignment to a recreation center to observe a year-round program facility.

2. PERMANENT CENTER ASSIGNMENT. The intern is then assigned to a recreation center, where he will be expected to carry out regular leadership functions on a 20-hours-per-week basis for the remainder of his internship. This assignment may also offer opportunities to work in areas of special interest, such as performing arts, street club programs, or activities for the handicapped. As part of the orientation process the intern receives brochures, manuals, schedules, and reports covering the entire work of the department.

3. WEEKLY INTERN ASSIGNMENTS. Baltimore N.R.P.A. interns also are expected to attend in-service training programs regularly, one morning a week, for 30 weeks of the year; to attend bi-weekly seminars conducted by the department superintendent; and to meet weekly with the superintendent.

4. OTHER MEETINGS. Interns take part in regular meetings with other municipal departments and organizations in order to learn the relationship

of these bodies to the Bureau of Recreation. These departments might include the Community Action Agency, the Health and Welfare Council, the Board of Education, and similar groups. In addition, interns should accompany the superintendent to budget planning sessions and hearings, to meetings of the Recreation and Parks Board, the Board of Estimates, City Council, Planning Commission, and a wide variety of special conferences, architectural planning meetings, and advisory sessions on recreation for the handicapped.

5. Special Projects. Finally, during the course of the year, interns are expected to complete one or more special projects which will be helpful to the Bureau of Recreation. These might include such projects as: (a) organizing the departmental library; (b) preparing bulletins or manuals on public relations procedures or other functions; (c) working with committees of teenagers or other community organizations; (d) assisting the superintendent in working on the annual budget; (e) participating and assisting in the planning of "street-club" group work conferences; or (f) initiating special studies of staff morale, maintenance problems, or other areas of departmental concern.

Obviously, such a varied and fully rounded experience during the course of an individual's first year of full-time professional employment can be of immense value as far as his career development is concerned. Over the past several years, the number and variety of N.R.P.A. internships have expanded, offering unusual opportunities for a growing number of young professionals.

Other Internship Programs

Other types of internship programs are frequently arranged. For example, the Indianapolis, Indiana, Department of Parks and Recreation has offered a 12-week program of Summer Internships to students representing eight colleges and universities. An internship offered the choice of four program options: (a) planning and engineering; (b) park resources; (c) park administration; and (d) park maintenance. Work experiences included park design, planning, and construction; forestry, greenhouse, conservatory and sod farm experience; exposure to budget and finance procedures; and daily park maintenance operations, as well as a series of special seminars and tours.

In some cases, state park systems have developed internship programs. For example, the Department of Conservation of the State of Illinois has developed an internship program which regularly involves students from several state university colleges. An unusual example of a state-sponsored internship program is in Idaho, where several state university students were assigned to operate the first state park in the country totally managed by college students—Indian Rocks State Park, near Pocatello.

Special Projects

While not specifically a form of field work or internship, many college recreation and park departments undertake unusual or innovative projects which give their students practical experience, contact with professionals, and other valuable benefits. For example, several Central Washington State seniors undertook the assignment of converting an unsightly garbage dump located along the Yakima River near Ellensburg into a waterfront park, complete with a "climbing rock." This man-made "rock" was constructed of rocks, concrete, and steel reinforcement; it was approximately 60 feet high and 100 feet long, included a separate chimney-spire of concrete, and was to be used to provide training for mountain climbing enthusiasts. In addition, the development was planned to include fishing areas, nature study and group campfire sites, an arboretum, and hiking trails.

Travel as Field Experience

One of the major benefits of the kind of internships just described is that they provide recreation and park students or recent graduates with the opportunity to work in new geographical settings. This affords young people a breadth of contacts, experiences, and new perspectives of the field. Some colleges and universities have developed extensive travel programs to make this opportunity possible.

Michigan State University Travel Program

The Department of Park and Recreation Resources at Michigan State University conducts a travel course intended to permit majors in the department to visit and observe a wide range of recreation and park agencies throughout the United States. Offered to upper-level students, the course is titled *Field Studies in Park Administration*. Each year, it covers a different itinerary. For example, in a recent year the tour visited 21 agencies in the Northeastern United States and Canada over a two-week period. Performing arts centers, Y.M.C.A.'s, ski areas, state and national parks and seashores, inner-city recreation centers, and a variety of other facilities were visited in the province of Ontario, and in states from Maine to West Virginia. Through this unique program students are able to sample real situations over an extensive geographical region, to be exposed to the personal philosophies of park and recreation educators, and to study unique developments, trends, programs, and facilities in operation.

Michigan State University has also made extensive use of field assignments in other classes, with students taking to the field to explore problems and develop solutions. It also uses tours as a teaching approach around which cooperative extension programs with county agents' annual summer schools are structured.

University of Illinois Travel Program Abroad

Encouraged by a university policy stating that each undergraduate student should have the opportunity to ". . . include an international cross-cultural component in his education," the Department of Recreation and Park Administration of the University of Illinois has developed a full-semester travel tour for undergraduate majors. In the first tour the United Kingdom was selected for study, since too few students were sufficiently fluent in a foreign language to justify extended periods in other countries. Students were given an intensive one-week orientation into British recreation, during which they visited most of the primary national organizations and a number of national recreation facilities. Two weeks of field work followed in a variety of settings. After this field work, students engaged in a four-week "Outward Bound" course involving climbing, canoeing, orienteering, and similar activities in the mountains of Wales. The students then had another two weeks of field work, tours through France and Spain, and an eight weeks' study experience in an English college.

In a later semester-abroad program a special interuniversity plan was developed, known as American Universities' International Program in Leisure Sciences. Consisting of 22 students from the University of Illinois and 6 students from other institutions, this tour included intensive study and field work in Scotland, and individually planned travel throughout Europe. Clearly, such international programs represent an excellent form of field experience, providing cross-cultural exposure and enriching students with knowledge both of American recreation and park programs and of the theory and practice found in other nations.

FIELD WORK AND INTERNSHIP IN PERSPECTIVE

As this chapter has demonstrated in detail, the field work experience, or other curricular ventures which expose students to a range of realistic programs and problems, is a vital part of both undergraduate and graduate education in recreation and parks. However, certain aspects should be noted about the field work policies which prevail in most colleges and universities today.

First, almost all field work and internship experiences are geared toward student placement in public recreation and park departments. While some college field work manuals refer to placement in voluntary and therapeutic agencies, these are distinctly in the minority. In view of the substantial number of job opportunities today for recreation graduates in therapeutic settings, such as psychiatric hospitals, nursing homes, or special schools for the retarded, it seems clear that greater emphasis should be given to encouraging field work in such agencies. Similarly, field work commitments should be developed in voluntary, industrial, commercial, and other kinds of agencies to a more extensive degree than is done at present.

Since many such organizations—as well as other public service departments like health and welfare, housing, and youth service agencies—do not have qualified recreation supervisors on their staffs, a question should be raised about the common requirement that field work students must be supervised by individuals holding recreation degrees. Although this requirement appears to support professionalism, in practice it frequently results in college recreation and park departments *not* sending field work students to a wide variety of agencies that are in a position to hire recreation personnel. Thus, the field loses out in terms of expanding professional contacts and influence. Although they may not have administrators with specialized backgrounds in recreation, many organizations, such as the Y.M.C.A. or Y.W.C.A., Boys' or Girls' Clubs, might provide excellent settings for field work students.

If a greater number of recreation students were assigned to field work in such agencies, it is probable that many would then find regular employment in them. This would have the effect of opening up "beachheads" for recreation as a preferred area of professional training over a period of time. Thus, opportunities for employment throughout the broad spectrum of social agencies would be enhanced—a particularly important goal today.

A second important need is to regard field work not just as a culminating experience, taken at the end of the student's course work, but rather as a continuum that begins as soon as a student has declared his major—and sometimes before.

Field Work as a Continuum of Experience

In the past, most college curricula tended to be extremely rigid, with a high percentage of required courses and limited opportunities for elective study, independent work, or community involvement. However, many colleges today have reduced their core, or liberal arts requirement, and are providing greater opportunities for more flexible individual programs of study. In many cases, colleges are granting academic credit for past professional work, and are encouraging creative projects or community service designed to meet individual student needs.

This trend makes it possible to provide more varied opportunities for field experience than in the past. In recognizing the importance of this curricular component, there should be an intelligently planned sequence of field work assignments. These might include any or all of the following:

Field Work as a Course Requirement

Field work may be offered as a course requirement in introductory courses in recreation leadership, programming, or group dynamics. Typically, the field work assignment might encompass no more than two or three hours a week, and might be taken as early as the freshman or sophomore year. It would provide an early acquaintanceship with the field and with various types of recreation agencies.

Required Summer Work

Recreation and park majors might be required to work for at least two summers or school quarters. Such field work assignments might involve not only camp counselor work, but also working for public recreation and park departments, voluntary agencies, or other organizations in the leisure services field. It should be possible for students to be paid for such positions, contrary to the policy in many field work manuals that they not be paid. Realistically, many college students count on the summer to earn money for living expenses throughout the year, and cannot afford to do volunteer work at this time. Beyond this, paid assignments frequently involve more meaningful work and more realistic experiences than strictly volunteer assignments.

Major Field Work or Internship Assignment

This assignment should continue to be emphasized as the student's chief exposure to professional practice, and every effort should be made to have it a full-time commitment in an agency of the highest possible quality. As in summer work, it should be possible to have students paid for doing field work — assuming that the field agency is prepared to budget for this commitment.

Special Field Projects

Finally, there should be the opportunity for students to undertake special field projects or unique assignments — either within the normal realm of leadership and supervision, or in functions related to research, public relations, planning, facilities development, or similar tasks. Such assignments might be undertaken at any point in the student's college career, but probably would be most appropriate in the junior or senior years, or as part of graduate study.

Having a continuum of field experiences in recreation, as suggested here, should be of great value to all students and faculty advisors in recreation and park curricula. Early field exposures provide an excellent means of screening out disinterested, apathetic or poorly equipped students, and of giving students a realistic picture of the field that will help them in making hard career decisions. Field experiences may also help to confirm the judgment of advisors by demonstrating that certain students have a high level of interest and ability and should be strongly encouraged — or to tell students that recreation *is* the field in which they really should carry on their life's work. Such knowledge should not have to wait until the end of the student's junior or senior year.

This chapter has described a key component of professional education in recreation and parks. Chapter Six deals in depth with job classification systems and with specific requirements for positions in the field.

Suggested Examination Questions or Topics for Student Reports

1. What are the major types or administrative arrangements of field work placement? Under what circumstances do you feel that each of these arrangements is most appropriate?
2. Based on examples given in this chapter, outline a set of guidelines for college field work programs in recreation agencies, covering such elements as selection of agencies, placement of students, and appropriate assignments.
3. Identify a hypothetical agency in your region, and prepare a semester-long outline of experiences and responsibilities for students who might be placed in this agency or department.
4. The text describes several innovative kinds of field assignments, such as travel courses. Can you identify some other kinds of unusual field courses which might be of value in your judgment?

Suggested Action Assignments for Students

1. Interview a group of students who are presently carrying out a field work assignment, or who have recently completed one. Have them evaluate this experience and make recommendations for its improvement.
2. Prepare a listing of agencies in your community or area that would be suitable for field work, indicating the special kinds of experiences or types of professional exposure they might offer.

personnel standards and selection

This chapter is concerned primarily with the processes of defining job responsibilities, classifying positions, and recruiting and selecting qualified professional personnel in recreation and park agencies. It examines the rationale underlying the classification procedure, and the methods of identifying individuals who meet professional standards, such as by certification and registration. After outlining Civil Service selection methods, the chapter presents job descriptions and requirements for a variety of agencies and specializations.

PROFESSIONAL EMPLOYMENT IN RECREATION AND PARKS

As Chapter One pointed out, there is an extremely wide range of professional employment opportunities in recreation and parks. The types of agencies employing full-time, year-round, paid professional leadership include public, voluntary, private, and commercial organizations.

PUBLIC AGENCIES. Federal, state, or provincial departments are primarily concerned with the administration of parks, seashores, or other large, natural resources used for outdoor recreation. Personnel employed in such agencies are generally resource-oriented, and are involved in the design, construction, maintenance and operation of varied park and recreation facilities. Others carry out planning, consultation, or research functions, while an additional group fills interpretive or "naturalist" positions.

On the federal level, recreation personnel are also employed in agencies related to health, education and welfare, the armed forces, housing, and other social programs. State governments employ large numbers of personnel in institutions, such as mental hospitals, correctional centers, special homes or schools for the retarded, or nursing home facilities. States may also employ rural extension personnel, who provide recreation services, and planners, researchers or consultants, who work with local recreation and park agencies.

On the local level, every type of government—be it city, town, village, county, or borough—employs recreation and park personnel. These individuals are most frequently attached to recreation and park departments, and have the responsibility of administering a wide range of facilities, such as parks, playgrounds, pools, community centers or other facilities, or of organizing varied leisure programs under direct leadership. In addition, many other units of local government, for example, youth boards, departments of education, housing authorities, and departments of welfare or social service, frequently operate recreation programs.

VOLUNTARY AGENCIES. Such organizations as the Boy Scouts, Girl Scouts, Boys' Clubs, Girls' Clubs, Young Men's and Young Women's Christian Association, Young Men's and Young Women's Hebrew Association, Catholic Youth Organization, Police Athletic League, Children's Aid Society, and a host of other nongovernmental, nonprofit, privately-supported agencies, employ recreation personnel. In many cases these are nationally organized and local chapters are parts of federations or other larger structures. In other cases, they are independent with respect to policy, funding, and control.

PRIVATE AGENCIES. There are many thousands of private membership organizations in the United States and Canada, such as country clubs, yacht clubs, golf clubs, tennis clubs, or other social organizations. Generally, they are geared to meeting the recreational needs of more affluent or elite groups, although in many newly developed communities recreation programs have been established for the exclusive use of residents, thus constituting a form of private recreation agency. Many individuals with recreation skills are employed by such organizations.

COMMERCIAL RECREATION AGENCIES. Probably the largest number of workers are employed by commercial organizations which sell recreation services, equipment, instruction, admission tickets, or similar products to the public at large. These include such ventures as sports stadiums, movie theaters, skating rinks, night clubs and bars, miniature golf courses, bowling alleys, ski centers, dance schools, vacation resorts, commercial tours, and a host of similar enterprises.

In addition to these four major categories of sponsors, a number of other types of agencies employ recreation personnel. The largest single category encompasses therapeutic recreation and consists of hospitals, special schools or homes, and so on. These may be sponsored by the government, or by voluntary or proprietary managements. Other categories include such areas as industrial recreation, college union programs, or camping facilities.

In general, government agencies tend to have clearly defined requirements for professional-level recreation and park positions. Standards have been established for work functions, educational and experiential requirements, and hiring procedures. The majority of professional positions in federal, state, and local government departments require at least a college degree – and many give preference to specialized degrees in recreation and parks.

Voluntary agencies usually have a greater degree of flexibility in hiring, although generally college degrees are required for supervisory or administrative positions. As a rule, private and commercial recreation agencies do not have professional standards or degree requirements for their personnel; instead, they seek primarily to hire individuals who are able to do the job, regardless of formal training or other qualifications.

In summary, the bulk of hiring of *professionally qualified* recreation and park personnel is done by government agencies, although great numbers of recreation workers are employed by other types of organizations. Therefore, the majority of guidelines and examples presented here are drawn from the personnel practices of government departments.

SELECTION PROCESS IN GOVERNMENT AGENCIES

The personnel selection process in government may be divided into several distinct phases: (a) the establishment of a position classification system; (b) the recruitment of qualified personnel; (c) the establishment of a merit system personnel screening process; and (d) the actual process of selecting and hiring workers, which is usually followed by a period of probation and ultimately by permanent employment.

Position Classification Systems

Position classification systems involve organizing positions into groups or classes on the basis of the specific duties or responsibilities of each position and on the qualifications or requirements that must be met by those applying for it. Such systems have the following purposes:

1. They help to determine what the functions of workers throughout an organization are, and to organize the assignment of work based on known competence and job responsibilities.
2. They provide a logical basis for controlling pay levels by developing whole classes of positions with common salary ranges.
3. They reduce a wide variety of occupations to manageable proportions, so recruitment, testing, hiring, and promotion of personnel can be done efficiently.
4. They offer a basis for determining orientation and job-training needs, and for systematically carrying out promotion procedures.

Stahl summarizes the importance of a position classification system by pointing out that without it, a confusing and bewildering array of titles would make administrative control all but impossible. He comments that neither the fiscal office nor the personnel department could properly perform its functions

> ... unless titles and their definitions describe the duties and responsibilities of the various positions and indicate the qualifications necessary to fill them. This need is apparent not only in connection with the problem of pay, but also in the matters of selection, placement, promotion, transfer, and training.[1]

A position classification system is not equivalent to a pay plan, although it may provide the structure for determining compensation levels; essentially, it is useful throughout the entire personnel administration process. The key elements of such a system are the concepts of *position, class,* and *series.*

Position refers to a specific job "slot" which normally would have a descriptive title and place in the personnel structure of an organization. It must be differentiated from the person who holds it in that the person may leave or change, while the position normally remains.

Class refers to a group of positions with roughly comparable responsibilities and qualifications. Positions within the same class or category may be found in different departments and usually are subject to the same policies with respect to selection, compensation, promotion, and similar personnel matters.

Series describes a vertical classification of employees within a common specialization who have a gradation of skills, education, or seniority, so that they have different levels of salary and status. Thus, a Recreation Therapist Series might run from Recreation Therapist Trainee to Senior Recreation Therapist.

Normally, a position classification would include each of these elements. It would define each position, place it within a class or series, assign it a salary range, and outline its responsibilities and required qualifications or credentials.

How are classification plans and specific job descriptions developed? There are four basic steps:

1. Analyzing and recording the duties and other distinctive characteristics of the positions to be classified.
2. Grouping the positions into classes on the basis of their similarities.
3. Writing standards or specifications for each class in order to show its general character, define its boundaries, and to serve as a general guide in assigning individual positions to the class.
4. Putting the system into effect by assigning individual positions to each class.

In carrying out these steps an administrator or supervisor might rely on the guidelines of professional organizations, such as those listing job functions for a particular level or series. Or, the administrator might develop job descriptions based on practices in his own organization by

---

[1] O. Glenn Stahl: *Public Personnel Administration.* New York, Harper and Row, 1962, p. 147.

carefully analyzing all functions within each position. He might do this by having those people presently holding the positions in question fill out at regular intervals detailed statements of their responsibilities. This method may be used to help evaluate the work of individuals and to provide a means of monitoring a position over a period of time in order to keep its description up to date.

In developing a total system of positions, classes, and series, the questions of career entrance and promotion must be considered. Typically, lower-level positions, at the bottom of certain series, are regarded as "entry-level" jobs. In many large municipal departments, a candidate may only enter at the lowest level of the "leader" series, and must then move up through the various grades by seniority, favorable personnel evaluations, or promotional examinations. In many cases, advancement through the ranks of a single series is fairly automatic, but advancement to a new series requires a more involved process of application and review.

A final important principle of position classification systems is that they must be kept up-to-date, and must be reviewed and revised regularly, if they are to be part of a dynamic, responsive personnel structure.

Recruitment of Qualified Personnel

Once an effective classification system has been established, the next step in the selection process is to recruit qualified applicants. In any large organization, such as a statewide hospital system or a big-city recreation and park department, there temporarily may not be openings at a given moment, but it is likely that before long several will appear. These may occur because of the transfer, firing, retirement, resignation, or promotion of individuals, and may demand the prompt appointment of new employees; therefore, it is customary to offer Civil Service examinations at regular intervals. The procedure is to use the examination to develop a list, or pool, of qualified applicants. Then, when openings appear, individuals from the top of the list may be appointed.

Before any examination can be given, however, it is necessary to attract the most highly qualified and capable individuals to apply for the position in question. It might be pointed out that in a period of relative abundance of qualified personnel and a limited number of openings, it is no longer necessary to recruit as actively as in the past. However, it still must be recognized that, unless the recruitment process is soundly conceived, it is unlikely that a top-quality professional staff can be assembled. Stahl describes recruitment methods in public administration as including the following:

1. Intensive cultivation of newspaper, radio, and television outlets for news about public job opportunities, usually on a "public service" basis.

2. Use of extensive mailing lists of schools, labor unions, vocational counseling offices, and organized occupational groups, such as professional, technical or trade associations.

3. Careful development of long-term relationships with teachers, editors, professional and technical personnel, and labor leaders.

4. Preparation and strategic distribution of well-illustrated pamphlets, or, within a large organization, a career directory showing varied job opportunities.

5. Periodic visits to college campuses, maintaining exhibits of departmental career fields at conventions, and holding open houses in appropriate locations.[2]

Each of these approaches may be useful for recreation and park agencies. As far as the field itself is concerned, it is important to think of recruitment from the very outset — that is, to encourage young people of high potential to enter professional study in the field. Thus, colleges and universities must make intensive efforts to attract capable high school graduates into recreation and park degree programs by means of career days, brochures, workshops, newsletters to high school guidance counselors, and similar methods.

Public departments or voluntary agencies that are seeking to employ qualified personnel may employ the following methods: (a) send listings of job openings to college placement offices or departmental advisors; (b) use professional newspapers, magazines, or placement services to advertise openings; (c) sponsor booths at professional conferences; and (d) prepare and distribute attractive brochures which describe the department and community, the nature of openings, or brief summaries of job responsibilities, qualifications, and details on applying or filing for an examination. In addition, many agencies also recruit full-time personnel from young men and women who have been working with them over a period of time as seasonal or part-time leaders. Recruitment should be an on-going, systematic process in which departments and agencies are on the lookout for capable new employees.

SELECTION OF QUALIFIED CANDIDATES

Within any public recreation and park system, there are three major approaches to determining the qualifications of individuals for professional employment. These consist of: (a) certification; (b) registration; and (c) Civil Service hiring procedures.

Certification

This term refers to a formal process by which an application for entry into a profession is reviewed and approved. In such fields as medicine, law,

---

[2] *Ibid.*, pp. 61–62.

accounting, or occupational therapy, it is customary for state certifying boards to attest to the certification of candidates within a given field. This may be based on the candidates' having completed a required course of study in an accredited institution, or on their passing an examination which is framed with the assistance of the major professional organization in the state, or on both. Certification is usually based on such criteria as the candidate's education, experience, performance on written and oral tests, and personal recommendations.

Once an individual is certified in a given field, he is in effect "licensed" to practice it anywhere within a state, or in other states which have reciprocal arrangements with the licensing state. In the field of recreation and parks, only a few states, such as New Jersey and Georgia, have established formal certification procedures which are used to identify qualified professsionals on a statewide basis. However, such plans are extremely flexible in that they permit the substitution of years of experience in the field of recreation for college training. This is done through "grandfather" clauses which permit those already in the field to become certified by virtue of their experience. What this has meant is that in a state like Georgia, which enacted a recreation certification law in 1968, within the first few years of enactment 136 professionals were certified as Administrators — with 128 of these qualifying under the "grandfather clause." Such plans are *permissive* rather than *mandatory*. They do not have the weight of law behind them in that public and voluntary agencies are not required to hire only certified applicants. Leavitt writes:

> Obviously, the (certification) bill was conceived and supported as a means of upgrading the recreation profession in Georgia, and consequently upgrading recreation for all Georgians. With stringent education, experience, and examining provisions, the law is designed to increase the caliber and stature of the professional and his program. The permissiveness of the certification compounds the problem of convincing the employer to hire only certified professionals. The day of total statewide professional certification for recreators is somewhere in the distant future. We may never see that day, since mandatory provisions are unlikely to ever become a reality.[3]

In Canada, a somewhat similar situation prevails. In the province of Ontario, for example, the State Department of Education issued a regulation in 1971 that clearly defined the requirements for Municipal Recreation Directors' Certificates. This regulation outlined five tracks through which individuals might qualify for an Interim Municipal Recreation Directors' Certificate. These included various combinations of study or actual degrees in approved universities, institutes of applied arts and technology, "reading courses," in-service training courses, and professional experience. Permanent Municipal Recreation Directors' Certification is given to those who meet one of these five types of qualifications and who have at

---

[3] H. Douglas Leavitt: "Certification." *Parks and Recreation*, January, 1971, pp. 123, 130.

least three years of full-time, paid professional experience. These qualifications would appear to insure that only highly qualified individuals would be able to hold such positions.

However, advertisements of job openings in professional recreation journals in Canada suggest that "preference will be given" to those holding the Permanent Municipal Recreation Directors' Certificate — rather than that this certificate is *required* for all candidates. Thus, in Canada as in the United States, while certification has been established, it is not mandatory in recreation and park hiring.

Registration Plans

The term "registration" refers to the process under which professional societies screen and identify qualified practioners in their respective fields.

Hines indicates that early registration programs came about chiefly because of the desire of professionals to upgrade qualifications and professional practice in recreation and parks. A report issued by the North Carolina Recreation Society in 1953 pointed out that ". . . in most of the United States, any barber can be a recreation leader, but no recreation leader can be a barber without a licence."[7] Registration plans were conceived of as being both substitutes for and preliminary steps toward certification. North Carolina in 1954 became the first state to initiate a registration plan for recreation administrators on a statewide basis. Societies in other states, such as California, New York, Wisconsin, Washington, Colorado, and Texas, also initiated voluntary registration plans during the 1950's.

Basically, such registration plans lack force in application. However, in some cases, they involve the cooperation of state governmental agencies. For example, in 1966, the Indiana General Assembly granted the Indiana Outdoor Recreation Council the power to set standards, establish leadership criteria, and formulate guidelines for local departments. The New York State Recreation and Park Society has a voluntary registration plan, which was begun in 1957 and amended in 1968, that was developed with the help of consultants from the New York State Division for Youth, the State Education Department, and the State Department of Civil Service. Thus, its recommended standards have had an impact on the qualifications established by these agencies.

On the national scene, the American Recreation Society maintained a registration program for recreation professionals during the 1950's and early 1960's. However, since the formation of the National Recreation and Park Association, there has been no national plan for registration. The view is widely held that this should be a state function, and that the N.R.P.A.'s role should be to develop a model licensing or certification act for the recreation profession that would set the pattern for the individual states.

Since 1970, the National Therapeutic Recreation Society has had a voluntary registration plan for individuals employed in the field of recreation therapy. This plan was widely recognized and, by 1973, over 1,000 professionals had been approved under its various categories. However, pressure from a number of veteran practitioners, who had many years of experience in the field, raised questions about the validity of having formal, degree-oriented education programs as the only route toward achieving various levels of registration. As a consequence, an "equivalency" procedure was developed under which alternatives to formal education might be approved for the registration of qualified therapeutic recreation specialists.

As with certification, the voluntary registration process is an effective means of screening personnel only for those public or voluntary agencies willing to adopt or respect it. Realistically, the screening process that has the greatest potential for upgrading the qualifications of recreation and park professionals in government agencies today must be found within the Civil Service system.

CIVIL SERVICE IN RECREATION AND PARKS

Civil Service refers to the governmental personnel structure which attempts to provide a politically neutral system of employment under which individuals are hired because of their formal qualifications rather than because of political patronage or favoritism. It provides job security rather than permit employees to be hired and fired at the whim of changing political administrations.

Operating on all levels of government, Civil Service involves a complicated job classification system, and a detailed procedure for appointments, probation, promotions, separation, and personnel benefits and rights. It embraces the bulk of governmental employees, although key administrative figures in government agencies are usually appointed rather than promoted through the normal career channels.

On the federal level, all full-time professional employees in such agencies as the National Park Service or the Veteran's Administration are part of the federal Civil Service system. Similarly, all state employees in hospitals, penal institutions, recreation and park departments, or other agencies are normally Civil Service employees, with the exception of upper-echelon administrators or part-time or seasonal workers.

On the local level, Civil Service Boards control most government hiring in counties, towns, cities, and villages through what is commonly known as "career service" or "competitive service." Those not subject to merit system regulations include elective officials, those appointed to special commissions or boards, the heads of departments, and sometimes individuals working under special contracts.

A

B

C

Paul Caramuto

Special Events. Many recreation departments and agencies offer a "smorgasbord" of varied activities and special events. In Mt. Vernon, New York, participants take part in a dog obedience class (*A*) and a surf-casting contest (*B*). Los Angeles children don costumes for a period piece (*C*). In Canada, Vancouver youths attend a science fair (*D*) and Montreal residents compete at chess (*E*). Finally, Hollywood, Florida, youngsters take part in a watermelon-eating contest (*F*).

D

E

F

Civil Service Procedures

How does the typical Civil Service system operate? In one large Eastern state, a state law passed in 1941 left the specific form of administration up to local option. There were three alternatives: (a) administration through the State Civil Service Commission; (b) administration by a County Personnel Officer; and (c) administration through a County Civil Service Commission. Each local jurisdiction was permitted to determine which of these plans it wished to adopt, although the rules and positions classification system of the plan were required to meet the approval of the State Civil Service Commission. Several forms of classified service, which are listed here, exist today in counties and cities:

1. COMPETITIVE CLASS.   All positions filled through competitive examination fall into this class, which covers the majority of full-time recreation and park employees.
2. NONCOMPETITIVE CLASS.   Positions with definite requirements, but for which a competitive written examination would not be practical, are placed in this class. Usually such factors as the candidate's education, work history, or armed forces record are evaluated as the basis for determining eligibility. Candidates may be given suitable tests in specific skills, but these need not be in competition with others.
3. LABOR CLASS.   This consists of all unskilled laborers in municipal or county service; it includes positions for which there are no educational or competency requirements but for which good physical condition is essential.

To become certified for appointment within the competitive class, a candidate must go through the following steps: (a) he must meet general requirements for the position that may include residency in the county or municipality concerned; and (b) he must take examinations, notices of which are posted in county newspapers to inform prospective candidates of their time and place. Examinations, although administered by the county, are usually constructed and graded by the State Civil Service Commission. Each person who passes the test and meets other requirements is put on a list in the order of his ranked grade (lists of eligible candidates usually have a duration of four years or less). The municipality must then send a "duty statement" to the Civil Service Commission for the position it wishes to fill. The Commission determines the correct title for the position and sends the certified list of eligible candidates. The municipality canvasses the list, holds interviews if it wishes, and makes an appointment from the top three eligible candidates who are willing to accept the position.

If eligible lists do not include approved candidates for vacancies in the competitive class, a municipality may nominate a candidate to the Civil Service Commission for a noncompetitive examination. Assuming that this individual is certified as qualified, he may receive a provisional appointment for the position. No such provisional appointment can continue for a period longer than nine months, and an individual appointed on this basis has no advantage over other persons competing for the eligible list when a competitive examination is finally held.

Examination Procedures

Examinations are usually of two basic types: *open* examinations which any qualified candidate may take; and *closed* examinations, which are usually for promotional purposes for candidates already employed in the agency or department. Examinations may involve assessment of written, oral, and skills competencies.

WRITTEN EXAMINATIONS.   These are intended to measure the individual's general knowledge of the field and his ability to perform in a special area of service or level of responsibility. Such tests are of two types: *objective* (short answer), and *subjective* (essay). It is generally agreed that the objective examination lends itself to more standardized, uniform grading, and avoids giving an excessive advantage to the candidate who uses language extremely well. It may also be used to measure the critical ability or judgment of a candidate, if properly developed. Objective tests are usually carefully planned to cover major subject areas of importance. For example, in a recent Civil Service examination for Recreation Supervisors in New York City, the following breakdown was made of key areas of knowledge as a basis for developing objective questions:

		Percentage
I.	Staff supervision, development, and evaluation.	20%
II.	Recreation and group work philosophy, principles, objectives, and techniques.	20%
III.	Recreation program development and activities.	20%
IV.	Community, public and human relations.	10%
V.	Relations with, and resources of, public, voluntary, and community agencies.	10%
VI.	Preparation and interpretation of reports.	10%
VII.	Current issues and trends in recreation service.	10%

ORAL EXAMINATION.   On higher levels of responsibility—for which there are fewer candidates and it is important to assess the candidate's skills of communication and analysis, his judgment, and even his personality —oral examinations are often used. These may be completely unstructured, or may consist of several brief but significant questions to which the candidate is asked to respond in depth. This is done before a small panel of interviewers or judges who are given several criteria on which to rate each candidate. Such examinations are not the same as job interviews, which tend to be used chiefly as "get-acquainted" sessions that allow hiring officials or key administrators to make personal judgments about candidates after the field has been narrowed down.

SKILLS TESTS.   In some departments, emphasis may be given to performance tests in such skills areas as arts and crafts, sports, dance, or music, to determine the leadership ability of program specialists in these areas.

Effectiveness of Civil Service Personnel Procedures

Although Civil Service has the potential for developing a true merit system of highly qualified recreation and park personnel in government service, too often it does not succeed in this task. Typically, it has the following weaknesses:

1. Within any geographical region, there tends to be a lack of uniform job titles, descriptions, qualifications, and pay scales for comparable positions. Counties, townships, cities, villages, and school districts frequently employ individuals doing essentially the same job under widely varying titles, position descriptions, and salaries. In addition, the existing Civil Service personnel standards are frequently far below the standards recommended by professional recreation and park societies.

2. Educational requirements for specific positions are usually so flexible, or are so poorly enforced, that a large proportion of professional Civil Service positions in recreation and parks continue to be filled by candidates who have not had specialized training in this field. Many agencies stipulate that candidates must have a degree in recreation, parks, or a "closely allied field." Too often, the closely allied field that is approved is as remote from recreation and parks as history, physics, or a foreign language.

3. The examination process tends to be meaningless when examinations are used that do not have sufficient relevance to the field of recreation and parks. In many cases, they concentrate narrowly on specific skills or knowledge of activities, or on knowledge of English or other areas of general information rather than on the important professional abilities that recreation and park professionals should possess.

4. One of the most vexing problems related to Civil Service personnel selection in recreation and parks stems from the fact that, although this system was intended to do away with patronage, political favoritism continues to operate to a great extent in many local government jurisdictions. Individuals connected with the political party in power may be given special treatment in notification of examinations, or assistance in preparation for them. Where competitive examinations are not required, it is common practice for seasonal, part-time, or specialist jobs to be awarded almost automatically to the "party faithful." High-level administrative jobs continue to be awarded to individuals with limited background in the field. As a single dramatic example of this problem, the following news item appeared in a recent issue of the

Leisure Service News, which is published by the New York State Recreation and Park Society:

Society Fights for Professional Head in Suffolk County

In a major effort to seek voluntary compliance with the State Society's personnel standards, the appointment of an unqualified nominee for the position of Commissioner of Parks, Recreation and Conservation for Sufflok County was temporarily blocked through action taken by the Society and its affiliate, the Suffolk County Recreation, Park and Conservation Association. After numerous articles appeared in . . . daily newspapers in the county and editorials were aired on local radio stations, the Suffolk County Legislature temporarily blocked the appointment of J＿＿＿＿ C＿＿＿＿＿, a two-year college graduate with 22 years of . . . administrative experience at the Brookhaven National Laboratory. Mr. C＿＿＿＿ indicated that he had no training or experience in recreation and park services.

W＿＿＿＿ S＿＿＿＿＿*, the State Society's Executive Director, in a public hearing before the Suffolk County Legislature, asked that the Legislators screen credentials of professional applicants before making a decision, and asked that someone be appointed who exceeded the Society's minimal standards. After C＿＿＿＿'s initial nomination was defeated, the State Society submitted resumés of highly qualified administrators from across the state, many of whom had countywide experience. That effort was ignored by the legislators and . . . they finally endorsed C＿＿＿＿＿'s nomination and he was appointed by the legislators earlier this month.[4]

In a similar case on Long Island, the Society fought — without success — the appointment of an assistant incinerator superintendent, who had no experience in parks and recreation, to the post of park and recreation superintendent of a large township. These cases illustrate the extent to which Civil Service procedures which permit political appointment of the top administrators of departments can circumvent professional standards in recreation and parks, resulting in the appointment of unqualified individuals to key posts. For all these reasons, it is essential that recreation and park personnel, working through their professional societies, labor unions, or other civic organizations, make vigorous efforts to upgrade Civil Service position standards and the procedures for recruitment, examination, and candidate selection. In general, such problems are most severe in very large cities. In smaller communities Civil Service tends to operate more effectively.

EXAMPLES OF JOB DESCRIPTIONS

The concluding section of this chapter provides illustrations of several job descriptions of recreation and park positions drawn from various com-

---

[4] *Leisure Service News.* New York State Recreation and Park Society, February, 1974, pp. 5–6.

munities and agencies throughout the United States. The descriptions vary considerably in their content but usually include the following: (a) the title of the position; (b) a general statement of duties characterizing the position; (c) specific examples of the work performed; (d) a listing of specific skills or competencies required; and (e) a listing of minimum qualifications for the position, in terms of education and experience.

Example I

AGENCY: State of Idaho, Department of Parks and Recreation

TITLE OF POSITION: Park Manager

Definition:

Under direction, to be responsible for the operation of an individual park within the state park system, to plan, organize, and supervise park employees in maintenance and construction work, and to do related work as required.

EXAMPLES OF WORK PERFORMED:

Plans, directs, and participates in the maintenance of park and recreation structures, facilities, and areas including public kitchens, bath houses, public docks, campgrounds, and trailer camps; plans and schedules the placing of men and machinery to perform a definite program of work; orders materials necessary; recommends the transferring or hiring of workers; recommends improvements in operating procedures; supervises the construction and maintenance of roads, boat ramps, recreational facilities, and picnic areas; supervises the maintenance of the park lighting and water systems for building and recreational facilities; supervises the mowing of large areas in the park; assigns, supervises, and trains staff in department policies and procedures; provides information for the public on the park and its uses, and assists visitors as necessary; maintains records and prepares reports.

MINIMUM QUALIFICATIONS:

Education and Experience

Graduation from an accredited four-year college in park management, forestry, recreation or closely related field, and one year full-time paid experience in park management or general construction work.

Knowledges and Abilities

1. Knowledge of the layout and construction of parks and their facilities.

2. Knowledge of the standards and desirable methods of providing parks and park facilities.

3. Knowlege of the principles, practices, and equipment used in parks and parks facilities construction and maintenance.

4. Knowledge of the proper seasonal timing of the activities for which he is responsible.

5. Ability to lay out, direct, and supervise the work of crews performing semi-skilled and unskilled work, and to obtain efficient results.

6. Ability to get along well with the general public, park visitors, and recreation participants.

Example II

AGENCY: Macon-Bibb County Recreation Department, Macon, Georgia

TITLE OF POSITION: Recreation Superintendent

DUTIES:

Assist and advise the governing authority on formulation of policies and basic procedures.

Execute policies, rules and regulations of the governing authority.

Plan, promote, organize, supervise, develop, and direct through executive, administrative and supervisory staff, program, services, and operations.

Instigate surveys and studies of recreation and park needs, and interpret them to the governing authority and to the people.

Formulate (with cooperation of governing authority and staff) long-range plans for acquiring, designing, developing, and constructing parks, areas, and facilities to meet the needs and demands of the people.

Administer total services assigned to the park and recreation department.

Develop and organize department in such a manner that the working relationships between his personnel and those of other departments are maintained at a high level of mutual understanding.

Interpret to all other department heads the needs and responsibilities of his department.

Encourage and lead his staff in full cooperation with all community agencies.

Work closely with all administrative and supervisory staff in directing and guiding them to a cooperative realization of department goals and objectives.

Hold membership with and participate in the programs offered by national, state, regional, and local professional recreation and park organizations, encouraging his staff to do the same.

Select, supervise and direct training of staff, encouraging and leading them in the acquisition of new knowledge and the development of new skills for an efficient performance of responsibilities by a program of in-service training and participation in workshops and institutes.

Prepare budgets, supervise expenditure of funds and be responsible for accurate accounting of funds.

QUALIFICATIONS:

A degree from an accredited college or university in Recreation Leadership or Park Management, or a Master's degree in Recreation and Park Administration.

A minimum of five years' experience as an executive in a recreation and park department with previous experience and/or training in related fields such as landscape architecture, physical education, horticulture, engineering, political science, finance, land, and personnel management.

A good character, with acceptable personal qualities and the ability to command respect and cooperation from a staff of specialists, members of the governing authority, and the public at large.

A thorough knowledge of the philosophy of recreation; appreciation of the activities which make up the community recreation program; ability to administer efficiently the areas and facilities comprising a recreation system;

capacity for cooperating with and interpreting recreation to city authorities, civic clubs, private agencies, and the public; understanding of the problems of the community in respect to recreation; ability to enlist the best efforts of a staff of employees; and other qualities which characterize the promoter, organizer, and executive.

Minimum age should be 30 years.

Example III

AGENCY: Flint, Michigan, Recreation and Park Board

TITLE OF POSITION: Senior Recreation Leader

GENERAL STATEMENT OF DUTIES:

Position title covers the following functional assignments: Supervisor of Boys' and Men's Activities; Supervisor of Girls' and Women's Activities; Supervisor of Senior Citizens' Activities; Recreation Activity Specialist; Swimming Pool Manager; Playground Area Supervisor.

Supervises and participates in planning, scheduling, organizing and directing recreational and social activities in the various municipal recreation centers; instructs assistants in phase of recreation work; performs related work as required.

SUPERVISION RECEIVED:

Works under the supervision of a Park Board recreation employee of higher grade who suggests programs and reviews work for effectiveness.

SUPERVISION EXERCISED:

Exercises working supervision over a few employees engaged in conducting recreational activities.

EXAMPLES OF DUTIES:

1. Supervises and coordinates a group of subordinates engaged in conducting individual and team sports and athletic activities of all types.

2. Demonstrates and explains techniques, procedures, materials, equipment and supplies used in dramatics, nature and outing, dancing, arts and crafts, music and social recreation.

3. Organizes, promotes, leads, teaches and conducts a comprehensive program of games, athletics, bowling, aquatics, and sports activities for all appropriate ages and for both sexes.

4. Consults with individuals and community groups to determine their recreational interests, needs and desires.

5. Leads a well-rounded program of diversified activities suited to the needs and interests of people who attend the center.

6. Organizes, leads and acts as an advisor to clubs and other community groups.

7. Assists in organizing, promoting, and directing tournaments, shows, pageants, socials, exhibits, and special events.

8. Visits various playgrounds or community centers to inspect grounds and equipment; reviews work of subordinates and makes suggestions for improvements.

9. Maintains discipline and safety; administers simple first aid.

10. Instructs new recreation assistants in work or various phases of specialized activities.

11. Participates in staff conferences concerning the recreation program; makes oral and written reports; acts as liaison officer for superior.

MINIMUM ENTRANCE REQUIREMENTS:

Graduation from a college with a bachelor's degree in Recreation or related field of education, *or* equivalent to two years of college, majoring in Recreation or related educational fields, and two years of experience in a recreational position.

Thorough knowledge of the more common physical and social activities, or one of the more specialized activities such as dramatics, manual arts or crafts, folk dancing, music, or rhythm.

Knowledge of the purposes and aims of organized recreational work.

Ability to follow written and oral instructions.

Ability to maintain cooperative working relationships with children and the general public.

Ability to meet the physical, mental and visual standards of the job.

Ability and willingness to work in a manner that will not needlessly endanger the safety to one's self, other persons, and equipment.

Example IV

AGENCY: State of Indiana, Department of Mental Health

TITLE OF POSITION: Recreational Director XII

GENERAL STATEMENT OF DUTIES:

Responsible administrative work directing the recreation program in a state institution. Employee is responsible for planning, organizing, and coordinating program activities, and for the supervision of lower-level employees working in the program. Work is performed independently to secure desired results, but matters of policy are discussed with the Coordinator of Activity Therapy or an administrative official.

EXAMPLES OF WORK (ILLUSTRATIVE ONLY):

Plans, directs, coordinates and integrates recreational activities to meet specific needs, interests and abilities of patients or inmates.

Supervises preparation of budget estimates for the recreation program, personnel, equipment, supplies and facilities.

Plans, assigns and supervises the work of recreation personnel in specific program areas and activities to assure a well-rounded, effective recreation program.

Directs the maintenance and compilation of records and statistics of the recreation program and reviews data.

Conducts studies and experiments for developing new recreation techniques.

In the Department of Mental Health, maintains contact with appropriate medical authorities in order to develop and conduct medically approved plans and policies which will meet the needs, capabilities, and interests of the patients.

Assists in the general rehabilitation of patients or inmates; performs related work as assigned.

REQUIREMENTS FOR WORK:

Extensive knowledge of the principles and practices of institutional recreation programs.

Extensive knowledge of the rules and regulations of a variety of sports, games and other recreation activities.

Working knowledge of the principles and practices of recreation administration.

Ability to plan, assign and supervise the work of others engaged in a recreation program.

Ability to adapt recreation policies, procedures, plans, methods, tools and techniques to specific situations.

Ability to establish and maintain harmonious relationships with patients or inmates of a state institution.

MINIMUM EXPERIENCE AND EDUCATIONAL REQUIREMENTS:

A Master's Degree in hospital recreation, recreation in rehabilitation, or recreational therapy, and one year of full-time paid experience in recreation
    or
A Master's Degree in recreation, and two years of full-time paid experience in recreation. In non-mental institutions, physical education is an acceptable field of education and experience.

It is obvious that these recreation and park positions in public agencies vary considerably. The functions are extremely diverse, and reflect the wide range of specializations in this field. Typically, a medium-sized city would have leadership and supervisory personnel assigned to such specialties as: (a) program areas, such as arts and crafts, music, aquatics, social and cultural activities, the aging, or the physically or mentally disabled; (b) various types of facilities, such as parks and playgrounds, nature centers, sports complexes, or community centers; (c) maintenance, such as tree crew foremen, maintenance engineers, construction foremen, custodians, or security supervisor; (d) administrative functions related to personnel direction, fiscal management, and a variety of other functions.

Again, in terms of education and experience requirements, no single system prevails. Some departments—particularly in the field of therapeutic recreation—maintain a strict requirement for specialized college degrees in the field. Others, including many municipal and county park departments, are prepared to accept a high school diploma and appropriate experience as adequate preparation for a position of considerable responsibility. A typical pattern is to balance the educational requirement with appropriate amounts of full-time, paid experience in recreation. In some cases, such experience is equated, year for year, with study. In others, it is based on a formula such as the following:

1. A Bachelor's degree in recreation and one year of paid, full-time experience in the field.
2. A Bachelor's degree in a closely allied field, and two years of paid, full-time experience in the field.
3. Any Bachelor's degree, and three years of paid, full-time experience in the field.

4. A two-year degree, and four years of paid, full-time experience in the field.

JOB REQUIREMENTS IN VOLUNTARY AGENCIES

Personnel standards in nongovernmental agencies are generally much more flexible than in public departments. In those organizations which are influenced strongly by policies of their national headquarters, such as the Boy Scouts of America or the Young Women's Christian Association, it is the national staff which may develop guidelines for professional positions as well as personnel training procedures and materials (see Chapter Seven). However, these organizations usually do not have standardized, sharply defined educational and experience requirements for professional-level positions, and it would be extremely rare for them to rely on a formal examination process to identify qualified candidates for a job opening.

As a single example, the Association for the Help of Retarded Children in New York City has a Group Work, Recreation and Camping Guide which outlines the responsibilities and needed qualifications for such positions as: Director, Supervisor, Group Leader, Assistant Group Leader, Children's Program Leader, or Trip Leader. Responsibilities of the Supervisor are stated as follows:

General Statement

Under the direction of the Director of Group Work, Recreation and Camping Services, assist with the planning and conduct of recreation and camping services for mentally retarded persons primarily by working directly with groups of mentally retarded persons on a long term and short term demonstration basis.

Examples of Work

1. Assist with the work involved in planning, organizing, and carrying out the department's total recreation services.
2. When so assigned, provide direct recreation leadership for groups of children and adults.
3. Teach recreation and leisure time skills both on a group and individual basis.
4. Supervise volunteers and other part-time personnel assigned to his program.
5. Assist with supervision and in-service training of total staff.
6. Maintain required records and reports.

In general, private or commercial recreation agencies are even less likely to have fixed educational or experience requirements for positions, or to have rigid hiring expectations or procedures. They are usually not as concerned with formal credentials as they are with demonstrated ability to do the job, as determined through past experience or references.

GETTING THE FIRST JOB – CONCLUDING STATEMENT

This chapter has been concerned with the nature of job requirements and the process through which community recreation and park agencies recruit and select personnel. Turning the coin around, what is the method through which young professionals *find* jobs? The examples of position descriptions provided here are typical in that a number of them specify the need for previous, full-time, paid experience. How does a college graduate find his or her *first job* in recreation? Before reaching this point, the student should have determined that he is in the right field. At an early point in his college study, he should have asked himself the following questions:

Self-Screening by Potential Recreation Professionals

Have you been actively involved as a participant in recreation programs in your childhood and youth? Do you have specific skills and interests in recreation that you might use in leadership roles?

Have you already had experience in leadership as an officer of youth groups, a volunteer or part-time leader in community centers, summer camps, or similar settings?

Do you find satisfaction in watching others recreate, or in making recreation opportunities available to others, such as family or friends?

Do you like people, and are you usually able to communicate well with them?

Are you as a rule well organized, a self-starter, enthusiastic, and able to accept and carry out responsibility? Can you see yourself in the role of supervisor or administrator? (Most professional-level recreation positions involve such functions.)

Are you willing to make some personal sacrifices – probably including much of your own leisure time – in order to carry out your job effectively?

If his answers to these questions are generally positive, the college student is probably well suited to the recreation field. If not, he should seriously question whether or not he is in the appropriate major department – and at as early a stage as possible. Following this early determination, it is important for the young recreation major to prepare himself as fully as possible throughout his college study rather than to wait until he is looking for a job before he examines his skills as they might appear to a potential employer.

Upgrading Skills and Experience

It is essential that the student get as much direct field experience as possible in volunteer or paid part-time jobs. Such assignments are valuable for the reasons cited in Chapter Five (page 100), and may be used — if they involve paid work — to meet Civil Service or other occupational requirements for previous professional experience.

In addition to such experience, the student should seek every opportunity to develop professionally. An important aspect of this is to join relevant professional organizations, particularly national associations or student sections of state or provincial societies, and other appropriate organizations. In so doing, the student will receive professional publications, will have the opportunity to attend conferences and special meetings, and will become more fully involved in the field. He will begin to have a sense of himself as a professional. Holding offices or being a committee member of a student section will be a positive experience, as it affords a way of getting to know older professionals and of learning to work as part of a team.

When the student has identified his special area of professional interest, he should make every effort to become knowledgeable and experienced in it. This may be done by visiting and observing such programs, holding volunteer or paid part-time or seasonal jobs in them, doing course papers or research on them, or taking special college courses intended to reinforce his strengths in the area (such as courses in social group work for the student who plans to work in a community social agency).

Assuming that he does all these things, the student will be well equipped to enter the field as a professional. How does he approach the critical challenge of getting his first full-time, paid job after graduation? There are many ways in which people get such positions in recreation. They include the following:

Strategies for Getting the First Job

1. JOB ANNOUNCEMENTS.   During the course of the year, the college or university recreation faculty should distribute announcements of job openings to their classes, as soon as the openings are brought to their attention. Also, job listings may be posted outside departmental offices.

2. WORD-OF-MOUTH.   Many positions are filled through informal, word-of-mouth communication. For this reason, it is extremely important to be active in the field and to know people working in it.

3. NEWSPAPER OR MAGAZINE ADVERTISEMENTS.   In large cities, agencies with openings frequently place advertisements requesting recreation personnel in the Sunday job listings. These must be read carefully, since recreation positions may be described as "group leaders," "therapists," "youth counselors," or "activity supervisors." Professional journals in the United States and Canada also sometimes include advertisements of positions.

4. PROFESSIONAL ORGANIZATIONS.   These provide placement services or publish lists of positions on a national or statewide basis. Professional conferences may have "job marts," at which administrators may interview applicants. Generally, they offer the opportunity for professional contact on varied levels, which leads to employment possibilities.

5. EMPLOYMENT AGENCIES.   Professional employment agencies and college

placement services should provide job notices. Particularly in large cities, one or more commercial employment agencies will be likely to specialize in government or social service jobs.

6. DIRECT APPLICATION. Some students send out applications directly to potential employers, and ask if they have job openings at present, or if they expect them. These applications should include covering letters and detailed, well-prepared résumés.

7. TAKING QUALIFYING EXAMINATIONS. Even if the student does not have a particular position in mind, he is wise to take the appropriate qualifying Civil Service examination well in advance of the time of applying for a job. For a position in the National Park Service, for example, the candidate must be rated eligible under the Federal Service Entrance Examination.

Finally, the student should recognize that the first job is *just* that – and not necessarily one in which he will be spending the next 30 years. Through it, he will begin to gain a livelihood, valuable experience and confidence, and will begin to make a professional contribution. If it is to be a successful and rewarding experience for him, and if he is to able to function to his full potential in this new setting, it is essential that he be provided with an adequate orientation process and an effective in-service education. These important supervisory responsibilities are dealt with in Chapter Seven.

Suggested Examination Questions or Topics for Student Reports

1. What are the functions or purposes of a job classification system, and how should it be developed? Describe the key elements in a job description form, based on examples given in this chapter.
2. Assess the strengths and weaknesses of certification, registration, and Civil Service selection procedures in recreation and parks, as described in this text.
3. Examine the selection and hiring process of public recreation and park employees in your community or state, and develop a set of recommendations for improving this process.
4. What methods would be most appropriate, in your judgment, for the recruitment and selection of part-time and seasonal recreation personnel?

Suggested Action Assignments for Students

1. Construct job description forms for several levels of positions in a public agency (federal, state or provincial, or local), and prepare outlines of examinations which would be used in connection with the selection process on each of these levels.
2. Select a large voluntary organization or therapeutic agency, and review its job standards and recruitment and selection procedures critically.

staff development: orientation, in-service training, and evaluation

This chapter deals with three key elements of staff development that are intended to upgrade the level of employee performance: *orientation, in-service training,* and *evaluation.* Although these services are generally found within any large business or governmental organization, they are particularly essential within the field of recreation and parks, for the following reasons:

Need for Staff Development Programs in Recreation

1. Many individuals entering work in recreation and parks tend not to have been prepared specifically in this field. Although they may have the needed leadership skills and personal qualities, it is important that they be given a fuller understanding of the goals of recreation, and of the agency that has employed them.

2. Recreation involves many different settings and types of services, all of which require knowledgeable and responsive leadership. In many cases, it is necessary to provide on-going training in specific areas of leadership methodology, group dynamics, and human relations. Since departmental approaches constantly undergo change to meet new community needs, personnel must also be encouraged to stay up-to-date and able to function meaningfully.

3. Evaluation is particularly crucial because work output in recreation is not as readily determined as in other fields, where it may be easier to measure an individual's accomplishment (caseload handled, number of insurance policies sold, or amount of products manufactured). Therefore, there is an important need to evaluate the competence and overall performance of recreation and park personnel for use in counseling purposes or for personnel decisions.

For readers of this text, an understanding of orientation, in-service training, and evaluation is important for two reasons: (a) the areas indicate what kinds of supervisory assistance a new employee should expect in a well-organized department; and (b) they outline the methods used in staff development, and so are of value to those with supervisory responsibilities.

ORIENTATION IN PERSONNEL MANAGEMENT

Orientation may be defined as the process of introducing new workers to a department by familiarizing them with its philosophy, policies and working procedures, the overall structure and physical setting, and their co-workers and supervisors. Its fundamental purpose is to provide new employees with the skills, knowledges, and minimal abilities needed to carry out work assignments during the initial period of employment, until they have participated in a fuller program of staff development.

The first days and weeks of any employee's beginning job experience should include a thorough exposure to: (a) the department or agency, which may include a tour of the departments's offices or facilities and familiarization with its various divisions and functions; (b) a detailed outline of all responsibilities and duties, including instructions for carrying these out, when necessary; and (c) a clear presentation of personnel policies relating to hours, sickness, leaves, vacations, health and medical insurance, and similar areas of personal responsibility or company benefits.

How is all this to be accomplished? There are two methods which may be used separately or in combination. These are *printed manuals*, and scheduled *orientation sessions or meetings*.

Personnel Manuals

Most cities or large organizations provide general personnel manuals to all employees that cover regulations and general information applicable to all departments. For example, the city of St. Petersburg, Florida, presents a general manual to all new employees that covers 21 major headings, such as employee performance evaluation, classification plan, pay plan, and safety regulations.

Many departments also publish printed manuals which cover such matters but also include special information relating to the recreation and park function. For example, the town of Hempstead, New York, presents new employees in its Parks and Recreation Department with a *Recreation Staff Handbook*. This manual includes both general information on administrative policies and personnel procedures, and on many elements related to leadership in recreation and parks, including regulations dealing with dress and appearance, staff meetings, in-service training, work schedules, inclement weather arrangements, and similar matters.

Printed staff manuals may also deal with leadership methodology. This is particularly true in therapeutic settings, where it is essential that new workers understand the institution's philosophy and method of operation. For example, the Recreation Therapy Department of the Evansville, Indiana, Psychiatric Children's Center issues a detailed Policy and Procedure Manual to new employees. This includes the following major sections:

1. Organization of Recreation Therapy Department
2. General Staff Relationships and Responsibilities
3. Program Responsibilities and Specific Job Assignments
4. Responsibilities of Supervisors
5. Time and Hours
6. Attire While on Duty
7. Responsibility and Relation to Volunteers
8. Responsibility with Patients
9. Equipment, Supplies and Area Requisitioning
10. Professional Attitude and Conduct

Under the final heading, the Evansville staff manual includes such guidelines as:

> It is the aim of this department to improve and raise its standards of operation to the level whereby it will become a more professional service. . . . The overall conduct and attitude displayed by the Recreation Therapy Staff members as a whole or individually . . . reflect on the department and affect its function. Following are guidelines each staff member will be expected to follow.
>
> No discussion is to be held outside the hospital about a patient's history and/or illness. This includes indiscreet remarks to any of our public about any information concerning patients.
>
> Show each patient respect and courtesy regardless of how ill he is, just as you would any other human being. Do not play jokes on patients or mimic or make fun of patients. Expressions of this type often reflect your attitude toward the patient. Never argue with a patient. . .

Orientation Meetings

Although such manuals are helpful, they cannot do an effective job of orientation by themselves. Instead, well-planned orientation sessions or programs are called for. Such sessions may take on a number of forms: they may be either formal or informal, may last several days or simply for a portion of one day, and may involve only one new employee or a large number of new employees.

The Parks and Recreation Department of Phoenix, Arizona, for example, holds a special orientation session in September for all new employees. In this meeting, key staff members make presentations acquainting the

A

B

Paul Caramuto

Senior Centers. Many departments and agencies today operate Senior Centers or Golden Age Centers. This is an extremely popular program in Mt. Vernon, New York, where participants take part in a choral group (*A*), a "hot lunch" program (*B*), an annual luncheon (*C*), and a mass checkers competition (*D*). Senior Citizen officers are sworn in by a city judge (*E*).

C

D

E

new employees with the history, structure, and goals of the department, the functions of the Recreation Division, personnel policies, and similar matters. The advantage of such meetings is that they provide the opportunity for give-and-take, for exploring problem areas in detail, and for helping new workers identify individuals associated with different administrative and program areas.

Another form of orientation would be to assign the beginning worker to an experienced employee who has been specifically trained to "break-in" new staff members by having them work side-by-side with him for a period of several weeks.

IN-SERVICE TRAINING

Following the orientation period, there should be a well-organized program of in-service education that serves to heighten the employee's understanding of his work, improve his skills, and generally enhance his professional growth. In many departments, workers are given little meaningful guidance and assistance in carrying out their responsibilities. However, authorities agree that it should be an important function of administration to provide such programs. The nature of professional responsibilities changes so rapidly in our society that it is necessary for most people to continue to learn and to change if they are to be successful in their work.

Dimock and Dimock write:

> The psychologist, Donald Michael, in *The Next Generation,* predicts that soon most people will regard education as a life-long pursuit. For one thing, continuing rapid social, economic and political change will mean that no one can afford to stand still . . .[1]

Another authority on personnel management, Nigro, agrees, and points out a dozen techniques which are widely employed to promote staff development. These include internships prior to formal entry into service, apprenticeships after entry, direct counseling, rotation and transfer of employment, opportunity for observation of other workers, supervised reading, lectures, discussions, and group dynamics meetings.

If in-service training is to be successful, it must be made a serious responsibility of supervisors, with strong staff support from personnel administrators in research, advice, and planning. In planning in-service training programs, a number of specific guidelines should be established. The following guidelines are drawn from the general literature on personnel management, and from specific examples of in-service training in recreation and park departments in the United States and Canada.

---

[1] See Marshall E. Dimock and Gladys O. Dimock: *Public Administration.* Holt, Rinehart and Winston, Inc., New York, 1969, p. 235.

Guidelines for In-Service Training

Identify Objectives. Each department should clearly identify specific objectives for each aspect of the program. These goals should not be developed by department administrators or supervisors alone but in collaboration with all staff members. It is common practice to carry out surveys to determine staff training needs. They may reveal that a variety of problems, such as accident records, absenteeism, resignations, or poor production, stem from a lack of adequate training, and they may identify clear objectives for such training. Review of personnel evaluations records may also indicate specific in-service training needs.

Assign Responsibility. Instead of being everyone's responsibility, the task of planning and organizing in-service training should be assigned to one or more supervisory-level individuals. They should be allowed an adequate amount of time apart from their routine work. To assist them, a committee of employees should be established to help in planning and carrying out specific in-service training projects.

Select Appropriate In-Service Training Projects. Those responsible for in-service training should determine which types of training projects should be selected to meet the specific needs of the department. An overall plan for a given year should be established, including all of the types of programs that have been selected.

Develop a Schedule. The exact dates and times of in-service programs must be established. At this point, a major policy question must be faced. Will in-service training meetings be carried on outside of work hours, with employees attending of their own volition? If so, they will lack status in the eyes of the staff, and attendance is likely to be weak, although the department may find ways to motivate people to attend by giving special certificates, by recording attendance in personnel records, and through similar devices.

A more constructive approach is to schedule in-service training sessions as part of the regular job commitment of employees. This may be done in a variety of ways. In some situations, a period of required attendance on a nonpaid basis may be scheduled before the actual work period; this is commonly done with summer playground leaders. In some departments, a given morning each week is devoted to in-service training. In others, a particular group of employees may be selected for full-time intensive training workshops and released from other job responsibilities while these are held.

Plan Sessions. The specific content of each workshop, clinic, or other training session should be carefully planned to meet departmental needs, focus on special problems, or prepare for new programs or responsibilities. Training sessions should be brief rather than drawn out. They should stimulate action rather than restrict it. The sessions should deal with real rather than theoretical concerns. They should make use of techniques that involve, interest, and influence participants rather than be passive, lecture-type methods that are dry and boring.

Arrange Staffing. Many departments use their own staff members to give courses or special training workshops, particularly if they have workers who are strong specialists in various program areas. Frequently, use is made of personnel from other city departments or agencies, such as police officials, fiscal officers, youth board workers, or other specialists. Faculty members from nearby colleges or universities, or representatives of professional organizations, may be drawn in as paid or unpaid speakers. It is essential that persons staffing training sessions have something significant to offer; *nothing* is more disheartening than to have those attending a training session feel that they know more or are more highly skilled than those presenting the material.

Evaluate Programs. It is essential to evaluate all in-service training programs to determine their effectiveness and to help in making recommendations for future activities. Too often there is little systematic evaluation of in-service training. Pfiffner and Fels comment, "Training conducted without research is like an automobile without a driver."[2]

TYPES OF IN-SERVICE TRAINING PROGRAMS

A wide variety of methods may be used to conduct in-service training. For example, the Richmond, Virginia, Department of Recreation and Parks lists 11 specific methods used for staff development: (a) special institutes; (b) city-wide and neighborhood staff meetings; (c) interchange of departmental personnel for special purposes; (d) regular in-service training meetings for staff (including roundtable discussion, demonstration, and workshops); (e) monthly evaluations and follow-up; (f) meetings with advisory councils and volunteer groups; (g) bulletin service; (h) professional library service and magazines; (i) planned visits to other units or activities; (h) provision of opportunities for sharing experiences; and (i) research and study.

Several of these will now be described in greater detail, followed by actual examples drawn from departments or organizations in the United States and Canada.

Staff Meetings

In various ways, staff meetings make an important contribution to in-service training. The staff of a large center or district, or even the entire recreation staff of a department, may meet regularly to be informed of departmental plans and policies and to take part in problem-solving discussions or project planning. Individual members of the staff may be

---

[2] John M. Pfiffner and Marshall Fels: *The Supervision of Personnel: Human Relations in the Management of Men.* Englewood Cliffs, New Jersey, Prentice-Hall, 1965, p. 270.

requested to report on their work, or committees may be appointed to study special problems and make recommendations at such meetings. Individuals who have attended professional conferences may be asked to share their experiences with the staff at the sessions.

Pre-Season Training Institutes

Customarily, pre-season training institutes are held before the summer, in the latter part of June. They are used to train seasonal employees for work on playgrounds or in other special programs.

In some cities, such workshops are held not only before the summer season but also before any major new programs are initiated, in order to train all personnel in their new responsibilities.

Special Workshops

These are special short-term, intensive in-service training programs which may last from a single afternoon or morning to several days of full-time attendance and participation. They may be concerned with the improvement of professional skills, involving clinics in major program areas, such as sports, nature activities, or the performing arts. They may serve to introduce new program features, such as mobile recreation units and services. They may be concerned with problems of community relations, youth discipline, vandalism, or other social problems. They may also be intended to improve personnel performance, encourage innovation, or improve morale in a department.

In-Service Training Courses

These are similar to special workshops, except that they usually extend over a longer period of time and cover more varied topics. Many departments offer one or more training courses on a given morning or afternoon of the week, throughout an entire season, for 12 or 15 weeks. Normally, such courses are compulsory in attendance when offered during working hours, although in some departments they are given on evenings or weekends, with voluntary attendance.

Other Methods

In addition to the preceding approaches, other recreation and park departments use the following methods:

They may encourage staff members to attend national or regional conferences by giving them professional leaves, and even assisting them financially with travel and registration costs.

Staff members may also be encouraged to attend college or university courses in recreation and parks and to work toward appropriate degrees; some departments help to pay tuition costs and arrange work schedules to facilitate attendance.

Professional libraries of books and magazines in the recreation and parks field may be maintained, and staff members encouraged to read these or use them as planning resources.

Staff members are usually encouraged to join professional organizations and take part in their activities, as an important stimulus to professional growth.

Departments may arrange visits and tours for staff members to observe recreation and park agencies in neighboring communities or special agencies as a form of in-service education.

EXAMPLES OF SPECIFIC TRAINING PROGRAMS

Several examples of specific training programs, as provided by public, therapeutic, and voluntary agencies, follow.

Pre-Season Training Institute: Reading, Pennsylvania

The Bureau of Recreation of Reading, Pennsylvania, sponsors an annual Pre-Season Playground Leaders' Workshop on three days in mid-June. All summer playground personnel are expected to attend. The schedule includes a variety of speeches, demonstrations, and participation in playground activities. The staff of the institute includes supervisory members of the department, who conduct workshops in special activity areas, and guest speakers, including a newspaper reporter, police official, city attorney, city councilman, and physician. The schedule is tightly organized, with a wide variety of presentations and clinics. In a recent year, it followed this plan:

Monday

9:00 a.m.	Introduction and welcome address.
9:30 a.m.	Playground Administration.
10:15 a.m.	Responsibilities of playground leaders; safety on the playground.
11:00 a.m.	Introduction to folk dancing.
1:00 p.m.	Opening exercises.
1:05 p.m.	Legal responsibilities.
1:20 p.m.	Introduction to tournament games.
3:00 p.m.	Introduction to athletic events; organization of tournaments.

4:00 p.m.   Playground publicity.
4:15 p.m.   Distribution of supplies.
6:30 p.m.   Dramatic activities: singing games.
7:30 p.m.   Introduction to handicrafts.

Tuesday

9:00 a.m.   Opening ceremonies.
9:15 a.m.   Police and the playgrounds.
9:30 a.m.   Explanation of departmental forms.
9:45 a.m.   Active and quiet games for small groups and places.
11:00 a.m.   Problems on the playground: panel discussion.
1:00 p.m.   Opening exercises.
1:10 p.m.   Handicrafts.
3:00 p.m.   Folk dancing (women leaders).
               Athletic games (men leaders).
4:00 p.m.   First aid on the playground.
6:30 p.m.   Music and drama.
7:00 p.m.   Planning a program.
7:45 p.m.   Playground publicity.
8:00 p.m.   Playgrounds in action.

Wednesday

9:00 a.m.   Opening ceremonies.
9:15 a.m.   Summer playground program.
10:00 a.m.   Advanced handicrafts.
11:00 a.m.   Dramatic activities; singing games.
11:30 a.m.   Low organized games.
1:00 p.m.   Opening exercises.
1:15 p.m.   Staff photo.
1:45 p.m.   Structure of athletic leagues and track meet.
2:45 p.m.   Advanced folk dancing and athletic games.
3:45 p.m.   Playground associations (neighborhood advisory councils).
4:00 p.m.   Playground assignments and conference.
5:30 p.m.   Playground federation picnic.

This institute is an example of an intensive in-service workshop for playground personnel. Many recreation and park departments have much less crowded schedules, cover a shorter period of time, and have more flexibility in the choice of sessions.

Pre-Season Training Programs: Hewlett-Woodmere, New York

An interesting approach to in-service training may be found in the Recreation Division of the Department of Community Services of the Hewlett-Woodmere, New York, public schools. This Department is responsible for four major areas of school services: Recreation, Adult Education, Senior Citizens, and Coordination of Drug Programs. The Recreation Division operates a major summer program, including morning playground activities for elementary school children at four school sites, and day and evening programs for junior and senior high school students. Teachers, college students, and high school students are employed as leaders in these programs.

The Recreation Division makes use of several different training approaches in preparing personnel for summer work, including a six-week course conducted for high school students who hope to work in the summer program. This is held weekly during the spring and covers the following topics:

1st week:	Philosophy of recreation and leisure; introduction to playground leadership.
2nd week:	Playground directors in charge of the previous summer's centers present slides of past programs, facilities and equipment, and discuss their programs.
3rd week:	Safety and first aid, accident procedures, and general responsibilities of playground leaders.
4th week:	Games and sports: demonstration of leadership methods by staff and students.
5th week:	Arts and crafts session, with demonstration of methods and student participation.
6th week:	Discussion of overall workshop; question-and-answer period, and examination.

Based on their performance during the six weeks, several of the most capable students are hired to work during the summer, filling vacancies created when members of the previous year's staff do not return. Other forms of in-service education include meetings and planning sessions with the college students, teachers, or playground specialists who will be in charge of programs during the summer.

In-Service Training Courses in Three Cities

During the regular year, many municipal recreation and park departments sponsor weekly courses for their personnel. One example is in the city of Detroit, where the department offers courses in different districts of the city from 12:30 to 2:30 p.m., three days of the week. Samples of the topics dealt with in these courses include: "Alcoholism," "You and Your Police Department," "Mental Health Program," "Personnel Policies and Procedures," "Vest Pocket Parks," "Recreation Advisory Committees," "Special Events," "Mobile Programs," and varied courses dealing with program activities and how to conduct them. Obviously, these sessions cover a wide range of subjects, including specific leadership skills, human relations, professional development, and community relations responsibilities.

The Philadelphia Recreation Department has a similarly diverse list of in-service training institutes, including courses that *must* be taken as part of each employee's professional development, and which are required to become eligible for promotion. For example, individuals who hope to become eligible for promotion to *Recreation Leader II* must take such basic courses as "Recreation Programming," "Facility Planning and Maintenance," and "Camping Organization and Administration." On a higher level of responsibility, in order to qualify for promotion to *District Supervisor* or *Senior Recreation Leader,* candidates must take such courses as "Recreation Administration and Personnel Practices," "Inner-City Operations and Federal Funding," "Fiscal Planning and Management," and "Recreation Supervision and Public Relations."

Probably the most ambitious single in-service training course to have been offered by a municipal recreation and park department was sponsored during the early 1970's by New York City's Parks, Recreation and Cultural Affairs Administration. This course was designed to give a thorough professional "re-treading" to selected supervisory or senior recreation directors as preparation for new assignments as "district superintendents" in areas throughout the city. The course involved attendance three full days a week over a period of several weeks, from early February to mid-April. Held at Teachers College, Columbia University, it was staffed by faculty members from that institution, and by dozens of speakers and consultants from varied government agencies in New York City, consultant planning firms, professional organizations, and representatives from other cities.

The curriculum involved a total examination of urban recreation service today, as shown below:

I. *Urban Environment.* A general orientation to the growth and present status of cities, combined with an analysis of New York City government, including various offices, councils, and commissions.

II. *Urban Recreation Service.* A general introduction to the philosophy and current trends of recreation and group work services provided in New York City by public, voluntary, and other agencies.

III. *Parks, Recreation and Cultural Affairs Administration.* An analysis of the city's major recreation and park agency: its goals, structure, functions and resources; also, its role with respect to city libraries, cultural institutions, and historical landmarks.

IV. *Community Life.* An analysis of "community" and "neighborhood" concepts, local power structures, differing needs of various communities based on ethnic, racial, religious, and economic factors; the role of school-sponsored recreation programs.

V. *Bio-Social Factors.* Principles of human development, patterns of family living in modern society, and needs and problems of various age groups, as they affect recreation and leisure.

VI. *Disabilities and Special Needs.* Examination of various types of physical, mental, and social disability and their effects; principles of designing special facilities and programs to serve special needs.

VII. *Administrative Principles.* Principles of office management, personnel practices, planning, and budget development and fiscal management.

VIII. *Staff Development Methods.* Development of in-service training, library and visual aids, role of professional organizations and labor union relations, use of research in personnel management, and supervision of volunteers.

IX. *Other Government Agencies.* Role of other federal and state agencies which provide recreation programs, or assist with funding or other resources.

Other class sessions dealt with problems of public and community relations, the design of playgrounds and other facilities, program development, and the proposed new district plan of decentralized recreation administration. The overall group of approximately 80 students was divided into four sub-groups, each of which was assigned to a community planning district in the city. Members of each sub-group did extensive field observation, developed master plans for their assigned districts, and presented recreation events in various institutions as part of their "action-oriented" experience in this course.

IN-SERVICE TRAINING IN OTHER SETTINGS

Obviously, other types of recreation agencies or departments also provide their personnel with in-service training opportunities. Examples are now given of four such settings: federal, voluntary, commercial, and therapeutic recreation.

National Park Service

This major agency in the United States Department of the Interior operates a huge network of national parks, seashores, and recreation areas. In order to provide on-going professional development for its personnel, it sponsors a number of special training centers, including the Stephen T. Mather Training Center, at Harpers Ferry, West Virginia; the Horace M. Albright Training Center, at the Grand Canyon National Park; and the National Capital Parks Center, in Washington, D.C.

Employees elect to take courses which will help them both in their present positions and in career advancement. If approved, they are sent to take courses which include practical management workshops and high-level executive development institutes given at appropriate training centers. Most such courses involve full-time attendance, ranging generally from five days to two weeks; some longer courses permit employees to remain on the job while undergoing training. Typical course titles include the following:

"Dealing with Unions at the Park Level"
"Executive Management Seminar"
"First Line Supervision"
"Basic Law Enforcement for Seasonal Park Rangers"
"Introduction to Park Planning"

"Introduction to Maintenance Management"
"Standards for Operations: Historical Areas"
"Environmental Interpretation"

In addition to these training opportunities, employees of the National Park Service are also encouraged to attend other centralized training programs provided by the federal government for employees from various federal agencies and departments.

Girl Scouts of the United States of America

This leading voluntary youth organization maintains an intensive training program—both for its professional staff and for the tremendous number of volunteer leaders who direct Girl Scout troops. In part, this training is done through workshops and institutes. However, because of the numbers involved and their scattered location throughout the United States and other countries, the organization must also rely heavily on printed training materials.

For example, in a pamphlet titled *Just Tell Us How*, the Training Division of the Girl Scouts lists a number of major questions regarding objectives and techniques: "What is Scouting supposed to do for girls?" "How does a leader really get acquainted with so many girls at once?" "What do we do in meetings? What are some good program activities? How do we carry on ceremonies?" "How do we keep the group from getting out of control?" It provides answers to these questions, and suggests additional training resources, such as packets, film strips, leadership handbooks, and similar materials. The Girl Scouts also publish and distribute materials intended for professional staff development, in which they outline goals and executive improvement techniques for their paid professional workers.

Boys' Clubs of America

Another outstanding voluntary agency is the Boys' Clubs of America. This organization's rationale for conducting in-service training programs has been stated in the following passage:[3]

> Competent leadership is the key to the success of the entire Boys' Club movement. To achieve and maintain high leadership standards, it is essential that all professional workers constantly increase their knowledge and understanding of boys in the Boys' Club setting and stay relevant to the demands imposed by a rapidly changing society. They should also continue to acquire better methods and techniques for organizing, operating and managing the Boys' Club itself, so as to achieve goals in the most efficient manner.
>
> Education and experience are important requisites for professional Boys'

---

[3] *National Orientation Program Manual.* Boys' Clubs of America, New York, 1973.

Club staff. However, every person should understand that he cannot get enough education and training before taking his first position to last his entire career. He should strive continually to improve those skills and abilities related to his present job. Also, whenever possible he should add layers of new skills and experiences which will equip him for advanced positions in the Boys' Club field.

Professional workers, of course, form only a part of the staff team. They are the nucleus, but the successful Boys' Club also utilizes part-time paid employees (who may be professionals in other settings), volunteers, junior leaders and supporting staff, as maintenance and clerical personnel, to achieve its objectives. All of these people must be developed to their fullest along with the professionals.

As the attitudinal and skill needs of an entire Boys' Club staff are considered, it becomes apparent that different kinds and different levels of training are required. One of the best ways to provide this is through an organized program of in-service training.

Careful guidelines are prepared by the National Boys' Club headquarters to assist local directors in developing in-service education programs. Extensive manuals have been prepared to guide them in assessing needs, available resources, and developing staff training models. Training personnel are guided in the use of innovative techniques, such as audiovisual materials, case studies, buzz groups, panels, programmed learning techniques, role playing, debates, and a variety of other methods.

In the early 1970's, the Boys' Clubs of America embarked on an elaborate plan for national upgrading of staff development programs. National conferences were held, and major committees appointed, to implement this effort. At present, employees are involved in a five-phase plan of professional training:

FIRST PHASE: NEW WORKER BRIEFING AND REGISTRATION. New employees receive extensive orientation materials outlining information about the Boys' Clubs, and informing them of training opportunities.

SECOND PHASE: ORIENTATION SEMINARS. Preferably during the first year of employment, Boys' Club workers participate in a five-day Orientation Seminar designed to serve 20 to 50 participants, and scheduled each month as part of a National Professional Training Plan in several different cities around the United States.

THIRD PHASE: ADVANCED PROGRAM SEMINARS. After two or three years in the field, professionals participate in Advanced Program Seminars, dealing with subjects such as program planning, principles of supervision, and intensive work in discipline and guidance.

FOURTH PHASE: MANAGEMENT PREPARATION PROGRAMS. After about three years, workers are encouraged to begin professional preparation for administrative responsibility. They take part in pre- or junior executive conferences concerned with such problems as working with boards of directors, fund raising, staff development, budgeting, and problem-solving.

FIFTH PHASE: EXECUTIVE TRAINING PROGRAMS. These are continued training experiences for executive personnel, to refresh them on basics, bring them up to date on new trends and approaches, and teach new job behaviors.

Commercial Recreation: Walt Disney World

Walt Disney World, in Lake Buena Vista, Florida, like its California cousin, Disneyland, operates a giant outdoor show on more than 27,000 acres of resort-hotels, campgrounds, golf courses, and the "Magic Kingdom Theme Park." In this huge undertaking, with thousands of employees and millions of patrons, very little is left to chance. Orientation, in-service training, and supervision of personnel are carefully planned and carried out. New employees are given colorful manuals welcoming them to Walt Disney World and outlining the organization's philosophy and working operation—as well as their own responsibilities. They learn quickly that they are part of "show business," on the "world's largest stage," and that the show is expected to be spectacular, fresh, new, and unique, every day of the year.

Employees must learn a new language as part of Walt Disney World's formula for "creating" happiness. Their role is to help their "guests" shed the problems of the outside world, and enter into a land of fantasy and excitement. They are "hosts and hostesses," "on stage at all times," following a careful code of costuming and appearance, speech, behavior, teamwork, and showmanship.

Each new employee goes through a careful training program conducted through the "University of Walt Disney World." This University is a nonaccredited training aspect of the company, and all employees take one, two, or more of the training programs each year. Beginning employees go through a one-day training program, called *Traditions I,* at the University center, which is equipped with training facilities, conference rooms, and special theater rooms. *Traditions I* involves an eight-hour orientation to the company's tradition, history, and philosophy—and to the basic concepts employees must follow in their contacts with the public.

On the second day of initial training, employees go to their respective Divisions for *Traditions II,* which covers all the information they need about their respective jobs. Little use is made of printed materials; instead, teaching aids, flow charts, talk boards, talks with various management personnel, and walk-throughs of the areas under the Division's responsibility are used. On the third day of training, each employee reports to his assigned area, where

> He meets the individual department head, and then is assigned to a qualified trainer (an employee who has proven himself capable, responsible and knowledgeable about a certain position). Each position from a Captain Nemo submarine operator to a lifeguard or a campground host has been assigned a certain number of training hours. The trainer works on a one-to-one basis with the employee, using a trainer check sheet, and the particular position's Standard Operation Procedure, in guiding the employee through the training period which goes anywhere from four hours to 110 hours.

Other training programs operated by Walt Disney University include classes to instruct teachers and "leads" (hourly employees who supervise

other workers); *Disney Way,* a six-day familiarization program for all salaried personnel; a *Disney Way Seminar,* a seven-day seminar for key managerial staff that is conducted at corporate headquarters in California; a *What
Can I Do For You?* series of half-day sessions for all supervisors and managers that deals with basic concepts of human relations; a *Management Awareness* program of management education in the area of minority relations
and sex discrimination for all salaried employees; and a number of other
specialized training programs.

IN-SERVICE TRAINING IN THERAPEUTIC SETTINGS

Programs of in-service training in the field of therapeutic recreation
are developed, in some cases, on a system-wide basis, in order to meet state-
wide requirements and guidelines. In others, they are planned and carried
out by individual institutions. Several examples of such staff development
programs follow.

Rainier School, State of Washington

This special school for the retarded provides a week-long course to
prepare all new personnel to work effectively with residents. Trainees come
from all school departments, and the purpose is to equip workers with a
basic understanding of the Rainier School's objectives, philosophy, and
working procedures. The approach is chiefly through lectures, discussion,
and observation of facilities and programs. The basic training course
follows the following format:

Day I.   Orientation to resident care; routine hall duties; dental care and
procedures; education department program; forms, records and
record-keeping procedures.

Day II.   First aid methods; special hall programs; supervision of residents;
handling of keys; planning the future for residents; medication and
treatment procedures.

Day III.   Resident life rules, regulations and procedures; laundry processing;
vocational experiences for residents; understanding the mentally
retarded; commissary tour; adult education program; understanding basic human needs.

Day IV.   Housekeeping service; farm tour; recreation services; resident
training methods and behavior modification; basic nursing techniques; safety.

Day V.   Normalization and dehumanization; restraints and isolation; seizures; pre-placement and placement (discharge) procedures; contacts with public and residents' families.

Regional In-Service Training Program: Province of Ontario

A growing trend in the staff development of rehabilitative personnel is to provide in-training courses on a statewide or regional basis. In the Province of Ontario, Canada, the Ministry of Health has sponsored regional training programs with the purposes of upgrading the work of personnel employed in provincial institutions, and of equipping staff members having less than a two-year College Diploma in Recreation with formal training and an equivalent standing in this field.

As an example, a series of workshops was held recently in the Western Ontario Region, with each such course covering a five-day period and one or more major topics. Topics dealt with such concerns as philosophies of recreation, play and leisure; the needs of special groups; leadership and group dynamics; the evaluation of recreation programs; community recreation programs; and Canadian social problems. They were given at the campus of the University of Waterloo, and the lecturers were drawn chiefly from the therapeutic recreation specialists in that institution's Department of Recreation.

State of Maryland: Department of Mental Hygiene

This department operates an extensive training program for Rehabilitation Therapist trainees, including recreation personnel. In the past, this program involved a year-long sequence that included a pre-class orientation, lectures and practicums, and finally a clinic assignment. Heavy emphasis was given to instruction in such clinical subjects as understanding of psychoneuroses and personality disorders, medical aspects of illness, and psychometric evaluation. Trainees were exposed to techniques of patient assessment, counseling and group dynamics methods, and specific skills in art, and occupational, industrial, and recreation therapy.

More recently, this state-wide training program has been reduced to a six-month period, which places less emphasis on theory and more on practical applications.

State of Minnesota: Department of Public Welfare

This final example of an institutional in-service training program illustrates changing approaches in the field of staff development in rehabilitation service. On various levels, such as *Human Development Services Specialists, Rehabilitation Therapists,* or *Rehabilitation Therapy Supervisors,* staff members must meet state-wide training requirements for certification in their current positions or for promotion.

For example, the *Human Development Services* career ladder requires a minimum of 120 hours of training in basic methods, which may be taken through relevant college courses or through approved in-service courses. Those promoted to supervisory positions are required by the State Commissioner of Personnel to take a minimum of 48 hours of training, which deal with supervisory principles and methods, through two three-day courses provided by the Training Division of the State Department of Personnel. There is an increasing attempt to make these requirements more meaningful to individual employees. Thomas Jung, the Rehabilitation Director of Hastings State Hospital, writes:

> The State of Minnesota is currently revamping its entire personnel system. Individual job descriptions are to be worked out by each employee and his supervisor. Standards will then be worked out and each employee will then be evaluated at least once annually against his job description and standards. The gap between what his job calls for and his performance will constitute his in-service training needs. The State has put together a management training course which all administrative types must take and a course on supervision which all supervisors must complete.
>
> This system leaves almost total freedom to the employee and supervisor in working out position descriptions . . .[4]

This attempt to individualize in-service training programs represents a desirable direction in current staff development approaches. However, it poses serious difficulties with respect to providing training in that a wide variety of workshops or courses would be needed to meet the full range of individual needs.

EVALUATION OF IN-SERVICE TRAINING PROGRAMS

As suggested earlier, it is essential to evaluate all in-service training programs. The professional literature in the field of personnel management suggests that the best way to do this objectively is to assess the on-the-job performance of those who have taken in-service courses or workshops, in order to determine whether their work has improved within these three specific areas: (a) improvement in general knowledge, awareness of professional principles and program needs; (b) direct improvement in job skills and daily performance; and (c) improvement in attitudes toward the job, and relationships with co-workers.

It is extremely difficult, however, to carry out such evaluations. Ideally, a training program should be designed to develop specific abilities in each staff member that might be consistently applied on the job. Training should give each individual the opportunity to develop his potential to the

---

[4] Letter from Thomas Jung, Hastings State Hospital, December 26, 1973.

fullest. However, the practicability of assessing such "ideal" programs is remote. Trainees often vary considerably in already acquired skills, experience, motivation, and trainability. Differences in job performance are affected by a great many other factors besides the efficacy of training. Finally, there is rarely the opportunity to assess directly the effects of training by comparing those who participated and those who did not ("experimental" vs. "control" groups), since most often all persons within an agency are required to participate in training sessions.

The method used in evaluating in-service training is therefore generally to have those who have gone through courses or workshops fill out anonymous rating forms or questionnaires. These usually ask questions about the value of the workshop, the contributions made by individual speakers or resource leaders, and the overall worth of the training experience. Two examples of such efforts follow.

Milwaukee, Wisconsin, Department of Municipal Recreation and Adult Education

This school-sponsored recreation department makes a consistent effort to evaluate all phases of its program, including leadership training. For example, Area Supervisors and District Directors are asked to evaluate In-Service Education Sessions with questionnaires covering the following points:

I. *Preparation for Playground Season*

    a. Was the April Preparatory Week of value?

    b. Was the teaching program as made out by the various committees satisfactory—or would you rather make out your own teaching plans?

    c. Pre-Season Staff Meeting—do you feel that this meeting is of value in clarifying procedures, policies, etc.?

II. *Opening Day Institute*

    a. Was the one-day session as valuable as the previous two-day sessions in: (1) lack of strain and pressure; (2) general preparedness of first-year leaders; (3) inclusion of pertinent information.

    b. General comments regarding this year's session: What did you like about it? What did you not like about it?

III. *Saturday In-Service Education Sessions*

    a. Were sessions planned to take care of play-leaders' needs in relation to timing?

    b. Did you see evidence of teaching on the playgrounds of activities taught on Saturdays? If no such evidence was found, why was this so, in your judgment?

c.   What features of the in-service education sessions do you feel were
     good? What features of the in-service sessions do you feel should be
     deleted or improved?

Evaluation of In-Service Training: Alexandria,
Virginia

The Department of Recreation and Cultural Activities of the city of
Alexandria, Virginia, carries out an extensive program of employee orientation and in-service training, including a pre-summer Recreation Workshop. All leaders attending this workshop in a recent year were required to
evaluate them anonymously. Examples of the kinds of comments made by
participants follow:

"I thought that the sensitivity groups and discussion groups were well
worth the time. I enjoyed most of the speakers, but I felt that we did not have
to have someone go through the manual for us. *We can read!*"

"In my opinion, the Summer Workshop was generally successful and
beneficial to the recreation staff. This is probably mainly due to the good organization, which is in contrast to last year's Workshop. The arts and crafts
and games demonstration were especially beneficial, although I think more
time could have been spent in these two areas. . . . Also, less time probably
could have been spent with the speakers on the first day."

"In general, the workshop was more beneficial than any I've attended in
the past (this is my fourth). Although the structure and "disciplinary" attitude
seemed harsh at first, I've come to realize that this was essential to the noticea-
ble improvement; I actually learned things."

"I am new to this program, and I felt that more time should have been
spent on explaining the manner in which our part of the overall program in-
terconnects with all of the other programs. A clearly organized timetable of
events within and without our program should have been formulated. Each
playground should have a schedule of events during the length of the program. I still am not sure who are my district supervisors, and who I go to for
help in securing resources and program planning . . ."

Similarly, both the supervisor responsible for in-service training and
the director of the department filled out detailed analyses of the strengths
and weaknesses of the Summer Workshop and the contributions made by
each of its session leaders. When these evaluations were combined with the
frank comments made by the participants, it was possible to develop useful
guidelines for future workshops.

EVALUATION OF RECREATION AND PARK
PERSONNEL

A final important concern of this chapter is the process of evaluating
departmental personnel. This is generally the responsibility of supervisors,

who are required to assess the ability and performance of leaders. However, supervisors themselves must be evaluated systematically by administrators, just as administrators must be evaluated in turn by city managers or mayors. Thus, on every level, personnel evaluation is a key aspect of recreation and park service.

Personnel evaluation may be defined as the process of appraising the quality of work performed by a member of the professional staff of an organization. Normally, it is reduced to a series of statements or conclusions which provide a general picture of the worker's strengths, weaknesses, and areas in which improvement may be needed.

In well-administered departments or organizations, it is customary to have supervisors fill out personnel rating forms for each employee on a regular basis, such as every six months or once a year. These forms are customarily inserted in the individual's personnel file. They provide information that may be used in making personnel recommendations or decisions regarding an individual's move from probationary to regular employee status, transfer, promotion, or other changes in status.

A second purpose of evaluation is to help supervisors do an informed and intelligent job of counseling staff members. Simply put, if evaluation demonstrates that a recreation leader has certain consistent weaknesses, these should become the focus of supervisor-leader conferences, in-service training, or other purposeful efforts to improve the leader's performance.

Many departments require that workers be shown their evaluation rating before the ratings are inserted in their personnel files, and that they be given the opportunity to discuss them and express their views on them. Although one might think that it would be the worker who is to be evaluated who dreads this process, research in the field of public personnel administration has shown that actually many supervisors find this task difficult and unpleasant. Often they resist the idea of sitting in judgment and, in effect, of "playing God." Specifically, they tend to dislike having to give *negative* judgments, while they enjoy being able to give *positive* ratings. Stone comments:

> ... while people dislike playing a *punitive* God, they tend to enjoy playing a *benevolent* one.[5]

In general, supervisors have consistently expressed a wish for help in this process, so that their judgments are objective, detailed, consistent, and based on sound evidence. Similarly, research has shown that workers who are evaluated are not only concerned about whether their ratings are favorable but also that those evaluating them be well-qualified, knowledgeable, and unbiased.

---

[5] Thomas H. Stone: "An Examination of Six Prevalent Assumptions Concerning Performance Appraisal." *Public Personnel Management,* November–December, 1973, pp. 408–414.

Methods of Personnel Evaluation

What are the most common methods of gathering and reporting information for the purpose of personnel evaluation? Several approaches are used.

DIRECT OBSERVATION.   The best way to determine the effectiveness of a leader is to observe him at work in a variety of situations. Such observations may be casual and informal, or may be regularly scheduled. The supervisor should keep notes of observations, especially of "critical incidents" which are particularly revealing about the worker's performance.

SUPERVISORY CONFERENCES.   Another important means of gathering relevant data for evaluation is through supervisory conferences with individual employees. These should be held regularly, for the specific purpose of discussing the employee's performance and progress on the job. The supervisor should tell the worker what he perceives as his strengths and weaknesses, not in a threatening or judgmental way but as part of an open and frank process of communication.

At the same time, the worker should help the supervisor understand his view of the operation and structure of the department, and how he might be helped to function more effectively. This two-way process should help the supervisor make more meaningful judgments about the worker's capability, and also should enable him to assist the worker in his day-by-day work.

REPORTS FROM PARTICIPANTS OR CO-WORKERS.   Another source of information to be used in the evaluation of personnel utilizes reports from individuals who participate in the program, or from co-workers in the department. Obviously, these may reflect bias, either because of special friendship with the worker involved or possibly because of antagonism or hostility. At the same time, they obviously have some merit, and if all participants and co-workers agree that a staff member has been doing an excellent job, their views must carry weight.

REVIEW OF ACCOMPLISHMENTS.   A final basis for personnel evaluation may be a careful review of work done by an individual over a period of time. What has his job performance been like, in terms of successful projects (tournaments, special events, attendance on the playground, relations with community people, or similar criteria)? Are his programs well attended? Have they achieved their objectives? Much of this information may be found in departmental records, with some of it in the form of reports submitted by the worker himself or by his direct superiors on the job.

In making use of all of these techniques for gathering information, it is customary to fill out a rating form which gives a total picture of the worker and his performance. Customarily, such forms present a number of important qualities or descriptive terms. The supervisor is asked to rate the individual on these traits, making use of a scale with a series of ratings, such as "excellent" through "poor," or "outstanding" through "unsatisfactory." These ratings may then be assigned point values, which may be used to develop a total performance rating for the individual, as well as a profile of his strengths and weaknesses.

Several examples of rating forms or approaches in municipal recreation and park departments follow.

Recreation and Parks Department
Montclair, New Jersey

Leadership Performance Evaluation

	Unsatisfactory	Below Standard	Satisfactory	Above Standard	Outstanding
Name:_____ Position:_____ Location:_____ Date: _____ 19__					
Factors Evaluated					
1. *Personality:* appearance, dress, poise and tact.					
2. *Cooperation:* cordial relations with staff and public.					
3. *Initiative:* works effectively without detailed instruction.					
4. *Organization:* plans and implements program according to needs and objectives.					
5. *Leadership:* rounded leadership ability.					
6. *Promotion:* submits timely, well-written publicity.					
7. *Dependability:* punctual, carries out assignments.					
8. *Emotional Stability:* can objectively accept suggestions and criticism.					
9. *Enthusiasm:* interested in work and reflects interest to others.					
10. *Reports:* submits reports correctly and promptly.					
11. *Skills:* knowledge and ability in varied activities.					
12. *Safety Hazards:* recognizes and eliminates them.					
13. *Facility Upkeep:* bulletin, play equipment, supplies and apparatus.					
Overall Evaluation:					

Evaluated By: _____   **Employee Signature:**_____

The leadership rating form used by the Montclair, New Jersey Recreation and Parks Department is a fairly simple one that makes use of a standardized set of ratings for each trait to be evaluated. In other departments, the evaluation form may provide illustrative comments which assist the evaluator in making his judgments.

Richmond, California, Recreation and Parks Department

This department has developed an Employee Performance Record form which has eight personality items to be measured: Knowledge of Work; Initiative and Application; Quality of Work; Quantity of Work; Relations with Other Workers; Dependability; Leadership; and Punctuality. Each of these must be rated according to its own set of five descriptions. For example, under *Initiative and Application,* the descriptions are:

> Exceptionally industrious. Highly resourceful and self reliant.   ____
> Energetic and conscientious. Goes ahead on own judgment.   ____
> Steady and willing worker. Requires little direction.   ____
> Inclined to take things easy. Requires occasional prompting.   ____
> Wastes time. Needs close supervision.   ____

In addition to rating each of the eight items based on such descriptive phrases, the supervisor must respond to a set of questions that include the following:

> Employee's strong points: _____
> Progress made since last evaluation
> or beginning of employment: _____
> Areas of needed improvement: _____
> Mutually agreed-on goals:
>   Short-term: _____
>   Long-range: _____
> Employee development plan: _____
> Supervisory recommendation: _____

Long Beach, California, Recreation Department

This department's Employee Appraisal System carries the approach of the Richmond, California rating method somewhat further. Each worker is asked to determine, in conference with his immediate supervisor, several "challenging, specific objectives" to be achieved during the next rating period. Such objectives should involve both regularly assigned tasks and new projects or measures for self-improvement. Estimated dates of completion should be given and, when possible, measures of successful performance included. Examples of possible objectives are given in the appraisal report:

> "Develop effective demonstration materials to aid teaching of new crafts skills."
> "Organize a soccer team in the fall."
> "Contact fifty families in the area within the next six months."
> "Eliminate a safety hazard."

A second interesting element in the Long Beach appraisal system is that the worker is asked to evaluate his supervisor anonymously, and to forward the confidential statement to him for his personal use. Such questions are asked as:

"In your opinion, what kind of job is this supervisor doing? Consider both his or her good points and weaknesses or areas needing improvement."
"Were you in his or her position, what would you do to improve and to bring about improvement in your employees?"
"How do you think your Area, District, or the Recreation Department as a whole could become more effective?"

This evaluation approach shows clearly how evaluation may be used not only to put a rating of the employee's work in his personnel folder but also to provide positive and helpful input that will assist him in growing as a professional.

Edmonton, Alberta, Canada, Parks and Recreation Department

In this department's employee evaluation system, both the leader and the supervisor play an active role.

LEADER'S RESPONSIBILITIES. The Edmonton recreation leader is required to fill out an extensive form which lists his job responsibilities under a number of major headings, and to assign each of them percentage figures, showing the amount of time given to each responsibility during the week. He must describe his work in detail, including: (a) statements about those who supervise him and those he works with in the department; (b) responsibility for financial matters or other administrative functions; (c) role in policy-making or explaining policies; (d) personal schedule, and role in supervising other employees; and (e) difficult or abnormal working conditions and similar information. This form provides a detailed record of the employee's job functions, as he perceives them.

SUPERVISOR'S RESPONSIBILITIES. The Edmonton recreation supervisor must list six of the employee's major responsibilities and evaluate how well he is performing them. Then he must write statements describing the employee's performance, using such topics as *Knowledge, Planning, Organizing Work, Personnel Management, Control, Communications,* and *Problem-Solving.* He then indicates his plans to promote improvement in these areas, listing the methods he intends to use (giving a priority to each) and providing a tentative timetable for action. Methods such as the following are suggested:

1. Directed self-development (reading, self-study, and so on).
2. Formal training program (department courses).
3. Outside educational programs (seminars, courses).
4. Counseling and coaching.
5. On-the-job training.

The entire plan must be discussed with the employee, and both he and the supervisor must sign it. Another section of the report requires appraisal of the employee's personal qualities, such as appearance, energy, adaptability, initiative, strengths, and areas requiring improvement. A final, confidential section describes the "promotional potential" of the employee, and gives the supervisor's judgment as to the best ways in which he can be used in the department.

EVALUATION IN OTHER AGENCIES

Evaluation methods in other types of recreation agencies tend to follow the systems just described, although the qualities or performance criteria reflect the specific objectives of each agency. For example, in therapeutic agencies such as psychiatric hospitals or community agencies serving the mentally retarded or physically disabled, evaluation forms might exam-

---

YMCA OF NASSAU-SUFFOLK

INDIVIDUAL PERFORMANCE—PROMOTABILITY RATING

BRANCH:_____PERSON BEING RATED:_____DATE:_____

EMPLOYEE'S AGE:_____YMCA TENURE:_____SEX:_____

CURRENT POSITION TENURE:_____PRESENT POSITION:____

    (DO NOT CHECK ITEMS UNLESS YOU ARE CERTAIN)

	Does Not Apply	Not Accept.	Below Avg.	Avg.	Above Avg.	Out-Standing
PERFORMANCE						
RESPONSE TO COMMUNITY NEEDS						
PEER WORK GROUP COOPERATION						
WORKING RELATIONSHIP TO SUPERIORS						
WORKING RELATIONSHIP TO SUBORDINATES						
USE OF RESOURCES						
WORKING WITH BOARDS AND COMMITTEES						
FOLLOW THROUGH						
SUPERVISORY SKILLS						

ine such traits as the employee's understanding of disability, ability to promote constructive participation, rapport with patients, or his effectiveness as part of the treatment team.

A final example of evaluation forms is drawn from a major youth-serving voluntary organization, the Young Men's Christian Association. In this example, it is possible to see how the items being rated are based on the overall goals of the organization.

Nassau-Suffolk County, New York, Young Men's Christian Association

A recent statement of operational goals of this large, suburban Y.M.C.A. included the following priorities:

1. Developing and implementing sound and progressive fiscal policies and practices.

YMCA OF NASSAU-SUFFOLK (continued)

	Does Not Apply	Not Accept.	Below Avg.	Avg.	Above Avg.	Out-Standing
EMOTIONAL STA-BILITY						
PROGRAM SKILLS						
RACIAL SENSITIV-ITY						
FUND RAISING ABILITY						
PLANNING ABILITY						
BUILDING AC-COUNTABILITY						
STATISTICAL AC-COUNTABILITY						
INITIATIVE						
FINANCIAL AC-COUNTABILITY						
COOPERATION WITH COMMU-NITY AGENCIES						
INVOLVEMENT OUTSIDE REGU-LAR POSITION						
INNOVATION						

2. Giving active leadership and support to closer collaboration with Y.M.C.A.'s and other public and private agencies on a local and regional basis for the purposes of planning, programming and funding.

3. Broadening present membership principles and implementing a unit program fee structure.

4. Recruiting, training and rewarding staff who are able to produce positive results.

These and other "Y" goals are directly reflected in the preceding evaluation form, which deals specifically with characteristics regarded as essential for success in this agency. At the end of the form, if the candidate is rated *Below Average* or *Not Acceptable,* the evaluator must indicate what action is being taken, or what training is recommended for the employee. He must also give a statement concerning the promotional potential of the individual.

SUMMARY OF STAFF DEVELOPMENT PROCESSES

This chapter has provided a detailed analysis of three of the key processes of recreation and parks staff development: orientation, in-service training, and evaluation. It has provided general guidelines as well as examples of manuals, courses, and forms used in each of these processes. Such staff development functions are extremely important to developing the maximum performance and effectiveness of all employees on leadership and supervisory levels.

Thus far, this text has dealt with the background of recreation leadership and supervision. It now examines the actual process of leadership. The following chapters present detailed guidelines for the effective presentation of recreation program activities.

Suggested Examination Questions or Topics for Student Reports

1. Make a strong case supporting the need for carefully organized and well-supported orientation and in-service training programs in recreation and parks.

2. Several different types of in-service training programs are described in the text. Describe several specific kinds of problem situations or needs for staff development as they might occur in a given agency, and show how a different kind of in-service training program might be planned to meet each need.

3. Review the guidelines for developing in-service training programs, as presented in this chapter. Discuss the merits of these guidelines, and add others that you believe are important.

4. Develop a philosophy of personnel evaluation that you believe is constructive and in harmony with modern principles of personnel management. Then show, specifically, how this philosophy would be carried out in the evaluation process in a given department.

Suggested Action Assignments for Students

1. Select a large agency (municipal, therapeutic, and so on), and examine its existing program of staff development. Based on principles suggested in this chapter, present recommendations for improving this program.
2. Develop a three-part evaluation form for a given agency, including these elements: (a) evaluation of leader by supervisor; (b) evaluation of supervisor by leader; and (c) self-evaluation by leader.

three

recreation
leadership
methods

activity leadership methods

The key to the success of every recreation leader is the ability to lead groups productively in varied forms of play activities. Obviously, the leader's role includes many other tasks and responsibilities. However, his or her basic concern is with selecting appropriate activities and presenting them to groups of participants so effectively that they will become deeply involved in satisfying and rewarding play.

APPROPRIATE SELECTION OF ACTIVITY

Three important factors should be considered in selecting recreation activities for inclusion in a public or voluntary program. These are: (a) whether the activity has appeal – that is, whether people *want* to take part in it and *enjoy* it; (b) whether it is socially acceptable and promotes positive or constructive values; and (c) whether the activity is administratively appropriate, in terms of the kinds of leadership, materials, equipment, or facilities it might require for participation.

Beyond these general factors, the choice of appropriate recreation activities for any group would depend on the following additional elements.

Factors Affecting the Choice of Activities

1. The *age* of the group, since one's tastes and interests with respect to leisure activity are affected by one's chronological age.

2. The *physical health* and general *fitness* level of the participants, which influence the choice of activity, or require that it be modified.

3. The *psychological* or *mental status* of the participants. Obviously, if one or all of the members of a group were emotionally disturbed or mentally retarded, it would affect their ability to participate satisfactorily in certain activities.

4. The *size* of the group. A very large group cannot receive the same degree of personal attention and instruction for each member that a much smaller group might.

177

5. The *amount of time* to be given to the activity. Certain activities require two or three hours or more to be carried out successfully, while others can be enjoyed in just a few moments.

6. The *facility* available to the group, and its potential for different types of program activities.

7. The *previous recreational experience* of the group, which provides a base for new learning and affects the group's attitude toward different forms of recreational activities.

In selecting activities for a group, the leader should be aware of all of these factors, and should choose experiences that will meet the needs and interests of group members as fully as possible. Beyond this, he should make sure that the activity is in harmony with the goals of the sponsoring organization as well as with his own philosophy of leadership.

The leader should be fully aware of the kinds of social experiences involved in the activity. What kinds of group relationships does it promote? Is it a game in which players compete vigorously against each other? Is it an arts and crafts activity in which participants are essentially on their own? Is it a dramatic presentation in which several members work together creatively to develop an improvised theatrical work? Depending on the needs of group members, each of these outcomes might be highly desirable.

Finally, the leader should encourage group members themselves to select and plan activities and, when possible, take on much of the direct responsibility for organizing and carrying them out.

EFFECTIVE LEADERSHIP PERSONALITY

There is obviously no single effective leadership personality. It is not possible to say that a leader must be highly gregarious or extroverted to be effective with groups, or that he or she should be extremely dynamic or commanding, or tall or short, loud- or soft-voiced, or possess other possible attributes.

However, it is obvious that the leader's personality and style will have a considerable effect on his ability to involve participants successfully in recreational activities. He should be enthusiastic and lively in his presentation, so that his warmth and interest in the activity are communicated to group members. He should be well organized, and able to help them enter into participation with a minimum of delay or confusion. He should be able to present the activity with the utmost clarity and efficiency. He should know it thoroughly, and have all the materials or equipment needed for participation ready. He should have control of the group, in the sense that its members look to him for help and direction.

Beyond this, he should be able to view the activity, not just as a single event or experience taking place at a given time, but as part of a continuing series of exposures and involvements in leisure pursuits for participants. In this sense, he must regard it as an opportunity for pleasure, for growth, for personal satisfaction, for healthy social involvement, and creative expression—and his leadership style must reflect these values.

Finally, he must be able to *teach*. It is true that much recreation leadership does not involve teaching; supervising children on a playground or taking them on a trip are not really teaching acts. However, under many circumstances, the leader is essentially a teacher. He introduces activities such as games, dances, music, arts and crafts, or sports. And, just as a teacher in a school or college does, he must teach participants the *skills* involved in the activity, if they are to carry it on successfully and enjoy it to its fullest.

Obviously, then, leaders should know how to teach activities, because teaching is an important part of their work. Supervisors should also be familiar with this process, because it is their responsibility to help leaders become *better* teachers. Thus, on both levels, effective teaching is a key concern of recreation professionals.

While many persons are instinctively good teachers, others have great difficulty in breaking down activities into their component parts, and in communicating them to participants. And, even those who are strong *natural* teachers can improve, if they become more fully aware of the principles of skilled teaching. It is therefore desirable for every recreation leader to be familiar with the basic concepts that have been developed by authorities in educational psychology through the years.

BASIC CONCEPTS OF TEACHING AND LEARNING

There has been a tremendous amount of research into the psychology of learning during the past several decades, resulting in certain widely accepted concepts which should be of great value to any individual concerned with the teaching process.

Awareness of Individual Differences

It is essential to recognize that each learner is an individual and must learn in his own way and at his own rate. He may benefit from different kinds of teaching methods or stimuli, and his retention of what has been learned also differs from others. The leader must be aware of the differences among individuals, and must avoid either a standardized approach toward teaching all participants in the same way or standardized expectations of how much and what they will learn.

Realistically, this does not mean that the typical recreation leader is able to devote tremendous amounts of time to each individual and to give him a full measure of uniquely designed instruction. It does mean that he is aware of each person as an individual, and of the progress he is making—even in teaching a large group of participants. He strives to use a variety of teaching techniques and gives individual encouragement and advice whenever possible.

Learning by Doing

In general, people learn best by *doing*. It is not enough to be told about an activity. It is usually necessary to take part in it, and to learn concrete skills by participation. It is not necessarily true that *all* learning requires overt responses from the learner. It is possible for some learning to occur while one is merely sitting, observing, or listening. However, the best learning occurs through involvement.

This does not always mean that a learner must be physically active. The nature of the doing depends on the activity. The only way to learn a sport, a dance skill, or a craft activity is to take part in it directly. However, listening and reading are effective ways of learning essentially verbal materials, and learning about music may be based on listening to a lecture and then to music—both physically passive acts. In any case, the leader must be aware of the need to get people involved in *doing* as rapidly and as meaningfully as possible, if they are to learn skills successfully.

Analyzing the Learning Task

It is necessary to analyze and understand the nature of the learning task in presenting any activity to participants. Exactly what are the key elements that they must learn? What actions or skills are not relevant or important? If the teacher is able to identify these components, and to make them crystal clear to participants, the learning process becomes immensely easier. On the other hand, if he is wasting energy and time in drilling participants on skills which are not crucial, or which keep them from learning the important techniques, the entire process of teaching and learning is frustrated.

For example, in presenting an active group game, the key task is to clarify the basic purpose of the game (i.e., whether it is a "tag" game, in which the purpose is to catch other players, or a "guessing" game, in which the purpose is to identify a title or object), and then the sequence of play. If a leader gives major emphasis at the outset to teaching minor rules or playing strategies of a game, and not to teaching its fundamental purpose and structure, he has not analyzed the learning task properly.

Selecting Appropriate Teaching Devices

When he has identified the skills or components of the task to be represented, the teacher must then identify the best ways in which to get them across to learners. In general, most recreation activities can best be taught through demonstration — by having the leader or a selected group of participants *show* the dance, the sports skills, or the arts and crafts technique. However, a variety of other inputs can and should be used. Verbal description or commentary, cues that prompt accurate response, or audiovisual aids such as diagrams, slides, loop-films or regular films, may all be useful in teaching skills. It is important to experiment and determine *which* teaching devices are most effective, since it is possible to "overload the channel" by providing too many kinds of teaching inputs.

In some cases, a problem-solving approach may be used, in which learners themselves discover the appropriate solution or skill that is at the heart of the activity. This is particularly true in movement education, creative dance, and arts and crafts activity, in which learners are often encouraged to learn the skill for themselves. Thus, the leader asks, "How many ways can you use to cross the floor?" rather than, "Follow me and do as I do."

"Whole" Versus "Part" Instruction

For years there has been a controversy about the best approach to organizing skills for instruction — whether to present the entire activity as a "whole," so that individuals may learn it all at once, or to present it by "parts," in step-by-step units of instruction.

Those supporting the "part" method were influenced by the early behaviorist psychologists, who held that it is best not to teach for generalized responses but for specific behaviors in clearly defined situations. It was believed that all tasks must be divided into parts that must be learned and practiced separately. Then, as in a dance involving several parts, they are learned as a total sequence and performed as a whole. Or in the case of an activity like swimming, which involves a number of separate skills (stroking, kicking, breathing), each skill must be identified and learned separately before the entire activity is performed simultaneously.

In contrast, those proposing the "whole" method argue that the most effective learning takes place when the task is perceived and approached in its entirety. Clearly, both approaches have merit, and both should be employed. An activity with several distinctly separate skills and sequences of action, such as a complicated craft activity, simply cannot be learned as a "whole" but must be taken by stages. On the other hand, many sports skills or other play activities can certainly be learned best in a single, continuous learning experience.

Motivation and Readiness for Learning

It is widely accepted today that unless individuals are motivated and ready to learn, the teaching process cannot be fully successful. Motivation

Marvin Richmond A

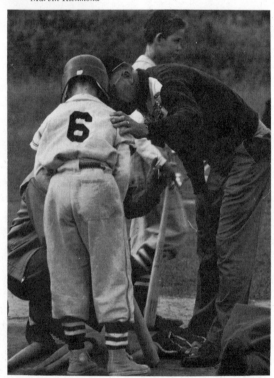

B

Marvin Richmond

Leadership Roles. Recreation leaders play an important role in helping participants develop healthy personal and social values. Here, a Worcester, Massachusetts, Little League player strikes out (*A*) and is consoled by his coach (*B*). In Mt. Vernon, New York, young men in a methadone maintenance program that includes athletics meet with their coach (*C*), while other Mt. Vernon youth take part in a special summer employment program (*D*).

C

Paul Caramuto

D

Paul Caramuto

refers to a general level of arousal and interest—a state of willingness or eagerness for activity. It was found that significant learning would not take place unless there was a basic physiological or psychological need in the learner that made him ready to learn. Further, he must be ready in the sense of being old enough, strong enough, or having had the earlier learning experiences that serve as preparation for new challenges.

The preparedness or "set" of the learner is important. He must be attentive and ready to learn. The leader who feels that he is not in charge, or that participants are not paying attention to him, should try to improve this situation before going ahead to teach an activity. Similarly, one does not learn simply by complying with instructions and going through the motions of activity. There must be a level of interest and attention in which learners are actively involved and seeking to develop insights before effective learning takes place.

Reinforcement of Learning

This important concept holds that when individuals perform correctly, their action should be immediately reinforced, so that it will be repeated correctly and ultimately fixed as a behavioral response to a stimulus. This theory was developed through the "stimulus-and-response" work of Pavlov, who developed reflex behaviors of involuntary action in response to certain stimuli in laboratory animals. An American educational psychologist, Thorndike, extended the "pleasure-pain" principle (we do what brings pleasure and avoid what brings pain) to a so-called *law of effect*. This held that when a connection between stimulus and response is made, and the subject discovers that carrying out a certain action will bring a reward, constructive learning takes place.

The use of punishment to modify behavior, or discourage incorrect or inappropriate responses, is an area of considerable disagreement. Some psychologists hold that it is not a desirable means of behavior modification, in that it only tends to suppress undesired responses temporarily, and may bring about undesirable complications. The essential point is that positive reinforcement is believed to be more effective than punishment, resulting in faster and more efficient learning. Skinner points out that in the early phases of training, it is important to reinforce every desired response. Once learning is well under way, reinforcement should become more and more intermittent, and may be discontinued as long as the desired learning behavior is maintained.

Transfer of Learning

Once a basic skill or understanding has been achieved, an individual finds it easier to learn related tasks. "Transfer" can be defined as the effect practice of one task has upon the learning of another task. In essence, a skill that has been learned in one activity can be readily transferred to another, provided that the tasks have strongly comparable elements and that the learner both has sufficient recall of the original skill and is able to recognize its place in the new task.

Practice of Skills

This is one of the most widely researched areas of educational psychology today, and is particularly applicable to the learning of physical skills in areas such as sports or dance. The "law of exercise" holds that connections between stimuli and desired responses are strengthened with use. However, practice must be distinguished from mere repetition, and should involve both rewards and new learnings. The amount of practice needed for a given activity will depend on its complexity as well as on the capabilities and past experience of the learner.

Practice may be "massed" (provided in longer and fewer sessions), or "distributed" (provided in a greater number of briefer sessions). Generally, massed practice may be more effective when the learner is highly motivated, while distributed practice is more likely to be helpful when learners are less highly motivated. Practice that is too extended may pass the point of effective learning when it keeps repeating what has already been learned, or when participants become fatigued, irritable, or inattentive.

Other Principles of Learning

A number of other concepts of effective teaching and learning may be briefly summarized:

Both "drill" and "problem-solving" approaches to learning may be used. In general, most learning psychologists today encourage the latter approach, in which the learner is encouraged to see the meaning of facts, the effect of different ways of accomplishing a task, and the insights that underly successful performance.

There is no single, optimum schedule for the learning of all skills. Instead, each skill or task must be analyzed and periods of instruction and practice scheduled according to the capacity, motivation, and stage of learning of participants.

The setting of goals is an important factor in successful learning. They should be high enough to challenge learners and provide them with an incentive for working hard. On the other hand, they should not be so high that they are unrealisitc or excessively difficult to accomplish. The successful achievement of a given task brings satisfaction and the willingness to attempt new tasks. Failure and frustration may result in the learner's unwillingness to continue the process or move on to other activities.

Ability grouping is a useful tool for learning activities in which it is necessary to direct the teaching method at the precise level of the group's ability, and where participants learn from each other as they pursue a common learning experience. However, placing participants in clearly defined and identifiable groups of "high ability" and "low ability" may have undesirable effects on their social attitudes and self-concepts, and should be used with caution by leaders.

Finally, effective leaders make use of the "teachable moment." Rather than try to impose their view of when and how people should learn, they focus on their readiness and state of motivation. They also make use of what happens in a teaching situation to implant key concepts or insights creatively, and at the point when they will have the greatest impact on learners.

LEADERSHIP METHODS IN SPECIFIC ACTIVITIES

Obviously, there is more to effective teaching than being aware of learning theories. Each type of activity, and each learning situation, imposes its own set of appropriate leadership methods. This section outlines a number of guidelines useful for recreation leaders in several major areas of program activity, including games, arts and crafts, sports, music, dance, dramatics, and nature activities.

The approaches presented here are drawn from the direct professional experience of the authors, and from manuals published by a number of municipal recreation and park agencies throughout the United States and Canada. The activities chosen are primarily found in playground and community center programs. Specific *examples* of activities are not presented, since this is not a program text. However, the Appendix includes a useful listing of books which may be used as resources by students and leaders seeking to practice the guidelines presented here, or to enrich their programs.

GAMES LEADERSHIP ON THE PLAYGROUND

There are many different types of games which may be used in community recreation. These include active group games, social games and mixers, dramatic games, mental games and puzzles, and a host of others. This section will concentrate on one of the most common types of game situations—the presentation of games of low organization, such as tag, relay, and simple ball games, in summer playground programs.

Goals of Playground Games

It is important to know *why* you are presenting any activity. The goals and purposes of playground games are as follows:

1. Games provide a useful means of organizing small group or team activities. Children enjoy playing together in such groups.

2. Games provide an opportunity for competition, and for the testing of agility, strength, skill and intelligence, under controlled circumstances.

3. Supervised games may be used to help develop such character traits as co-operation, self-control, willingness to obey rules, obedience to officials, and habits of fair play and sportsmanship.

4. Games provide an enjoyable form of physical exercise, and help to teach skills which will later be useful in playing sports.

5. Games represent an economical use of space and equipment, and a means of working with a large group of participants at one time.

Selection of Appropriate Games

The success of playground games will depend on whether you have chosen games that are suitable to the participants. Factors to be considered include:

1. Games should be selected primarily on the basis of age group rather than sex. It should be possible to play a wide variety of low-organized games with boys and girls together. Generally, games for children up to the age of eight years should

   a. be fairly vigorous, involving fundamental skills of running, jumping, hopping, starting, stopping, throwing, and catching

   b. be in simple formations, and have fairly simple rules

   c. involve individual achievement rather than place a heavy stress on complicated team play

2. Games for children over the age of eight may be more complicated, of longer duration, and involve team play to a greater degree.

3. Games should be selected on the basis of adequate space and numbers of participants, i.e., if you have a large area and a considerable number of players, you would attempt to involve them all in mass games. If space and players are not available, the reverse would be true.

4. Game selection should consider the weather; choose active games for a cold day, and quiet games for a hot day.

5. Have variety in the choice of games. Provide both some new games, for learning and challenge, and also some old favorites. Mix active and quiet games, and those with and without equipment.

Preparation for Leading Games

To be a capable games leader, make sure you are ready, *before* the game session, in the following ways:

1. Select a number of games appropriate to the age, ability, and interest of the group. Have more games ready than you will need. List them on a card, so you will have them readily available.

2. Review the game in your own mind. Make sure you are thoroughly famil-
    iar with its rules and playing strategy. If necessary, practice it in advance
    with a group of players.

3. Make sure that any needed equipment is available, and that boundary
    lines are marked, if necessary.

4. Arouse the interest of the boys and girls in the games session by announc-
    ing it in advance, "talking it up," or having posters advertising play-
    ground games at a regular time.   *

Organizing Teams or Groups

Most playground games involve breaking the overall group up into
smaller groups or teams. This is done in the following ways:

1. Generally, it is best to have the leader pick the teams, alternately choosing
    players for teams A and B, and keeping their size and ability in mind.

2. A second approach is to have players form a line based on size (from the
    tallest to the shortest) or a large circle, and to count them off into appro-
    priate groups or teams, based on this.

3. Although children tend to want to form their own teams, this is usually
    not a good idea because: (a) the better players are chosen first and the
    weaker ones last, giving them a feeling of rejection; (b) bigger children
    tend to want to be on the same team, making the sides uneven; and (c)
    there is a risk that you will wind up with one-sex groups, i.e., boys playing
    against girls, which creates unnecessary antagonism.

4. Before starting the game, make sure that all teams have an equal number.
    If players of two or more teams "mingle" during the game, make sure
    that they are marked in some way, so they can be readily identified.

Teaching the Game

There are many ways of teaching games. Here are several useful
guidelines.

1. After you have gotten the group into the proper teams or formation,
    make sure you have their attention. If you have a whistle, blow it as a sig-
    nal for quiet. Do not over-use it. Make sure that you have everyone's at-
    tention; do not talk over crowd noise.

2. When presenting the game, stand where the maximum number of
    players can see you and hear you, and where you will be facing them,
    rather than with your back to them.

3. Create an air of expectancy by your own enthusiasm. Quickly announce
    the game with a brief introduction, and then begin to teach it.

4. Make your explanations clear, brief, and correct. If necessary, use one
    or more players to demonstrate the activity. If it is at all complicated,
    repeat this.

5. Ask for questions if any of the players seem confused. Then start the game without further delay.

6. Minor errors or faults in play may be corrected by blowing the whistle, stopping the game briefly, showing the correct action, and continuing play.

7. If an activity is going badly, with much confusion, stop it. Demonstrate it again, explain the rules, ask for questions and answer them — and then begin it again.

8. Make sure that rules are obeyed. If necessary, stop the game to enforce them, and then continue.

9. Keep interest high, and encourage the players enthusiastically.

10. If the game involves keeping score, let the players know the team scores from time to time.

11. End the game while interest is still relatively high rather than let it drag on and become boring.

Controlling Behavior of Participants

One of the great advantages of games is that they provide an opportunity for children to play vigorously and to express their energy in constructive ways. However, they may tend to become overexcited and wild, and the leader will need to control this.

1. Allow some noise and shouting; they are natural expression of enjoyment and show that the game is successful. However, do not permit uncontrolled "bedlam." When you blow a whistle to signify the end of play or the selection of new players, make sure players understand that they must all be quiet.

2. Keep safety factors in mind. Make sure that equipment is used correctly, and that physical contact is kept under control.

3. A general condition of order must be maintained, and "horse-play" should be stopped at its first appearance.

4. Insist on fair play, and enforce the rules strictly.

5. Children sometimes misbehave because they are losing and are dispirited. Give encouragement to losing teams, and rotate team memberships between different games.

General Leadership Style

The leader's overall style or manner with the group can help to determine his success in leading games.

1. Always try to be at ease, and optimistic and positive in manner. Do not get over-excited or "flustered," no matter how excited children may become.

2. Throughout your leading, emphasize the positive, not the negative. Use "do's" rather than "don'ts."

3. Project your voice at all times. Speak clearly and distinctly in a pleasing but firm voice. Give one command at a time.

4. Let your interest and enthusiasm be contagious. As a leader, have fun yourself. Stress the fun and play element of games, and do not be afraid to appreciate humorous situations.

5. Depending on the game situation, you may play in the game with the children. This may be done particularly to even up the sides but not if it means displacing one child player.

6. Emphasize team spirit and loyalty. Do not over-praise gifted individual players, or permit them to dominate play.

7. Try to have every child participate successfully. Help shy or hesitant children join in. If children are physically disabled, have them play if possible; if not, let them participate in some way — as scorer, time-keeper, judge, and so on.

8. Throughout the game session, keep active. Be a coach to the players as well as a referee.

Evaluating the Game Session

When the game session is over, the conscientious leader should review it carefully, asking the following questions:

1. Did the children enjoy the games and take part whole-heartedly? Were some of them left out, and if so, why?

2. Were the games successful? Which ones did not work out? Why not? Should these games be played again?

3. In selecting the games, was there a good variety of activities that continued to challenge and interest the players?

4. Did you maintain effective discipline, or was there a behavior problem? How could you handle this more effectively? Did the children show respect for your leadership?

5. How could your teaching of the individual games have been improved? Were children given a voice in the selection of games?

6. Did you keep a record of the games session for use in planning future activities?

MUSIC LEADERSHIP: COMMUNITY SINGING

Recreational music may include instrumental music instruction, bands and orchestras, barber shop quartets and choral groups, rhythm bands, and many other activities. However, community singing is probably the most useful and widely found music activity in general recreation programs.

Values of Community Singing

Music is one of the most appealing forms of recreational activity for participants for every age and type. Community singing, in particular, has the following values:

1. It can be enjoyed by all ages, and by those with limited physical capability, unlike more strenuous forms of recreation.

2. It brings the unique gift of fellowship; for many centuries, people have sung together in order to affirm their comradeship, and singing still has this unusual power.

3. Community singing may be enjoyed in almost any setting and does not require any special facilities, equipment, or high level of leadership ability.

4. Singing offers a constructive outlet for excess energy, and can be a useful way of quieting a group after activity.

5. Singing offers the opportunity for creative expression, and can give participants a sense of personal accomplishment and satisfaction.

6. Singing may be approached as an informal, impromptu experience, or, with sufficient practice and training, may be used for performances and entertainment of others.

Preparation for Song Leadership

It is not necessary for the leader to be a highly skilled musician, or to have an outstanding voice. However, he should be able to carry a tune and sing with a fairly pleasing quality. The chief qualities of the successful song leader are enthusiasm, the ability to instill a sense of good fellowship and enjoyment of music, and to teach and direct a variety of appealing songs.

1. In selecting songs, the leader should pick several that are familiar to the group as well as others that will be new to them and should be taught.

2. He should practice these songs and know them thoroughly, so he does not have to refer to a book or songsheet while leading.

3. In a small group no musical accompaniment is usually necessary. In a larger group, it helps if the leader or a friend can play an instrument such as a guitar or accordion. In a very large group, the most useful accompaniment is provided by a skilled pianist.

4. In a songfest with a new group, or one unaccustomed to community singing, the leader might wish to prepare songsheets for them, or to use slides with the verses on them to help people learn the words quickly.

Steps of Leading a Song

There is no one, cut-and-dried method of leading a song. However, most successful song leaders follow this sequence:

1. Get the group's attention, and announce the song clearly. Give it a brief introduction to arouse interest.

2. Sing the first verse through, in order to give the participants a sense of what the song is like.

3. If the words are difficult, you might teach them first without the melody, one line at a time, having the participants repeat them after you. Otherwise, teach both words and music together, a line or two at a time. When an entire verse has been learned in this way, have the group learn the chorus, or the next verse.

4. Sing the entire song. If the participants are doing it correctly and enjoying it, continue it until the end. If not, stop them and correct the singing.

5. Go on to new song. Continue singing as long as interest is high.

Guides for Improving Singing

The steps of actually leading a song are rather simple. It is somewhat more difficult, however, to get people to sing *well,* and to enjoy it to the fullest.

1. It is necessary to pitch the song correctly for them. If you have an accompanist, he may know the proper pitch. If not, select a key that is in a comfortable range for you and see if the group members find it suits their voices. Remember, children usually prefer a higher pitch.

2. In beginning a song, get the group "set," or ready, and then start with an introduction from the accompanist, or a sharp, clear movement which will bring all singers in together. "Attack" and "release" each section of the song clearly.

3. Begin singing with a familiar and well-liked song. Then move on to an appealing variety—including folk songs, patriotic songs, action and novelty songs, songs with repeated choruses, songs from other lands, old show tunes, and others which will have broad appeal.

4. If the group is singing well, break them up into sections for rounds and part songs. Encourage harmony, changes in volume (moving from loud to soft), and urge people to *listen* to each other, which always improves singing.

5. Recognize all sections of the audience, and reach out to them with your leadership rather than to just a few singers in front of the group. Encourage all to take part, but do not force anyone.

6. Sing along with the group, but do not dominate them, particularly if you have a very strong voice or are using a microphone.

7. Praise and encourage the group for singing well. If you correct them, do it pleasantly and constructively.

8. Ask for requests, but select those that you feel will be most suitable for the group. Do *not* overteach; a community singing session is not a formal instruction period, and it should be lively and spontaneous.

Use of Hand Gestures

Most community song leaders use hand gestures to conduct singing, although it is not absolutely necessary.

1. With very small groups, leading with hands may be unnecessary, and the leader may accomplish the same purpose with his own singing and facial expressions.

2. With large groups, or when more polished singing is desired, the leader may use the traditional gestures to indicate the rhythm and tempo.

3. In "conducting," make large gestures, particularly if you are leading a large group. Make generous strokes away from your body, using your arms in one graceful extension from the shoulder to the fingers; the total up-and-down movement should not be more than 12 inches.

4. Raise your hands and arms high enough for all to see, and cup your hands slightly, as if shaking hands.

5. In using hand gestures, try to eliminate mannerisms, and move in a natural, relaxed way. Use vigorous movements for lively songs, and more flowing or graceful movements for quieter selections.

6. Do not feel that you must use the gestures throughout a song, but do use them to emphasize the tempo or beat, to lead the group in terms of "feeling," volume, richness of sound, or other qualities. Also, be sure to use them in beginning and ending a song.

Leadership Style in Community Singing

In more than almost any other activity, the song leader and the participants share a sense of friendship and pleasant cooperation as they sing together. This can best be achieved in the following ways.

1. The experience must be a relaxed, pleasant one in which the leader and the participants have a sense of "sharing" an enjoyable experience with each other.

2. The leader should feel free to express his sense of humor (although never ridiculing any of the participants) and to encourage others to join in with comments (although not to the point of making the song session a "gabfest").

3. The singing should be kept well paced, with no dead spots. As indicated, it should include songs of many different types and qualities. The sheer beauty of singing should be emphasized whenever possible, along with novelty, humor, or other song qualities.

4. In ending the song session, wind up with a familiar song that everyone enjoys, and that will not require teaching. In some settings, such as club meetings, camps, or similar situations, the last song is approached as a ceremony, with all participants standing in a circle holding hands.

CREATIVE DRAMATICS FOR CHILDREN

Most community recreation programs have a wide range of drama activities in which individuals may take part—gradually building skill and confidence in dramatic self-expression. These include charades, pantomimes, skits, story plays, puppetry, story telling, pageants, informal dramatics, and, finally, actual theater programs for all ages. The urge to act is universal, and finds its greatest release among younger children. For this age group, creative dramatics are useful both as a form of enjoyable activity in playgrounds and community centers, and as a lead-up to more advanced forms of theatrical experience.

Values of Creative Dramatics

Creative dramatics may be defined simply as an informal approach to children's theater that makes use of creative, spontaneous, or improvised forms of expressive activity rather than of structured or formal plays. It has the following specific goals and purposes:

1. Dramatic activity encourages the development of poise and confidence, the improvement of speech and diction, and a more expressive, graceful, and well-coordinated body.

2. Creative dramatics promote imagination and creative expression as well as a deeper appreciation of theater as an art form.

3. Emotional release is an important outcome of dramatic experience; children are able to express their feelings through acting and to enter deeply into the situations and roles they are portraying.

4. Creative dramatics are a valuable form of group experience; children learn to cooperate and work closely with others, and thus develop important social skills.

5. Dramatic play provides an additional dimension to the community recreation program, and appeal to participants who may not be as skilled in games, sports, or other typical playground activities.

Lead-up Activities in Creative Dramatics

The intelligent recreation leader does not attempt to begin dramatics with children by having them take part in full-fledged group presentations. Instead, he makes use of a variety of lead-up activities, such as improvisations, story telling, skits and dramatic stunts, and pantomimes, as preparation for group dramatic play.

1. Improvisations represent simple forms of dramatic play in which children act out characters from stories, simple themes of daily life, moods, or other familiar themes. They may be approached as individual stunts or as small group activities. Typical improvisations that may be suggested to younger children include the following:

    a. pretending to cook, iron, have a tea party, care for a baby, sweep the floor, or rake leaves

    b. playing different sports, such as playing tennis, riding a bicycle, dribbling a basketball, or throwing a baseball

    c. feeling different moods, such as "happy," "sad," "angry," or "frightened"

    d. other household activities, such as brushing teeth, combing hair, answering the telephone, or shoveling snow

2. Story telling is a popular activity for younger children. After a story has been told, children may act out different characters from it, or take key parts of the action and pantomime these events. Such stories might include traditional folk tales, like *Rumplestiltskin, Cinderella,* the *Sleeping Beauty,* or *Jack and the Beanstalk,* or well-known nursery rhymes, like *Jack and Jill, Simple Simon,* or *Little Miss Muffet.*

3. Skits and dramatic stunts may be carried on in varied ways:

    a. the leader may tell a story, such as the *Lion Hunt,* in which, as he tells the tale, children pantomime each event or happening

    b. the leader may prepare a "bag of props," in which several familiar objects (paintbrush, flashlight, cap, etc.) are placed. Small groups of children are given these props and work out simple stories which they act out, based on them

    c. the leader may use charades as a "lead-up" activity by having individual children act out book, song, movie or other titles, proverbs, or famous characters for others to guess

    d. imaginary situations may be developed in which children are given a one-line "skeleton story to act out" such as: "you are trying to study with a tooth ache," "you are bringing a poor report card home to your father," or "you are walking past a graveyard late at night"

4. Pantomimes may be used in any of the other types of creative dramatic activities, or may be presented as a separate activity. There are dozens of good ideas for pantomime, including:

    a. you are at an amusement park; act out any of the things that happen there (eating spun candy, shooting at targets, riding the roller-coaster);

    b. you are Santa Claus, and you take presents out of your sack for a group of children. What are they?

    c. you take a trip to a farm, and act out the different chores that farm boys and girls do each day (pitching hay, milking cows, finding eggs, feeding chickens, etc.); and

    d. you join a symphony orchestra, and act out any of the players (drum, piano, violin, horn, or conductor).

Presenting Group Dramatic Experiences

After children have enjoyed activities of this types for a period of time, and have gained confidence and skill in presenting ideas through movement and speech, they are ready to engage in more structured group dramatic experiences. These may be based on stories, poems, songs, or real life happenings. Although there is no single method for developing such group presentations, the following sequence is fairly typical of how success-ful children's dramatics leaders approach this task.

1. Select a story. This may be based on a story which the leader tells the children, or it may be one that the children develop independently.

2. The leader tells the story in a relaxed, informal manner, bringing out the humor or suspense in it, and using direct dialogue wherever possible. The story should have interesting action and characters but should not have too complicated a plot.

3. The children and the leader discuss the story, analyzing its meaning, the different characters, the most important scenes and exciting moments.

4. Children should be selected to take different parts. They may volunteer for different roles themselves, or the leader may assign them. If the group is large enough, it may divide into several smaller groups, each of which undertakes to act out the play and assign roles to its members.

5. The story should be reviewed to develop the basic plot outline, which con-sists of the most important scenes that will be acted out. Then children begin to act it out. They should be encouraged:

    a. to be natural, and to use gestures, movements or speech which feel comfortable to them

    b. to pace themselves, to speak slowly, clearly, and with a sense of being the character

    c. to begin to think of how they "feel" toward the other characters, and how the stage action may be laid out so it is most effective

6. After each of the scenes has been played, children should review the en-tire experience. They should be helped to analyze both themselves and others in constructive and supportive ways, and to make sound sugges-tions for improvement.

7. If the children wish to, the story may then be played out in its entirety for other children on the playground, or for an audience of parents. It is never necessary, in informal dramatics, to have an audience. However, if children wish to, they may get great satisfaction from performing their work for others.

Leadership Guidelines

As the previous section has shown, the creative dramatics leader must operate in an informal, unstructured way. He is *not* a strict or authoritarian play director. He is not using a script that children must follow precisely, and performance with props, costumes, lighting and similar details is not the group's goal. The process is far more important than the product in in-formal dramatics. Nonetheless, the leader does play an important role in this enterprise.

1. First, he must help children gain the confidence to express themselves; his encouragement, assistance, and skill in establishing a comfortable, ac-cepting group climate are essential if this is to be done.

2. He must be able to present good stories or themes to children for them to consider acting out. As they discuss these, his ability to help them make judgments and decisions will prevent aimless wrangling and confusion.

3. His flexibility will keep the enterprise responsive to the needs of individual children, and his enthusiasm and good humor will keep it fun for all.

4. If the group develops enough interest in dramatics to wish to put on more formal presentations, he must have a thorough knowledge of the process, including the following tasks:

    a. selecting appropriate scripts

    b. outlining a regular schedule of meeting days and hours, and setting up specific rehearsal hours that will be observed by all

    c. casting the play, and assigning other responsibilities (costumes, props, stagecraft, and so forth) to children who will not be acting

    d. teaching simple rules of stage movement, the use of voice, acting, etc., to participants

    e. getting help from arts and crafts leaders or other skilled persons in designing and making props and costumes, and assisting with lights and public-address systems, if necessary

    f. involving parents, as volunteer aides in the project, in making costumes, helping with transportation and publicity or in other needed ways

    g. maintaining the motivation and interest of the players through the entire process, including reassuring those who lose confidence and wish to withdraw

    h. carrying out final "technical" and "dress" rehearsals, and polishing the performance

    i. putting on the final performance or performances

ARTS AND CRAFTS LEADERSHIP

Arts and crafts activities are enjoyed by all age groups, both sexes, and by individuals with a wide range of abilities and interests. The term "arts and crafts" is used very broadly. It covers a full range of art activities, from sculpture and oil painting to the simplest kind of sketching, and crafts, from ceramics or weaving approached as a complex and advanced profession using highly skilled techniques and equipment to extremely basic hobby-craft activities for the playground.

Values of Arts and Crafts Activities

Arts and crafts are an extremely important element in most recreation programs, for the following reasons:

1. They stimulate and encourage self-expression, imagination, and creativity, and help to develop an appreciation of design and color.

2. They provide a sense of accomplishment and satisfaction in the final product.

3. They help to encourage such desirable personality traits as orderliness (when applied to the care of equipment and crafts facilities), working patiently toward a final product, good manners toward others, and cooperation.

4. They result in final products which may be shown in exhibitions or displays, providing favorable public relations for the recreation department, or which the individual may sell or use as a gift to friends or relatives.

5. They provide hours of self-absorbed enjoyment. Arts and crafts are easy to direct. They can be carried on individually or in small groups, with any age group, in limited surroundings, and at almost no cost.

General Guidelines for Leadership

The task of arts and crafts leadership involves both the skilled teaching of individual crafts or projects and the overall management or direction of arts and crafts as a program activity. The successful arts and crafts leader should be

1. Personally interested in arts and crafts as an enjoyable hobby activity, and convinced that this pastime represents a vital part of the overall recreation program.

2. Able to select appropriate activities that will suit the varied needs and interests of participants, and to present these in simple, clear ways that will motivate others to take part.

3. Well-organized in the planning of projects, gathering of materials, and management of the overall program.

4. Enthusiastic and positive in his approach to the activity. On the playground, for example, he should

   a. Encourage and praise participants for their efforts in a sincere way, as children can easily spot "phonies."

   b. Encourage children to finish every job they start. If a child is not able to do this while the rest of the group completes a project, special time should be set aside for him to return to it.

   c. Provide a wide variety of arts and crafts projects, so that every child, regardless of age or ability, can find interesting and rewarding activities in this area.

5. Aware of the creative values of arts and crafts. Instead of presenting mechanical or ready-made arts and crafts projects, in which the participant uses a hobby kit or "grinds" out a standardized product, he should present activities which provide the opportunity to be original and expressive.

Management of Arts and Crafts Sessions

Arts and crafts may be approached on many different levels in community recreation. They may be the partial responsibility of a playground leader or director who does not have special skill or background in this area but who can direct a number of fairly simple projects. In such situations, arts and crafts are usually provided at regular times each week, as part of the playground schedule, for all participants who wish to take part. In community centers, arts and crafts instruction is usually approached in more formal ways, with actual classes being set up based on age levels, degree of skill, or type of activity being presented. Often, a special room or workshop is set aside only for arts and crafts, with special equipment and storage areas, and with a highly skilled specialist in charge of the program.

While each of these situations may impose its own requirements or approaches, the following guidelines apply to the management of all arts and crafts activities in recreation settings:

1. Schedule arts and crafts activities on a regular basis, at least two or three times weekly. Make sure this is known to all participants through posters, fliers, and announcements. Encourage participation in advance.

2. Keep a regular display of finished arts and crafts projects, as a means of praising those who have done good work in the activity and interesting others to take part.

3. Know in advance what projects you will be presenting. Have a sample of the product to show participants at the previous session to encourage attendance.

4. Be sure you have all the materials and equipment you will need for the project set out and ready to go.

5. Demonstrate each step of the craft activity clearly and precisely as you progress. Encourage children to ask questions, and make sure they are fully answered. As the group works, keep them closely supervised at all times, giving help as needed. Do *not* do the work for them.

6. Make your program so enjoyable that participants will want to come. Do not encourage onlookers; get them involved in activity. First get regular participants started with their project, and then pay attention to newcomers.

7. Allow enough time to complete the activity. If it cannot be done in a single session, make sure that all work in progress can be safely stored until the next time.

8. Maintain good discipline and order in the crafts session in order to avoid accidents and to permit all participants to work seriously on their projects in a quiet, controlled atmosphere.

9. Allow enough time for clean-up, and expect all participants to join in this, as a matter of group responsibility. Keep a clean, well-organized area, and make sure that damaged equipment is repaired or replaced. Since it usually takes time for arts and crafts materials to be ordered and sent, requisition all needed materials well in advance.

10. If possible, plan for a playground arts and crafts exhibit, and invite parents and other community members. Although your goal is not to over-emphasize competition, it is a good idea to give awards (ribbons, scrolls, and so on) to the best artists or craftsmen in a number of categories.

11. In addition to exhibits, plan other special events or projects which make

use of arts and crafts, or integrate them with other recreation activities, such as puppet shows, costume-making projects for drama programs, kite contests, poster displays, nature crafts exhibits, and so on. A communitywide Arts and Crafts Fair, including both children's and adults' work, is a good year's end activity.

Many useful and enjoyable arts and crafts projects and activities are described in the manuals and texts listed in the Appendix of this text. As the leader works with these to direct groups in creative activities, it is important that he stress two sets of goals: (a) personal expressiveness and growth, in terms of artistic creativity; and (b) the development of technique, or craft, in the creation of products. While the arts and crafts leader is interested in encouraging all participants to discover their full potential within this area of activity, he is also concerned about identifying those participants who have special gifts or talents. Often, such individuals realize for the first time in an arts and crafts program that they have unique talents and abilities, and may be encouraged to join special classes or undertake more demanding and challenging types of craft hobbies.

LEADERSHIP IN DANCE ACTIVITIES

Dance in its various forms is a popular recreation activity which may be enjoyed by all ages, in a variety of settings. Younger children on the playground or in community centers may take part in creative rhythmics, singing games, and simple folk and square dances. Older children, teenagers, and young adults are more likely to enjoy social dancing, more advanced folk and square dancing, or the creative types of dance—such as modern dance, ballet, or jazz dance. Even senior citizens take part in social dancing and simple folk or square dancing in Golden Age clubs or special community programs. Thus, dance is a uniquely useful recreation activity.

Values of Dance in Recreation

While these vary according to the type of dance that is being done, dance generally has the following goals or purposes:

1. It is a valuable form of physical experience—both in terms of developing one's neuromuscular skill and such attributes as balance, agility, or coordination, and in terms of promoting healthy physical fitness.

2. Dance is a highly social activity; in most of its forms, it is carried on as a group experience, and provides companionship and confidence in social settings.

3. Dance enhances creative and artistic growth; particularly in such activities as modern dance or ballet, it is a recognized theatrical art form, and so enriches the aesthetic awareness and skills of the participant.

4. Generally, dance promotes one's poise, confidence, and grace. Both for boys and girls, it is a way of getting over a sense of awkwardness and gaining confidence in one's appearance and in contact with others.

5. Dance is an important cultural element in many societies, and represents important folk and ethnic traditions. It may be performed as part of the cultural heritage of minority racial or national groups, or in sharing intercultural customs and holidays.

6. As suggested, when children learn dance at an early age, it has the potential for becoming an enjoyable and creative leisure activity or hobby that they can take part in throughout their lifetimes.

Guidelines for Dance Leadership

One need not be a highly skilled dancer or dance teacher in order to present dance activities to children in community recreation settings, or to conduct simple folk and square dance activities for teenagers or adults. With a minimum of preparation, such as a basic course or two, a departmental clinic or workshop, and use of appropriate manuals, most leaders can be reasonably successful in this activity. However, for more advanced or established groups in any area of dance activity, specially trained leadership is essential. Some municipal recreation and park departments hire dance specialists, who go from playground to playground during the summer and lead special sessions for all participants, and who also conduct training clinics, or other leaders in dance activities. In some cases, it is the responsibility of the specialists to plan exhibitions, concerts, festivals, or other large-scale special performances.

The teaching of dance—beyond a very basic level—requires knowledge of steps, skills, techniques, and basic principles. This is true whether the teacher is presenting folk or square dance (each of which can be highly complex activities), or modern dance or ballet (both of which demand years of training, in order to become an advanced performer). On a recreational level, the following leadership guidelines apply:

1. The leader should know his subject well, and make a point of observing other programs, gathering useful materials, and attending classes or workshops which will strengthen his leadership skills.

2. He should plan dance sessions carefully, so that they are well publicized, set at a regular time, and involve continuity and improvement in skills over a period of time.

3. Dance classes, clubs, or playground sessions should be publicized as fully as possible, and an attempt made to involve boys as participants; in the past, dance has been falsely regarded as a primarily feminine activity, and it should be recognized that boys can enjoy it and be highly successful in it.

4. Demonstrate enthusiasm and enjoyment of the subject; the leader's approach to participants should be warm and encouraging rather than highly critical. Dance must be made fun as well as instructive.

5. Maintain control of the teaching situation; particularly among younger children or pre-teenagers; coeducational dance sessions can be boisterous if the leader does not expect and demand good behavior.

6. Plan special events, such as performances, festivals, or other exhibits, at which participants can show what they have learned. These provide a goal to aim at, and enhance motivation and regular attendance in the playground or center dance activity.

7. Integrate dance instruction as fully as possible with other program activities, such as music, theater, or arts and crafts.

Specific Leadership Skills

Dance leadership skills are presented here in two categories of activity: (a) creative dance and rhythms for younger children; and (b) basic folk or square dance instruction for all ages.

Creative Dance Teaching Methods

The approach used in this field is very much like that used in creative dramatics; it places primary importance on the child's own exploration of movement rather than on the "rote" learning of dance techniques.

1. The leader should have specific goals in mind. Usually, these relate to the following:

   a. helping children understand how the body moves, and giving them experiences in a total range of movement exploration

   b. promoting their awareness of different qualities of movement that use the body as a means of communication

   c. developing musical understandings related to rhythm, tempo, phrasing and form, and relating these to movement

   d. developing personal expressiveness and creativity, and relating creative movement to other aesthetic experiences, such as art, literature, or music

   e. giving early experiences in making dances by exploring elements such as direction, levels, and floor patterns

2. The leader should use a variety of approaches to stimulate movement exploration. These may include:

   a. exploration of locomotor movement—walking, running, skipping, sliding, running, leaping

   b. exploration of axial (nonlocomotor) movement—swinging, striking, bending, stretching, shaking, bouncing

   c. use of suggested movement sequences, in which the leader suggests combinations of actions, and children interpret individually

   d. use of images as basis for movement, such as moving like animals, machines, vehicles, fairy tale characters

   e. use of music or percussive accompaniment to stimulate movement

   f. use of moods to suggest movement, such as sadness, happiness, anger, loneliness

   g. exploration of movement possibilities of parts of the body: arms, hands, head, feet

   h. use of pictures, stories, or poems to suggest movement sequences

3. The teacher should move from simple, basic movement expression to more complex combinations and skills with young children:

   a. more difficult challenges may be presented, in terms of combinations of movement

   b. gradually, movement skills may be introduced in which children deliberately work on such elements as flexibility, strength, coordination, or balance

   c. different types of elements may be combined, such as floor patterns, levels, directions, and rhythmic sequences

   d. from exploring movement individually, young children can gradually move to working in pairs or small groups

   e. from sheer spontaneous expression, children may be guided into *planning* dance sequences, working them out more carefully and showing them to others

Throughout this process, the leader should not be concerned about the child's technique, although an obvious outcome of creative movement experiences should be the steady improvement of the body as an instrument of dance. As children gain in ability and motivation, they will want to know how to *dance* (in a more literal sense), and it will be possible to provide increasing elements of actual instruction in dance techniques. However, pleasure and creative expression should be emphasized throughout, and learning routines and drills should not be the focus of instruction.

Folk and Square Dance Leadership Methods

Essentially, teaching folk dancing involves the presentation of basic skills of movement, along with individual dances, thus building a repertoire of performing ability. The leader therefore is teaching *set* material to participants and must do so in as enjoyable and informal a manner as possible. Initially, many young children and teenagers have a dislike for dance because of the way it may have been presented to them in their school physical education classes. Therefore, it must be made a pleasant experience on the playground or in the community center rather than a grim, forced exercise.

GENERAL GUIDELINES FOR LEADERSHIP

1. The leader should present a wide variety of dances of different national or ethnic backgrounds, including American square dances. These should

be geared for the skill level of the participants, and should involve sequential learning so that they improve steadily in dance skills.

2. Folk and square dancing should be presented at set times in recreation settings, with strong publicity urging attendance. Both boys and girls should be involved.

3. Dances of different patterns should be used, including couple dances, lines, squares, and circle dances without partners. The latter are particularly useful if there is resistance on the part of boys about dancing with girls as partners.

4. In planning any dance session, it is necessary to concentrate on teaching basic skills (specific steps, such as waltz, polka, schottische, mazurka, and so on), not as drills but by including them in enjoyable and interesting dances.

5. The leader should seek to have everyone take part but should not insist that they do so.

6. It is wise to begin a folk or square dance session with familiar, easy dances, and then to include several new or more challenging dances if it is basically an instruction period. If the program is a party or festival, it is best chiefly to do dances which have already been learned and will require little instruction on the spot.

7. The leader should gear his material generally to the bulk of dancers within the group rather than to the very expert or experienced dancers or to those who are having considerable difficulty.

PRESENTING A SINGLE DANCE

In addition to such general suggestions, the leader should know the specific guidelines that are useful in presenting a single dance to a group.

1. Select an appropriate dance, in terms of the level of the group and the skill progression that you have planned.

2. Prepare yourself, making sure that you understand the dance thoroughly and can demonstrate it clearly. Make sure you have the needed record (or sheet music for an accompanist), that your record player is operating properly, and that any other needed materials are available.

3. Have the group take the appropriate function. Stand where all the participants can see and hear you most effectively, and where the accompanist (if you have one) can observe your signals.

4. Briefly introduce the dance, giving some information regarding its source or background and playing a portion of its music, to arouse interest in it.

5. Demonstrate the dance yourself, with a partner, or with a group of participants.

   a. If it has several distinct sections, show these one at a time. After each one has been demonstrated, have the entire group repeat the action as you give verbal cues or directions.

   b. If the dance is fairly simple, or has only one or two sections, it may be best to demonstrate it all at once, and then have the entire group repeat the action.

6. Repeat step (5) with musical accompaniment, making sure that the parti-

cipants understand the dance and are performing it correctly. Then have them go through the entire dance, section by section, without stopping.

7. If the dancers are having no difficulty, have them do the entire dance to the music. If they are having trouble, stop and re-teach the section that is giving trouble. Then have them do the dance again.

8. Other guides for effective folk dance teaching are:

    a. Use a distinct signal with which to start the dancers and the music (assuming that you are using an accompanist), such as, "Ready — begin!"

    b. As you demonstrate, stand at different points on the floor, so all can observe or hear the directions and have you close to them at some point. In some circle dances, it may be best to have participants form a line, standing behind you, in order to learn the dance best.

    c. Change partners from time to time, to promote social interaction and help dancers learn from each other.

    d. Do not over-teach. Progress as rapidly as is possible for your group.

    e. Keep a record of all dance sessions — what you have taught, when, and how well the group performed the dance.

    f. Plan to have special events, such as festivals and demonstrations, as culminating activities and to improve interest and motivation.

NATURE ACTIVITY LEADERSHIP

Nature activities have been an important part of public and voluntary recreation programs for many years. Today, with the increasing concern with the environment and the need to promote effective conservation practices, many agencies see this as a high-priority area. The types of services and programs provided by recreation and park agencies in the field of nature fall into the following categories: nature clubs and outing groups; operation of nature centers and museums; playground zoos or aquariums; playground activities such as nature games, hobbies, collections or craft activities; construction or conservation projects; gardening projects; weather study and practice of such skills as knotcraft, using a compass, canoeing, snow skiing or use of snowshoes, camp cookery and fire-making, and a wide variety of other activities.

Those recreation and park departments that operate extensive outdoor areas, such as nature preserves or beachfronts, are able to provide rich programs of nature study and camping in these sites. Other departments have more limited resources and must make use of county or state park facilities for trips, camping, and nature projects.

Goals of Nature Activity

As in all program areas, it is important to have a clear picture of the values and purposes of nature activity. These include the following:

1. Nature activities help to put young people — particularly those who live in

urban settings—in touch with the natural environment of plants, trees, and animals which should be an important part of their heritage.

2. Nature activities, particulary those which involve exploration, overnight camping, hiking, and exposure to more remote settings, provide an opportunity for adventure and challenge.

3. Children should be encouraged to develop an awareness of nature, and a respect for the environment; these values are crucial if mankind is to succeed in preventing further pollution and degradation of parks, waterways, and natural wildlife.

4. Nature provides a laboratory for children to learn facts and principles of science in the most meaningful and direct way. Thus, recreation-sponsored nature programs serve to broaden and enrich school-sponsored education.

5. Nature activities offer a medium through which recreation and park agencies may mobilize community resources and enlist "youth power" in conservation and antipollution projects. They can make an important contribution to community life.

6. Nature activities are *fun,* and worth doing if for no other reasons than purely recreational ones.

General Leadership Guidelines

There are no cut-and-dried rules for success in the leadership of nature activities. However, several important guidelines follow. First, the leader *must* have expertise in this area. It is not possible to introduce children and youth to nature in meaningful ways unless one has a solid background of knowledge and understanding of the natural environment. To improve his competence, the leader should attend workshops and courses, reading, visiting nature centers, and learning all he can about the subject. In addition, he should bring in guest lecturers or other experts, and use films, displays, or other learning resources, thereby enriching the program as fully as possible.

1. The leader should recognize that children's attitudes about nature will vary considerably because of their past experiences. They may range from enthusiasm and interest to boredom or even fear. To build positive attitudes and interests will take patience and encouragement.

2. The leader should demonstrative a positive and constructive attitude toward nature; his interest and enthusiasm and love for the environment will be "catching."

3. Nature cannot be experienced properly indoors; it must be learned through doing. Children should be involved in trips, outings, camping, visits to nature centers, and other real experiences.

4. Much learning comes from discovery and use of "teachable moments" as the unexpected occurs. Thus, the leader must be alert to such possibilities at all times.

5. Participants should share in planning projects, outings, or other activities.

They should be given real responsibilities and should be expected to live up to them, if the nature experience is to be meaningful for them.

6. In all learning experiences, it is best to begin not with the scientific study of names, facts, or processes, but rather with observation and exposure to natural experiences that will prompt interest in further study.

7. Teach sound nature principles from the outset. Do not destroy living things in putting together a collection. If collecting live specimens such as salamanders, snakes, or squirrels, keep them only for a short time and then release them, unless you are certain that they can live in a healthy way in your collection. Even then, respect for animal life raises a question as to whether you have a right to take them from their homes.

Examples of Nature Projects and Activities

The list of possible nature activities is almost endless. However, here are a number of appealing projects which children and youth will enjoy, and which do not require tremendous expertise on the part of the leader.

1. *Nature Hobbies and Crafts.* These may encompass any of the following:

    a. preparing labels for tree or plant identification

    b. doing spatter-printing with leaves, or doing leaf-printing on wood sections

    c. making pine needle whisk-brooms

    d. making pine cone bird-feeders

    e. constructing and maintaining terrariums and aquariums

    f. making Christmas tree ornaments out of seed pods, pine cones, or other natural objects

    g. doing sketching, painting, or photography of nature subjects

    h. doing creative writing on nature themes for camp, center, or playground newspapers

2. *Nature Science Experiments.* These involve more formal projects, with careful observation and recording of results over a period of time. Examples are:

    a. observing how long it takes beans or other types of seeds to germinate under different conditions (type of soil, light, warmth, and so forth)

    b. building simple weather stations and recording temperature, humidity, wind changes, and similar information

    c. doing careful observation of plant flowering, tree leafing, bird migration, correct times for planting, and so on

    d. doing careful collections of rocks, minerals, fossils, tree leaves, insects, driftwood, weeds, or forms of water life, and analyzing and classifying these

3. *Special Conservation Projects.* Older children, with adult help, can become involved in a wide variety of such projects on school grounds, campsites, or in parks or natural preserves:

    a. property improvement and beautification through relocation of walks and paths, construction of retaining walls, replanting, or soil erosion measures

b. stream and pond improvement, through cleaning of refuse, construction of small dams, planting of fish, or controlling of bank erosion

c. new planting of plants and shrubs which provide food and shelter for wildlife

d. waste clean-up drives and community campaigns

4. *Campcraft Activities.* These may be learned in playground settings to prepare children for overnight or longer camping trips. They include:

a. Basic camping skills, such as pitching a tent, lashing methods to construct camp "furniture," knotcraft, or fire-making and camp cookery

b. Survival methods, including compass reading, locating natural foods, Morse code signal sending, and so forth

c. Skills in fishing, boat handling, or similar recreational activities (assuming that the recreation and parks department has ponds for instruction)

5. *Nature Games.* There are many games which are specially suited for the natural environment that promote observation and awareness of the outdoors.

a. Nature retrieving or treasure hunt games involving races or relays in collecting natural objects

b. Nature sounds and smells—observing the environment and recording sights, sounds, smells, or other observable phenomena as a form of contest

c. Trailing games, or races to get to particular locations, using maps and compasses

d. Nature word games or memory contests, based on knowledge of the outdoors

Any or all of these activities may be undertaken as part of daily playground or community center programming, and will have great appeal for children. They should all lead to the ultimate goal, as expressed by Albert Schweitzer, of "reverence for life."

SPORTS LEADERSHIP IN COMMUNITY RECREATION

Probably the most popular and widely distributed area of activity in community recreation is sports. Certainly it ranks as the activity with the highest level of active participation for children, youth, and young adults in both public recreation and park departments and many voluntary youth organizations. Public recreation agencies tend to operate the major sports facilities in any community, such as ballfields, golf courses, tennis courts, and swimming pools. Sports have a tremendous attraction for the public and represent an important area of recreation programming and leader-ship concern.

Goals and Purposes of Community Sports Programs

Since sports can be used for exploitative or undesirable purposes — as evidenced by many high-pressure college athletic programs — it is essential that the objectives of community sports programs be clearly defined. An excellent example of stated goals of athletics is found in the Program Book of the Recreation Division of the Chicago Park District:

We affirm our fundamental belief in democratic principles as a way of life, and through the annual program of activities we seek:

1. To emphasize for individuals and groups, the importance of sound physical and mental health habits and practices;

2. To encourage individuals and groups to assume a role of leadership in the planning and conduct of our physical activities programs;

3. To emphasize and enlist the participation of many in community tournaments rather than a select few in highly specialized competition for those of greater ability and interest;

4. To allow programs to be adjusted to meet the needs of groups and communities and to cooperate with other agencies in meeting these needs;

5. To provide a guided outlet in carefully planned and controlled competition for community groups;

6. To avoid highly regimented programs of competition;

7. To encourage instructors to develop local programs with ample opportunity to consider the individual as well as the group in an endeavor to see that concomitant learnings, as well as direct learnings, may prosper;

8. To conduct orderly, progressive, and purposeful programs in the teaching of fundamental skills and activities; and to encourage the learning of carry over activities;

9. To foster initiative and experimentation in administrative practices on the part of each local instructional staff.

We believe the very soul of athletic sports and games lies in competition, but we feel that it should be competition for all, well-planned, well-conducted and guided in safe and healthful channels.

Obviously, different organizations may have different kinds of goals for their sports programs. This is illustrated in the directives issued to base sports programs by the Special Services Program of the United States Army Air Force:

1. To provide a wide variety of sports activities which will provide op-

portunities and encourage maximum participation throughout the year.

2. To provide a program of sports which will meet the leisure-time needs and interests of Air Force personnel.

3. To give Air Force personnel the opportunity to develop skills and recreational capacities in a variety of sports and habits of participating therein.

4. To promote the development and maintenance of physical fitness and health.

5. To develop an enthusiastic appreciation of sports and of skilled performance.

6. To provide, for entertainment purposes, events of spectator interest.

7. To contribute to the development of such traits and qualities as will make for an integrated personality, capable of displaying leadership, followership, competitive and cooperative spirit, sociability, and teamwork.

8. To develop safety capacities enabling one to care for one's self and to aid others in sudden emergencies.

9. To add to the personal growth and social enrichment of the individual by providing a means for the participant to make new acquaintanceships and form new friendships.

10. To contribute to the development of unit solidarity, esprit de corps, and individual and group morale.

Each agency or department that sponsors programs of sports activity should develop its own set of goals and principles in accordance with its overall philosophy and role in the community.

Range of Department Functions and Services

This may vary considerably according to the nature of the department or agency, the population it serves, its physical and staff resources, and its overall philosophy. The small recreation department with limited facilities is likely to offer only a few basic programs in the most popular sports. On the other hand, a big-city recreation and park department with hundreds of specialized facilities is likely to offer an extremely wide range of opportunities. For example, the Chicago Park District provides sports activities in the following team and individual sports: archery, baseball, basketball, football, handball, horseshoes, ice skating, softball, swimming, tennis, touch football, track and field, trampoline, volleyball, and wrestling. In each of these areas, it may provide basic instruction, organized competition, testing programs, or special events that promote community interest. It cooperates with community organizations by providing facilities or other forms of assistance to their programs.

In many cases, the Chicago Park District will provide several levels of involvement for a single sport. For example, in such sports as baseball, basketball, or softball, it sponsors basic instruction and competitive leagues for boys, men, girls, and women, and also school-based teams. In addition to the above sports, it provides instruction or competition in such areas as bicycle derbies, bait casting, checkers and chess, dog training, golf, fishing marble tournaments, pinochle, sailing, roller skating, and table tennis.

General Principles of Sports Leadership

While these depend in part on specific program objectives, the following principles of sports leadership should apply to all situations:

1. The involvement of any participant in sports activity should take into consideration the following individual characteristics: age, physique, interests, ability, experience, and the participant's stage of physiological, emotional, and social maturity.

2. Involvement in athletics must be based on a comprehensive and reliable evaluation of the health status of the participant, with careful restriction of participation when possible risk is involved.

3. The leader should seek to develop the skill of all participants, using a wide variety of careful, effective instructional procedures. He should follow accepted principles of teaching methodology and not rely on players learning skills "on their own."

4. Of equal importance is the need to promote healthy values toward competition, good sportsmanship, obedience to rules, and team play. The effective leader must incorporate these values in his own behavior, and must constantly reaffirm them in his leadership practices.

5. The leader should make arrangements so that all players can participate and compete on appropriate levels of ability, so that they learn to meet challenges with a reasonable degree of opportunity for success.

6. The leader is responsible for making all physical arrangements for sports participation related to scheduling, registration, provision and maintenance of sports facilities, assignment of officials, and presentation of awards or trophies.

7. The leader must formulate and enforce, either individually or in cooperation with community sports associations, appropriate policies with respect to eligibility, practice, team make-up, forfeits, protests, and similar competitive concerns.

8. The leader should involve, as fully as possible, youth, parents, and other interested representatives of the community, in teaching, coaching, managing or officiating roles, either on a voluntary or paid basis. Community representatives should also be involved in planning events and determining policies of the sports program.

Guides for Management of Sports Programs

Sports specialists or supervisors in municipal or voluntary recreation agencies have a major responsibility for organizing major sports tournaments, league play, or other large-scale events. The following listing of an Area Chairman's Duties and Responsibilities for carrying out a specific Chicago Park District sports activity provides a useful illustration of how such procedures are carried out.

To successfully conduct the activity to which you have been assigned, the following details are of utmost importance. It may be necessary to add or delete some of the following, depending on the activity.

1. Consult the program bulletin and activity calendar, and check on the date and/or length of time in which the activity is scheduled to be conducted.

2. Consult with your Area Supervisor as to date (rain date if necessary), location, time, officials, P.A. System, physical set-up of gymnasium, assembly hall, or outdoor facility.

3. Consult with the supervisor at the location where the event is to be located and discuss all details, locker room facilities, lighting, ventilation, necessary equipment, etc.

4. If it is necessary to initiate orders for special marking of a field, gymnasium floor, or setting up of any equipment, or transportation of heavy items, do so through your area supervisor.

5. After the location has been selected, then notify all parks in your area by bulletin or letter as to the nature of the event, who is qualified, when entries are due, date of event, time and location.

6. Submit to your Area Supervisor a listing of the officials needed to conduct the activity. After receiving his approval, then notify all officials as to time, date, duties and proper uniform.

7. Secure from the Physical Section Office the necessary forms pertaining to your event, such as: registration sheets, heat sheets, chief judges cards, summary sheets, bout cards, numbers, pins.

8. Notify your local district police station.

9. Whether it be an individual or team activity, you are expected to know the rules of eligibility and to enforce them.

10. Set up the activity in as efficient a manner as possible. For example, for a track and field meet you will need an order of events sheet for the contestants and officials; registration tables for the contestants; proper signs, such as "junior", "intermediate" and "senior"; and officials list and their duties. Always use a Public Address system where possible, and have a good announcer.

11. If you are called upon to render a decision for an infraction of a rule or interpretation, use good judgment and show no partiality.

12. At the close of any event, have the winners announced over the P.A. system.

13. If meet records are available, announce the tied or new meet records.

14. If medals, trophies or certificates are supplied for the winners, individual or team, have the presentation made in such a manner that the recipient feels proud of the honor bestowed.

15. A summary of the activity should be prepared and sent to all parks in

the area for local park record and display on the bulletin board. Also send a copy of the report to the Physical Activities Supervisor in charge of the event.

16. Prepare an article for the local newspaper and send a copy to the Park District publicity office.

17. Immediately following the conclusion of the area event, prepare the special report form which was forwarded to you by the Physical Activities Supervisor. Then forward this report to your Area Supervisor. Do not delay, as this information is vital in preparing for the City Championships. . . .

18. Review all phases of the activity just conducted and make notes for improving the conduct of the activity the following season.

19. Make sure that all loaned equipment is returned immediately.

20. Keep an up-to-date file on the activity either for yourself, or to pass on to the next Area Chairman selected to conduct the activity.

This outline of responsibilities, while it applies primarily to a track-and-field event, demonstrates the careful and logical sequence of responsibilities that must be carried out in organizing any sports event or competition.

Guidelines for Teaching Sports Skills

An important responsibility in all community sports programs is the instruction of basic sports skills. While much of this is done in school physical education departments, many municipal recreation and park agencies offer sports that are *not* taught in the schools. Even when they are, it is often necessary to provide basic skills instruction to participants who have not learned the rudiments of play, or who wish to have advanced instruction.

Effective teaching is based on a general knowledge of teaching principles, and on the ability to organize sequences of instruction and to carry them out clearly and in a logical progression of skills. Guidelines for the effective teaching of sports skills are found in many physical education texts. However, the following key principles are identified here:

1. To the extent that it is possible, learners should be grouped on appropriate skill and ability levels: beginner, intermediate and advanced.

2. Learners should be organized most effectively to permit demonstration and practice of the skill components of the sport. If at all possible, when working with large numbers of learners, they should be spaced so all of them can be active all of the time. For example:

   a. In teaching baseball skills, it is common practice to assign players to groups based on specific skills, such as hitting, pitching, and infield and outfield practice. Working with separate instructors, each player gets instruction and practice for a maximum amount of time.

   b. In a sport like tennis, where normally only two or four players would be on a court at a time, learners should be organized in groups so they practice basic strokes and then rotate rapidly in hitting the ball.

3. Emphasis should be given to learning the correct way to perform each skill, but the instructor should be able to accept each individual's style or movement or unique way of performing. It is not possible to fit all players to a mold, in any sport.

4. Periods of demonstration and practice should be followed by periods of actual play—in order to keep interest high, and to give learners a chance to practice what they have learned. However, the instructor should not hesitate to interrupt such periods of "practice-play," as in the case of a basketball scrimmage, to make teaching points.

5. As basic skills are mastered, the instructor should move players on to more advanced skills and to other areas of learning, such as rules, scoring, and strategy.

6. In planning any course, the instructor should outline the major areas of learning, and fit them into a logical order or course of study. For example, in a basic tennis course offered by the Department of Recreation and Parks of the City of Richmond, Virginia, in cooperation with the National Recreation and Park Association, and the Lifetime Sports Foundation, the following sessions were scheduled:

Session A: Presentation of basic position and forehand stroke.
              Practice of forehand grip and stroke.

Session B: Review and practice of forehand stroke.
              Presentation and practice of forehand stroke.

Session C: Review and practice of forehand and backhand strokes, in teaching court, practice court, and against backboard.

Session D: Teach principles of tennis courtesy.
              Practice forehand and backhand strokes, emphasizing positioning on court.

Session E: Introduce game scoring rules, and show demonstration game, analyzing each play and having group keep score.
              Play practice games.

Session F: Introduce serve with demonstration.
              Players practice serve.

Session G: Players review and practice serve.
              Practice forehand and backhand.
              Practice games, using correct serve.

Session H: Start "ladder" competition for strongest players and play complete set.
              Work on weaknesses at backboard: backhand and serve.

Session I: Continue ladder competition.
              Continue working on weak strokes.
              Introduce lob, volley, and overhead strokes to better players.

Session J: Demonstrate doubles rules and teamwork strategy.
              Practice singles games.

Work on weaknesses.
Try to find a tennis team for strongest players to challenge.

Session K: Continue ladder competition.
Practice doubles.
Work on weaknesses.

Session L: Singles elimination tournament.
Doubles elimination tournament.

7. As the preceding outline demonstrates, the instructor should provide basic lessons each day in fundamental skills for all players, and at the same time work on individual needs, permitting more highly skilled players to move ahead, in order to maximize their learning and increase their motivation.

Human Relations in Coaching

Throughout the coaching process, it is important to be keenly aware of the human relations aspect of sports participation. Little League Baseball, which has often been accused of exploiting youngsters by subjecting them to excessive competitive pressure, makes a vigorous effort to indoctrinate its volunteer coaches and managers in positive principles of working with boys. In one of its nationally distributed publications, "My Coach Says . . .," it stresses the important role of the coach in shaping the values of young players and serving as a healthy adult model for them. This pamphlet, prepared by Dr. Thomas P. Johnson, a leading psychiatrist and former Little League player, coach, and umpire, deals with the following kinds of concerns:

"How does a coach earn respect from his players?"
"How does he get a boy to care, and to be strongly motivated?"
"How does he make use of praise – and how does he handle criticism?"
"How does he help boys who are unable to make the team?"
"How does he handle such chronic problems as swearing, dissension on the team, back talk, quarreling and fighting, or temper tantrums?"
"How does he deal with special cases, such as the 'I'm not any good' boy, the 'scapegoat,' the 'bragger,' the 'clown,' the 'tattletale,' or the injured youngster?"
"How does he help boys to handle winning streaks, slumps, or the 'big game'?"
"How does he work with parents who interfere, with boys who want to quit the team, or with subs, scrubs and benchwarmers?"

Under each of these headings, it is made clear that the coach's role is to deal positively and constructively with young people, to place winning and losing in perspective, and to help each player gain a sense of respect for himself and his teammates as well as the other important values that should come from sports participation.

Other Leadership Functions

There are a number of other important leadership functions within the broad area of sports leadership. One of these is officiating. While the professional recreation leader or supervisor is not usually expected to serve as an official as a routine responsibility, he may be expected to do so on occasion, or to act as a supervisor to officials. Many municipal departments therefore develop detailed procedures and guidelines for officials who work in their programs. The Milwaukee County Recreation Department, for example, publishes a detailed Officials Guide for individuals employed in their baseball and softball program. This manual gives precise procedures and rules under over 78 headings for umpires, scoremarkers, and scoreboard officials, such as:

Agreements	Playoff Games
Availability of Officials	Protests
Complaints	Rain-Outs
Condition of Field	Rates of Payment
Conduct of Players	Re-Entry Rules
Ejection (Player)	Sign-up Sheets
Field Locations	Suspensions
Forfeits	Tie Games
Foul Balls	Time Limits
Game Rules	Trips to Mound
Injuries	Uniforms
Light Failure	Women and Girls' Rules
Masks	

As a single example, the following guidelines are provided to insure that officials behave correctly at all times:

Officials' Conduct and Actions. As an official, you must realize the importance of your responsibility. You are a representative of this department and must at all times uphold the dignity which your position demands. There is far more to good umpiring than mere knowledge of the rules.

1. *Alertness.* Be alert at all times; follow every play closely.

   a. Keep your eye on the ball.

   b. Be alive on the field. When changing positions, run, don't walk. Hustle!

   c. Be ready! Decisions must be made in a split second. Keep in mind you don't have time to think about the play.

   d. Be emphatic. Make your call in a decisive way that leaves no doubt as to the correctness of your judgment.

   e. Always bear down. Never take anything for granted.

2. *Fraternization.* Officials are not to *socialize* or *fraternize* with partici-

pants or spectators at any time before, during, or just after a game. *Do not hold valuables for participants.*

3. *Personal Control*

   a. Control your temper at all times. Be patient and keep your poise no matter how angry those around you appear.

   b. Never be sarcastic or antagonistic toward players, managers, spectators, or other officials.

   c. Do not follow or charge a player and above all do not point your finger and yell at a player.

   d. Every game is a new game. Do not hold a grudge.

   e. *Control the game* at all times. This means from the time you arrive at the field until the time you leave.

   f. Once a game has been completed and you have no further responsibility, *leave.* Do not stand around and discuss or argue about any decision you made earlier.

4. *Teamwork* on the part of officials is a *must.* Help each other out, whenever and wherever possible. Never make adverse statements about another official.

Guidelines of this type are essential for the successful conduct of sports programs by recreation departments and agencies. Particularly since so much sports leadership is carried on by part-time or seasonal coaches, managers, or instructors — many of whom lack formal preparation in the field — it is essential that full-time personnel have a very clear idea of departmental goals, policies, and recommended procedures.

Suggested Examination Questions or Topics for Student Reports

1. Identify and discuss several key principles of teaching, drawn from this chapter, and illustrate them with your own experience in recreation situations, either as a teacher (leader) or learner (participant).

2. Critically review one of the sets of guidelines for teaching an activity (such as a game, song, dance, or dramatic activity) presented in this chapter. Based on your own experience, add useful hints for successful leadership.

3. Based on your own experience as a leader or participant, what are some of the key problems faced in working with a given age level in one of these areas of activity?

4. Develop an overall program of activity and a set of leadership guidelines within a major area of activity (such as sports or nature) for a large playground or community center.

Suggested Action Assignments for Students

1. In class, present a given activity, such as a game, song or dance, for participation by other class members. The class will then evaluate the effectiveness of your leadership performance.

2. Observe a leader at work in an actual agency program, and carefully record his approach to the group in presenting specific activities. Evaluate this approach, both in terms of teaching methods and according to the guidelines for leadership practices outlined in Chapters One, Two, and Three.

special events leadership

Another important aspect of recreation leadership is the ability to plan, organize, and carry out special events. Such events are useful in providing highlights for a summer playground program, or in maintaining interest and attendance throughout the year. Hjelte and Shivers describe their value:

> The special events at every recreational facility are the occasions that give "spice" to the program. They attract new patrons, discover new talent, provide an incentive to practice, give an everchanging flavor or emphasis to the program, and create opportunity to secure some educational outcomes not otherwise possible. Their variety is endless and limited only by the imagination of the recreationist in charge and the participants who may assist in the planning.[1]

The commonest types of special events are:

Parties or Celebrations.   These include such events as festivals, carnivals, and other novelty events which are carried on with special themes or to celebrate particular occasions.

Exhibitions and Demonstrations.   In these, the emphasis is on showing the work that has been accomplished, either as a display or through direct performance.

Competitions.   These are one-day tournaments, playdays, or field days, in which competing individuals or teams come together in a single location.

Trips and Outings.   These include picnics, group excursions, camping trips, and similar outings.

Each of these types of special events may make use of the various types of recreation activities described in the previous chapter, or may provide culminating experiences which build upon these activities. Therefore, the leader's skill in planning and carrying out special events is important to the conduct of the entire recreation program.

---

[1] George Hjelte and Jay S. Shivers: *Public Administration of Recreational Services.* Philadelphia, Lea and Febiger, 1972, p. 443.

PARTIES AND CELEBRATIONS

These range from small-scale novelty events which may be carried out for a short time on a single playground to large-scale events, such as carnivals or huge community get-togethers that may extend over a day or more. The list of possible themes of such parties and celebrations is almost endless. Some may involve a single novelty contest with prizes, while others combine a number of different events. Here are examples of such programs:

Accuracy Day	Kite Contest
Amateur Show	Mother and Daughter
Barnyard Day	Afternoon
Bicycle Rodeo	Paper Airplane Sailing
Backwards Day	Contest
Bubble Blowing Contest	Pet Fair
Bring a Friend Day	Picnic
Circus Day	Pioneer Party
Clown Day	Pirate Party
Crazy Hat Day	Physical Fitness Day
Caveman Day	Potato Races
Country Fair	Puppet Show
Doll Show	Sand Castle Contest
Dress Up Day	Scavenger Hunt
Family Day	Science Fiction Party
Freckle Contest	Smelling, Spelling or
Funny Relay Day	Tasting Bees
Gay 90's Day	Soap Bubble Blowing
Gypsy Party	Contest
Globetrotters Day	Talent Show
Haunted House	Tongue Twister Contest
Hat Show	Treasure Hunt
Hobo Day Picnic	Turtle Race
Hobby Show	Water Relays
Hula Hoop Contest	Watermelon Bust
Hi-Neighbor Night	

Examples of several novelty parties or contests follow:

Clown Day. Award prizes for different categories of costumes, and for the best two-minute clown act show.

Decorate Anything Day. Children decorate anything—hats, baby carriages, shoes, coats. Prizes are given for the funniest, most unusual, most artistic, and other types of decorations.

Gold Rush Day. Plant rocks of different sizes, painted with gold, around the playground. Then children search for them. Prizes are given for the largest, smallest, lightest, heaviest, and other kinds of gold "nuggets."

Grasshopper Day. Children compete in various types of jumping or hopping contests, such as hop tag, leap frog, broad jumping, or folk dances involving hopping.

Photograph Contest. Children bring in their favorite photographs, mounted for display. Prizes are given for: most unusual, funniest, prettiest, and so on.

In addition to such novelty events, recreation leaders may plan special parties or celebrations built around humorous or unusual themes or at holiday times. Examples of such special parties include:

Halloween	Thanksgiving
Christmas	New Year's Day
Washington's Birthday	St. Valentine's Day
Lincoln's Birthday	St. Patrick's Day
April Fool's Day	Easter
Passover	May Day
Independence Day	Labor Day
Veterans' Day	Columbus Day
Rodeo Party	Hawaiian Luau
Father and Son Party	Mother and Daughter Party
Doll Party	Deck the Tree Party
Space party	Indian Pow Wow Party
Easter Egg Hunt Party	Take a Cruise Party
Olympics party	Beach Party

Party Planning

To carry out any large-scale carnival, celebration, festival, holiday party or other special event, the best procedure is to form a "planning" or "steering" committee that will put together the program, develop a schedule, and make all necessary arrangements. This committee would be responsible for the following arrangements:

Program. This includes the actual planning and scheduling of activities, games, contests, demonstrations, dancing, performances, music, and the awarding of prizes.

Publicity. This involves getting out the word, in the form of press releases, posters, or personal invitations to individuals or organizations that are invited to attend.

Physical Arrangements. This involves obtaining the site, such as a hall, auditorium, school gymnasium, or field (assuming that special arrangements must be made) and also arranging the physical set-up — such as chairs or bleachers, public address system, or other equipment.

Financial Planning. It may be necessary to plan a budget authorizing expenditures and estimating income for the event. This might also include responsibility for ticket sales and for organizing raffles, auctions, bazaars, sales of refreshments, and so on.

Refreshments. In a small party, this might involve having cider and doughnuts, or broiled frankfurters and hamburgers, and hot coffee. At a large-scale celebration, there are often several food counters with varied refreshments. In some cases, dozens of people may bring pot-luck casseroles, desserts, or similar refreshments.

Floor Committees. These individuals might assist in handling the crowd, taking care of emergencies, assisting with automobile parking, and generally making sure that events flow smoothly.

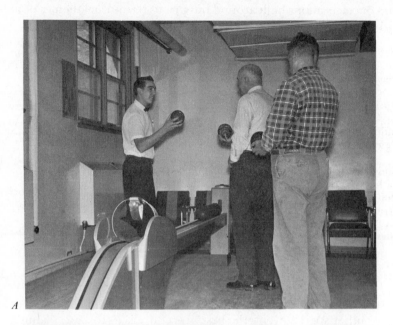

A

B

Leadership in Institutions. Many hospitals, rehabilitation centers and special schools or homes provide extensive recreation activities. In a Weyburn, Saskatchewan, Canada, psychiatric hospital, older patients take part in bowling (*A*) and weaving (*B*). Boy Scout Troop 50 leads the Labor Day Parade at the Rainier School for retarded youngsters at Buckley, Washington (*C*), and patients from the National Institutes of Health Hospital at Bethesda, Maryland, visit a famous Washington, D.C., monument(*D*).

C

D   *Thomas Jay*

Other responsibilities, depending on the situation, might include: (a) getting permits to hold the event; (b) obtaining police coverage; (c) making arrangements for music, guest speakers, or featured entertainers; (d) having a "trouble shooter" for the loudspeaker system; (e) obtaining prizes; (f) soliciting contributions from local merchants; (g) printing a program or journal for the event; (h) making travel arrangements; and (i) setting up first-aid or lost-child booths, portable toilets, or similar facilities. Many communities or organizations that hold large numbers of special events prepare guidelines or simple manuals to make sure the events are carried out efficiently. For example, the Joliet, Illinois park and recreation department publishes a special events manual giving many suggestions for organizing such programs. Under the heading of "Playground Carnival," it offers the following suggestions:

The Playground Carnival is one of the biggest attractions on the playground, where participants and their parents both get involved. You should allow enough time before the carnival in order to construct the booths, make assignments, and finalize all aspects of this special event.

Personnel: The more responsible children should be chosen to handle the booths where money is being exchanged (i.e., prize, food, ticket booths).

Publicity: You should devise ways of advertising on and off your playground. Flyers and posters should be made by the children and posted around the neighborhood and on the playground in the most conspicuous places. Another means of publicizing your event is to organize a minstrel group, with a barker and parade through the neighborhood thus announcing the event.

Finances: The leader should provide the petty cash needed for change-making purposes.

The proceeds derived from the carnival may be utilized as a donation to a charitable institution, for a year end picnic, etc. However, the amount taken in and the use must be reported at the Staff meeting following the event.

Refreshments: For refreshments you may wish to have Kool Aid, lemonade, pop, etc. Parents may be willing to donate cake, cookies, cup cakes, or some other food item. Pop corn, candy bars and ice cream might also be good money makers. Signs should be made telling the prices for each item available.

Clean-Up: When the carnival is over your grounds should be neat and clean. If any refreshments are left make sure they go to the individuals who helped in the clean-up process.

Booths: Your carnival booths may be constructed of cardboard boxes (the larger type, such as refrigerator boxes are best), rope tied to picnic tables, trees, etc. When ropes are used crepe paper streamers should be attached.

Ticket Booth: Have children get tickets for all booths here.

Prize Booth: Prizes can be handled at one booth rather than at each booth. Prize tickets will be given at the game booths and are to be exchanged for prizes at the central booth.

In some situations, such as treatment centers, it is necessary to make careful arrangements with other staff members when planning any special event. For example, the Connecticut State Department of Health, which works closely with activity directors in nursing homes and hospitals throughout the state, publishes a handbook on recreation programs in institutions and extend care facilities. It suggests the following guidelines for party planning:

1. Pre-plan with Administrator for all special events.
2. Check with Director of Nurses regarding patients' condition and activities planned.
3. Arrange with dietary department regarding refreshments.
4. Encourage patients to assist with planning, preparation and leadership.
5. Advise volunteers of specific duties for event.
6. Arrange with housekeeping staff for any special set-up of recreation area.
7. Have camera ready to take snapshots or slides to be shown at a later program.
8. Arrange well in advance of date for staff coverage of event.

EXHIBITIONS AND DEMONSTRATIONS

There are many different kinds of exhibitions and demonstrations which may be sponsored by recreation departments. Typical examples include the following:

Performing Arts: presentations by musical groups, concerts, choral presentations; folk, square, ballet or modern dance performances; readings, one-act plays, or other dramatic works.

Arts and Crafts Exhibits: displays of paintings, drawings, ceramics, leathercraft, metalwork, and other crafts products.

Performance of Sports Skills: featured performances of athletes showing activities such as fencing, gymnastics, figure skating, diving, water ballet, or similar activites.

Animal Shows: pet shows, dog obedience demonstrations, or horse shows of various types are popular events.

Each of these may be approached on a simple basis on a local playground or in a center, or may be presented much more elaborately on a communitywide basis. In some cases, for example, the adult arts and crafts program in a community may hold an art show once a year, presenting high-quality work by dozens of artists and craftsmen for sale to the public. Theater festivals may be held with the assistance of local drama associations, and animal shows with the assistance of organizations which set the standards and provide officials for judging such contests.

Such events boost interest and participation in public recreation programs and enhance community awareness and approval of the department's services. In planning them, the recreation leader or supervisor may assign responsibilities for program development, publicity, and physical arrangements to other staff members or participants, although it is his responsibility in the long run to make sure that these tasks are being carried out properly.

COMPETITIONS AND TOURNAMENTS

Another form of special event is the competition or tournament. This may be carried on over a period of days or weeks in separate locations, or may be concentrated into a single day's play, as in a track-and-field or wrestling competition, or a play day involving a variety of different events. There are several different patterns of tournaments, chiefly in the area of sports, although card and chess tournaments may also be held. Several of the most common arrangements follow:

Individual Best-Score Tournament. In a sport such as golf or riflery, a large number of players compete. After a set number of rounds, the player with the best score is the winner. In such tournaments, there may be a preliminary round to determine eligibility, or eligibility may be determined by previous tournament play.

Team Competitions. There are several types of team competitions, of which the elimination tournament is most common. In this, several teams compete through a series of rounds. When a team loses a game or match it is eliminated, and the team to win the final round is the tournament winner. In another form of team competition, such as track-and-field meets, each team has a number of players who compete in different events as individual contests. The team to amass the highest number of points (through individual team members' scoring) is the winner. This may be done through players competing in different weight classes, as in wrestling, or in different events, as in swimming.

The leader who is responsible for conducting tournaments should be thoroughly familiar with the various types of competitions, such as *elimination* tournaments; *round robin* tournaments; *challenge* tournaments and others. He should also be familiar with the operation of each type of tournament, and with specific details of tournament structures, such as "brackets," "rounds," "drawings," "byes," "seeding," and similar arrangements.

Other Types of Competitions

There are many other types of special events which involve competition, not as a formal tournament, but as a single program offering different events or varied forms of play. Such programs are usually known as field days or play days. They may be planned to offer contests in several different sports or games for different age levels, or may have several events based on a single sport or activity.

For example, the Parks and Recreation Department of Phoenix, Arizona, offers field days in which the following events are provided for different age classes:

Table tennis (singles and doubles)	Mock track meet (novelty events)
Checkers and chinese checkers	Softball throw for accuracy
Badminton	Jacks
Soccer ball kick for accuracy	Home run derby
Base running against time	Hopscotch
	Horseshoes

Sometimes, several different events may be developed around a single sport, such as the Baseball or Softball Field Days sponsored by the Chicago Park District. These involve competitions in the following events for both baseball and softball: (a) throw for distance; (b) fungo hit for distance; (c) circling the bases for time; and (d) throwing the ball around the bases relay, for teams of four players. Contestants are divided into two age classes (11 and under, and 12 to 14), and boys take part in both baseball and softball competitions, while girls engage only in softball.

Another type of competition is the "Bicycle Rodeo." Many communities sponsor such events. Normally, about six or eight different events would be selected, and competition would be organized on several age or grade levels. Examples of such events may be found in a games manual published by the Stockton, California, Department of Parks and Recreation:

Wheels Day—Bike Rodeo

Instruction: you may have to adapt some bike events to your individual playground areas. Keep safety factors for both participants and pedestrians in mind.

1. *Steering Test:*   Have participant ride at comfortable speed for 30 feet between parallel lines 4 inches apart without getting onto or over lines. This will be easiest to judge if you place pairs of blocks, etc., on sidelines at 6 ft. intervals. Deduct 5 points from 100 if rider touches a line, 10 if he goes outside a line and 15 if he loses control of his bike.

2. *Circle Riding:*   Mark two concentric circles with diameters of 16 feet and 12 feet to make a circular path two feet wide. Have each participant stay within the path while riding 4 times around. Deduct 5 points from 100 for hitting a line, 10 for getting outside patch, 15 for losing control.

3. *Balancing at Slow Speed:*   Make a lane 3 feet wide and 50 feet long. Rider must go slowly enough to take at least 30 seconds to complete the distance without losing his balance.

4. *Maneuvering:*   Lay out a weaving type of course with boxes, blocks, etc., at twenty-five feet interval spacing in a straight line. This would require 7 markers to set up a distance of 150 feet. Participant may ride at comfortable speed weaving to pass on alternate sides from marker to marker.

Deduct 5 points from 100 for touching any marker, or 10 points if he loses control of bike.

5. *Bicycle Kick Ball Race:* Set up on 100 yard distance if possible with riders well spaced out across field. Each rider will have a kickball placed 10 yards in front of him at starting line. On time signal, the riders mount and start dribbling (must impel ball with foot only) down the field to finish line.

Guidelines for Organizing Event

In organizing a play day of this type, the following assignments must be carried out successfully: (a) planning the event; (b) obtaining a location, such as a large school parking area, which provides a smooth, safe surface; (c) publicizing the program; (d) signing up contestants (often this is done through specific grade levels in the public schools); (e) pre-registering contestants; (f) obtaining volunteer teenage or adult leaders to help run the events; (g) obtaining needed materials, such as measuring tape, chalk or flour, wooden blocks, cans or milk cartons for markers, loudspeaker equipment, certificates or ribbons; (h) organizing the event on the given day, with scorers and officials running the individual events so contestants can rotate from area to area; (i) arranging places for spectators that will be safe and will not interfere with the players; and (j) awarding prizes and preparing news releases for publicity coverage.

In scheduling special events, it is helpful to work out a master calendar well in advance to insure that participants are given basic instruction in appropriate activity areas and to permit coordination of a department's specialists and other resources. To illustrate, the Atlanta, Georgia, Department of Parks and Recreation has each playground district prepare an advance schedule of special events before the summer begins. Playgrounds within the district then structure their programs based on this master schedule. A typical schedule for the Southwest district of Atlanta during a recent summer follows:

Week of:	*Tournaments and Contests*	*Weekly Themes*
June 11	Checkers/Marbles Contests	Ecology Week
June 18	Carrom Tournament	International Week
June 25	Hula Hoop/Frisbee	Bicycle Week
July 2	Table Soccer Contest	Space Week
July 9	Horseshoe Contest	Nature Week
July 16	Basketball Free Throw Contest	Hobo Week
July 23	Tennis Tournament	Hawaiian Week
July 30	Table Tennis Tournament	Down on the Farm Week
Aug. 6	Cultural Arts Festival	Fantasy Week

The Phoenix, Arizona, Department of Parks and Recreation also outlines a week-by-week series of program ideas and playground themes. It suggests that special events be featured on Tuesday afternoons, with a postponement date on Wednesdays in case of bad weather. Tournaments and contests should be scheduled on Thursdays, with Fridays as postponement days. Other activities, such as ball games, drama, dance, crafts, story telling, nature activities, hikes and quiet games, would be fitted into the schedule at regular times on other days, and during the mornings and late afternoons. A sample schedule follows:

Suggested Ten-Week Program, Phoenix, Arizona

Week	Designation	Feature Special Event	Tournament or Contest
1	Organization–Get acquainted–Safety on the Playground	Learn use of equipment; Clean-up; Treasure Hunt	Checkers Rope Jumping
2	Learn to Swim Week	Instruction–swimming & water safety. Bicycle Club hike	Horseshoes Bean Bag Toss
3	Games of Low Organization	Parade on Wheels Bicycle Rodeo Band Concert	Paddle tennis Hand tennis Jackstones
4	Independence Week	Celebrate July 4th Pet Show Hobby Show Camera & Movie Exhibits	Box Hockey Pick-Up-Sticks
5	Sports Week	Track & Field Day Progressive Game Day Tennis Instruction Water Carnival	Bull Board Scoop
6	Nature Week	Nature games-crafts Nature hike Activity with other playgrounds	Deck tennis Hopscotch
7	Know Your Community	Trips to historical spots, State Park. Visit industry Radio programs	Clock golf Bubble blowing
8	Arts & Crafts Week	Exhibit of crafts made on playground Sidewalk art show Flower show	Table Tennis Puzzles
9	Hobby Week	Hobby Show Model Train-all types Band Concert	Peteca Yo-Yo
10	All Nations Celebration	City-wide Playground Closing Event Games from other lands Songs and dances of other lands Water Show	Tetherball Mumblety-Peg

TRIPS AND OUTINGS

A final category of special events consists of trips and outings. These may involve very brief half-day trips to neighborhood parks, beaches, or pools, or outings to nearby museums or sites of special interest. Transportation may be on foot, with volunteer automobile drivers, or by bus. Outings may also include more elaborate trips over longer distances and periods of time, using chartered forms of transportation. Some communities schedule weekly trips for all the children on city playgrounds, visiting places of interest on a regular day each week. Organizations serving adults, such as industrial recreation departments or Golden Age clubs, sometimes schedule charter flights and vacation tours to scenic destinations.

Trips provide a "break" from the routine, and offer novelty, excitement, and the opportunity for new experience. They *must,* however, be carefully planned and supervised. A poorly organized trip or outing can be a disaster. Planning should include the following important elements:

1. Selecting a destination, and making arrangement with individuals to receive those making the trip.

2. Publicizing the outing, registering those who will go, and obtaining parental permission slips (in the case of trips for children and youth).

3. Making arrangements for transportation, and collecting fees, if necessary.

4. Preparing those who are about to go on the trip with necessary details (time, place, schedule, appropriate clothing, other information).

5. Providing adequate supervision while on the trip, including safety practices and activities for the group to carry on while traveling.

6. Planning for supervision while at the destination, particularly if the group is a large one and is breaking up into smaller units.

7. Gathering the group together and making the return trip home.

8. Evaluating the trip, basing other recreation activities on it, and sending notes of appreciation to those who have assisted or cooperated with the leaders.

Guidelines for Trips—New Haven, Connecticut

Many agencies develop detailed guidelines for the conduct of trips and outings. The following set of suggestions is drawn from the Trip Planning Manual published by the New Haven, Connecticut, Department of Parks and Recreation.

Pre-Planning. Trips should not be extemporaneous, but carefully planned. Planning should be done well in advance of the actual date. If making a trip to a state or national park, you should inquire as to what facilities are available to you, the best dates to bring a large group, possible admission fees, and the length of time the trip will take. Travel time should always be estimated conservatively, allowing for possible road construction, rush hour traffic, or other slowdowns.

Prepare Group in Advance.   Have all playground directors give children detailed information about the trip, including what the park or amusement center has to offer. If there are charges for special activities, let them know this. Make sure that they have appropriate clothing, swim suits, or sports equipment.

Register Participants.   After this has been done, set a date for the trip, publicize the event, and register those who will be going. Have permission slips signed by parents, and include the following information: (a) the sponsoring agency; (b) the destination; (c) date; (d) time of departure; (e) time of return; and (f) supervisor in charge of trip. The permission slip should have the parents' telephone numbers so they can be reached in case of an emergency.

Departure and Return.   Most trips are made by bus. The supervisor in charge should have a roster with the name of every child on the bus before departure; the roster should agree with the permission slips. Before departing, children should be told what group they will be with, and what staff member will be responsible for them. The supervisor should let staff members know the exact time they must have their groups back at the designated meeting place for the trip home.

When the group is ready for the bus trip home, the supervisor should check each child's name against the roster before permitting him to enter the bus. When all names have been accounted for, the bus may leave on the return trip. If any child is missing, the staff member responsible for that child should search for him. Never permit other children to look for lost or late children. You should delay the bus until a missing child is located, although it may be necessary to start the trip back after an hour has passed. In this case, the staff member responsible for the child remains behind. Do not hesitate to call on the police for assistance. With proper staff coverage, children should not be lost for more than a brief time.

Other Trip Guidelines

Particularly when a trip is being made to a state park or other large park area, it is necessary to make arrangements with the host agency, and to observe rules they may set up. For example, the Atlanta, Georgia, Department of Parks and Recreation has established the following regulations for playground bus trips to Georgia state parks:

1.   The State Park Superintendent will be notified by the central office of the Atlanta Parks and Recreation Department when a trip is scheduled to his park.

2.   Trips are scheduled for ages five to 15 years. Children who do not meet the age classification will not be permitted to board the bus. Parental permission slips must be obtained for all children going on a trip.

3. There must be one leader for every ten children. The leader must stay with his group at all times during the trip. Each group should be limited to one bus load or its equivalent.

4. Leaders must have a planned program of games and activities and carry all necessary equipment with them on the bus. They will be expected to have the group under control at all times while in the park.

5. Group leaders must be easily identified, and should introduce themselves to the Park Superintendent immediately upon arrival.

6. Atlanta Parks and Recreation pays established fees (admission, parking, etc.), but does not pay individual swimming admissions fees.

7. Swimmers must wear swimming suits rather than cut-off jeans, whenever possible.

8. Groups will not be allowed in family camping or cottage areas, may not rent or otherwise use park boats, and must picnic only in designated picnic areas.

9. Groups must restrict their trips to weekdays only, and must limit their stay at parks to a maximum of four hours.

10. Parks which provide planned programs given by their Naturalists will do so only if the request is made two days in advance of group visit.

These rules, which are based in part upon policies established by the State Park system, illustrate the need for careful controls and preparation in all trips and outing.

Suggested Examination Questions or Topics for Student Reports

1. Describe the major types of special events found in community recreation, and indicate their values in enriching the total program.
2. Select one major type of special event, such as a carnival, play day, festival or community celebration. Outline a set of guidelines for developing such a program, indicating the kinds of assistance you might need from volunteers and other community organizations.
3. Prepare a description of several different types of tournaments which are most commonly used in sports or other forms of competition. Describe the types of sports or games or circumstances of participation that are suited for each kind of tournament.
4. Trips and outings are extremely useful recreation program elements. What are the major problems to be faced in organizing such events, and what are the solutions to these problems?

Suggested Action Assignments for Students

1. Investigate a variety of possible locations to which recreation agencies in your community might plan trips and outings. Select the best of

these, and prepare a brochure or manual describing them and such elements as distance, travel time, activities and special features, costs, restrictions, or other factors.

2. Plan and carry out an outing or other major event, as a class, for participants in a community agency, or as a special project for other students in your college. Evaluate this assignment thoroughly when it has been completed.

other leadership functions

Recreation leadership involves considerably more than simply teaching or directing activities. In addition, the leader must carry out a variety of other important interpersonal or managerial tasks if his or her program is to go smoothly.

This chapter describes a number of these additional leadership functions, and presents guidelines for carrying them out effectively. They include such tasks as planning and carrying out programs, developing effective public relations and community involvement, maintaining control of participants' behavior, and practicing careful, thorough safety and accident procedures.

Such responsibilities are found not only in recreation and park department but in other types of social or therapeutic agencies as well. However, for purposes of simplification, this chapter deals only with two basic types of settings: playgrounds and community center programs, chiefly serving children and youth, that are sponsored by public recreation and park departments.

OVERALL PROGRAM LEADERSHIP
RESPONSIBILITY

The responsibilities of recreation leaders are outlined in many departmental manuals. For example, the Stockton, California, Recreation and Park Department Manual points out that leaders are expected to function in the following ways:

As an Organizer. Make a survey of your playground and neighborhood to find out what it has and what it needs. Organize and develop such activities as will . . . produce the best physical, mental and moral results.

As a Leader. Teach games, both old and new; direct club organizations and promote indoor and outdoor activities as outlined by the supervisors and in accordance with the policies of the Department.

As a Host.   Encourage all persons attending the playground or center to enter into the various activities . . .

As a Coach.   Develop teams and competitive events of all kinds, giving instructions when necessary . . .

As a Teacher.   Promote literature and study clubs, dramatics, hand work, and nature lore . . .

As an Advertiser.   Provide a bulletin board. Plan a program at least one day ahead. See that all announcements are attractively displayed . . .

As a Clerk.   See that all reports are submitted *on time* to the main office . . .

As a First-Aider.   Apply first aid *only* in emergency. Know the accident procedure completely and thoroughly.

As an Authority.   Supervise carefully lavatories and *out-of-the-way* places. Do not permit marking on walls of buildings or fences. Eliminate all smoking, swearing, rowdyism and gambling, etc . . .

As a Friend.   One of your most important jobs as a leader is to be a friend to all who participate on your playground . . .

A similar but somewhat more imaginative list, published by the Oakland, California, Recreation Department, tells the leader that he is the "ten most-wanted people." It tells him that he is, among other things, "an artist — with people, instead of paint," "a friend — to everyone, big or little," "a builder — of health and character," "a pioneer — in trying out new ideas," "a reformer — of bad habits or poor sportsmanship," and "a believer — in the best of everyone." This list emphasizes the social role of the recreation leader, particularly in terms of working constructively with young people in playgrounds and community centers.

In organizing and carrying out the overall playground or community center program, the leader should follow a number of general guidelines or principles. First, he should provide a wide range of activities, including sports and games, creative activities, and hobby and social pastimes. These should be suited for both sexes and as broad an age range as possible. Many playgrounds and community centers serve neighborhood populations that run the gamut from pre-schoolers to senior citizens. The leader should seek to alternate strenuous with quiet activities, team games with individual play, and competitive with cooperative games and projects.

The program should be planned in advance for each day as part of an overall schedule of regular events and program features organized at the beginning of the summer. However, the leader should not hesitate to change this plan when special circumstances demand it. Weather should be considered in outlining the program schedule, with active sports planned for the morning or late afternoon and quiet activities held during the warmer part of the day. The leader should also consider the following suggestions:

Offer a diversified program, including both old and new activities. *Plan* special events at regular intervals to heighten interest and participation. These should occur at least once a week at a time most convenient to all, and whenever possible should be closely correlated with routine program activities. *Strive* for maximum participation in such special events; they are not just for highly skilled "champions" but for *all* children or youth on the playground. *Plan* a progressive program, with culminating activities at the end of units, tournaments in various sports, and major playground events, such as festivals or carnivals, at the end of the summer.

Encourage informal, self-organized activity by providing definite times when no specific activities are scheduled but when play equipment is available. *Arrange* time periods so that if projects or activities are not completed within scheduled times, they may be carried over without interfering with the overall program. The leader's time should be divided fairly between different age groups, boys and girls, and different types of activity.

In planning program activities, all those concerned (including recreation aides or assistants, volunteers, and the participants themselves) should be involved. Always *follow through* on all advertised plans or special features. If you are unable to do it yourself, make sure that another leader takes over responsibility for it. If it is absolutely necessary to cancel an announced activity or special event, make sure that everyone knows about it. It reduces interest to postpone events or fail to live up to promised program plans.

For specific examples of program schedules, the reader should consult other textbooks. This text is primarily concerned with the process of leadership rather than with program development.

PUBLIC AND COMMUNITY RELATIONS

The recreation leader plays an important role in promoting effective public and community relations. In any recreation department or agency, public relations are essential for the following reasons: (a) to create a favorable public image of the department and to encourage positive official or legislative support; (b) to encourage maximum attendance at regular programs and special events; (c) to enlist volunteers to help in the program; (d) to overcome public misconceptions or distortions about the program; and (e) to develop a public constituency that will support budget requests for facilities, staff, equipment, or materials, or that will help the department attack its operational problems most successfully.

Public relations must not be left to chance. Individuals skilled in this field should be given the responsibility for arranging major public relations events, such as interviews, tours, radio or television programs, and for preparing newspaper releases, magazine articles, reports, brochures, and other publicity materials. However, *all* public relations cannot be carried on effectively by central office specialists. Instead, they must also be the direct responsibility of recreation leaders on the grass roots level, in community centers or playgrounds.

How do recreation leaders carry out this important assignment? This

A

B

Bill Cogan

Other Programs for the Disabled. Millions of disabled participants are served in community-based or therapeutic camping programs. In Edmonton, Canada, "co-ed" wheelchair basketball provides excitement (*A*). At the Lake Merced summer camp sponsored by the San Francisco Recreation Center for the Handicapped, young campers participate in flag ceremonies (*B*), and learn to fish (*C*). Wheelchair bowlers take part in a program sponsored by the Cincinnati, Ohio, United Cerebral Palsy Association (*D*). Children enjoy a cook-out with their counselors at the Kentucky Easter Seal Society's Camp Kysoc (*E*), and, in a reverse of the usual situation, a Rochester, Minnesota, coach in a wheelchair teaches basic hockey skills (*F*).

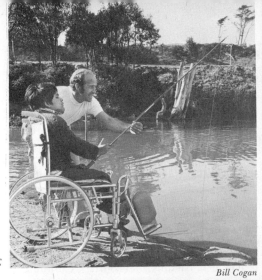

C

D

E

F

is done essentially in two ways: (a) through personal relationships; and (b) through use of the formal media of public relations.

Personal Relationships

All recreation leaders should seek to do the following in dealing with the public:

1. Acquaint themselves with the neighborhood as fully as possible—its streets, buildings, businesses, churches, and other organizations. Whenever possible, chat with parents and program participants. Special efforts should be made to help each participant feel that he or she is wanted in the program, and that there is a helpful, friendly, and courteous attitude on the part of all staff members.
2. When there are requests or problems, treat them with sincere interest and respect. Each problem should be given prompt attention and handling. Policies should be explained fully and tactfully when they are challenged. Use all available information or resources to solve problems or meet requests of residents.
3. Set a positive image for the public. Neat appearance and responsible conduct on the part of recreation and park employees will help give neighborhood residents a favorable view of the department. Facilities and equipment should also be maintained in the best possible condition. If department morale is high and recreation workers project a strong, optimistic view of their program, public attitudes will reflect this.

Use of Public Relations Media

In addition, it is necessary for recreation leaders to take specific steps to bring information to the public. This may be done through the use of traditional publicity media—some of which the recreation leader may send out or initiate himself (subject to departmental policy), and some of which come from the central administrative office. These include:

Newspapers. Recreation leaders should submit, through regular departmental channels, suggestions for news releases or photographs which would make good publicity. They should keep the central office accurately advised of all games, tournaments, and special events, with emphasis on good "human interest" stories. Guidelines for preparing newspaper copy include:

a. Type all stories double-spaced.
b. Identify the name and address of the playground or center at the top of the sheet, along with the date of the release.
c. Keep stories brief, colorful, and interesting.
d. Include the main facts of the story in the "lead," or first paragraph.
e. Keep a carbon copy of all stories for the file.
f. Know newspaper release deadlines and observe them.
g. When reporters are sent to cover stories, have accurate lists of partici-

pants, program events, and other information that will help them prepare copy.

Magazine Articles. These are more difficult to prepare and not as timely in their impact as newspaper stories. However, they can be used to reach specialized audiences, either through magazines that serve a particular age group or region, or through those concerned with a particular hobby or activity.

Brochures, Leaflets, and Newsletters. Most recreation and park departments prepare brochures advertising seasonal programs on a citywide basis. However, the local playground or community center leader should also prepare and publish such printed materials, advertising his own program or special events.

Bulletin Boards and Posters. These should be used to display topical and interesting announcements. In addition to locating them on the recreation department's facilities, posters may be placed in stores, schools, churches, and other locations.

Audiovisual Materials. Many departments prepare color slides and films depicting department activities, facilities, and programs. These may be used for presentations in schools, Parent-Teacher Associations, local service clubs, and similar organizations to promote recreation programs.

Exhibits and Displays. Demonstrations of sports, dance, drama or music, as well as displays of arts and crafts, nature projects, and similar program activities offer an excellent means of publicizing a recreation department.

Tours and Open Houses. These are particularly useful in getting publicity for new facilities or unusual programs. Generally, a department arranges an interesting series of events or presentations, provides transportation, and invites newspaper reporters (including reporters from schools and colleges nearby), as well as television reporters or news editors.

Although he may not be able to carry through on all such public relations projects himself, the recreation leader is the *key* contact person with the public at large, and should be in a position of constantly feeding publicity ideas and program suggestions to those who do direct public relations.

Community Relations

The playground or community center recreation leader should consult frequently with school principals, heads of civic associations and service clubs, various committees or planning groups, and with residents of all ages and backgrounds. He should also be thoroughly familiar with other community agencies, such as the Y.M.C.A. or Y.W.C.A., Boy Scouts and Girl Scouts, Boys' Clubs, or the operators of private recreation facilities, such as commercial bowling alleys, pools, or skating rinks. Whenever possible, he should cooperate closely with such agencies in sharing facilities, coordinating schedules, planning to meet community needs, and attacking social problems.

One of the most effective ways in which recreation leaders can develop constructive community relations is by forming neighborhood advisory councils. Such councils are groups of citizens, both adults and youths, who are sincerely interested in the recreation program and willing to assist it. Although they have no legal status as boards and commissions do, local advisory councils can be invaluable in determining the leisure needs and interests of the community, and interpreting these to playground or community center directors. They are helpful in advising the recreation staff on needed policies, and in assisting in the development of programs. Similarly, they serve as a two-way communication link by helping to inform neighborhood residents about the objectives of the program and publicizing specific activities and events. When favorable testimony is needed before city councils or governmental officials, representatives of local advisory councils can play an important role. Finally, they can be extremely helpful in providing volunteer assistance or in carrying on fund-raising to finance special projects or purchase needed equipment that is not included in the regular budget.

Advisory councils may be selected in a number of ways. In some communities, there is a formal election process, while in others the procedure is to ask a number of neighborhood organizations or clubs to delegate representatives. In others, members are simply informally invited by the recreation leader or supervisor to join the council. The quality of the members, and their enthusiasm and willingness to work is more important than the way in which they are selected.

Generally, advisory councils consist of between eight and twelve persons who have a genuine interest in the program and who represent a cross-section of the neighborhood or community. Members need not be "key" people in the community; in fact it is often better to avoid such persons because they tend not to have enough time to give to the recreation council. While political experience and contacts are helpful, they are not essential. The most important elements are leadership ability, good judgment, and willingness to give time to the council's work.

It is up to the recreation leader or supervisor to work closely with such councils, assisting them in their work and seeking advice and help from them. Skill in community relations is one of the most important attributes a leader can have; it involves a willingness to listen, respect for the views of others, and the ability to serve as an intermediary between the formal structure of the recreation and park agency and the people it serves.

DISCIPLINE AND CONTROL FUNCTIONS

An extremely important area of recreation leadership responsibility today relates to the supervision of participants' behavior and the handling of discipline problems. In any recreation situation involving youth, a certain number of participants are likely to be mischievous, destructive, or hostile. However, in recent years this problem has grown in severity. The increase in juvenile delinquency and antisocial gang activity has been accompanied in many communities by drug abuse and interracial hostility among young people.

Any recreation facility should provide a safe and wholesome atmosphere for young people. There must therefore be certain rules of behavior which protect the safety and security of staff members and participants, and prevent vandalism, destruction, theft, or physical aggression. In general, such rules are directed at preventing or controlling the following kinds of misbehavior: smoking or drinking in the playground or community center, fighting or excessive horseplay, carrying or threatening others with weapons, destruction or defacement of property, profanity, or the use of liquor or drugs.

How should the recreation leader deal with the problem of maintaining discipline? Essentially, there are two kinds of approaches. The first consists of categorizing certain forms of unacceptable behavior, and outlining the specific steps that must be taken in preventing them, or punishing those responsible for them. The other approach involves understanding the cause of misbehavior, and developing a human relations philosophy that is basically preventative rather than punitive.

Disciplinary Guidelines

Most recreation and park departments provide specific guidelines for their staff members that outline procedures to be followed in case of violation of department rules. For example, the Oklahoma City, Oklahoma, Parks and Recreation Department makes clear that leaders must interpret departmental policies or city ordinances to participants on playgrounds or in community centers. The following steps are to be taken in the case of serious violation of rules:

1. One recourse in case of infraction of rules is dismissal from the playground. Leaders may not handle patrons with physical force.

2. Before dismissing a patron from the grounds be sure that he knew the rules. If he did not, he should be given a chance to prove himself.

3. The period of suspension should be based on the severity of the infraction of the rule. One effective plan is not to impose a specific length of time but require that the patron return with parent or guardian when he thinks that he is ready and have a conference with recreation staff before reinstatement.

4. The senior leader in charge should call the parents or guardian of all patrons suspended and outline reasons and ask for cooperation.

In Topeka, Kansas:

Directors or managers of facilities under the jurisdiction of the Recreation Commission shall have the authority to suspend any person who violates the rules and regulations of the said facility for a period of not more than three activity days. Supervisors shall have the authority to suspend an individual for a period not to exceed ten days. Further banishment from the facilities shall be authorized by the Recreation Commission.

In some cases, specific departmental procedures are outlined to deal with special types of problems. For example, the Hollywood, Florida, Parks and Recreation Department has a detailed set of guidelines dealing with problems of smoking, drinking, and drug abuse. It makes clear that all staff members are expected to seek out and eliminate drug abusers from recreation programs. The following guidelines suggest actions that leaders may take:

1. Suspension from area, from one night to an indefinite period, as immediate action. Use your own judgment in dealing with each individual infraction.

2. Request those believed to be under drug influence to leave area immediately with friends, if one of friends is "straight." Keep girls in office until they can be released safely.

3. Call parents if they will not, or cannot leave. It is inadvisable to call parents and accuse youth of using drugs. Tell parent the child is acting ill and needs attention.

4. Do not hesitate to call police should any trouble occur.

5. If you believe someone is pushing drugs but cannot prove it, you should suspend him from the area for another valid cause. Immediately make a report of suspicions to office.

6. No unauthorized selling of *any* product on recreation facilities is permitted.

7. If definite selling of narcotics is noticed, call police immediately and make reports.

8. Take license number of any car you suspect of being a stakeout for selling drugs.

9. Watch for unusual signals (signs with thumb or feet, etc.). These may be signals to pass drugs or alcohol.

10. All reports to police and leader's reports should be filled out (see Incident Report) in duplicate. Keep one and send one to office.

Still other departments may outline a range of possible offenses or infractions and develop procedures for dealing with each level of antisocial behavior. For example, the Recreation Department of the City of Oakland, California, has developed a manual describing three levels of problems: minor, serious, and extremely serious. These are described as follows: (a) *minor* offenses are routine behaviors which are socially unacceptable or in violation of center or playground safety rules, such as scuffling, fighting, unauthorized attempts to enter facilities, destruction of property, or disturbing organized programs; (b) *serious* offenses are technically misdemeanors, such as using a gun or other weapon, morals offenses, being under the influence of intoxicants, or refusing to leave the premises for violation of Recreation Commission regulations; and (c) *very serious* offenses involve more hazardous control situations, such as potential riots, rumbles, or major incidents. The appropriate measures that should be taken for each level of difficulty are clearly outlined for recreation leaders.

HUMAN RELATIONS APPROACH TO DISCIPLINE

A second major approach to the problem of controlling antisocial behavior places emphasis on understanding the causes of the problem and attempting to deal with them constructively. First, leaders are encouraged to understand the wide variety of children and youth they must deal with, including those who are relatively happy and well adjusted as well as those who are hard to reach or difficult to handle. They must understand that many children come from family backgrounds that have not nurtured them properly, and so are hostile, aggressive, unsure of themselves, and insecure with others. They may also have physical or mental disabilities that have hampered their social development.

While it may be difficult to accept children who are frequently hostile or disruptive, the recreation leader must be patient in working with such youngsters, and should never ignore or reject them. Whenever possible, he must show personal interest and concern for them and be generous with his smiles, words, time, and encouragement. Rules should be simple and clear, and should be consistently enforced. Children should have a voice in the making of rules, and should know why it is necessary to have them, and why certain forms of behavior are undesirable.

Staff members are encouraged to prevent antisocial behavior wherever possible by building a favorable atmosphere of participation and developing constructive relationships with participants. The leader who is consistent and fair, who knows individual children or youth well, who identifies and works with natural leaders in youth groups, and who is alert to the signs of unrest or difficulty, will usually succeed in averting serious behavior problems. Leaders must recognize that expulsion from a playground does not really solve the problem for an individual child. Every effort should be made to keep him active within the program, and to work constructively with him.

In most communities, the level of antisocial activity on playgrounds or in community centers can be tolerated and worked with. Particularly if the recreation leader is able to call upon his district supervisor for assistance when necessary, and to get help from the police (some police departments maintain juvenile divisions that handle such matters), the problem is not excessive.

However, under some circumstances, discipline becomes a much more difficult task. This is true most often in the poorest areas of large cities, where, in crowded and run-down slum neighborhoods, teenage gangs and social pathology of all kinds tend to flourish. It is not at all uncommon to have delinquent groups of youth who dominate playgrounds or small parks and prevent others from using them. If a leader attempts to oust them, they will often retaliate physically.

Some small parks or playgrounds are so dominated by derelicts or alcoholics that parents fear sending their young children into them. In some community centers, older youth or adults sell drugs and "shoot up," again making such settings unsuitable for constructive recreation participation. How does the recreation leader handle such situations? The answer is that he cannot handle them by himself any more than he can change the total social situation of poverty and deprivation. Physical enforcement of regulations should not be his responsibility, just as it would not be expected of bank tellers that they engage in pitched gun battles with hold-up men.

Instead, the recreation leader should receive assistance from other municipal departments, such as youth boards or drug service agencies, in working with such situations. In addition, he should receive consistent, strong police protection and support if he is to maintain his facility as a viable setting for community recreation.

SAFETY PROCEDURES AND ACCIDENT PREVENTION

In any well-organized recreation program, safety and accident prevention are important responsibilities of all leaders and supervisors. Conscientious leaders should be aware of the dangers that may exist in play areas where children and youth participate in active games or use varied types of equipment.

General Safety Principles

1. Safety is a basic consideration in playground and pool operation, and well-managed recreation facilities must provide safe places to play.

2. *All* accidents have causes, and every effort should be made to prevent them before they can occur.

3. Professional recreation personnel should be safety-conscious, and should instill this attitude in other leaders, volunteers, and participants.

4. All recreation staff members should know their own responsibility and degree of liability with respect to accidents, and also understand the department's liability.

5. All recreation staff members should know the procedures for handling accidents and injuries. These procedures should be outlined in staff meetings or orientation sessions, and should be printed in departmental leadership manuals.

6. Leaders should be trained in basic first aid techniques, and should be carefully informed of departmental policy about using these in case of

accidents. Well-stocked first aid kits should be kept at all recreation facilities.

Specific Safety Practices

These general principles should be supported by a number of procedures which minimize the possibility of accidents occurring. These include the following:

1. Prepare, post, and enforce simple rules of safety for your playground or other facility.

   a. Prohibit climbing on fences, buildings, or other structures not intended for this purpose.

   b. Prohibit bicycle riding on the playground, and restrict the use of skateboards, scooters, roller skates, jump ropes, and similar equipment to specific areas.

   c. Prohibit climbing on apparatus when wet and slippery.

   d. Prohibit rough-housing, unnecessary pushing, or throwing of sticks, stones, or other objects.

2. Inspect all equipment, grounds, and facilities daily, and carry out the following measures:

   a. If any piece of equipment or apparatus is not in working condition, place it "out-of-order," and notify the maintenance department immediately.

   b. Keep play areas and sanitary facilities clean at all times.

   c. Keep all pointed or sharp-edged tools out of reach when they are not in use.

   d. Restrict play activities in areas where surfaces are slippery or not suitable for use.

   e. Keep animals off grounds, except for organized playground activities, such as pet shows.

   f. Establish "safety zones" around areas such as swings, giant strides, or merry-go-rounds, so children can move past them safely.

   g. Locate active games involving batted or kicked balls in areas where they will not interfere with or endanger "tot" playgrounds or other quiet activities.

   h. Generally, keep play areas free of congestion.

3. In carrying on active games, sports, gymnastics, or similar activities, observe the following guidelines:

   a. See to it that children have proper conditioning or preparation before engaging in strenuous activity.

   b. Require physical examinations before organized competition.

   c. Require children to have suitable equipment and uniforms (such as batting helmets in baseball) for specific activities.

d. Exclude children who are recognizably ill from activity, and stop activities before fatigue sets in.

e. Gear activities to the physical capabilities and skill level of groups.

4. Make sure that apparatus is used correctly at all times. Children should be taught its proper use, and should be carefully supervised by leaders. Apparatus should be restricted to the particular age group it is intended to serve. Children should learn to take turns in use of equipment, and should not be permitted to engage in speed contests on equipment.

It is a generally accepted principle that municipalities conducting playgrounds or other recreation programs, and the individuals in charge of programs and facilities, are not liable for damages in case of accident unless negligence can be proved or equipment was known to be defective. Therefore, if recreation leaders take careful precautions to assure safe conditions for play, they should be reasonably assured that they will not be liable if accidents occur. However, it is essential that they be familiar with the necessary steps to be taken in case of accidents or other emergencies – and that they follow these exactly, both to assure proper care of injured persons and to avoid possible post-accident liability.

There is no single set of prescribed procedures which all public recreation and park departments follow in the event of accident. However, most departments require their employees to carry out the following steps:

Minor Injury.   Most accidents on the playground will be of a minor nature. Within prescribed limitations (see page 250), the leader should apply first aid as needed, following procedures outlined by the National American Red Cross or departmental first aid guidelines. It is then customary to send the child home or have a parent or another responsible relative call for him.

Major Injury.   In the event of a more serious accident, or an injury which the recreation leader feels *may* be more serious, the following steps should be taken:

1. Make the injured person as comfortable as possible, covering him to keep him warm. Do *not* move him, since this may aggravate the injury.

2. In the event of severe bleeding or stoppage of breathing, apply emergency first aid measures. Do not apply any other treatment; do not probe injuries, test the movement of limbs, or attempt to set fractures.

3. Immediately call for appropriate medical assistance if the injury appears to be of an emergency nature:

a. In some departments, the procedure is to call the police or sheriff's office directly, to have them call for an ambulance.

b. In other departments, the procedure is to call a special police emergency squad which normally transports individuals to hospitals after giving expert first aid.

c. In other situations, the recreation leader must call the ambulance directly.

4. Call parents or guardians immediately. In some departmental guidelines it is required that this be done *before* sending for medical assistance, to have them make needed decisions. If the injury is extremely severe, or if it is not possible to contact parents, the recreation leader must send for an ambulance first.

5. Notify the recreation department of the accident, and fill out a report form, giving full details of the incident. Meanwhile, other participants should be encouraged to continue with the recreation program.

Other Guidelines. Most departments stipulate that their employees should follow these procedures when injuries of any sort occur, chiefly to protect the individual leader and the department in the event of a possible lawsuit:

1. In the event of serious injury, be sure to secure signed statements from all witnesses, including other employees. This may be done by a departmental supervisor.

2. The playground leader must not use his own car, or that of any other private person, to transport an injured person to a doctor or hospital.

3. Under no circumstances should the recreation leader discuss or promise financial reimbursement or municipal liability in the event of an accident; he should not discuss the accident with anyone other than appropriate department or municipal officials.

4. If the playground leader gives parents or relatives any information regarding doctors, clinics, or hospitals where an injured person may be treated, he must state clearly that the department has no facilities or financial provision for paying for medical care.

5. The person in charge of the facility, the staff member in whose program the accident occurred, and any other staff member who witnessed the accident should remain at the location until medical help has come and investigating officers have gathered all the information they need.

6. A follow-up telephone call or visit to the injured person and his parents or family should be made after the accident, both as a matter of personal concern and interest and as a desirable departmental procedure.

7. When a child who has been injured returns to the playground after recovery, special care should be given to insure that he is brought back into participation as normally as possible.

It should be recognized that special circumstances may require different procedures from those suggested here. For example, in California park and recreation programs, state law requires that parental permission be obtained *before* minors are given medical service. Therefore, in this state it is essential to notify parents or guardians before sending for an ambulance, or to make every effort to reach them at the same time that emergency medical assistance is being called.

First Aid Procedures

It cannot be over-emphasized that there should be strict limitations to the actions taken by recreation leaders with respect to first aid to injured persons. First aid should only be offered under two circumstances: (a) if the injury is a minor one, of a type that the recreation leader is equipped for and authorized to deal with; and (b) if it is an emergency situation requiring immediate action while more expert medical assistance is on the way. It is essential that leaders realize that they are subject to a lawsuit if they apply incorrect procedures, or if they violate policies governing the appropriate assistance that may be given.

Within these limits, a sound knowledge of first aid procedures is an important requisite for playground or other recreation leaders. When minor accidents occur, prompt and careful treatment may be invaluable in relieving the discomfort of injured persons and reducing or eliminating the danger of infection.

The most common types of injuries occurring in recreation settings are small cuts and abrasions, splinters, insect stings, animal bites, puncture wounds, more serious cuts or injuries causing bleeding, shock, heat stroke and heat exhaustion, fractures, and dislocations. Appropriate procedures for dealing with such injuries are provided in many recreation leadership manuals. Several examples of such guidelines follow:

Small Cuts, Scratches, and Abrasions. Remove grit or other foreign matter with sterile tweezers or with the tip of sterile gauze, moistened with sterile water. Apply mild tincture of iodine (2%) or Merthiolate (5%). Allow to dry thoroughly before applying sterile dressing, which is held in place with adhesive or bandage. If wound is deep or bleeding seriously, have injured person see a doctor immediately. In this case, do not apply antiseptic, but simply cover with sterile dressing.

Splinters and Puncture Wounds. Wipe area of wound with alcohol and remove splinter with sterile tweezers or a needle properly sterilized. Apply antiseptic. In the case of a puncture wound, allow wound to bleed by permitting injured part of body to be lowered. Cover with sterile dressing and have person see a doctor promptly.

Insect Stings. These may be quite painful and poisonous, depending on the susceptibility of the person stung. Infection may occur from scratching. Remove the sting, if it is visible. Apply a paste made of baking soda and water or cold cream, or a compress moistened with ammonia water. Applications of ice may reduce pain. If patient shows severe allergic symptoms to an insect bite, such as serious swelling or difficulty in breathing, have him see a doctor immediately for appropriate medication.

Animal Bites. Apart from the injury itself, these are always serious because of the risk of rabies. Immediately wash the wound thoroughly with quantities of soap and water. Mild tincture of iodine or Merthiolate may be applied. Cover with sterile dressing, and have the individual see a doctor at once. Do not destroy the animal but, if possible, capture it and have it confined for observation by health authorities. Remember — dogs are not the only rabies carriers; small rodents and other wild or domestic animals may be infected.

Bleeding. If serious bleeding occurs, use first aid dressing or sterile cloth to apply steady pressure directly over the wound or at appropriate pressure points. Get medical assistance immediately. Nosebleeds are dealt with by having the individual sit in a chair, with his head hanging backward and his clothing loosened. Place a roll of paper or gauze under the upper lip (between it and the gum). If the nosebleed continues, place a piece of cotton or gauze in the nostril and press it in gently.

HOUSEKEEPING FUNCTIONS: CARE OF THE FACILITY, EQUIPMENT, AND SUPPLIES

Although most recreation facilities have their own maintenance personnel (janitors, custodians, or laborers) who carry out routine cleaning, repairs, and other maintenance, it is the job of the recreation leader or supervisor to be certain that housekeeping duties are carried out properly.

The leader or supervisor is normally responsible for carrying out inventories of supplies and equipment, requisitioning new materials, ordering repairs, and storing supplies. It is essential to use all equipment and apparatus carefully, to have them repaired when necessary, and to ration all supplies or expendable materials with care.

Care of Facility and Equipment

From a health and accident-prevention point of view, the following guidelines should be followed regularly. If the recreation leader is not directly responsible for doing these tasks, he should still make sure that they are being carried out properly.

1. All equipment must be safely checked before each opening of a playground (this means twice a day).
2. Storage facilities should be kept neat and in good order.
3. Play areas should be sprinkled to eliminate dust. Sand in the sandbox should be sprinkled and raked each day, and loose sand swept up daily.
4. Lavatories, drinking fountains, and showers (when available) should be inspected regularly and kept clean. Playground directors should encourage hand-washing and showers, when facilities are available.
5. The facility should be cleaned up daily, including arts and crafts scraps, paper cups and napkins, broken glass, and other kinds of refuse.
6. Make sure that grass is cut regularly, broken windows are repaired, and that all problems are immediately dealt with or reported to the responsible office.

Supplies and Expendable Materials

Staff members are generally held responsible for supplies and materials in their respective locations, including the process of requisitioning, storing, handling, or returning all small pieces of equipment or materials that are not used. Supplies should be stored in such a manner that inventories can be carried out promptly and efficiently. Lost or stolen equipment should be reported immediately, and records kept until the needed item is replaced or a new inventory carried out. Generally, requisitioning major blocks of supplies and materials is done at the beginning of the summer or other seasonal program, when allocations are made to all playgrounds and centers in a community. However, it is usually possible to make additional requisitions on an emergency basis.

In some departments, supplies and materials are divided into two categories: expendable and unexpendable. Expendable items are those which are expected to wear out or to be used up during the course of the season, such as arts and crafts supplies, or tennis or ping pong balls. While staff members are expected to exercise care in the use of such materials, they need not usually make a report as the supplies depreciate or are used up. Unexpendable items are those which are *not* used up, and which must be accounted for in a final inventory at the end of a season. Whenever equipment is worn out or damaged beyond use, it is common practice to require that it not be discarded or disposed of by playground leaders. Instead, broken or damaged items should be exchanged for new ones, using the regular requisition process. This is intended to prevent casual disposal of equipment and materials, which might encourage participants or even staff members to "help themselves" to needed items, explaining their disappearance by saying, "It was broken, and we threw it out."

In general, the key guidelines with respect to the use and care of supplies and equipment are that they must be systematically stored and handled, given as long a life as possible, and accounted for at all times.

PREPARING REQUIRED REPORTS AND EVALUATING THE PROGRAM

A final important function of recreation leaders in playgrounds or community centers is to maintain accurate records and submit required reports to their departmental supervisors. Linked to this is the responsibility for evaluating programs regularly and systematically.

Weekly and Monthly Reports

Many departments require staff members to maintain accurate records of programs, and to submit regular reports, usually on a weekly or monthly basis. In addition, special reports must be submitted under certain circumstances, as in the case of accidents or theft. Regular reports fall into the following categories:

Program Reports.   These usually must follow prescribed formats, in which the individual responsible for a facility must describe the general activities which were carried on, special events, and other matters of concern. Membership and/or attendance figures are usually requested, and any problems or suggestions should be noted. If these reports are routine, no action may be taken on them. If they raise serious problems or reveal inadequacies, they may become the basis of staff meetings or other supervisory action.

Personnel Reports. Individual staff members normally submit time cards, noting latenesses, overtime, illness, special leaves, and similar information. District supervisors review these and, in addition, must submit reports dealing with problem situations, such as violations of departmental policies, infractions of rules, or other information which should go into personnel records.

Attendance Records. Accurate attendance records should be kept for all recreation programs, and should go into departmental files. This information is to be used in reviewing programs and providing the basis for future planning. In some cases, attendance records are not as accurate as they should be — either because of the desire of recreation leaders and supervisors to paint as favorable a picture as possible, or because of the difficulty in getting precise statistics of attendance.

In situations where each person is registered by name, or must purchase an admissions ticket or pay for transportation, it should be possible to keep a completely accurate record of attendance. In other facilities, such as community centers or club programs where only registered members may attend, it is also possible to get fairly precise head-counts of the participants involved in activity groups. Playground attendance is generally more difficult to record, because of the transient nature of much participation. Therefore, special formulas have been used to count attendance at the peak time in the morning and again in the afternoon and evening, with a specified percentage added to account for "come-and-go" participants. Obviously, such estimates amount to little more than guesswork, and stronger efforts should be made to get completely accurate figures of attendance.

Special Events Reports. These are reports of major programs that are carried on, usually on a district-wide or community-wide basis, as opposed to special events at a single facility. They should sum up the major details of the event, how it was planned and carried out, those who participated, and other relevant information. Such reports serve as a basis for helping to determine for future use whether given programs should be repeated and exactly how previous arrangements were made.

Other Reports. As previous passages in this text have indicated, most departments also require that reports be submitted dealing with the following: (a) accidents and personal injury, either to participants or staff members; (b) permission slips for trips; (c) vandalism, damage, and theft reports; (d) reports of disciplinary problems on playgrounds or in centers, and of actions taken, such as suspension or expulsion; (e) inventory reports regarding equipment and supplies; (f) facility or apparatus condition reports; and (g) reports dealing with monies collected by the department (for memberships, transportation, or other fees), or the use of petty cash funds.

Within each of these areas, most departments have specific procedural guidelines and require precise and detailed reports. For example, one department has the following statement governing reports dealing with monies collected by the department:

Handling City Money

All employees who must handle City money as part of the job are personally responsible for following established procedures. No money is accepted by an employee without the proper financial records being completed. Under no circumstances may the employee spend city money, nor may he refund money previously collected. Copies of all receipts and forms properly completed, and all monies collected, must be turned in to the Treasurer's office daily. No money is to be retained on a recreation area overnight. Refunds may be transacted only through the City Treasurer.

While it *is* essential that accurate records be kept in each of the areas that have been cited, it is also important to keep "paper-shuffling" to a minimum, and to require only those reporting procedures that are really necessary and make a contribution to the work of a department. A comparable example might be found in some hospitals, in which recreation staff members are involved in so many planning sessions and team meetings (interdisciplinary meetings, meetings of ward or unit teams, "grand rounds" to review individual patients, staff development meetings, and so on) that little time is available during the week to provide actual programs and services for patients. Paper work should be carried out as quickly and efficiently as possible, and either filed systematically or forwarded to the appropriate office.

Evaluation of Programs

This involves the process of determining how effective the recreation program is — either at a single facility, within a district, or on a community-wide basis. At each level, an appropriate individual should be designated to carry out the evaluation, although persons who are higher in the chain of command then review his analysis and conclusions.

Evaluation is carried out in a variety of ways. It may involve measuring the performance of individual leaders throughout the season or year, and the success of all regular programs or specially scheduled activities. Some departments require elaborate forms to be filled out for every playground or community center on a regular basis. For example, one municipal recreation department has its recreation center directors fill out narrative reports twice a month that deal with the following points:

1. Economic and cultural group in area to be considered.
2. Types of program – diversified activities for all desired interests.
3. Does scheduling of program meet the needs of the community?
4. Do the activities bring in the desired attendance?
5. Are publicity methods adequate?
6. Does staff show initiative and imagination in programming?

For departments that wish to carry out a thorough self-evaluation, the National Recreation and Park Association has formulated a detailed instrument for measurement of all the major aspects of recreation and park operations, with suggested standards and criteria for performance. While it would not normally be the responsibility of a recreation leader or supervisor to carry out such an evaluation, he might well be part of it, and would certainly be expected to assist in the evaluation of programs for which he is directly responsible. Such evaluation might be based on a variety of elements, such as: (a) attendance, as a basic criterion of interest; (b) nature of participation by those attending; (c) interest and support by members of the community; (d) success in achieving specific goals or carrying out desired projects and programs. Based on guidelines found in the literature, such questions might be asked as:

"Are diversified programs being provided that meet the needs of all age groups, both sexes, and varied socioeconomic groups in the community?"
"Has behavior and cooperation of participants generally been favorable, or have there been many instances of behavior problems, such as fights or tensions between groups?"
"Have members of the community supported the program by serving as volunteers or in other ways?"
"Have programs received public attention through favorable coverage by newspapers or other media?"
"Has the program been carried out in cooperation with other public agencies or voluntary or private organizations?"
"Has the net impact of the program been to enrich the leisure life of the community and to strengthen desirable human values and development?"

As indicated, an important element in program evaluation may involve the observation and appraisal of *participants*. This is particularly true in hospitals or other treatment centers, where regular records are kept of the progress of individual patients. Their involvement in recreational activities, their social participation, and their ability to function in such situations is recorded and related to treatment goals and recommendations for future involvement or recreation experience. Such records should be used in staff meetings which review patient progress and in conferences with patients themselves.

In general, whatever form of evaluation is carried out, it will be meaningful only if it is honest, thorough, and systematic. When a recreation leader is called upon to present a report of his own programs and, in effect, to evaluate his own work, he should feel free to point out all strengths and weaknesses rather than gloss over flaws and exaggerate successes. In order to do this, he must be assured that his own self-evaluation will not be used against him by his supervisor. Instead, it will be used constructively to help assist him and improve his program.

This chapter has presented descriptions of the varied functions held by recreation leaders, in addition to the familiar tasks of presenting program activities. It has given primary emphasis to playground and community center settings found in all public recreation and park departments, and it has dealt chiefly with children and youth as participants. However, many leaders must function in more specialized settings, dealing with populations of different ages and with special needs or interests. Often, these programs are sponsored, not by public agencies, but by voluntary, private, or other organizations. The chapter that follows examines a number of such settings, with specific emphasis on their unique requirements for recreation leadership.

Suggested Examination Questions or Topics for Student Reports

1. Apart from the obvious function of leading recreation activities, what are several of the other key responsibilities of recreation leaders in playgrounds and community centers? Which of these do you feel are of the greatest importance? Why?
2. Discipline and control of participants' behavior are key functions of recreation leaders. Based on this chapter and on your own experience, what do you regard as the key elements in carrying out this responsibility successfully?
3. Outline a set of basic principles for promoting safety in recreation and park settings. What are the most important steps to be taken when an accident does occur, based on the text and on your own experience?
4. Why is it important to evaluate programs, and what are some of the ways in which this can be done objectively?

Suggested Action Assignments for Students

1. Examine the specific guidelines for first aid, as outlined in the recreation leadership or summer program manual of your community — assuming that such guidelines are provided. Then contrast these with recommended guidelines in American Red Cross manuals, and make suggestions for their improvement or correction.
2. As an exercise in public relations, plan a hypothetical event or recreation program, and carefully prepare several newspaper releases for it that would appear before, during, and after the event.

leadership in special settings

Earlier chapters of this text have dealt with the most familiar aspects of leadership, and with playgrounds and community centers which primarily serve children and youth. However, it is obvious that many recreation leaders are employed today in situations which impose special needs or leadership approaches, or which serve populations that have unusual needs. Particularly in working with groups with disability, the leader may assume functions related to counseling and guidance, social service, or behavior modification. Increasingly, he must cooperate closely with representatives of other disciplines or services, such as psychologists, psychiatrists, social workers, or penologists.

None of this is completely new. For decades, recreation leaders have worked with gang members in city streets, or with the mentally ill in psychiatric institutions. However, the programs and approaches themselves have changed markedly, and it is necessary for recreation leaders to have new skills and a new degree of sophistication that will help them fulfill new service roles. This chapter therefore examines eight settings or areas of service:

1. Recreation programs for teenage youth.
2. Outreach programs for "problem" youth.
3. Therapeutic camping programs.
4. Industrial recreation programs.
5. Armed forces recreation.
6. Recreation in psychiatric treatment settings.
7. Recreation in senior centers.
8. Recreation in nursing homes.

In each case, the nature of the participants, their unique needs and interests, the goals of recreation programs serving them, and appropriate guidelines for leadership are presented. As the reader combines this chapter with the preceding ones, it should be possible for him to get a full

257

picture of the wide variety of functions that recreation leaders serve in modern society—and the kinds of skills and techniques they must possess to work in different settings. The basic principles of leadership, group dynamics, effective teaching, and sound organization apply in all situations. However, the emphasis and methods used vary in each situation.

RECREATION PROGRAMS FOR TEENAGE YOUTH

One of the most important contributions any recreation department or agency can make is to provide constructive and attractive programs for teenage youth. The period of adolescence is one in which many young people seek to affirm their identity and to establish themselves as autonomous beings. It is also a time in which many individuals are in a state of conflict or turmoil, in which they rebel strongly against adult codes or moral values. Many adolescents engage in forms of leisure behavior during this period that express their rebellion in potentially self-destructive and negative ways, in violent gang activity, dangerous car racing, promiscuous sexual involvement, or the abuse of drugs and alcohol.

Helping teenagers move successfully through this period is obviously the responsibility of a number of community agencies or forces, including schools, religious authorities, and parents. The special contribution of a community recreation program for teenagers is threefold: (a) it provides challenging and constructive leisure activities which may serve as an appealing alternative to the many forms of antisocial play that tempt adolescents; (b) it provides a specific form of release for many of the drives and energies of young people, and meets many of their psychological, social, and physical needs; and (c) it provides an opportunity for teenagers to make their own decisions, gain experiences in self-government, and contribute to society.

There are many different types of agencies which seek to serve teenage boys and girls. Of these, three models are described here: (a) religious youth-serving agencies; (b) public recreation departments; and (c) independent youth canteens or "drop-in" centers.

Religiously Affiliated Youth Programs

Each of the three major faiths—Catholic, Protestant, and Jewish—provides organized programs for youth. As an example, one might examine the work of the Catholic Youth Organization in the Archdiocese of New York. In this organization, recreation is regarded as an important need of young people, and a crucial area of character development. For example, the C.Y.O. Pledge of Sportsmanship states:

I pledge myself, upon my honor, to be loyal to my God, to my Church, and to my Country. I pledge myself to live a clean and honest life and to fulfill all my duties as a Christian. I bind myself to promote by word and example clean and wholesome recreation. I shall work and pray to be in all things, a generous winner and a gracious loser.

Catholic Youth Organization leadership manuals stress that the very nature of one's daily leisure activity has serious religious meaning; play should be regarded as "spiritual sacrifices acceptable to God." Sports in particular are seen as a means of training young people in Christian behavior, fairness, teamwork, honesty, sportsmanship, and other forms of virtue. At the same time, they provide a way of strengthening morale and a sense of affiliation in parish life:

> A spirit should be built up in each parish. Enthusiasm for the different teams, encouraging parents to come out to see their children compete; pulpit and parish bulletin announcements concerning parish team games; posters announcing different events; all contribute to good parish participation.
>
> Uniforms for a parish team can be a big boost to morale. Parish CYO banners help build a spirit. Parish cheers, songs, and . . . cheerleaders add a great deal to build up a good spirit.

Obviously, the program is not restricted to sports. C.Y.O. sponsors a five-fold program of spiritual, cultural, apostolic, social, and athletic activities for youth in the Archdiocese. It maintains youth centers throughout the city that sponsor daily programs, as well as a number of summer camps open to underprivileged children, regardless of age or creed. It offers specialized group projects in 17 parish areas of the Archdiocese, in cooperation with the New York City Youth Services Agency. It sponsors numerous scout troops, special programs for handicapped youths, and a wide variety of recreational activities. These include the following, both as regular activities and special events:

> Major sports programs in baseball, softball, basketball, soccer, track and field, swimming, and "roller hockey."
>
> Oratorical contests, "Christmas Crib" contests, religious quiz contests, essay contests, music, art, and theater programs.
>
> Social and club programs, leadership training seminars and projects, retreats, youth centers, and numerous other activities.

The bulk of leadership throughout the Catholic Youth Organization is provided by volunteers, in the form of interested adults coaching teams or working with young people in other special activities. However, the central Archdiocese staff and a number of the center directors are full-time professionals. They must provide extensive field services, and act as consultants in helping local parishes establish their own programs as well as in setting up many Archdiocesan activities. Their role is very predominately an organizational one, and is enacted within a highly structured system. They need to be able to work closely with parish priests or nuns, with other school personnel, with parents, with directors of other city agencies, and with large numbers of volunteers.

The Catholic Youth Organization recreation program places emphasis on traditional recreation activities carried out under Church auspices in carefully structured clubs, leagues, or other groups. It is not a program which tends to reach out to problem youths or is able to accept deviant behavior. The role of the professional leader is chiefly one of setting up large-scale programs, obtaining facilities, carrying out scheduling, publicizing events, arranging banquets, clinics and training sessions, and other managerial tasks.

Programs Sponsored by Public Recreation Departments

Many municipal recreation and park departments provide a broad range of activities specially designed for teenage youth. While primary emphasis tends to be given to team sports principally designated for this age group, other activities are offered.

For example, the Phoenix, Arizona, Parks and Recreation Department offers the following categories of special "teen" activities: *Arts and Crafts,* such as girls' "fixit" classes, woodworking, and other crafts; *Community Service Activities,* including a teenage volunteer service and employment program; *Dramatics,* including one-act plays, puppetry, stage shows, and movie making; *Hobbies and Special Interests,* such as "charm" classes, sewing clubs, model car contests, and boys' and girls' cooking classes; and varied other musical, camping, physical fitness, and hobby activities. The Phoenix program includes many social activities, such as dances, canteens, and parties with special themes.

Municipal departments that wish to provide more extensive programs for adolescents often sponsor or encourage the formation of "teen clubs." For example, the Montgomery County, Maryland, Department of Recreation has sponsored or assisted a number of successful clubs which are organized by young people and adult advisors in local communities or school districts. This involves a number of important ingredients: *planning* on the part of teenagers, their parents, and the Recreation Department; *organization* and active committee work; *publicity;* the development of *community support;* well-planned *by-laws* and *regulations;* varied and attractive *programs;* and, above all, good *leadership.*

Programs of such teen clubs in Montgomery County fall under several headings: "at home" recreation events; "away" events; and service projects. Examples are given of each.

At Home Events: pizza parties, picnics, buffet suppers, table games, costume or holiday dances, band dances, talent shows, rock-and-roll contests, novelty dances, and square dancing.

Away Events: cookouts, roller or ice skating outings, swimming parties, bowling, visiting other teen clubs, attending athletic events, barge trips, and visiting amusement parks.

Service Projects: fund-raising drives or volunteer work for March of

Dimes, Heart Fund, UNICEF, American Cancer Society; or volunteer leadership with county welfare projects, summer camp for underprivileged children, summer playgrounds or programs serving retarded children.

Such programs generally tend to serve teenagers who are willing to enter into socially approved and constructive programs, and who will accept the regulations imposed by adult authorities. For example, many public recreation and park departments or schools that sponsor teenage canteens and dances have rigid codes of admission, dress, behavior, and other regulations. These are necessary in their view — and yet they tend to restrict or exclude other adolescents who are not willing or able to accept these limitations.

New Approaches to Developing Youth Centers

A final approach to serving young people today in organized programs may be found in a number of communities around the United States and Canada, in which attempts to provide more contemporary and realistic programs for teenagers have been made. The rationale for these programs is that young people have changed so radically in their interests and attitudes that the traditionally conceived recreation program, with its emphasis on carefully chaperoned social activities, is no longer acceptable or attractive to them. Following an intensive study of teenage recreation in Los Angeles County, the Los Angeles Recreation and Youth Services Council concluded:

> Traditional agencies created to serve the recreation needs of teenagers must pioneer a new form of program and administration, only partially comparable to teenage centers as we have known them in the past and as we know them today.[1]

Based on a study carried out by Springfield College of many teen centers around the United States, it was concluded that three major concepts should be recognized in planning teen centers:

1. Young people should take the lead in the responsibility for their own affairs.

2. The program should be based on the needs and desires of youth . . . as they see them.

3. Serious youth problems should be faced realistically.

The Springfield College report, *A Youth Center for the 70's*, stressed the need to serve diverse groups of young people with meaningful social experiences:

> A teen center should be for all young people in the community. There are those who believe that teen-age cliques exist which are as different from

[1] *A Profile of Recreation and Youth Services in the Pasadena-Foothill Area.* County of Los Angeles, Recreation and Youth Services Planning Council, February, 1969.

one another as the differences that exist between the generations. However, a center should be diverse enough in its makeup, representation, and programming to provide for:

The Swingers and the Clingers
The Squares and the Long Hairs
The Blacks and the Whites
The Normal and the Handicapped . . .
The Junior High and the Senior High (although usually programmed separately), and frequently
Post-High School young people . . .[2]

Activities should provide the opportunity for social interaction, and for young people to "do their own thing." Programs should be determined with the help of questionnaires, youth conferences, bull sessions, suggestion boxes, and careful planning. They should include a wide range of informal, "drop-in" activities, such as listening to records, playing ping pong, pool, or table shuffleboard, eating and talking, coffee house programs, and similar elements. Special events, including camping, skiing trips, theatre parties, fishing, surfing, picnics and similar outings, or carnivals, street dances, games, tournaments, skating, bowling, or car rallies, are offered in many centers. In addition, special interest groups involving such activities as hi-fi building, photography, music, physical fitness, judo or karate, boating, or other specialized areas are often found in teen centers.

Beyond this, if teen centers are to be fully meaningful to young people today, they must involve the opportunity to deal with real issues and problems. The Springfield report suggests that teenagers may want to rap about "pollution, drugs, ecology, population, women's liberation, materialism vs. humanism, the racial situation, youth involvement, war, etc."

Services offered in some communities have included the following:

Tutoring	Job Referral
Drug Counseling and Referral	Family Counseling
Rap Line (Emergency)	Welfare Assistance
Draft Counseling	Free School

Community involvement programs may include:

Youth-Government Day	Teen Council
Youth Conferences	Adult-Teen Dialogues
Anti-Litter Campaigns	Service to Handicapped or Elderly
Playground Assistance	Environmental Projects
UNICEF Drives	Information Service

In developing centers with such programs, much help is needed. They simply cannot be accomplished successfully by community organizations or departments that provide staff, set policies, and dominate the entire operation. Instead, young people must take the lead in organizing the programs

---

[2] Donald Bridgman, Project Director: *A Youth Center for the 70's.* Springfield, Massachusetts, Springfield College Report, 1971, p. 7.

—although they will need considerable assistance from adults in terms of obtaining facilities and funding, getting legal advice, handling problems, and insuring continuity. The Pennsylvania Youth Advisory Council, in a pamphlet, *Let's Listen to Youth,* sets the limits of adult involvement:

> Youth need the backing of adults. Successful youth councils have continuing adult assistance without adult domination. Adult advisors must be helpful, when needed, but must give youth great latitude in making plans, reaching their own decisions, and carrying out their activities. The quickest way to kill a youth council is to spoon-feed it with projects which adults think youth should carry out.[3]

Thus, the role of adult leaders will be to help teenagers carry as much of the responsibility as possible for planning their own programs and for center operation.

It is obvious that much of the self-destructive or hostile behavior of young people arises because they feel a sense of helplessness or frustration at being "irrelevant" to the adult society all around them. Teen centers may serve to provide both causes and meaningful tasks for young people that can absorb their energies and are relevant to their psychosocial needs. Taking responsibility for themselves and carrying out meaningful programs is essential to their own healthy growth—as well as to the success of the teen center itself.

Obviously, limits must be set by adults. Teen centers cannot be permitted to operate with members frankly using alcohol and drugs, and regulations governing such behavior must be enforced. But, the Springfield Report suggests, the existence of problems in this area does *not* mean that programs should be discontinued:

> Problems will arise from time to time in or around a youth center. Young people will appear on the scene obviously under the influence of alcohol or drugs; pushers might even show up. These problems are also found in schools, but schools are not closed; education, after all, provides an important and vital service. The contention here is that a youth center also provides an important and vital service that should not be jeopardized by the misadventures of a few . . .
>
> Our contention is not that drugs should be permitted. They should not. But we do make a plea for a realistic approach to the problem. *A youth center should not be abandoned as a failure because occasional problems arise.* It is at this very point that support for young people is most significant—after all, what support is required when things are running smoothly?
>
> A youth center is frequently sought out by the teen-ager who has problems and is not involved in traditional forms of recreation. If we accept the viewpoint that many young people try drugs as an escape from unpleasant realities and because they have not found meaning in life, a relevant youth center and wise, understanding leadership might contribute to the prevention of drug abuse . . .[4]

---

[3] Cited in *A Youth Center for the 70's,* p. 46.
[4] Cited in *A Youth Center for the 70's,* p. 49.

The implications here for leadership of teenage recreation programs are clear. Programs which are planned, organized, and carefully supervised by adults can provide interesting and valuable recreation activities for a segment of the youth population. In order to serve a much broader segment, however, it is also necessary to provide activities and programs which significantly involve young people who are less conforming in their values and behavior, and who not only need the opportunity for meaningful involvement but who also can make an important contribution to community life. While this represents a difficult challenge for recreation leaders, it is a challenge that must be met if this population group is to be effectively served.

COMMUNITY OUTREACH PROGRAMS FOR YOUTH

In recent years, a serious problem has arisen in many community recreation departments which have been attempting to serve young people in disadvantaged, inner-city neighborhoods. Large numbers of teenagers in crowded, urban slums are school dropouts and, even at an early age, have been in trouble with the police because of delinquent behavior. Often they are alienated from any constructive contact with adults or community agencies, and are active members of antisocial gangs. It has been extremely difficult for traditional recreation programs or youth organizations to involve such young people.

Since the 1950's, such cities as New York, Philadelphia, Washington, Richmond, and Los Angeles, plagued by growing juvenile delinquency and warring gangs, have employed special workers to serve unaffiliated, "problem" youths. A number of different titles have been applied to such workers: "roving leaders," "outreach leaders," and "street gang" or "street club" workers. Bannon describes such leaders in the following terms:

> A roving leader is an outreach worker assigned to a specific community to stimulate hard-to-reach youth to participate in wholesome recreation programs. A basic purpose of this outreach service is to help disadvantaged youth use their free time constructively and, at the same time, assist them in effectively using community resources in education, health, employment and related social service.[5]

The task of outreach workers encompasses far more than traditional recreation leadership. He — or she (some departments have both male and female street workers) — has the mission of making contact with antisocial gangs, gaining their confidence, and attempting to re-orient their values and behavior in more constructive directions. The Washington, D.C., Recreation Department, which has had such a program since 1956, sees its

---

[5] Joseph J. Bannon: "The Roving Leaders: A New Look." *Parks and Recreation*, February, 1972, p. 23.

general function as preventing, neutralizing, and controlling the hostile behavior of youth groups and individuals. The specific goals of outreach workers include the following:

1. To help adolescents make use of community resources that are available to them.

2. To encourage drop-outs to return to school.

3. To direct youth behavior into more constructive social outlets, and to promote more productive and positive channels of communication between youth and the adult community.

4. To reduce the severity and frequency of offenses, such as vandalism, theft, and gang violence.

5. To intervene on behalf of youth with schools, police and the courts, and to assist them in their relationships with all community authorities.

6. To help youth understand the consequences of their anti-social behavior, and to promote a desire to become part of the larger society.

7. To identify conflict-producing elements in the community, and to work constructively with these.

8. To create opportunities for youth to assume more significant roles in society.

General Leadership Approaches

Outreach workers or roving leaders usually follow a somewhat similar plan of operation. Initially, the leader establishes informal contact with groups or individual youths in their neighborhoods, on the streets, or in informal hangouts. He develops rapport with them, helps them in small ways, and gradually attempts to gain acceptance as a friendly adult. Once a relationship has been established, he meets periodically with group members and attempts to lead them into constructive activities. Recognizing that they will distrust and resist any attempt at domination, he must employ a considerable amount of tact and discretion. He must adjust himself to the needs of the group, meeting them in places and at times convenient to them. The Richmond, Virginia, Department of Parks and Recreation describes his functions as follows:

> Upon stimulating general interest among groups and individuals, the Roving Leader channels their general interests and desires into constructive activities by organizing athletic events, securing employment for them, forming clubs and special interest groups, assisting them in developing hobbies, gaining admittance for them to movies, concerts, and to special events and activities sponsored by the Department and introducing them to recreation units where they may participate in organized athletics, social activities, arts and crafts, etc. He maintains continued close relationship and follow-up to assure their modification of attitudes and social behavior.
>
> The Roving Leader maintains close relationships and has numerous contacts with such individuals, groups and agencies as the Juvenile Aid

Division, Juvenile Court, Public Schools, Youth Councils and youth-serving agencies, civic organizations, churches, Parent-Teacher Associations, parents, public and private recreation centers, and the United States Employment Service.

The roving leader may also attempt to help individuals with personal problems or disability by referring them to group-work or family case-work agencies, to psychiatric, health and dental clinics, public employment services, or to religious and educational institutions, and then by continuing to assist them in appropriate ways. In terms of specific recreation-related activities, outreach workers may involve youth groups in a wide range of sports, cultural, and social programs. Typically, the Washington, D.C., Recreation Department's roving leaders involve disadvantaged, inner-city youths in the following summer activities:

1. Trips to amusement parks.

2. Roller-skating outings.

3. Trips to theatres and art galleries, and to professional soccer, football, baseball, and basketball games.

4. Classes in English, nursing, life sciences, and other subjects.

5. Census-taking and other community service projects.

6. Trips to talent shows, bowling, skating, picnics, and fishing, and for boat and airplane rides.

In most cases outreach workers are not attached to a particular facility, but are simply assigned to a neighborhood, and are given responsibility for a designated number of groups. In Washington, for example, the workload of a roving leader varies from two to four groups, depending on the needs of the community and the severity of the problem. A worker may be assigned only two groups, if they are extremely hostile and aggressive, but may have three or four, if they pose less serious problems.

The Department of Recreation and Parks in Los Angeles, California, has a different approach. This department has a Special Problems Unit which is assigned the task of working with antisocial and disruptive youth in and around recreation centers. Customarily, Youth Counselors, as they are titled in Los Angeles, are assigned to two or more recreation facilities, which may include centers, swimming pools, or other areas.

Qualifications of Outreach Workers

Formal qualifications for outreach workers and roving leaders vary from city to city. In some departments they are required to have college degrees; in others, they may be on a "career ladder" which permits them to work in this position while studying for a college degree. Specialized training in recreation is not usually required and, in fact, the background and personal qualities of street workers are usually considered to be more important than formal credentials. Theoretical knowledge of group dynamics, juvenile delinquency, or social work is not as important as knowledge of the slum milieu, personal experience, and character traits that are needed to work with alienated and hostile youth. The Los Angeles Special Problems Unit has developed the following statement of the desired qualities and skills of its youth workers:

1. First of all, a Youth Counselor must have commitment. He must be committed to what he's doing and know above all else that what he's doing is most important for the youth.

2. A Youth Counselor has to have persistence. He needs the drive to go from hangout to hangout and from street corner to street corner – constantly talking to youth.

3. A Youth Counselor has to be tough enough to be forceful both with others and with himself, yet at the same time, he must be sensitive to the needs of those around him.

4. A Youth Counselor has to develop and encourage youth leaders in his group. This requires that he be tough on his ego and let others receive the recognition, and also be prepared for the day he must back out. He is not building his own organization, but an organization of the youth.

5. A Youth Counselor must build trust. He must trust the youth with whom he works and they must be able to trust him.

6. A Youth Counselor has to listen so he will know what's going on in his area at all times.

7. A Youth Counselor must not be a phony. He must be himself and be natural. He can have a "bag of tricks," but must be comfortable with them.

8. A Youth Counselor must learn never to make promises that he can't keep, or threats he can't back up.

9. A Youth Counselor must know his area inside and out. He has to do a lot of research to find out about his area, but must never let this be an excuse for not doing his work. He must train others by involving them in this process.

10. A Youth Counselor must get youth to work for him. He must be able to involve youth on a personal level.

11. A Youth Counselor must recognize self-interest as one of the important motivations for human action and must, therefore, give a service which is needed and of value.

Careful training and constant supervision are essential for outreach workers. They must be aware of clearly defined departmental policies governing such difficult areas as: (a) how to handle threats from gang members; (b) how to deal with knowledge of a gang's past or present criminal activities; (c) what to do with respect to drug activities, possession of firearms, threatened gang "rumbles," and other critical situations; and (d) relations with the police and other community agencies. Whenever possible, the ultimate goal of roving leader programs is not only to use recreation as a positive tool for working constructively with problem youth but also to draw gang members and individuals into organized community programs.

Not all agencies that work with delinquent or pre-delinquent youth make use of the outreach worker approach. In some cases, special recreation projects are devised that have a unique appeal for young people, and that may have remarkable benefits in helping to move them in desirable social directions.

Each One Teach One

This unusual program had its origins in the work of Holcombe Rucker, a black playground leader in New York City, who was a force for good in the lives of many hundreds of Harlem youngsters. Through his coaching and personal influence, he helped them gain skill in basketball, with dozens of them becoming leading college and professional athletes. In addition, he counseled, inspired, and tutored them, so that many boys who came from the most deprived environments and were well on the way to lives of crime or drug addiction changed their values, returned to school, and went on to productive—and in many cases, distinguished—careers. With little assistance from city agencies, Rucker formed the Junior Basketball League in a Harlem playground in 1946. As many of the boys he worked with went on to college, they returned to work with him and help younger boys. Gradually, Rucker expanded the program to include girls' teams and junior high, high school, college, and professional leagues. During the summers, outstanding college and professional players took part in what became known as the Holcombe Rucker Tournament, playing before huge crowds on summer weekends.

After Ruckers' death in 1965, several of the young men he influenced who had become outstanding athletes, including Fred Crawford and Bob McCullough, carried on his work. They expanded the tournament and created Harlem Professionals, Inc., a nonprofit organization designed to establish sports clinics and camps, and to use sports as a means of counseling and working with youth to promote their overall welfare. Assisted by businesses and foundations, they established the "Each One Teach One" program, a unique project geared to using recreation—and particularly basketball—to reach inner-city youngsters. With the help of many professional athletes who have donated their time, this program makes use of the fascination that sports hold for disadvantaged youths. Top athletes hold clinics and compete, and serve as role models for youth. Carefully planned tutoring, vocational and career guidance, and college referral services are combined with drug addiction services, "rap" sessions, and first aid and health instruction to meet the needs of Harlem youth.

In a number of other cities, similar programs have been initiated. The

Industrial Recreation. Recreation staff members of the Xerox Recreation Association in Rochester, New York, are responsible for supervising women's team sports, including softball (*A*). Other program activities are varied clubs and hobbies, such as a Pistol Club (*B*) and an extensive physical conditioning program (*C*).

A

B

C

point they make is clear—that, by itself, recreation will do little to prevent or reduce juvenile delinquency. However, when intelligently combined with other remedial, counseling, and instructional services, recreation can become an attractive and enjoyable means of reaching problem youth and helping them to move in positive directions.

National Youth Project Using Minibikes

This unusual delinquency prevention project (known as NYPUM) is sponsored by the National Board of the Young Men's Christian Association. It makes use of outreach methods to work with small groups of young people of junior high school age who have resisted other community program services. The Y.M.C.A. undertook this project in recognition of the fact that youth crime in the United States is rising at a rate seven times faster than adult crime, with nearly half of the nation's serious crimes being committed by juveniles. Additionally, 74 percent of young delinquents are "repeaters," with the likelihood of becoming adult criminals.

The "minibike" project involves forming groups of about fifteen 11- to 15-year-old boys who have not been served by the Y.M.C.A. in the past, and who have been referred by schools or youth authorities for serious behavior problems. The youngsters are taught how to ride minibikes and how to maintain them properly as a first step. An attempt is then made to channel the boys into other types of constructive, socially desirable programs.

The first successful pilot program using minibikes was sponsored at the Northeast Y.M.C.A. in Los Angeles. With the assistance of the American Honda Motor Company, which donated 10,000 minibikes to the National Board of the Y.M.C.A., a national project was carried on throughout the United States. The results, compiled by Western Center Consultants in Los Angeles, showed positive results in behavior modification, community cooperation, and safety training. An additional grant from the Law Enforcement Assistance Administration of the United States Department of Justice was used to start new NYPUM's, and to carry on scientific evaluations of the entire program. By 1973, approximately 300 separate projects were initiated throughout the United States.

As the program got under way, several concepts were developed:

1. Collaboration of all agencies, business, voluntary agencies, government and private individuals was necessary, along with cooperation from police, courts, and probation authorities.

2. The minibikes were perceived as an exciting and attractive activity involving shared adventure, the learning of skills, exercise of discipline and responsibility, and respect for self and others.

3. Within each NYPUM group, the minibike activities quickly became a means to an end—the growing relationship between the group worker and the group members, in which trust between child and adult was established and the leader was able to act as a counselor, teacher, and friend.

Judges, probation officers, and other community workers have concluded that NYPUM has been an effective way of reaching and influencing delinquency-prone youth. There is an extremely low recidivism rate among first and second offenders who have been involved in the program.

The Y.M.C.A. minibike project demonstrates again how recreational activities may be used in carefully designed programs to meet the needs of delinquent and socially alienated youth. It is important to recognize that it is not the individual activity that is the major factor in creating behavior change. Instead, it is the quality of leadership, the bond built between the leader and the participants, the other services which are offered, and the fact that ultimately the socially constructive and desirable program becomes more rewarding and attractive to the youngster than his former antisocial associations and behavior.

THERAPEUTIC CAMPING PROGRAMS

Another major area of specialized service in the field of recreation involves organized camping programs that serve the mentally, physically, or psychologically impaired. Such programs have developed rapidly in recent years. They include several different types of camps: resident camps, trip camps, and day camps.

Resident Camps. Over 250 resident camps are listed in the *Easter Seal Directory of Resident Camps for Persons With Special Health Needs.* In such camps, residents stay at the camp for periods ranging usually from one to two weeks.

Day Camps. While the precise number of such camps is not known, a considerable number of camps have been established in which the camper comes to the campsite each day to participate in varied activities and returns home each night.

Trip Camps. Such camps do not use a central facility; instead, they set up temporary facilities to permit camping in natural surroundings.

According to a recent national survey of camping programs and services for the handicapped, sponsors of such camps fall into the following categories: (a) youth agency camps; (b) private independent camps; (c) church camps or those with religious affiliations; and (d) specialized camps. In those camps not specially designed for the handicapped, approximately three to ten per cent of the campers have been identified as having some significant disability. Specialized camps tend to serve primarily those with physical disabilities, although many are designed for the mentally retarded as well.[6]

---

[6] John A. Nesbitt, Curtis C. Hansen, Barbara J. Bates, and Larry L. Neal: *Training Needs and Strategies in Camping for the Handicapped.* San Jose, California, Therapeutic Recreation Service for Handicapped Children Project. Center of Leisure Studies, University of Oregon, 1972. pp. 27–28.

The rationale for providing therapeutic camping programs is that all handicapped individuals have the right to experience positive recreation and leisure pursuits, to grow in terms of independence and self-reliance, and to achieve satisfying peer relationships. A recent national conference identified the following specific needs of handicapped persons for camping experiences. These include:

> To experience the growth and development provided by camping which is normally denied the handicapped.
> To experience independence from the family, and build self-confidence.
> To experience successful activity, including satisfying and beneficial physical activity.
> To recognize his/her relationship to the natural world.
> To gain functional interdependence with others, and to experience relationships which extend beyond the camping opportunity.
> To learn carry-over recreation and leisure skills, and enrich one's lifestyle.[7]

While it is true that only a small proportion of the nation's estimated seven million handicapped children are today involved in therapeutic camping programs, there is growing pressure to expand such opportunities. A number of outstanding therapeutic camps have been developed in the United States and Canada, two of which are described here.

Camp Spindrift, San Francisco

This outstanding day camp is sponsored by the Recreation Center for the Handicapped, a pioneering program founded in San Francisco in 1952 to provide year-round social, cultural, and educational opportunities for children and youths with physical and mental disabilities.[8] Camp Spindrift is a carefully supervised program designed to provide a close-to-home camping experience for boys and girls who would not otherwise have camping opportunities. A recent camp report describes its program in the following terms:

> Activities for the Day Camp are selected, adapted, modified, or invented, to meet the needs of mentally retarded and handicapped children and to help them to grow and develop as individuals. Each child will have the opportunity to cook, and to eat, out-of-doors; to go on collection hikes, nature observation walks, exploring hunts; to become acquainted with trees, plants, animals, birds, and to enjoy campfires. They may go on field trips to the zoo, to a farm, to museums, parks and other areas which will expand their horizons and offer new living experiences. They will listen to stories and music, sing, dance, play games, participate in simple pantomime or drama activities, and enjoy worthwhile craft projects designed to be within the area of individual capabilities.

---

[7] Cited in *Training Needs and Strategies in Camping for the Handicapped,* pp. 12–13.

[8] Janet Pomeroy: "The San Francisco Recreation Center for the Handicapped: A Brief Description." *Therapeutic Recreation Journal,* Fourth Quarter, 1969, pp. 15–19.

The schedule is flexible and the program is carried out in an atmosphere of relaxed enjoyment . . .

Essentially, the camp's policies and operational procedures are not very different from those of a normal day camp, except that extreme care is taken to select mature and responsible staff members, with a ratio of at least one adult counselor for every four campers. Counselors are carefully trained and supervised throughout the camping period, and a strong effort is made to have a sufficient number of staff members returning from year to year to give stability, cohesion, and continuity to the program. The program offers a wide variety of activities, as indicated earlier, with opportunity for individual participation, small group activities, and events involving the entire camp. The tempo is leisurely, and campers have the opportunity to help plan activities and make their own choices. All camp procedures related to transportation, diet, medication, health and safety, and the modification of activities, are carefully planned in advance. Detailed records are kept of the progress of all campers, and staff members are thoroughly briefed about their individual needs and capabilities, their health care problems, and how to deal with emergencies that may arise, such as seizures.

Numerous other camps exist throughout the United States and Canada that deal either with mixed groups of disabled campers, as Camp Spindrift does, or with groups having a single major class of disability, such as blindness, mental retardation, or a physical handicap.

Camp Confidence, Brainerd, Minnesota

Known officially as the Northern Minnesota Therapeutic Camp, this facility provides year-round camping and outdoor education opportunities for the residents of Brainerd State Hospital and other mentally retarded individuals in the state of Minnesota. It represents a unique example of teamwork among many individuals and public and voluntary organizations in obtaining a large wilderness site on Sylvan Lake, and developing an outstanding camping facility with docks, tent campsites, cabins, nature playgrounds, a ski slope and chalet, skating rink and warming house, nature trails, fish houses, wheelchair walks, and numerous other special units. Camp Confidence is the only year-round camping and outdoor education program for the mentally retarded in the northern half of the United States, and provides the following different types of services:

1. *Day Camping.* Primarily intended as a camping experience from which to develop skills in camping and outdoor education in preparing for resident camping.

2. *Independent Living Skills Resident Camp.* Conducted at separate tent sites or individual cabin units, with emphasis on the camp living skills portion of the outdoor education curriculum.

3. *Wilderness Camping.* Considered an ultimate goal as individuals become proficient in various phases of the outdoor education curriculum.

4. *Recreation Camping.* Primarily intended for industrial residents who have little or no vacation opportunities.

5. *Vocational Training Center.* Located in a resort area, the camp provides skills training in various phases of resort work for selected individuals, to assist them in finding appropriate employment.

6. *Family Tent and Trailer Camping Area.* Provides opportunity for parents of the retarded to enjoy family camping and meet other parents and friends of the retarded.

Leadership for the Mentally Retarded. In working with the mentally retarded, it is necessary to structure activities carefully and to involve participants in appropriate activities, based on their readiness and observed levels of capability. While trial-and-error and experimentation are necessary at all times, the Camp Confidence program has developed the following guidelines for leadership with the mentally retarded:

1. Verbal directions should be brief and simple, with a calm, well-controlled voice, rather than a high-pitched, excited one. The leader's facial expression and tone of voice must convey a feeling of friendliness and warmth.

2. Present new skills carefully, efficiently and clearly, using demonstration as a teaching device and to motivate interest.

3. Praise and encouragement are essential at all times; even when an individual is unsuccessful, his effort should be given approval. Do not expect immediate results in the learning of skills.

4. Although it is generally believed that retardates necessarily have short attention spans, this often stems from disinterest, boredom, or lack of understanding. When motivated and interested, and when they see progress in a meaningful activity, retarded children may show considerable interest and ability to stick to a task. When interest wanes, activities should be kept short and changed frequently.

5. Repetition, drill, and review of skills are needed more than with the non-retarded. Keep the fun in fundamentals; the "game" approach in teaching fundamentals is effective. Visual aids of all types are valuable supplementary tools.

6. Activities should be constantly evaluated in terms of the individual's needs and objectives, and then modified as needed. The same activity with appropriate modifications often has possibilities for use over the entire range of mental retardation.

7. In presenting activities, the leader should attempt to stimulate as many of the participant's senses as possible — seeing, listening, feeling and touching are better than any of these alone. Since motivation plays such a key part in the retardate's participation and achievement, the leader must seek a variety of ways to stimulate his desire and interest in the program, and to reinforce learning.

8. Discipline must be consistent and firm, but without threats and within the

understanding and capabilities of the retarded participants. There is no room for corporal punishment in this program at any time.

This set of guidelines shows how a particular disability calls for special leadership approaches. The same is true of a number of other major disabilities. For example, in working with the emotionally disturbed child an entirely different method is used.

Therapeutic Camping for Emotionally Disturbed Children

In working with emotionally disturbed children, it has been commented that nonresidential treatment programs, such as those provided by guidance clinics, school counselors, or group therapy sessions, often are ineffectual because they cannot control the child's total environment strongly enough to bring about positive change. On the other hand, residential therapeutic programs, which *are* able to control the total environment, have the disadvantage of separating the child from his parents and peers over a period of time, and tend to damage the child's self-concept and create problems for adjustment upon his return to the community. Rawson points out that one solution to this problem is to provide programs that represent a "compromise"—short enough to minimize the difficulties inherent in separation, yet controlled enough to permit a large degree of influence over environmental factors.

Short-term therapeutic camping programs have been used in a number of instances to serve emotionally disturbed children. One such program was first organized during the summer of 1970 at a church-owned facility, Englishton Park, which is operated by the United Presbyterian Church as a national service mission, and is affiliated with Hanover College, in Hanover, Indiana. The program consisted of two intensive 10-day sessions, the first for boys aged 8 to 11, and the second for boys aged 11 to 14. Many of the participants were chronic school truants, highly disruptive when in school, and often extremely weak in their academic work. They tended to have poor peer and adult relationships, with negative social prognoses, if successful intervention did not take place.

Rawson described the goals of this therapeutic camping program, which has been held each summer since 1970, and which has now served several hundred boys and girls. Three specific goals were established:

1. The program would aim at significant alteration of specific behavior patterns which seemed to be causing the child the greatest difficulty in relation to others.

2. The program would make every effort to improve a child's academic skills and attitudes, since chronic frustration in school situations was probably aggravating the child's disturbance.

3. The program would direct itself toward highly reinforcing modeling and

identification relationships with teachers and therapists in an effort to teach the child more effective skills of interpersonal relationships.[9]

Although the staff included a psychologist, an outdoor educator, an academic remediation specialist, and several social workers, the major round-the-clock therapeutic work was carried out by four male and four female college-age leaders who acted as "teacher-therapists." These individuals, selected for their sex-typing modeling potential and their strong interest in working with children, along with their interpersonal skills, were given a month-long orientation session in program goals and methods prior to the beginning of camp. A male and female were assigned as a team to each group of six children, to simulate a "family-type" situation, so that children would have to learn to relate to both sex roles in teaching, work, play, and therapeutic activities. Male leaders were assigned the dominant role in groups of boy campers, and female leaders were dominant figures in girls' groups.

Behavior Modification Techniques

Behavior modification, as a method, has been widely explored in recent years. A variety of techniques have been used in psychiatric rehabilitation, drug therapy, correctional institutions, and other settings. Rawson describes the rationale of behavior modification, as it has been used at the Englishton Park therapeutic camp:

> Behavior modification theory places heavy emphasis upon the early extinction of socially maladaptive behaviors and immediate and consistent reinforcement of socially appropriate behavior. Put in its simplest terms, the basic assumption of this theory is that most behavior, good or bad, is in fact learned, and it was originally learned because it was reinforced socially or otherwise. Therefore, deliberate, consistent manipulation of reinforcements as a consequence of specific behaviors leads to unlearning of previous behaviors (which no longer lead to positive reinforcements) and simultaneous learning of new alternate behaviors which now lead to positive reinforcements.[10]

Before each child arrived at the camp, an intensive "behavior prescription" was drawn up for him, based upon study of family case histories, school and teacher reports, psychometric test findings, and parental reports. Based on this, the teacher-therapists sought to achieve specific behavior modification goals, using a number of positive and negative reinforcements to either reward or inhibit behavior. Positive reinforcements were: (a) verbal praise; (b) physical gestures of affection and approval; (c)

---

[9] For a description of this program, see: Harve E. Rawson: "Residential Short-Term Camping for Children With Behavior Problems: A Behavior-Modification Approach." *Child Welfare,* October, 1973, pp. 511–520.

[10] Cited in "Residential Short-Term Camping for Children With Behavior Problems: A Behavior-Modification Approach," p. 513.

award of candy pellets; (d) award of gummed stars on name badges, which could be traded for candy bars, soft drinks, or ice cream; (e) fancy certificates of merit given in public ceremonials; and (f) the right to participate in highly desired activities, such as evening swimming or overnight campouts. Negative reinforcements were: (a) complete ignoral (turning one's back on a child, despite his attention-getting pleas); and (b) withdrawal from a highly desired activity for a period of several minutes.

Rawson cites an example of a prescription for a hostile-aggressive boy with extremely poor interpersonal relationships, characterized by frequent fighting:

> *Primary goal:* to decrease fighting behavior. *Methods:* male teacher should be warm and supportive at all times and utilize a great deal of physical gestures of approval and affection, such as hugging, holding, etc.; set up token reinforcement system for self-control of overt aggression toward others, starting at 10-minute intervals and increasing to 30-minute intervals; reinforce immediately with verbal praise (and at first candy pellets) for any assertive positive social or work relationship with peers.
>
> If he fights, stand between him and aggressed, turning your back toward him in total ignoral and immediately reinforce aggressed for non-retaliation and others in group for not paying attention to the distraction; all attention-seeking behaviors, such as verbal annoyance, backtalking, talking too much, gross exaggeration, punching others, etc., should lead to immediate physical ignoral and reinforcement of others in the group for not paying attention; reserve leadership role as a coveted activity, but utilize immediately for socially desired behavior; be very firm and consistent with this camper at all times and make sure he understands your expectations, repeating them often; utilize maximum peer pressure where possible to alter inappropriate behavior, including halt of coveted activity for entire group.[11]

On the other hand, a prescription for a girl marked by excessive shyness, limited verbalization, and extreme withdrawal might be:

> *Primary goal:* to increase assertive behavior. *Methods:* female teacher should be very warm and supportive at all times and throughout session, and utilize a great deal of physical gestures of approval and affection; set up token reinforcement system for assertive vocalization behavior . . .; reinforce immediately for any appropriate assertive verbalization response; reinforce immediately for any assertive positive social or work relationship with peers; make sure this girl gets appropriate public ceremonial awards for any social appropriate behavior; wait for all responses with no exhibit of anxiety or 'hurry-up' clues if this child stutters or stammers.[12]

Psychological tests administered to emotionally disturbed children in this therapeutic camping program demonstrated that they had improved markedly in such areas as response to authority, self-concept, frustration tolerance, and attitudes toward parents and school. While the behavior

---

[11] Cited in "Residential Short-Term Camping for Children with Behavior Problems: A Behavior-Modification Approach," p. 514.

[12] Ibid., p. 514.

modification techniques used in this program might be regarded as controversial, they demonstrate how techniques for changing behavior and bringing about constructive change may be carefully designed to meet the needs of individual campers or patients.

ARMED FORCES RECREATION

Another special setting in which large numbers of recreation leaders are employed is the broad field of armed forces recreation. Both civilians and military personnel have the responsibility for providing recreation programs and facilities for men and women in the United States Army, Air Force, Navy, and Marine Corps and, in many cases, for their families. The philosophy underlying this program may be seen in an official handbook outlining the Air Force Special Services program:

Mission of the Program

The Special Services program fulfills the recreation needs and interests of Air Force personnel and their families by providing maximum opportunities for them to participate in leisure-time activities that help to stimulate, develop, and maintain their mental, physical, and social well-being. Recreation is a fundamental part of the American way of life; and Air Force military personnel and their families need and deserve self-rewarding creative recreation programs and opportunities equal in variety and quality to the best offered in the most progressive civilian communities. Proper recreation activities improve the individual's mental state, character growth, and job performance. Moreover, military personnel and their families who participate in recreation activities are more likely to have favorable attitudes toward an Air Force career.[13]

The Air Force recreation program includes the following types of activities: (a) sports, including self-directed, competitive, instructional, and spectator programs; (b) motion pictures; (c) service clubs and entertainment, including dramatic and musical activities; (d) crafts and hobbies; (e) youth activities for children of Air Force families; (f) special interest groups, such as aero, automotive, motorcycle, and power boat clubs, or hiking, sky-diving, or rod and gun clubs; (g) rest centers and recreation areas; (h) open messes; and (i) libraries. Base commanders are required to establish Special Service programs which are sufficiently diversified to provide a broad variety of activities for all those residents on the base, within manpower authorizations and available funding.

One of the key areas of armed forces recreation is sports, which are

---

[13] *Air Force Sports Program Manual.* Washington, D.C., Air Force Publication No. 215-1, July, 1966, p. 1.

designed to accomplish the following objectives:

1. To promote physical fitness and dispel fatigue and boredom.

2. To assist in the adjustment of military personnel to the service.

3. To create a socializing influence among military personnel, counteracting possible feelings of isolation and loneliness.

4. To provide opportunity to express socially approved forms of aggressive behavior.

5. To promote healthy personality development.

6. To strengthen military morale, fighting spirit, and esprit de corps.

7. To promote military discipline, respect for authority, and acceptance of rules and regulations.

8. To encourage wholesome use of leisure.

9. To provide, through sports, entertainment of a satisfying, vicarious nature, for large numbers of spectators.

As in all specialized areas of recreation, the goals reflect the unique mission of the sponsoring agency. This is best demonstrated in the description in the Air Force Special Services Manual of how sports contribute to "fighting spirit," "unity and esprit de corps," and military discipline. The manual states:

> *Fighting Spirit.* Morale is synonymous with fighting spirit. Its psychological basis is founded in the need for survival. Courage, determination, initiative, and aggressiveness are certainly desirable qualities for a soldier. They become mandatory in time of war. Nowhere is the fighting spirit and the will to win held in higher esteem than in the field of sports. . . . The will to win, to endure, the courage to carry on, is built continuously through a program of sport . . .

> *Unity and Esprit de Corps.* Sports develop a spirit of unity. Social distinction, race, and creed are forgotten in the light of the common task. Nothing in the Air Force program will so unify an Air Force base, a flight squadron, or group, as sports. It is through participation on the base or squadron team that an airman may gain . . . identification with his squadron, with the base, and with the Air Force . . .

> *Military Discipline.* Cheerful obedience to orders and to superiors is a military necessity. Discipline and respect for authority are a must in the service. Every agency which can make a contribution to discipline should be used fully. Respect for authority, acceptance of rules, and self-imposed obedience of the spirit of the rules are the essence of sports competition . . .[14]

It becomes the responsibility of recreation personnel in the Air Force to promote these goals vigorously. This is done through an extensive program of sports, which includes six major elements: (a) *instruction* in basic sports skills; (b) a *"self-directed"* phase of informal participation in sports

---

[14] *Air Force Sports Program Manual.* Washington, D.C., Air Force Publication No. 215–2, October, 1966, p. 4.

under minimum supervision or direction; (c) an *intramural* program, in which personnel assigned to a particular base compete with others at the same base; (d) an *extramural* program, which includes competition between the intramural teams of different air force bases, or with teams from neighboring communities; (e) a *varsity* program, which involves high-level competition with players selected for their advanced skills, who compete on a broader national or international scale; and (f) a program for *women* in the Air Force.

The task of organizing this extensive program is an extremely complex one. The individual serving as sports director must carry on a wide variety of functions. Working with a sports council that consists of the squadron sports directors, members of base standing committees, team managers, and squadron representatives, he must formulate policies and be responsible for the proper conduct of the base intramural program. This includes the following responsibilities:

1. Plan, direct, and supervise the general conduct of all intramural activities.

2. Assist group and squadron sports directors and team managers in an advisory capacity.

3. Develop intramural policies in collaboration with the base sports director, the sports council, sports staff, and the participants.

4. Systematically publicize and promote the program.

5. Draw up schedules, organize leagues, meets, tournaments, and plan special events.

6. Select, train, assign, and supervise intramural officials.

7. Interpret the intramural program to base personnel.

8. Provide for the safety and well-being of all participants.

9. Evaluate the program.

10. Compile and publish game results and individual and team records.

11. Develop and publish rules relating to program administration.

12. Develop and supply to squadron sports directors and organization managers the necessary forms for reporting game results, signing out equipment, reserving practice areas, making a protest, and so forth.

13. Control equipment furnished for contests.

14. Prepare budget estimates.

Although this listing of responsibilities refers to the intramural sports program in the Air Force, it provides a useful overall picture of the function of recreation personnel in all the armed forces. The task of recreation personnel includes a number of key supervisory and administrative functions. While many specialists are employed in specific areas of recreation interest, the general role is one which requires the ability to organize, work through appropriate channels, motivate participation, and carry out program elements within the total framework of the military structure. The successful recreation director in the armed forces must have enthusiasm, drive, and imagination, and must be able to turn his or her ideas into program realities through "know-how" of the bureaucratic structure.

INDUSTRIAL RECREATION PROGRAMS

Another important area of recreation service which is primarily directed at adults is industrial recreation. This consists of recreation programs which are offered by, or in conjunction with, industries and companies, to serve employees and, in many cases, their families.

Scope of Industrial Recreation

This form of recreation sponsorship has grown rapidly in the last three decades. Approximately a thousand major industries or companies provide extensive recreation programs, many under professional leadership. Essentially, their purposes are three-fold: (a) to *improve employer-employee relationships* by developing attractive and comprehensive activity programs as part of the overall personnel services and "fringe" benefits offered by the company; (b) to *promote employee efficiency* by helping to reduce absenteeism, accidents, or even sabotage (studies have indicated that these may stem from boredom and the psychological problems of workers), and by promoting the physical fitness of workers; and (c) to *improve the public image and recruitment appeal* of industries, which is particularly important for concerns that are located in remote geographical areas or that must compete with other companies for skilled employees who may be in short supply.

Patterns of sponsorship vary considerably in different companies around the United States and Canada. In some cases, the industry may take full responsibility for providing facilities, leadership, and financial support for a diversified program of activities; frequently this is done with the assistance of an advisory council of employees. In other cases, the facilities are provided by the company, while the employees, through a recreation association or council, take responsibility for organizing and staffing the program. In still other cases, the employees take the major responsibility for financing and operating the program, using facilities that are chiefly away from the place of employment.

To illustrate the patterns of industrial recreation that are provided today, a detailed description of the program at one major industrial concern is provided here.

Xerox Corporation, Rochester, New York

The Xerox Corporation offers a leading example of how a major company may provide outstanding recreation opportunities for its employees.

The responsibility for organizing and carrying out this program is assigned to the Xerox Recreation Association. This incorporated, nonprofit body was formed in 1965 through the combined efforts of the Xerox management and a number of interested employees.

Facilities and Funding

The Xerox Recreation Association offers programs at three company locations: at Xerox Square in the center of Rochester, and in two suburban settings, at Henrietta and Webster, New York. Xerox Square offers conference rooms, an executive fitness laboratory and lockers, physical fitness areas, saunas, gymnasiums, an auditorium, and an ice skating rink. The Webster complex has a multipurpose recreation building, including an exercise area with physical fitness equipment, lockers and showers, and a general purpose area for meetings of clubs and organizations. Its outdoor facilities include four lighted and two unlighted baseball diamonds, a putting green, a jogging and cycling path, lighted basketball and tennis courts, and facilities for horsehoes and archery. At Henrietta, there is an indoor recreation area with equipment similar to the Webster complex, in addition to a mile-long jogging path and two unlighted baseball diamonds.

In addition to providing and maintaining these facilities, the Xerox Corporation supports the Recreation Association in two ways — through total and partial subsidies.

Total Subsidy.　This is given in the form of salaries for full-time professional personnel, payment of outside services, purchase of major equipment, and similar costs.

Partial Subsidy.　Fees are collected for participation in all recreation activities. However, these may not pay the full cost of conducting them. When a surplus occurs, money is returned to the Xerox Recreation Association's treasury. When a surplus does not occur, and when serious deficits are incurred in supporting certain activities, the corporation may assist in paying for instructors, umpires, supplies, and other charges.

This arrangement, in which both the employees and the company share the cost of operating the recreation program, represents a form of cooperative sponsorship in which employees not only pay for a major portion of what is provided them but also supply much leadership and direction, thus gaining greater interest and desire to participate.

Program Elements

The Xerox Recreation Association offers a wide variety of opportunities in such areas as sports competition, physical fitness activities, cultural participation, special interest groups and clubs, travel tours, and discount tickets to special events. An overall schedule for a recent year is provided in

TABLE 11-1. Xerox Recreation Association Program Schedule

SPORTS & ATHLETICS	LOCATION*	SEASON AVAILABLE
BASKETBALL—Leagues & Tournaments	1,3,4	November—March
BOWLING—Leagues, Tournaments, & Fun Nights	4	September—April
FLAG FOOTBALL—Leagues	1	August—October
GOLF—Instruction, Leagues, Putting Green, Tournaments	1,4	May—September
HORSEBACK RIDING—Open Riding & Instruction	4	Year Round
HORSESHOES—Courts & Tournaments	1,4	May—November
ICE SKATING—Rink, Open Skating & Instruction	2	November—March
JUDO & KARATE—Instruction	4	September—May
PHYSICAL FITNESS— Executive, Men, & Women	1,2,3	Year Round
ROLLER SKATING	4	Spring & Fall
SCUBA—Instruction	4	October—April
SOCCER CLUB	1,3	May—September
SOFTBALL—Slo-pitch, Men's & Women's Leagues & Tournaments	1,3	May—September
TENNIS—Exhibitions, Instruction, Leagues & Tournaments	1,2,4	April—October
VOLLEYBALL—Men's & Women's Tournaments & Co-Rec. Play	1,4	Year Round

CLUBS & SPECIAL INTEREST GROUPS		
ANTIQUE CLUB	2,4	September—June
ARCHERY CLUB—Ranges	1,3,4	Year Round
AUTO CLUB	1,4	April—October
BRIDGE—Instruction & Club	1,2,3	September—May
PHOTO CLUB	2,4	September—June
PISTOL CLUB	4	Year Round
SAILING CLUB	2,4	April—October
SKI CLUB	1,2,4	September—April
TABLE TENNIS CLUB	1	Year Round
XEROX PLAYERS—Drama Club	2	Year Round

SOCIAL & CULTURAL		
DANCING—Ballroom	1	September—May
DANCING—Square Dance Club	1	Year Round
EDUCATION—Language, Music, Sewing	1,2,3,4	Year Round
FASHION SHOWS	1,2,3	Year Round
HEALTH—Diet Workshop	1,2,3,4	Year Round
PICNIC KITS	1,2,3	April—September
TICKET SALES—Athletic, Social, & Cultural	1,2,3	Year Round
TOASTMASTERS	4	Year Round
TRAVEL TOURS—Domestic & Foreign	4	Year Round
XEROX PIONEERS—Retirees Club	2,4	Year Round

* 1 Webster, 800 Phillips Road
 2 Xerox Square, Rochester
 3 Henrietta, 1350 Jefferson Road
 4 Sites located outside Xerox property

Table 11–1, which describes the activities offered, the seasons when they are available, and the locations where they may be found.

In addition to the customary activities, several of the program elements deserve fuller description. These are: (a) the travel program; (b) the inner-city youth program; and (c) the physical fitness program.

Travel Program. A wide variety of travel tours are planned as chartered discount flights to countries all over the world. These trips are formally sponsored by the Xerox Recreation Association, which signs up the travelers, in conjunction with Leisurac, Incorporated, a travel company located in the Rochester area. Leisurac makes all of the detailed arrangements for the flights and provides experienced tour guides. In a recent year, chartered jet flights were sponsored to Curaçao, Puerto Rico, Barbados, Disney World, the Costa del Sol (Spain), and for a tour of the Soviet Union. In addition, the Xerox Ski Club sets up trips for a weekend or longer to outstanding ski areas in the United States and abroad, including Vermont, Lake Tahoe (in the High Sierras), and Innsbruck, Austria.

Inner-City Youth Program. The Xerox Corporation recognizes its obligation to assist the city of Rochester in a variety of social concerns. Although it is an attractive and economically viable community, Rochester has a seriously disadvantaged inner-city population, and has had summer disturbances related to this problem. Xerox therefore initiated a summer inner-city youth program called CONTACT. As part of its project, CONTACT took inner-city youth, mostly black, to the University of Rochester campus, where they participated in activities such as baseball, soccer, swimming, and arts and crafts, which were planned for them by the Xerox Recreation Association staff.

Physical Fitness Program. Recognizing that, in an age of mechanization and automation, many individuals get insufficient exercise, the Xerox management has strongly supported a sound physical fitness program for the prevention of cardiorespiratory diseases. It is provided on two levels: (a) an executive fitness program, and (b) a general fitness program for other employees.

The executive program is provided in Xerox Square. It offers an elaborate circuit interval training program which makes use of eight Universal weightlifting stations, a mechanical treadmill, and a bicycle ergometer, along with an ultraviolet room and sauna. Medical diagnoses are made of the executives participating in the program, and the physical fitness specialist keeps a close check and maintains daily progressive records on each. It has been found that this fitness program is valuable in preventing the cardiovascular problems and other disabilities faced by executives, who are often challenged by stressful, deskbound daily routines. The general fitness program offered for other employees at all three locations provides basically the same indoor equipment for fitness, along with guidance from a fitness specialist who maintains records of employees on a daily basis.

Leadership

The Xerox recreation staff consists of seven professionally trained staff members, three of whom have advanced degrees in this field. In addition, there are full-time secretaries and a bookkeeper. Considering the number of employees served—today over 8,000 persons—this is an excellent ratio of staff to participants. Detailed position descriptions have been developed for professional staff members on five levels: Recreation Specialist, Senior Recreation Specialist, Recreation Supervisor, Manager of Recreation Programs, and Manager of Corporate Recreation Services. These position descriptions include the following statement of needed skills and abilities in industrial recreation:

> Foremost, the recreation professional must be able to deal effectively with men and women with varied ages, interests, education, economic levels, and abilities. He must be able to communicate effectively with superiors and subordinates, and to tactfully and diplomatically make constructive criticism. He also must provide the necessary encouragement to program participants and to generally make employee experiences with recreation enjoyable and beneficial. Natural leadership ability and knowledge of leadership skills cannot be overemphasized.
>
> Each professional staff member must be able to project a favorable image of his company and himself. In short, he must be skilled in all aspects of administration, with major emphasis in the management of finances. Additionally, he must be skilled in supervising subordinates while being able to take positive action with superiors. He must also be able to adapt quickly to new situations and to study and grow with new program, facility, and staff developments. . . . He must have a sound philosophy of recreation consistent with current trends in municipal and industrial recreation.[15]

A fuller statement of the skills essential for success as an industrial recreation professional would include the following elements:

1. The ability to work closely with all levels of management and to communicate effectively with line-level personnel.

2. The ability to make contact and work with community groups, school principals, and similar officials, to make cooperative program or facilities arrangements.

3. The ability to be an "enabler," to help members get their own clubs or special interest groups formed, and to take on many of their own responsibilities.

4. The ability to manage a variety of facilities—including assisting the conceptualizing and designing of facilities, as well as maintaining and scheduling them properly.

5. The ability to develop and carry out a variety of sometimes complicated financial arrangements for the support of programs, and to make judgments about the allocation of company resources.

---

[15] *Professional Staff Standards.* Rochester, New York, Xerox Recreation Association, June, 1969.

6. The ability to carry out effective promotional procedures. Just as in any other department, employee participation in recreation is not assured, and the leader must be highly skilled in publicizing activities offered by his service.

7. The ability to have the interests of both employees and management at heart; he must be able to represent both groups in an equitable and fair manner.

8. Finally, the ability to envision a program that incorporates a wide variety of recreation elements, but that may also include other personnel services which can legitimately be attached to this department.

The industrial recreation specialist must have many of the same kinds of qualities as those described for armed forces recreation workers. He must be able to function effectively within a large bureaucratic structure, and to justify his program and work closely with key executives or management personnel. He must be an excellent organizer and administrator, in part because his task is so complex that it requires these skills, and in part because he is employed by an organization that values these qualities highly. Finally, he must be an initiator, a self-starter, and a "do-er."

RECREATION PROGRAMS IN PSYCHIATRIC REHABILITATION

One of the major specializations within the broad field of therapeutic recreation service involves working with psychiatric patients. Until recently, mental patients comprised one half of all the hospital patients in the United States. In general, recreation has been accepted as one of the important rehabilitative services in psychiatric hospitals or treatment units, and is viewed as meeting the following important patient needs:

1. To help patients become involved in reality situations.

2. To help withdrawn patients become resocialized.

3. To provide emotional release and interests outside self.

4. To improve the self-concept of patients.

5. To create patient awareness of leisure needs, and improve motivation for participation.

6. To provide information useful for diagnosis or treatment.

7. To provide release for hostility and aggression.

8. To keep patient morale high.

9. To teach skills useful for leisure, after discharge from hospital.[16]

---

[16] Richard Kraus: *Recreation and Related Therapies in Psychiatric Rehabilitation.* New York, Faculty Research Award Program, Herbert H. Lehman College, November, 1972, p. 23.

TABLE 11-2.   Activities Offered in Recreational Therapy Programs[17]

Activity	Percent of Hospitals	Activity	Percent of Hospitals
Cards	97.3	Crafts	82.7
Sports	97.3	Bowling	81.3
Bingo	96.0	Hobbies	80.0
Music Listening	96.0	Music Classes	78.7
Social Activities	93.3	Cooking	77.3
Movies	93.3	Swimming	76.0
Arts	93.3	Talent Show	73.3
Professional		Drama	72.0
Entertainment	90.7	Gardening	71.7
Discussion Groups	89.5	Creative Writing	58.6
Game Room	89.5	Newspaper	54.7
Trips	88.0	Ham Radio	10.7
Television	86.7		

A recent study of recreation activities provided in psychiatric hospitals in the New York-New Jersey-Connecticut region indicated the following list of program activities (Table 11-2).

In the past, such activities generally were organized carefully and scheduled in most hospitals, with weekly calendars of activity comparable to what might be found in most community centers or other large-scale recreation programs. They tended to be planned by professional staff members, and patients were expected to attend the programs they were assigned to; if they did not, or if they did not take part, it was regarded as evidence of inability to function socially and a sign of continuing illness. In recent years, however, changes have occurred within the broad field of psychiatric care which have modified the nature of recreation—both in terms of its goals and its treatment methods.

Breakdown of the Locked Hospital, Custodial Approach

The most significant change has been the administrative shift away from large, custodial hospitals located at a considerable distance from the home communities of many mental patients, and toward smaller treatment units located in or close to the patients' places of residence. This has been accompanied by a much greater emphasis on short-time care. Instead of accepting as inevitable that the majority of patients must be locked up in hospitals where they remain for several months or years before being discharged, the effort today is to provide "crash" treatment, with an intensive effort made to get people out of the hospital as quickly as possible or, better than that, to avoid hospitalization completely.

---

[17] Cited in *Recreation and Related Therapies in Psychiatric Rehabilitation,* p. 24.

With the use of a variety of new drugs, mental hospital authorities found it possible to have many mental patients reside in the community while attending day clinics, night clinics, or even weekend programs in mental health centers. Increasing numbers of patients who have been discharged live in halfway houses or attend after-care centers or special social clubs for discharged mental patients. Many states and provinces have reduced their mental hospital populations sharply, and in some cases have eliminated the need for entire hospitals. Mentally ill individuals today live in the community—in some cases, in special hotels, in other cases, in apartment units where they have responsibility for self-care.

Within this new approach, recreation has come to be viewed in a new light. Several of the key aspects of the contemporary use of therapeutic recreation in psychiatric settings include: (a) the milieu therapy approach; (b) the development of activity therapies; and (c) leisure counseling.

Milieu Therapy Approach

This approach is based on the conviction that the entire institution should provide a total environment in which the patient is respected as an individual, has a meaningful voice in developing hospital plans and programs, and is able to play a real part in his own recovery. It argues that mentally ill individuals have lost their ability to relate effectively to others, or to handle environmental pressures and demands in the outside world. The effort of the psychiatric hospital should be to provide a new setting in which the patient will be able to function meaningfully, and in which he will develop a sense of reality and self-confidence in his ability to communicate with people. He will take part in social situations, and deal with real challenges and responsibilities.

Within this framework, the mental patient should be able to make meaningful decisions about his own experiences while in the hospital. In some cases, patients take over responsibility for housekeeping or cooking duties. In others, they serve on hospital committees or councils, and make recommendations to hospital administrators. On all levels, each member of the hospital staff is expected to play a significant part in the treatment program, and to use himself in therapeutic ways in all contacts with patients. Obviously, within this approach, recreation therapy must assume new roles. For instance, patients are not *required* to take part in activity. They have a real voice in developing programs; schedules tend to be less structured, and to involve new and different kinds of creative programming.

Development of Activity Therapies

Over a period of time, many psychiatric hospitals have developed a variety of different types of nonmedical therapies, including recreational, occupational, physical, educational, and industrial therapy, in addition to a number of other therapies in music, art, and dance. By their very number, these services have tended to create confusion and overlap in many hospitals. For this reason, and for administrative efficiency, an increasing number of hospitals have been combining the various adjunctive therapies under the heading of "activity therapies."

This trend has generally meant that recreation workers have been assigned new kinds of responsibilities, and are now expected to work much more closely with other staff members in other treatment disciplines. In many hospitals, there is greater emphasis on recreation as a medium through which patients plan their own trips to the community, or organize their own events or activities. Activities of daily living that are offered by activity therapies departments typically include the following types of elements: (a) grooming and self-care classes or sessions; (b) social awareness discussions or encounter groups; (c) home and family management discussion groups or projects; (d) clerical work groups, which carry on office work for the hospital and teach work skills; (e) "boutiques" or other sheltered workshops that produce craft articles for sale in the hospital; (f) ward clean-up assignments; and (g) shopping trips to the community to re-establish competence in dealing with typical tasks of independent living.

Such activities represent a conscious effort to make the program helpful in preparing people to return to the community. Instead of having them take part in recreational activities which, while enjoyable and constructive in the present, might not be readily available to them in the future, the effort is made to have them gain practical experiences that will be directly helpful in building competence for independent living.

Leisure Counseling

Leisure counseling—or recreation counseling, as it is frequently called —is a process of working closely with patients to assure that they will be able to use their leisure constructively upon return to the community rather than become involved in negative or self-destructive patterns of free time use. One of the the first programs of recreation counseling for psychiatric patients was established at the Veteran's Administration Hospital in Kansas City, Missouri, in 1955. The objectives of this program were to.

1. Assist the patient to maintain and strengthen his existing affiliations with family, friends, church, lodge, and civic groups.

2. Help the patient form new ties with individuals and groups.

3. Teach the patient how to make use of available community resources for recreation.

4. Stimulate the patient's awareness of his own recreational needs.

5. Mobilize community resources for fostering mental health.

Group therapy sessions with patients on the neurological ward were scheduled with a committee that included representatives of the psychiatric staff, psychologists, recreation therapists, and a representative of the public recreation department. This program has been described by Olson and McCormack:

> It has been our experience that with sustained psychiatric treatment in the hospital environment, withdrawn patients have come to participate with apparent enjoyment in social-recreational activities. Contact with patients who have required rehospitalization here or at nearby psychiatric centers indicates that some tend to lapse into solitary ways on discharge and thus set the stage for reactivation of old pathological patterns of behavior. Our observations suggested that in several of these cases, specific guidance in this area — living through the non-working hours — was indicated. As a consequence, a new patient service was instituted which we called Recreation Counseling. . . .
>
> Recreation Counseling is available to patients on both an individual and a group basis. Individual counseling is done where the psychiatric staff feels that use of leisure time or need for social contact or group affiliation is a prime factor in the current illness. . . . The counselor and the patient explore the patient's needs in this area and work together toward its resolution. In this type of counseling, the patient contact is done by the psychologist. He is able to call upon the hospital recreation section for help with regard to the patient's current situation and on the city recreation worker for advice with regard to opportunities for the patient after discharge. The team members work together in helping the patient make contacts that can last after discharge. The therapist is able to follow up on these contacts and work through whatever practical difficulties might come.[18]

An important element in recreation counseling is the group discussion, in which patients are encouraged to discuss their experiences, problems, and expectations for the future. Each staff member participating in these meetings clarifies problems or offers assistance on the basis of his own specialized expertise, while the representative of the city recreation department helps to provide knowledge of community programs and facilities. In addition, patients, through their counseling groups, visit many places in the nearby community, such as sports centers, community centers, schools, clubs, and similar facilities.

Evaluation over a period of years indicated that the Kansas City Veteran's Administration Hospital recreation counseling program has been extremely effective in helping patients strengthen existing affiliations with community groups, form new ties, and learn to avail themselves of facilities and programs that they had not formerly used.

Many other hospitals throughout the United States and Canada have developed leisure or recreation counseling programs in recent years. The Binghamton, New York, State Hospital, for example, has initiated a so-called "Gateway Program," a pilot project intended to assist discharged patients in returning to the community through both a systematic and

---

[18] William E. Olson and John B. McCormack: "Recreation Counseling in the Psychiatric Service of a General Hospital." *Journal of Nervous and Mental Disease,* May–June, 1957.

carefully designed selection of patients, and a series of experiences and planned exposures which provide them with a solid base of recreational opportunity. A major element in this program was the preparation of the community to receive and work with the discharged mental patient:

> After some experience in Gateway's Community-Readiness phase, we became aware of a void in continuity which existed on the community side of our program. To draw an analogy from vocational practices and goals, we had not developed the appropriate relationships with community recreation resources: for example, the Division of Vocational Rehabilitation regularly relates to employers, community employment agencies, and sheltered workshop programs. It was felt ... we should develop a network of communication and understanding between the institution and those individuals in the community who represent leisure-activity involvement for not only the convalescing mental patient but the entire "population at risk" within our institution's catchment area.
>
> In order to initiate this understanding, we began a series of educationally oriented workshops for community recreation agency personnel; administrators, as well as program people. Via these workshop experiences, an attempt was made to point out the responsibility the community has in dealing with *all* disabled individuals. Recreation professionals in the community presently make efforts to adapt their program to include the more obviously handicapped, and it therefore became our intention to point out the over-riding need that a similar effort be made on behalf of the convalescing mental patient. . . .[19]

Following these meetings, the Binghamton Gateway project developed a community referral plan which involved cooperating groups that represented local, state, and county recreation organizations, school and university representatives, public and private recreation agencies, church groups, and community volunteer associations. This process included post-discharge communication, through which guidance was given to community agencies serving discharged mental patients, with the hospital receiving feedback on their progress. It was decided, as this system began to yield positive results, to establish a community-based, leisure-use education and adjustment clinic, which was to become the base of operations for an expanded system of community referral agencies. In addition, detailed plans were developed to educate the public with the improved understanding of the needs of discharged mental patients, and to focus on providing instruction in this area in professional preparation programs offered to recreation and physical education personnel in nearby colleges and universities.

A final example of the strong effort being made to equip discharged mental patients to use their leisure effectively may be found in the Mental Health Centre in Penetanguishene, Ontario, Canada. This regional mental health facility makes a clear distinction between three phases of recreational service: (a) general recreation activities, which are intended to make the patient's stay at the hospital as pleasant as possible but are not for

---

[19] *Report of Gateway Pilot Program.* Binghamton, New York, State Hospital, February, 1969, pp. 5–6.

achieving therapeutic goals; (b) a therapeutic phase, involving assessment of the patient's status and needs, including development of a treatment plan, counseling services, and effective referral; and (c) a carefully designed research program, which is carried on to evaluate needs and outcomes.

The Penetanguishene Mental Health Centre examines the social and recreational patterns, interests, and needs of entering patients, in order to provide a basis for developing treatment plans. Following an anonymous observation of the patient attending evening activities, a series of seven sessions is scheduled to explore the entire problem. The first session is a videotaped interview between the assessor and the client that examines the patient's general attitudes toward recreation, his pre-hospital and present recreation activities and interests, and his perception of future involvements. The remaining sessions include the administration of the Guilford-Zimmerman Temperament Survey, a psychological projective test designed to complement the assessor's observations, and a series of meetings that involve the patient's actual exposure to social situations, games, and recreational areas, and careful analysis of his reactions and involvement.

Much of the information gathered through these sessions is used as the basis for counseling patients while at the hospital, or for guiding them in the use of available recreational opportunities, both in the hospital and in the community. The Penetanguishene staff makes an intensive effort to involve patients in community programs throughout their treatment stay, in order to avoid the harmful effects of institutionalization and to promote healthy ties with community leisure resources. Patients take bus trips to local community recreation events; they attend church, go shopping regularly in the community, use a local Y.M.C.A. swimming pool, and attend movies, harness racing events, wrestling matches, and other entertainment activities in and around Penetanguishene.

At the same time, intensive efforts are made to help those in the local community become aware of the recreational needs of the Centre's patient population:

> Members of the recreation staff attend local community council meetings and take active roles in community affairs. Recreation staff have been used as recreation resource persons within the local communities of Penetanguishene and Midland as well as the Simcoe County area. The dual role as participants and resource persons within the community is an important facet that assists in the integration and education of the community toward the recreational needs of the patient population.[20]

The examples that have just been cited show how recreation professionals in the field of psychiatric care must today operate as "social systems" specialists. They help to prepare individuals for successful return to the community, involve community representatives in the hospital program,

---

[20] *Staff Manual:* Description of Community Involvement Program at Penetanguishene, Ontario, Mental Health Centre, 1973.

make extensive use of community resources and, through follow-up and referral programs, they actually continue to sustain and assist patients through the difficult process of transition. Obviously, such programs tend to represent the vanguard of new treatment approaches in the most advanced states or provinces in the United States and Canada. They demonstrate one of the ways in which recreation leadership and supervision has adapted to meet pressing contemporary needs in an important area of public service.

LEADERSHIP IN SENIOR CENTERS

This chapter now turns to the needs of aging persons in modern society. Today, over 20 million citizens of the United States are over 65, and it is estimated that by the year 1980, one out of every seven persons will be in this age group. Although in some societies older citizens are highly respected and cared for, this is not generally true of the Western world, which tends to be youth-oriented and to denigrate the aging.

Social isolation becomes a particularly important problem for the old. Often they are seriously economically disadvantaged, living on only a fraction of the income of younger persons. In 1967, the United States Bureau of Labor Statistics found that 36 per cent of all retired couples could not afford the recommended budget for the lowest standard of living ($2,671), while 56 per cent could not afford the intermediate budget ($3,857), and 75 per cent could not afford the highest budget ($6,039). Thus, it becomes difficult for them to travel, or to make use of commercial recreation opportunities. The problem of isolation is made more acute by the fact that so many older persons live alone, having been widowed or divorced, and having lost many of their earlier friends and associations.

Health problems tend to be increasingly severe as one grows older. Limited mobility, poverty, and fear of venturing out keep many elderly persons from securing the services they need in the area of health. Similar factors make it difficult for them to shop and cook properly, with the result that nutrition becomes a serious problem for older persons. Mental illness becomes an increasingly important hazard, with the availability and adequacy of psychiatric care for older persons being seriously limited.

Role of Senior Centers

For the past two or three decades, there has been an increasing trend toward the development of community-based senior centers or Golden Age Clubs which are geared to serve older persons with recreational opportunities and other badly needed social programs. Project FIND (Friendless, Isolated, Needy and Disabled), sponsored by the National Council on the Aging, sought to locate the elderly poor, and to learn the source and amount of their incomes, their problems related to health, housing, isolation, and similar needs. It was found that the most serious difficulties lay in the area of need for social contacts and recreation. The National Council on the Aging, after evaluating data gathered by FIND, recommended the multi-purpose center as a means of meeting the social and service needs of the elderly, and urged that such centers be established in all communities, along with national programs of volunteer "friendly" visiting and tele-phone reassurance for homebound older persons.

A number of organizations, such as the National Council on the Aging, the National Council of Senior Citizens, and the 1971 White House Con-ference on Aging, have developed guidelines for the establishment of sen-ior centers for older persons. In 1971, the State of Michigan recommended to the White House Conference on Aging:

> . . . that consideration must be given to multi-purpose senior centers in full recognition that such centers' activities are not only recreational, but an essen-tial element in the maintenance of good mental and physical health for the older person.

The trend has been for the development of multi-service centers that offer at least three out of five basic services: (a) recreation; (b) counseling; (c) nutrition; (d) health programs; and (e) adult education programs. In defining such centers, the distinction has been made that generally Golden Age Centers meet only once or twice a week, have programs that are primarily social or recreational, and are under volunteer or nonprofessional leadership. In contrast, the term Senior Center is generally applied to centers that meet each day, provide a variety of recreational and other social services, and operate under professional leadership.

Multi-purpose Senior Centers today are regarded as places where all elderly persons, particularly the economically disadvantaged, can find social contacts, and the opportunity for self-expression and mental stimula-tion. Here, they may receive needed personal services, and are offered the opportunity to play significant social roles and, generally, to find mean-ingful life enrichment.

The goals of Senior Centers include the following:

1. Providing older persons with the opportunity for meaningful and satisfy-ing group and individual relationships.

2. Helping them learn new skills for enrichment and self-expression in the arts, in music, drama, nature, language, current events, dance, crafts, games, and similar activities.

3. Offering opportunities for them to be useful and provide service to others through volunteer action programs, thus re-assuming a valued role in society and gaining a strengthened self-concept.

4. Assisting them in maintaining good physical health, through programs of exercise, nutrition, and medical and dental care.

5. Promoting mental health, through the use and development of creative

abilities, exposure to a healthy social environment that counteracts social isolation, and provision of counseling services, where needed.

6. Helping the individual to keep informed about changes in the community and the world, and to become active in programs and organizations serving older persons.

7. Giving older persons the opportunity to assume leadership roles, and strengthening their personal effectiveness in working with others.

8. Offering guidance and, where necessary, formal assistance in a wide range of personal or legal service areas, such as housing, Social Security, or similar problems.

Typical Recreation Programs

The most commonly found recreation activities in today's Senior Centers are the following:

1. Arts and crafts, including such activities as oil and watercolor painting, sketching, woodworking, ceramics, needlepoint, sculpture, rugmaking, basketry, quilt making, and jewelry making.

2. Games, mixers, and social activities, including card playing, Bingo, parties, dances, chess, checkers, and similar activities.

3. Physical activities, such as dancing, exercise groups, lawn bowling, shuffleboard, horseshoes, or billiards.

4. Music, including community singing, small instrumental groups, choruses, music listening, or entertainment by performing groups.

5. Literary activities, such as having a center newspaper, book review or current events discussion, writing classes, debates, or visiting speakers.

6. Hobby and club groups related to such interests as sewing, knitting, photography, history, languages, stamp-collecting, or armchair travel.

7. Trips and outings to such settings as parks, scenic locations, major amusement complexes and beaches, or to concerts, plays, political rallies or conventions of older persons, boat trips, picnics, and similar excursions.

Usually, such programs are scheduled so that the most popular activities are offered daily at a regular hour, while other activities are provided once or twice a week. Often, programs reflect the particular ethnic or religious make-up of the group, such as Senior Centers in some locations that offer dramatic clubs, language groups, and other activities related to particular nationality backgrounds. In some cases, individuals may be exposed to an activity, or may attend classes in which they develop a strong interest, and may then be encouraged to attend the adult extension program of nearby colleges.

In some cases, an individual center's program may be tied to events promoted on a city-wide basis for senior citizens. For example, the Senior Citizen Section of the Department of Recreation and Parks of the City of Los Angeles offers many special events on a city-wide or district basis.

These promote the work of neighborhood centers and provide a second level of participation for active center members. In a recent year, the following events were scheduled for the month of June:

Senior Citizen Master Calendar for June

June 7–10	City-wide Art Finals, City Hall Rotunda
June 8	West Area Federation Meeting, Baldwin Hills Recreation Center
June 9	City-wide Federation Meeting, Hoover Recreation Center
June 15–17	Annual Shuffleboard Tournament, Sportsmen's Park
June 19	City-wide Talent Show Finals, Hollywood High School Auditorium
June 19	Senior Citizens Evening at the Hollywood Palladium, with Lawrence Welk and his T.V. Musical Family
June 21	Valley Area Federation Meeting, Van Nuys–Sherman Oaks
June 26	Disney on Parade
June 27	Mayor's Senior Citizen Day at the Greek Theatre
June 29	Senior Citizen Day at Hollywood Park

Health Services in Senior Centers

These may include classes, lectures, and workshops or special clinics on all aspects of health, disease prevention, diagnosis, and care. Specific health maintenance services may include any or all of the following: medical examinations, blood tests, X-rays, and special eye, ear, or dental clinics. In some cases, multi-service centers may have their own medical or dental facilities which are provided by public or voluntary agencies that may open up a service center, for example, within a housing complex attached to the social or recreational center. In other cases, a visiting team of doctors or nurses may come to the center on a weekly or monthly basis. In still others, centers may schedule organized trips to a nearby glaucoma inspection center, or to other health facilities.

Multi-service centers may also provide home care or home health aides as part of their health service program. They may also provide assistance in such areas as Social Security, Welfare, food stamps, housing, legal aid, Medicare, and similar concerns. Nutrition programs may include cafeteria service at the center (for example, the Associated Y.M.H.A.–Y.W.H.A.'s of Greater New York recently received a grant of over $800,000 from the City of New York to develop seven Senior Citizen Centers to provide one hot meal a day to the needy, as well as for other social welfare and recreation programs). The programs may also deliver meals from the center to homebound elderly persons, provide surplus foods, arrange for supermarkets to accept food stamps, and set up food purchasing cooperatives.

Community Service Programs

There are many ways in which older persons accept important social responsibilities in a multi-service center. In addition to assuming leadership roles in the center itself, they may act as delegates to other city-wide or state-wide associations for the elderly, or to senior center federations. They may engage in such service projects as making things for hospital patients, putting together Christmas packages for the homebound or institutionalized in cooperation with service clubs, telephoning voters on election days, raising funds for worthy causes, doing clerical work for social agencies, or assisting in children's day-care programs.

In some cases, specially funded programs have been established through which older persons are paid to work with emotionally disturbed or mentally retarded children. The important element is that they are able to use their lives in productive ways — whether or not they are paid — and thus regain a sense of value and importance to society.

Organization of Senior Centers

Senior Centers operate under a variety of auspices. As they have grown in size and scope, and have received funding from government and community fund drives, they have tended to be sponsored by organizations that are capable of providing thorough and efficient administration. Many

TABLE 11–3. Organization Chart for Multi-Purpose Senior Center, Recommended by National Council on the Aging

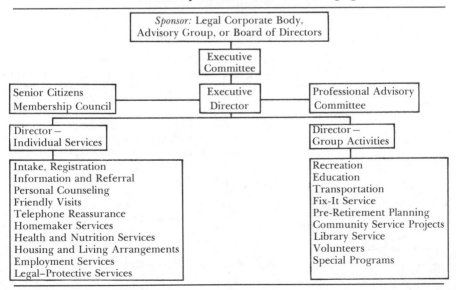

have assumed formal structures based on the model proposed by the National Council on the Aging (Table 11–3).

Many such centers are separate entities which operate under funds annually granted by the city or sponsored by voluntary agencies. In other cases, they are part of recreation and park departments with personnel hired through the Civil Service structure. They may use existing community centers, with special rooms being set aside for senior programs during the day, or they may operate in facilities that have been specially built for exclusive use by elderly persons. In many cases, these facilities are being attached to low-income housing projects.

In planning multi-purpose senior centers, the following rooms are generally provided: a combination auditorium–social hall–dining hall, multi-purpose meeting rooms, craft shops, health maintenance offices, library, lounge, kitchen, and administrative offices. Centers should be located with good accessibility to main roads or public transportation, and should be designed with ramps and other architectural features, so that it is possible for the physically disabled needing wheelchairs or with other limitations to use them conveniently. Some communities have constructed major facilities in the area of greatest density of senior citizens, and then have established satellite centers in other neighborhoods.

Hopefully, as the number of retired persons increases, we will rid ourselves of the last vestiges of the Protestant work ethic, which values only paid work and tends to make us feel guilt ridden about leisure and play. In such a liberated society, older persons may be able to use their time more easily in a wide range of enjoyable ways which are not economically productive but which bring pleasure and a sense of self-worth.

The task of leadership in centers for the aging requires certain unique talents and abilities. The Milwaukee, Wisconsin, Department of Municipal Recreation and Adult Education operates an extensive network of Golden Age Centers. It describes the role of leaders in such centers in the following terms:

> The backbone of the entire program is leadership. Leaders must bring to their assignments sympathy, patience, humility, a willingness and capacity to understand the problems of the older person, and the ability to lead and guide.
>
> The same basic group-work philosophy and principles apply to the old as well as to the young. It is necessary that the leader develop a sensitivity to the needs, feelings, and desires of the individuals in her group and discover opportunities for their recognition and fulfillment. It is important that a leader know when and how and to what extent to gradually transfer this to the club officers and committees. Her professional knowledge and competence is always important in recognizing the sort of activities that will meet the interest span of members, that will obtain the highest degree of participation, that will help develop wholesome attitudes, that will fit into the time schedule and facilities available, and that will meet the physical limitations of the members.[21]

---

[21] *Manual on Golden Age Centers.* Milwaukee, Wisconsin, Department of Municipal Recreation and Adult Education, p. 3.

Beyond this, it is essential that center directors and leaders bring a strong degree of warmth and enthusiasm to their work, providing older persons with acceptance and support while building upon their strengths and capabilities. Leaders must be able to work effectively with representatives of different organizations and disciplines in a unified team effort. In addition to recruiting and sustaining membership, leaders must also be able to involve volunteers successfully, and obtain assistance in the form of financial contributions, gifts, or other helpful services from many different sources. In a number of colleges and universities, special graduate programs in gerontology have been established through the funding of the Administration on Aging, in order to equip professionals to work with older persons. In many cases, such curricula have been attached to departments of recreation and park administration.

It seems clear that the specialized field of working with the aging will continue to be a more and more important aspect of recreation leadership, and will require an increasingly high level of expertise in the future.

RECREATION PROGRAMS IN NURSING HOMES

A major area of recreation service that has expanded markedly during the past several years consists of nursing homes serving individuals with a significant degree of physical or mental disability who are unable to live independently in the community. Depending on the nature and degree of disability and the level of medical and nursing care provided, such institutions may be called "extended care" or "health-related" facilities. Although in many cases they may also serve younger individuals who have suffered severe illnesses and are undergoing rehabilitation, generally nursing homes are for persons over the age of 65. In most cases, they are separate institutions, although some state hospitals operate geriatric units that house patients similar to the more regressed residents of nursing homes.

The Background of Nursing Homes

In earlier societies, little social assistance was given to poor, sick, or aged persons. Often, they were placed in the poorhouse, or almshouse, which was comprised of persons of all ages and disabilities, including the mentally ill. Only later were special institutions developed to care for dependent children, the retarded, the mentally ill, and similar groups in need.

Gradually, county poorhouses began to serve only aged, indigent persons in need of special care. Many other organizations, such as religious bodies or fraternal orders, also established group care homes for dependent older persons. Increasingly, private family homes also began to meet this growing need. In the United States, federal and state governments began to provide funding to assist older persons in paying the cost of such care. In 1954, for example the Hill-Burton Law provided state and federal reimbursement to public old-age homes and voluntary nursing homes. Proprietary (privately operated) nursing homes were able to obtain loans guaranteed by the Federal Housing Authority, beginning in 1959. With such assistance, nursing homes expanded rapidly, and shifted to much larger institutions which were run by management-oriented personnel.

With the establishment of Medicare and Medicaid, which pay the major portion of costs for eligible persons, great numbers of elderly indigent persons have been placed in nursing homes today. The monthly fees are paid almost completely by these agencies; individuals who have modest savings must use them up, and then are covered by local welfare programs which, in turn, have federal subsidies supporting them. As a consequence, nursing homes have become a billion-dollar business. Although such facilities are regulated by municipal or state departments of health or social welfare, and are approved nationally by nongovernmental agencies organized under the American Medical Association, the American Association of Nursing Homes, and the American Association of Homes for the Aged, too often they are shabby, unsanitary, unsafe, and provide only limited health care and activity programs. This situation results from two factors: (a) the profit motive, impelling many unscrupulous home operators to skimp on essential services in order to clear the greatest margin of financial return; and (b) that fact that nursing homes are supervised by a bureaucratic maze of agencies, unclear standards, and conflicting regulations, with inadequate numbers of supervisors.

Nursing homes actually fall into several categories today: *governmental* homes (sponsored by state, county, or municipal government); *voluntary* homes (sponsored by nonprofit agencies, usually of a philanthropic or religious type); and *proprietary* homes (privately operated for profit). They serve patients who have a wide range of disease or disability, including cancer, heart conditions, stroke, multiple sclerosis, and other illnesses or impairments. Typically, patients have not only physical but social and emotional problems. Aged persons often enter nursing homes or extended care facilities fearing that they have been abandoned by their families, and with a great sense of loss and despair. This is accentuated by the nature of living in a nursing home. This includes the fact that patients suffer a loss of privacy and independence, and are too often cared for by untrained and inexperienced aides who lack sensitivity and compassion. While medical and nursing staff members play a leading role in nursing homes, it is also clear that psychological, social service, and recreational and occupational therapy are also key elements in meeting the varied needs of aged residents.

Nursing homes must provide activity programs that permit each patient to be as alert and active as his individual physical, mental, and emotional health permits. The White Plains, New York, Center for Nursing Care has described the goals of its social rehabilitation program (which includes occupational therapy and recreation as key elements) in the following terms.

Purpose of a Social Rehabilitation Program

General Aim of such a program is to help each patient to function to his or her optimal level — physically, emotionally and socially. The successful program assists patients achieve the most vital way of life commensurate with their illness and disability. It encourages both individual and group enterprise and motivation. As such, it is an important segment of the total rehabilitation process.

Specific Goals are as follows:

To alleviate patients' fears of loneliness, abandonment and impending death

To provide stimulation and pleasure

To discourage the withdrawal tendencies so prevalent in the elderly sick, by encouraging patients to share activities and experiences with their peers in group situations, thus fostering the we-are-not-alone feeling

To re-awaken latent skills and interests, and in this way help patients revive their normal life patterns

To build self-confidence and self-respect, and lessen self-pity, by encouraging patients to communicate and to function

To make patients feel that they are not forgotten but are still part of current life in the community, by bringing members of the community into the nursing facility to entertain, to instruct, to give volunteer services

To encourage patients' sense of responsibility toward others, and to demonstrate to them that they can still be useful to society, by providing opportunities for them to participate in civic projects

According to standards that have been developed for nursing homes and extended care facilities by the National Therapeutic Recreation Society, programs should include both active and passive pursuits, individual and group activities, and varied forms of social, physical, and creative recreation. Federal regulations for extended care facilities operating with Medicare funding include the following guidelines for patients' activity programs:

1. The person in charge of patient recreation uses, to the fullest possible extent, all community, social and recreational resources, including personnel, supplies, equipment, facilities and programs.

2. Patients are encouraged, but not forced, to participate in recreational activities. Suitable activities are provided for patients who are unable to leave their rooms.

3. Suitable space is provided for the conduct of daily recreational programs, including areas designated for: (a) individual recreational pursuits, and (b) privacy for visits with friends, relatives, or clergymen.

4. The facility makes available a variety of supplies and equipment adequate

to satisfy the individual interests of patients. Examples are: books and magazines, daily newspapers, games, stationery, radio, and television.[22]

Specific examples of program activities in a given nursing home include the following:

Entertainment.   Arrangements are made with many individuals or groups from the nearby community to provide dance, drama, vocal, instrumental, or other entertainment. In some cases, groups which are preparing for formal concerts or shows elsewhere will hold their rehearsals at the home.

Parties.   Several times each month, parties, teas, or holiday or religious celebrations are held. Birthdays are celebrated en masse once a month, and frequent summer barbeques are provided.

Movies and Slide Presentations.   Free movies are obtained from corporations and similar sources. Patients particularly enjoy travel films, or films or slides which are shown by visitors to the home from the community.

Music.   Record players or strolling players are used to provide music at special events, or sometimes in the various living areas of the hospital.

Creative Arts.   Patients enjoy arts and crafts, including painting and sculpture, as well as sewing and needlework, cooking and food preparation, assisting at barbecues, gardening and flower arranging.

Sports.   These are necessarily limited but may include shuffleboard, ball tossing, rhythmic exercise or marching drills, dancing, a modified form of bowling, and table games.

Spiritual and Cultural Activities.   Religious services are held regularly; in addition, group discussions, lectures, a weekly story hour, a circulating book cart, reading therapy sessions, and a "talking book" machine are all provided.

Outings.   With medical and family approval, patients are taken on outings such as community picnics, boat trips, visits to museums or art shows, churches and synagogues, or social occasions at local homes or organizations. Usually these events serve ambulatory patients, although special arrangements may be made for those in wheelchairs.

Patients who are capable of such activity are drawn into community service projects, or into other roles which keep them active and provide them with meaningful responsibilities. In some institutions, patients have developed Welcoming Committees, which help to orient new patients to the nursing home and its program, and assist with the social adjustment that is often so difficult for them. In other nursing homes, patients are responsible for planning and editing a newsletter or newspaper which comes out weekly or monthly. In still other settings, patient councils have been formed that represent the various wards or floors in meetings held with staff members to discuss patient needs and grievances, to make

---

[22] Jean R. Tague: "The Status of Therapeutic Recreation in Extended Care Facilities: A Challenge and an Opportunity." *Therapeutic Recreation Journal,* Third Quarter, 1970, pp. 13–14.

requests for change, or to work cooperatively in planning new programs. At the White Plains, New York, Center for Nursing Care, community service oriented programs include the following:

Civic Projects.   Patients who contribute to the community continue to feel a part of the community. Patient-volunteers make cancer dressings for a hospital, roll bandages for a church group, stuff, seal and stamp envelopes for a fund-raising drive. These are good examples of useful services within the range of patient capabilities.

Fund-Raising.   Fairs are held twice a year for a worthy community organization or, sometimes, for the facility itself. Although staff participation is heavy and welcome, patients themselves make many of the articles sold, help with decorations and, if able, serve as sales personnel. Many patients have been similarly involved with bazaars and fairs in the past, during their healthier years, and thus enjoy this type of endeavor.

Voting Participation.   Good citizenship is encouraged, with shut-in patients voting via absentee ballots. Candidates for local offices are invited to present their platforms to patients. Representatives of the local chapter of the League of Women Voters visit to discuss issues; they return to assist with voting procedures. Civic leaders visit from time to time to discuss local problems and to report on progress in such areas as urban renewal.

Senior Citizen Visitors.   A continuing effort is made to invite senior citizen neighbors regularly to the facility to join patients in activities. Following the formal program they are invited to stay for refreshments and conversation. In this way, patients have an opportunity to form friendships with local people outside the institution.

Many nursing home patients may not be capable of taking part in such activities. These patients may be severely withdrawn or regressed, and unable to interact with their environments or to respond to stimuli. In some cases their behavior varies, and they are able to engage from time to time in meaningful activity or conversation, while also having intermittent periods of withdrawal or depression. In other cases, patients will cry or babble continuously, strike their hand or arm or head regularly against a table or the wall, or simply sit or lie motionlessly. Patients of this type are generally referred to as "regressed," "disoriented," or suffering from "chronic brain syndrome." Their condition may stem from a variety of causes, including physical, psychological, or social factors.

Whenever possible, these patients should be involved in program activities geared to their capabilities and interests—such as simple rhythmic activities or exercises, modified arts and crafts, singing, or other participant or spectator pursuits. In addition to such approaches, two special methods have been developed for working with highly regressed and disoriented patients. These methods are known as "remotivation" and "sensory training."

Remotivation

This consists of a technique promoting group interaction which recreation leaders, nurses, or specially trained aides may use with patients in both nursing homes and psychiatric facilities. When patients do not respond well to other types of therapy, remotivation is often tried. Its essential purpose is to improve alertness, involvement, and communication, and thus to help the patient develop other involvements and interpersonal relationships.

Remotivation was originated by Mrs. Dorothy Hoskins Smith at the Philadelphia State Hospital in 1956. Smith, Kline, and French Laboratories gave support to the program and before long it was being used by hospitals, mental health clinics, and nursing homes throughout the United States and Canada. With the assistance of the American Psychiatric Association, classes, seminars, and demonstrations have been provided to train leaders in this method. By the late 1960's, it was estimated that there were over 15,000 leaders participating in remotivation programs.

Essentially, the method consists of a series of patient meetings held once or twice a week under the supervision of a leader. Usually, there are 12 such meetings, with each session lasting from 30 minutes to an hour and involving from 10 to 15 patients. Patients are encouraged to come but should never be forced to do so. The basic method of remotivation involves an attempt to help the senile, regressed patient to come out of his shell, to become more fully aware of things outside himself, and of other persons. Remotivation sessions are highly structured and follow a five-step sequence, briefly summarized as follows:

1. *Climate of Acceptance.* The leader addresses the group and expresses appreciation to its members for coming to the meeting. The leader moves around the group greeting each member, calling them by name, or introducing herself to them. She compliments them on their appearance, or attempts to establish contact in similar ways. The purpose of this first step is to attempt to involve the group member in a social setting, and to provide a comfortable relaxed atmosphere.

2. *A Bridge to Reality.* The leader uses some sort of clipping, poem, or article to gain the attention of the group. She may read the poem slowly and rhythmically, or may move around the room asking each patient to read a line, or, if it is an article, to look at photographs it may contain, or read from it.

3. *Sharing the World We Live In.* This step seeks to develop a topic to be covered by the group, which may have been introduced in the previous step. The leader may bring some articles to show the group to provoke their responses, or may prepare a number of specific objective questions to ask them about it. Varied topics related to leisure, recreation, family life or personal interests may be developed; however, the method usually avoids topics which may arouse controversy or disturb patients, such as religion or racial prejudice.

4. *The World of Work.* Here the effort is to discuss work as a focus of activity, and (particularly in psychiatric hospitals, where patients may be returning to the community) to encourage patients to give their own perceptions of work and feelings about it. This step may be less relevant to senile, regressed patients. Whenever possible, similar themes or examples should be used through steps 2, 3 and 4, to establish a continuity in the session.

5. *Climate of Appreciation.* The leader thanks each patient for coming to the meeting and indicates that she is pleased with the group. She announces when the next meeting will be held, and urges group members to attend.[23]

In some institutions, evaluation reports and progress notes are kept for all remotivation group members. Groups on different levels of capability and participation may be established so that, as patients improve, they may be moved along to the next highest level. In may cases, remotivation sessions are held before having patients take part in recreation programs.

Sensory Training

Sensory training is a method that was developed originally in the early 1960's for children with perceptual-motor impairment. It has since come to be used very widely in work with regressed and disoriented psychiatric patients or residents in nursing homes suffering from chronic brain syndrome. While it has some elements in common with remotivation, the basic emphasis is to rehabilitate function or prevent further deterioration of regressed geriatric patients by providing various types of stimuli that arouse the patient's various senses and promote awareness and meaningful responses. Richman describes the methods in the following terms:

1. Sensory training is designed for the patient who is regressed, blind, or wheelchair-bound, and does not participate in off-ward activities.

2. Sensory training is a structured, sequential process, which is a shared group/individual experience.

3. The program provides the person with differentiated stimuli to improve his perception and his response to the environment.

4. All sense receptors are stimulated: auditory, olfactory, tactile, vision, taste, proprioception and kinesthetic.

5. Sensory training is specifically ordered, structured and designed to increase sensitivity to stimuli by the individual's discrimination and response to stimuli. A "response-feedback" system is inherent in the group interactional setting.[24]

Customarily, four to seven patients are involved in each sensory training group. Sessions last from a half hour to an hour, and may be held daily or less frequently. The general goals of each session are to stimulate the patient's awareness of self and of others, to orient him to reality, to increase his alertness to environmental stimuli, and to improve his level of functioning, including such aspects as concentration, tolerance, judgment, and manual dexterity.

---

[23] Alice M. Robinson: *Remotivation Technique: A Manual for Use in Nursing Homes.* New York, American Psychiatric Association, and Smith, Kline and French Laboratories, 1968.

[24] Leona Richman: *Manual of Sensory Training Techniques.* New York, Bronx State Hospital Geriatric Unit, 1968, p. 1.

To begin a session, patients are usually brought together and seated in a close circle. Both the leader and the patients are given name tags. The leader and the group members introduce themselves. The leader should shake hands with each patient, speaking loudly, slowly, and clearly, and repeating phrases when necessary. If patients do not know their names, he should try patiently to get them to say their names. Tactile contact, with much hand touching, holding, shaking, or clapping is repeated frequently. When introductions are over, the leader begins to orient the group to the time, the place, the date, the day, and the fact that they are in the hospital because they are ill or need treatment and special care. The purposes of the sensory training session are explained, and repeated carefully and slowly. Important ideas may be written on a blackboard or bulletin board. At this point, the leader should go through the series of stimulation exercises that follows:

Kinesthetic and Proprioceptive Exercises.   These exercises deal with awareness of the movement of the joint, and the awareness of different parts of the body. Patients are asked to identify and move different parts of their bodies – the shoulder joint, arms, legs, and head. In a sitting position, the patients go through various flexion and extension movements.

Tactile Exercises.   These exercises, which involve touching and identifying objects, are intended to sharpen the patient's awareness of the environment, and of his own reactions to it. The leader presents various types of materials or objects to patients for them to feel or touch; he may also rub them or brush them with the objects. Examples of materials might include a piece of wood, sponge, brush, ball, or piece of cotton. Patients are asked how they feel about the various objects or materials, what the sensation received from it is like, and which ones they prefer.

Olfactory Exercises.   The leader presents patients with different substances or materials which have distinct odors, such as tobacco, mustard, perfume, or garlic. In each case, he tries to get them to identify the substance, based on its odor, to indicate their feelings about it, and possibly also to say what it is used for.

Other senses, such as *hearing, vision,* and *taste,* are also focused on, with use of appropriate stimuli and exercises. Patients are worked with in terms of their level of capability and alertness; patients functioning at higher levels are pressed to respond more fully than those who are extremely regressed.

Often the leader may have mirrors available, so that patients may look at themselves. In every way possible, they are bombarded with stimuli – by touch, sound, sight, smell, and taste – and with suggestions and nonthreatening opportunities for social interaction. At the end of the sensory training session, the group may join together in some simple, purposeful group activity, such as singing a folk song. The leader shakes hands with each patient, announces that the meeting has ended, and reminds them of the date of the next session.[25]

---

[25] Cited in *Manual of Sensory Training Techniques,* 1970 supplement, pp. 1–4. See also Leona Richman: "Sensory Training for Geriatric Patients." *American Journal of Occupational Therapy,* May–June, 1969, pp. 254–257.

Both "remotivation" and "sensory training" represent techniques which are carried out by recreation leaders in many hospitals and nursing homes. While specialized leadership training should be had for both methods, they are not highly complicated techniques and may readily be mastered with careful preparation and supervision.

SCOPE OF SERVICE IN SPECIAL SETTINGS

This chapter has demonstrated how recreation leadership today may require unique or special skills and abilities, depending on the type of setting in which the leader functions. The examples of "behavior modification," "remotivation," and "sensory training" demonstrate how new and sophisticated methods of leadership are constantly being developed, particularly within the field of therapeutic recreation.

Obviously, no recreation leader is likely to face all of the kinds of challenges or job demands described in this chapter. Instead, what is essential is that the leader develop broad-based competence, and then move ahead to gain the kinds of special expertise or skills required within his unique job situation. Throughout this process, the role of the supervisor is a key one. It is the supervisor who is primarily responsible for guiding and directing recreation leaders and promoting their professional growth. The chapters that follow deal with the process and philosophy of effective supervision in recreation and parks.

Suggested Examination Questions or Topics for Student Reports

1. Compare the traditional approach to working with youth to some of the newer, more innovative methods described in this chapter.
2. What are the unique values in therapeutic camping for special populations? Describe some of the practices in camping for the mentally retarded or emotionally disturbed, as outlined in this chapter.
3. Both armed forces recreation and industrial recreation make certain demands upon professional leadership personnel that are different from those found in other types of settings. What are the key requirements of leaders in these two fields, in terms of personal qualities and skills?
4. The needs of aging persons have become increasingly important in our society. Describe these in detail, and then show how they are met by recreation personnel, either in multi-service Senior Centers or in nursing homes.

Suggested Action Assignments for Students

1. Select one of the four following methods or techniques: "leisure counseling," "behavior modification," "sensory training," or "remotivation."

Carry out additional research on it, either in the literature or by observation, and then write a brief manual indicating how it can be used in recreation or activity therapy programs.

2. Many psychiatric rehabilitation programs have been moved to community mental health settings (day clinics, after-care centers, and so on). Carefully observe one such program, and gather as much information on it as you can. Then evaluate its effectiveness and review the use of recreation as a treatment method in this setting.

four

principles and problems in recreation supervision

the supervisor's role

Particularly in smaller communities or voluntary organizations with limited staffs, the major responsibility for planning, organizing, and carrying out programs is held by supervisors, while the bulk of the actual program leadership is done by part-time or seasonal employees or volunteers. In almost all recreation and park departments, the supervisor plays a pivotal role in determining needs, carrying out middle management functions, and mobilizing the total efforts of the agency.

This chapter deals with the basic concepts and process of supervision. It provides five elements: (a) a definition of supervision as a key function in governmental and voluntary agency management; (b) a general description of the roles of supervisors; (c) a more detailed description of such roles within typical recreation and park agencies; (d) a philosophy of supervision based on contemporary teaching in administration and human relations; and (e) a set of guidelines for effective supervision in recreation and parks today.

SUPERVISION DEFINED

Supervision may be defined both in technical terms and in terms of its broad purposes. From a technical point of view, the National Labor-Management Relations Act has defined a supervisor as any individual having authority, in the interest of the employer, to hire, transfer, suspend, lay off, recall, promote, discharge, assign, reward, or discipline other employees, or having responsibility to direct them, or to adjust their grievances, or effectively to recommend such action, if in connection with the foregoing the exercise of such authority is not of a merely routine or clerical nature but requires the use of independent judgment.[1]

---

[1] William R. Spriegel, Edward Schulz, and William B. Spriegel: *Elements of Supervision.* New York, John Wiley and Sons, 1957, p. 1.

Williamson defines supervision in the following terms:

> . . . any person who is responsible (1) for the conduct of others in the achieve-
> ment of a particular task, (2) for the maintenance of quality standards, (3) for
> the protection and care of materials, and (4) for services to be rendered to
> those under his control.[2]

He suggests that supervision must be viewed as a process by which
both paid and volunteer workers are helped by a designated member to
make the best use of their knowledge and skills, and to carry out their responsibilities more effectively. The ultimate objective of supervision is to
improve the agency's total functioning through more effective employee
functioning. Such definitions place emphasis upon the "personnel management" aspect of supervision. In many recreation and park agencies, the responsibility of supervisors extends beyond this definition to carrying out a
wide variety of tasks of an administrative nature which are *not*, strictly
speaking, personnel management functions.

In recreation and park service, supervision should be regarded as the
administrative level on which professional employees assume responsibility
for a major division of service. This may be a geographical area or district,
an important unit of departmental operations or program service, or a key
facility. Within this division of service, the supervisor is responsible for
planning, organizing, and carrying out program activities, and for directing a variety of support services. It is his task to develop district or unit
budget plans and requests, to carry out public relations, to assist in facility
planning, and a number of other similar tasks. In addition, he has the
major responsibility of helping to direct and assist all subordinate employees in the district or unit, improving their work attitudes and performance,
and building an effective work team. Finally, it is his function to serve as a
channel for communication between top management and line employees.

Within recreation and parks, there are three distinct types of supervisors: (a) District Supervisors; (b) Supervisors of Special Services; and (c)
Supervisors of Major Centers or Facilities.

DISTRICT SUPERVISORS. These are middle-management employees
who are placed in charge of either recreation or recreation and park operations within a major geographical area of a community, such as a district,
borough, sector, or other political subdivision. Such individuals tend to
have a generalist background, with an overall responsibility for coordinating program services, supervising personnel, and carrying out budgetary,
facilities planning, public relations, and similar responsibilities.

SUPERVISORS OF SPECIAL SERVICES. These individuals have responsibility for major areas of service, involving either a particular type of activity
(such as performing arts, outdoor education, or sports programs) or a
population group to be served (such as the mentally or physically disabled,
children and youth, or the aging). In some cases, a supervisor of special ser-

---

[2] Ibid., p. 1.

vices may be assigned responsibility for all playgrounds, community centers, or pools within a city. In most cases, the supervisor of special services has an in-depth background of training and experience in his area of responsibility. It is his function to promote and carry on services related to his area throughout the city. For example, a Supervisor of Performing Arts in a typical, medium-sized city might be expected to plan music, dance, theater activities, and special events throughout the city, to train leaders in this area, and to coordinate departmental programs with other organizations active in the performing arts.

Supervisors of Major Centers or Facilities. Positions of this type involve the responsibility of administering a large recreation center with a diversified program and a substantial number of staff members. The center might consist of a large-scale arts and crafts operation, a varied aquatic facility, a senior center, a cultural arts center, or a similar facility. In a sense, such supervisors are similar to each of the other two types in that they must fulfill the functions of the District Supervisor (although within a limited geographical setting) and must often have the in-depth capabilities of the Supervisor of Special Services.

GENERAL RESPONSIBILITIES OF SUPERVISORS

While job functions may vary considerably in different types of agencies or departments, the International City Management Association, in a series of publications on "Effective Supervisory Practices," outlines the following typical duties of supervisors in public employment:

1. Getting the right man on the job at the right time.
2. Economical use and placement of materials and equipment.
3. Attendance control (absence and tardiness).
4. Accident prevention and control of hazards.
5. Maintaining morale.
6. Adjusting complaints and grievances.
7. Improving discipline.
8. Keeping records and making reports.
9. Improving quality and quantity of work.
10. Planning and scheduling work.
11. Training workers.
12. Getting tools, equipment, and materials on the job.
13. Inspection, care, and preservation of tools and equipment.
14. Making work assignments.
15. Cooperating with other city agencies.

A

B

C

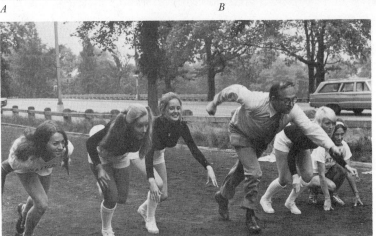

D

Public Relations. Administrators must be alert to all good opportunities to publicize their programs—in person, if necessary. Joseph Halper, Commissioner of Recreation in New York City during the early 1970's, introduces inner-city youngsters to his department's new Zoo-Mobile (*A*), proclaims Physical Fitness Week with then-Mayor John V. Lindsay (*B*), puts his reputation on the line in a foot race with several Playboy Club Bunnies (*C*), and reaches new heights on the trampoline at City Hall (*D*).

16. Checking and inspecting work.

17. Settling differences among employees.

18. Encouraging teamwork.

19. Explaining rules, policies, procedures, and so forth.

20. Maintaining good housekeeping on the job.

21. Safety training.[3]

A good example of the overall tasks of a recreation supervisor may be found in the following passage. It is excerpted from the *Job Manual* of the Recreation Department of the City of Long Beach, California. It describes the varied responsibilities of the Supervisor of District II in that city, an area which includes five parks, two recreation centers, and two playgrounds.

District Supervisor, City of Long Beach

Major Responsibilities

1. *To the Public:* Surveys community attitudes and meets changing needs and interests of the public through provision of high quality, diversified, recreational activities within the district for all groups and individuals.

   a. Assists in establishing and maintaining communications with Advisory Councils . . .

   b. Maintains contact with community groups . . .

   c. Uses professional expertise and experience.

   d. Communicates with other recreation departments and individuals in the field.

   e. Sees that leaders in area are providing programs needed by residents of area.

2. *To Subordinates:* Recruits, trains, assigns, schedules, evaluates, counsels and supervises general and specialized personnel at recreation facilities within the district.

   a. Interviews and recommends for appointment to the Assistant Director for Programs and Facilities all applicants for positions in the district.

   b. Assists in setting objectives for each employee and evaluating him on achieving objectives and job performance.

   c. Conducts in-service training and staff meetings.

   d. Reviews employee schedules.

   e. Observes leaders' performance and counsels them on weaknesses and needed improvement; offers recognition for good performance.

---

[3] Robert E. Bouton: *Effective Supervisory Practices.* Washington, D.C., International City Management Association, 1965, 1971, Bulletin 1, "The Supervisor Looks at His Job," p. 3.

3. *To Co-Workers and Administrators:* Coordinates all aspects of program with administrators and other supervisors, offering assistance wherever appropriate.

   a. Attends weekly staff meetings of Program and Facilities Division.

   b. Works closely with Program Section Supervisor to determine and meet needs and desires of community, and coordinates classes offered.

   c. Works with Publicity Supervisor in providing articles, tapes, programs.

   d. Works with Cultural Arts Supervisors to resolve problems in class scheduling or other difficulties.

   e. Works with Special Activities Supervisor in planning and staging special events.

4. *For Program:* Plans, organizes, promotes, coordinates, supervises and evaluates the city recreation program in the district.

   a. Inspects and evaluates adequacy of recreation services.

   b. Promotes and publicizes the program through brochures, public speaking, and other public information media.

   c. Is responsible for coordinating all playground program schedules with other departmental personnel.

   d. Reviews and approves new program ideas from leaders and other sources.

   e. Supervises and coordinates district special events, such as tournaments, beach days, etc. . . .

5. *For Facilities:* Oversees general development, use, and upkeep of recreational facilities, equipment, and supplies.

   a. Assists in developing long-range capital improvements.

   b. Prepares purchase requisitions and approves purchase of district supplies and equipment.

   c. Submits work orders requesting maintenance and repairs.

   d. Requests assistance from Projects Coordinator with small construction projects.

   e. Reviews use of facilities by "permit" groups.

   f. Coordinates supervision of caretakers with Superintendent of Building Services.

6. *For Administration:* Reviews and/or prepares all reports and documents produced in the district, maintaining necessary records, and managing district finances.

   a. Prepares district budget and continuously reviews budget status.

   b. Supervises use of district "incidental" funds and other special allotments.

Within each of these categories, the District Supervisor must follow procedures outlined in the departmental policy handbook, and must work closely with other appropriate officials. In addition, the *Job Manual* describes the following responsibilities for this position:

> Attends conferences, workshops, and training sessions; prepares reports as requested by Assistant Director of Program and Facilities.

> Assumes supervision of additional areas during the absence of other District Supervisors.

> Supervises the assigning of substitutes for recreation areas, and coordinates the hiring, assigning, orientation, and supervision of Student Workers, Neighborhood Youth Corps Workers, and other special aides in district.

> Cooperates with Co-op Nurseries using recreation areas in district.

> Checks with "What's New," the departmental newsletter twice each month for accuracy and policy matters.

In addition, the Program Supervisor must carry out a wide range of daily or weekly responsibilities related to receiving and acting on memoranda and requests; verifying and reviewing reports of income, time sheets, and overtime reports; submitting publicity items; submitting employee evaluations and reports on seasonal programs; meeting with various departmental groups; and carrying out other similar responsibilities.

Supervision as Middle Management

In a broad sense, supervision must be viewed as a somewhat lower, "action-oriented" level of management or administration. For the past several decades, business administrators have sought to have supervisors trained and officially recognized as representatives of management.

> Practically every supervisory training program emphasizes this fact. The National Labor-Management Relations Act recognizes the foreman as management's representative, and under this Act management is not required to recognize a union of foremen. The supervisor not only *represents* management to the men, but to the average employee the supervisor *is* the company . . .[4]

Because of their position midway between top management and line personnel, supervisors in effect share responsibilities of both groups. They work closely with administrators in working out policies, strategies, plans for budget development, major program development, facilities acquisition, and similar departmental functions. At the same time, many authorities regard them as having a "secondary leadership" function, in which they supplement the work of primary leaders, assisting and guiding them, and acting as a helping person, counselor, problem-solver and, at times, a coworker. This middle management role is described in the following terms:

> In the administrative process, the forces of leadership flow upwards, downwards, and sideways, and all lines of communication meet in the middle; in many respects, therefore, middle managers are the key people in adminis-

---

[4] Cited in Spriegel, Schulz, and Spriegel, *Elements of Supervision,* p. 42.

tration. It is they who transmit orders, decisions, and guidance from the top down, and in turn, communicate problems, difficulties, viewpoints, complaints, and suggestions from the lower ranks to the top.[5]

Personnel Management Function

The most important single responsibility of supervisors is generally considered to be personnel management. Although we refer to individuals serving as supervisors of programs or facilities, their key role is as supervisors of *people!* The art of building creative and effective human relationships is at the heart of successful supervision. Specifically, the supervisor is called upon to do the following:

1. To regularly observe the performance of line personnel, and to provide technical assistance in helping them solve problems and carry out their assignments more effectively.

2. To provide leadership, in the sense of acting as a spokesman for the organization, and a builder of incentives and positive motivation.

3. To act as a trainer and teacher of his subordinates, both in formal training programs, and in day-by-day contacts.

4. To help to resolve conflicts that may exist among personnel and to build cooperation and teamwork among them.

5. To help line personnel realistically understand their own strengths and weaknesses and work consciously toward improving their overall performance.

6. To serve as a key official in personnel administration, enforcing or communicating departmental regulations or policies, and assisting employees with respect to personnel requests such as leaves, vacations, reassignments, or similar matters.

7. To make recommendations with respect to promotions, demotions, transfers, or special job assignments.

8. To evaluate the overall performance of personnel, for use in service ratings and other departmental decisions.

It is essential that supervisors have technical competence, in the sense of knowing *how* the job is to be done accurately and efficiently. However, it is also necessary that they be able to operate within a total framework of intelligent, contemporary philosophy that provides a sound basis for judgment and logical decision-making.

PHILOSOPHY OF EFFECTIVE SUPERVISION

Supervision, viewed primarily as the process of personnel management, has obviously developed a substantial body of literature during the

---

[5] Marshall E. Dimock and Gladys O. Dimock: *Public Administration.* New York, Holt, Rinehart and Winston, 1969, p. 350.

past several decades. Principles have been developed relating to structural patterns of administration and supervision, such as the "staff and line" concept that those employees who are directly concerned with the delivery of service are known as "line" personnel, while those who assist them as planners, researchers, consultants, and so forth are "staff" personnel.

A number of similar concepts of staff relationships and functions, such as "span of control" "unity of command," "delegation of authority," "chain of command," and the "scalar principle," generally describe how responsibilities are assigned within a department, and how authority is exercised. Such principles are described in detail in other texts on recreation and park administration, or on public administration in general,[6] and will not be presented here. Instead, emphasis here is given to alternative approaches to supervision. Dimock and Dimock describe three common models of supervisors:

> The *bureaucratic* type has a passion for detail, for reducing every aspect of his job to systems and minutely prescribed procedures: this man is tied to his desk and rarely has a chance to think beyond the demands of his daily schedule. The *crisis* type has more energy but seems to reserve it for crises and "drives," which he often deliberately arranges. Almost invariably he lacks judgment and the capacity to plan ahead.... Finally, the *strategic* type delegates as much detailed supervision as he can, plans his "drives" to synchronize with the rest of the work, and reserves his best energies for innovation and planning for the future.[7]

In general, the most effective supervisors are those who, as in the "strategic" model, have good judgment, plan ahead, work toward tangible goals, and are able to motivate others to perform to their highest capacity. They are skillful in using group methods of supervision to build cohesive work groups with high performance goals, based on many of the principles of group dynamics which were described in Chapter Three.

The process of successful supervision involves several key elements. First, the supervisor must be sharply aware of his objectives, and those of his organization, and must bend every effort to work directly and efficiently toward these. Second, he must concentrate on improving motivation and releasing the "will to work" of his subordinates. Third, he must make effective use of communication at all times, in order to improve his relationship with other staff members and to strengthen overall departmental performance. Fourth, he must develop specific techniques which are useful in directing and overseeing work performance. Fifth, he must be able to exert sufficient discipline, where this is needed, to compel adherence to the rules and practices of his organization, to give reprimands when necessary, and to deal with employee complaints and grievances. Sixth, he must be skillful in observing other employees at work, and make judgments

---

[6] See for example Richard Kraus and Joseph Curtis: *Creative Administration in Recreation and Parks.* St. Louis, C.V. Mosby, 1973, pp. 17–25.

[7] Cited in Dimock and Dimock, *Public Administration,* p. 352.

regarding their performance which provide the basis for continuous counseling and guidance designed to improve their work.

Supervising by Objectives

A frequently expressed principle is that managers must learn to "administer by objectives." The purpose of this approach is to clearly define and express all of the objectives of a department or agency. When objectives are understood and accepted by all staff members, it is possible to place less reliance on mechanical rules, procedural manuals, and detailed instructions—which often tend to make an organization bureaucratic, sluggish, and lacking in innovation. Instead, authority can be more freely delegated to a wide mix of staff members who have the right to make decisions at lower levels of responsibility.

To be meaningful, objectives cannot be determined solely by the department administrator or supervisor, and then presented to employees. If this is done, employees will not necessarily understand or accept them. Instead, all employees should be consulted and should participate in the development of objectives. Such discussions should extend to the best ways of achieving objectives—the most useful and effective techniques of working, organizing programs, and delegating responsibility.

Realistically speaking, if this approach—which has been enthusiastically supported by many authorities in personnel management—is to work, the key agent in carrying it out is the supervisor. His tact, judgment, and skill in involving personnel in defining objectives and agreeing on work approaches are essential for team success.

Freeing the Will to Work

A traditional view of the supervisor's role was that he was an overseer, a sort of grim, coercive foreman who had to watch constantly over other employees to make sure that they were not loafing and stayed on the job. McGregor comments that we have widely assumed that:

> ... the average human being has an inherent dislike of work and will avoid it if he can. ... Because of this human characteristic of dislike of work, most people must be coerced, controlled, directed, threatened with punishment to get them to put forth adequate effort ....[8]

However, McGregor and other authorities in personnel management argue strongly that individuals generally want to work and to have the satisfaction of knowing that they have performed well, provided that certain

---

[8] Douglas McGregor: *The Human Side of Enterprise.* New York, McGraw-Hill Book Co., 1960, pp. 33–34.

conditions can be met. Too often, we assume that financial reward is the only important source of motivation – that employees work for an organization chiefly for pay. While this is unfortunately true of many workers who do not enjoy their work or lack a sense of self-realization or meaningful involvement in it, it is not necessarily true of all forms of employment or job situations. Stahl points out that in societies where it is generally possible to find employment that satisfies basic human wants, other factors than pay loom larger in personnel motivations:

> In an affluent society with a high minimum standard of "creature comfort," pay is rarely the number one motivator. Research studies time and again have shown that in public service and industrial environments in the United States pay usually ranks second or third, and sometimes lower, on a scale of morale factors. Ahead of it . . . are such factors as credit and recognition, challenging work, a congenial work group, freedom for decision-making, security of tenure, fair and equal opportunity for advancement, and the quality of supervision.[9]

Morale should then be regarded as a key factor in whether or not individuals in any work setting are highly motivated and able to be fully productive. Morale has been defined as the capacity of a group to pull together persistently and steadily in pursuit of common goals. It is based very heavily on the confidence that individual members of a group have in their leadership and in each other, the degree of support they give to the group's goals, and the extent to which the group has been efficiently organized to carry out its work functions. Probably the key factor in achieving favorable motivation is whether or not the basic emotional needs of workers are being met. As suggested earlier, they must have a strong sense of security, of success based on achievement and recognition, and of belonging.

Workers respond favorably to supervisors who consult with them frequently, who have high standards of performance, and who evidence concern for their welfare. The landmark study in the field of human relations in work settings was the experiment carried out at the Hawthorne plant of the Western Electric Company in Chicago, beginning in the late 1920's.[10] This research revealed that more than any other factor, the motivation and productivity of employees was improved when they were given the feeling of being important, of not being "bossed" arbitrarily, of being consulted and cared about. The physical factors of the work environment were not as important as the emotional climate – in terms of encouraging the will to work. Horney sums up the point by writing:

> The improvement of working conditions, raising salaries or shuffling work assignments alone will not motivate employees. The motivating factors

---

[9] O. Glenn Stahl: *Public Personnel Administration.* New York, Harper and Row, 1962, p. 199.
[10] Descriptions of this study have appeared in many social psychology texts. A useful summary appears in Stuart Chase: *Men at Work.* New York, Harcourt, Brace, and World, Inc., 1941, Chapter Two.

that are intrinsic to the employee's job assignment are: achievement, recognition for achievement, the work itself, responsibility and advancement.[11]

Effective Communication

One of the key factors in establishing favorable relationships between supervisors and line personnel, and in promoting favorable "team" attitudes, is effective communication. Too often, people are unable to communicate their feelings, ideas, and wishes and, although they think they are making themselves clear, are not actually doing so. Effective communication is essential in all staff development and supervisory processes.

Communication involves far more than the transmission of verbal or written messages. It is a basic tool of understanding, agreement, discussion, and decision-making within any organization. Horney points out that faulty communication is responsible for most human relation breakdowns, and that when it is not corrected, rumors develop, staff efficiency drops, and frustrations, mistrust, insecurity, and fear result. Stahl sums up the following important elements of communication:

1. Communication — oral and written — is the lifeblood of an enterprise. It is the means by which human beings work together.

2. Communication is a two-way process. Employees should know the goals of the organization, why management is proceeding the way it is, what changes are in the works. Management should know what employees are thinking and feeling, what ideas they have to get the job done.

3. Communication involves *receiving* and *understanding* as well as *telling*. Words, ideas, or proposals do not always mean the same thing to the receiver and the transmitter. A breakdown in understanding can occur because the communicator does not put himself in the other fellow's shoes. . . .

4. Normally, the more freedom and encouragement given to self-expression and the more care taken to provide people with the reasons for action, the less communication difficulty there will be.

5. Good communication is an essential concomitant of delegation of authority and reliance on the good sense and good intentions of the staff. Along with participation, it is the "stuff" of the decision-making process.[12]

Within traditional administrative theory, a number of basic principles of effective communication were established. Barnard, for example, developed the following rules based on administrative practice: (a) the channels of communication must be definitely known; (b) a formal channel of communication must extend to every member of the organization, and it must

---

[11] Robert L. Horney: "Administration by Motivation." *Parks and Recreation,* August, 1968, p. 15.

[12] Cited in Stahl, *Public Personnel Administration,* p. 211.

be as direct and short as possible; (c) the lines of communicaton should generally be respected (people should communicate through formal channels); and (d) lines of communication should not be interrupted during exchanges, and every communication should be authenticated or confirmed.[13] These somewhat formal and limited approaches to communication have gradually been expanded into a broader understanding of communication as a process which is heavily affected by the previous experiences and expectations of the parties involved, by the methods used to communicate, the language used, and the emotional tone of the exchange. Dooher and Marquis have developed a set of guidelines which should be helpful to supervisors in improving their communicative skills:

1. *Seek to clarify your ideas before communicating.* The more systematically we analyze the problem or idea to be communicated, the clearer it becomes. . . . Management communications commonly fail because of inadequate planning. Good planning must consider the goals and attitudes of those who will receive the communication and those who will be affected by it.

2. *Examine the true purpose of each communication.* Before you communicate, ask yourself what you *really* want to accomplish with your message — obtain information, initiate action, change another person's attitude? Identify your most important goal and then adapt your language, tone, and total approach to serve that specific objective. Don't try to accomplish too much with each communication. . . .

3. *Consider the total physical and human setting whenever you communicate.* Meaning and intent are conveyed by more than words alone. . . .

4. *Consult with others, where appropriate, in planning communications.* Frequently it is desirable or necessary to seek the participation of others in planning a communication or developing the facts on which to base it. Such consultation often helps to lend additional insight and objectivity to your message. Moreover, those who have helped plan your communication will give it their active support.

5. *Be mindful, while you communicate, of the overtones as well as the basic content of your message.* Your tone of voice, your expression, your apparent receptiveness to the responses of others — all have tremendous impact on those you wish to reach. . . .

6. *Take the opportunity, when it arises, to convey something of help or value to the receiver.* Consideration of the other person's interests and needs — the habit of trying to look at things from his point of view — will frequently point up opportunities to convey something of immediate benefit or long-range value to him. . . .

7. *Follow-up your communication.* Our best efforts at communication may be wasted, and we may never know whether we have succeeded in expressing our true meaning and intent, if we do not follow-up . . . by asking questions, by encouraging the receiver to express his reactions, by . . . subsequent review of performance. . . .

---

[13] Chester Barnard: *The Function of the Executive.* Cambridge, Massachusetts, Harvard Business School, 1938, pp. 175–180.

8. *Communicate for tomorrow as well as today.* While communications may be aimed primarily at meeting the demands of an immediate situation, they must be planned with the past in mind if they are to maintain consistency in the receiver's view; but, most of all, they must be consistent with long-range interests and goals. . . .

9. *Be sure your actions support your communication.* In the final analysis, the most persuasive kind of communication is not what you say but what you do. When a man's actions or attitudes contradict his words, we tend to discount what he has said — and perhaps to view it as an attempt to mislead us.

10. *Seek not only to be understood but to understand — be a good listener.* When we start talking we often cease to listen — in the larger sense of being attuned to the other person's unspoken reactions and attitudes. . . . Listening is one of the most important, most difficult — and most neglected — skills in communication. . . .[14]

Directing Work Performance

One of the key responsibilities of the supervisor in recreation and park agencies is the task of organizing and assigning work to subordinate employees. The International City Manager's Association's guidelines for effective supervisory practices suggest that supervisors need to think in advance about *what* shall be done, *how* it shall be done, by *whom, when, where,* and *why.* It is essential that work directions be precise and clear, involve a reasonable level of accomplishment, and give the employee receiving them the opportunity to use his own judgment or initiative in carrying them out. Directions may be given in several forms:

Commands or orders, which are usually used only when there is some immediate danger or urgency, or when an employee has been lax or insubordinate about carrying out assignments.

Requests, which are the most appropriate form of direction for routine work. Often these are put in the form of a question, like, "Would you be able to get the bleachers set up by this afternoon?" These are generally as explicit as commands, but give the subordinate worker some input and show some fuller respect for his role.

Suggestions, which permit the worker flexibility in carrying out the assignment, are particularly useful when he is more knowledgeable than the supervisor about how it should be done. However, not all employees will respond favorably to them, and they should be used only with workers who consistently show their responsibility and initiative.

Volunteer directions, in which the supervisor asks for subordinates to volunteer to carry out an assignment, tend to be used only when there are assignments that are difficult, dangerous or disagreeable, or beyond the normal range of job expectations. They should therefore be used sparingly.[15]

---

[14] M. Joseph Dooher and Vivienne Marquis, Eds.: *Effective Communication on the Job.* New York, American Management Association, 1956, pp. 21–23.

[15] Cited in Bouton, *Effective Supervisory Practices,* Bulletin No. 5. pp. 1–2.

After work directions have been given, supervisors should attempt to follow up to determine whether they are being carried out properly. Without actually hanging over the employee's shoulder in a threatening or repressive way, the supervisor should review the assignment at an early point, to determine whether the directions have been understood and the work performed properly. If not, the supervisor should consider: (a) whether the directions were not clear; (b) whether the task itself was too difficult or unreasonable; or (c) whether the employee simply had not carried it out with sufficient effort and understanding. In general, as he learns that a given employee carries out routine tasks successfully, less supervisory follow-up will be called for.

Several devices or techniques usually are used to review performance in a systematic way. These include the following:

1. *Direct inspection of the program or other work situation* is the best way of getting information about how assignments are being carried out.

2. *Measurement of work output* through quantitative procedures, such as measurement of attendance, games played, sessions held, or similar elements.

3. *Reports from employees, advisory groups, or program participants.* These may be written or oral.

4. *Flow charts,* or other forms of "production measurement" devices, in which the specific steps needed to carry out an assignment or develop a project are outlined, along with deadlines for each step of the process.

5. *Employee diaries or project books.* Some organizations require employees to keep track of their time and tasks accomplished by maintaining personal record books showing their schedules. In general, this method has not been used in municipal government, where it smacks of a "time-clock" approach. However, such organizations as the United States Forest Service have used individual field diaries as techniques for reviewing the work of field supervisors.

In general, the most useful approach, as suggested here, is to directly observe the employee at work. This, in turn, provides information not only about the immediate work being done in response to supervisory directions but also general information that will be useful in staff conferences and meetings.

Maintaining Discipline and Dealing with Problems

Just as the playground leader or other line worker must be prepared to carry out disciplinary procedures with groups of participants, so the supervisor must expect a level of responsibility and compliance with departmental policies from subordinate staff workers. If this level is not met satisfactorily, it is his responsibility to apply needed disciplinary action. Discipline, positively conceived, means that workers are aware of the right and wrong ways of doing a job, have good work attitudes, and conform to departmental expectations and regulations. If this is not the case, the supervisor should attempt to determine why there is a problem rather than automatically assume that the worker is to blame.

The first question to be asked in reviewing a problem of inadequate employee performance is, "Was his responsibility clear to him, and did he know how to carry it out?" Through organization charts showing staff lines of authority, job descriptions, flow charts showing work processes, procedural manuals, and orientation and in-service training, staff members should be fully aware of their responsibilities. The supervisor should have made clear to the leader or other employees how specific tasks were to be performed. Departmental policy statements or manuals should also make absolutely clear the rules regarding work performance, hours of work, behavior on the job, use of department vehicles, handling of money, drinking, or similar concerns.

If, despite these factors, employees have continued to perform inadequately or to disregard or fail to live up to personnel regulations, the supervisor should attempt to determine *why*. A number of factors may be responsible. In some cases, workers fail to do the job properly because of boredom, lack of interest in the work, inadequate supervision, unclear directions, or poor communications. In such situations, the supervisor should attempt to remedy the situation by getting at the specific causes of difficulty.

Often, disciplinary problems occur because of friction between or among groups of employees. If this cannot be solved through the supervisor's intervention and team meetings devoted to improving staff relations, it may be necessary to reassign workers to other job settings. In some cases, where it is apparent that an employee is emotionally disturbed, the supervisor should attempt to give what assistance he can, in personal counseling sessions. If the problem is a severe one, the department's administrator or personnel director should be advised of it, and the possibility of recommending that the individual seek skilled counseling or psychological help should be considered.

When, despite these efforts, disciplinary problems continue, the supervisor has a responsibility to act. Many departments have guidelines which suggest procedures to follow; for instance, when an employee has failed to perform adequately over a period of time, or has broken departmental regulations, the supervisor should meet with him — not with the immediate thought that he is going to punish or "tear him down," but rather with the intention of improving his behavior and work attitudes. Specific guidelines would include:

1. Arrange for a private meeting, in a location where the discussion will not be heard by other employees.

2. Try first to get all the pertinent facts. Begin with a question or series of questions which will give the employee the opportunity to give his side of the case rather than start immediately with criticism or accusations.

3. Maintain your own calm, regardless of the employee's behavior. Never

lose your temper, become impatient or angry, or "bawl out" the employee.

4. Face the issue by outlining clearly the problem as you see it rather than skirting around it. Make sure that the employee has a chance to know the full extent of the problem as it is viewed by management, and to respond to it completely.

5. If the problem is fairly simple and the solution self-evident, action may be taken immediately in the form of a reprimand, set of suggestions, or other supervisory action.

6. If the problem is more complex, the supervisor may suggest that a second meeting be held, to explore the problem further. This may give him the opportunity to consult with other department administrators or personnel officers.

7. Whatever action is taken, close the meeting as pleasantly and positively as possible, making an effort to restore the employee's self-confidence, if necessary.

Possible actions to be taken in the case of serious employee infractions or poor job performance include the following: (a) *warnings,* either written or oral, which tell the worker that his behavior or job performance must improve, or other action will be taken; (b) formal *reprimands,* which inform a worker of the serious nature of his failure to perform or violation of department rules and warn him that more serious action may be taken; (c) *fines, assignment to overtime work, reassignment* to other duties, or various forms of *demerits;* (d) *loss of seniority* rights or *negative service ratings;* (e) *suspension without pay* for a set period of time, or subject to a hearing before a personnel board or review by top management; (f) *demotion or discharge,* with continuing disqualifications for re-employment; and (g) most serious of all, *judicial prosecution,* which obviously would be applied only to misbehavior involving criminal action.

While it is desirable to avoid the more serious kinds of punitive action, in some cases there is no choice and it becomes necessary to suspend or discharge an employee. At this point, the possibility of his carrying out a grievance procedure should be considered, and the effect of the union contract and possible intervention by the union reviewed. Usually, at this level of concern, problems of appeals, grievance procedures, or lawsuits become the responsibility of departmental personnel officers rather than of the supervisor.

Supervisory Conferences

In general, supervisors attempt to forestall such problems by carrying out a continuing process of employee observation and conferences which are intended to maximize job output and improve staff morale, motivation, and relationships. Typically, supervisors seek to *avoid* grievances and difficulties by keeping on the lookout for lack of enthusiasm for the job or department; excessive complaints; lateness, loafing, absenteeism, or excessive short-term illness; an abundance of errors on the job; or a marked decline in work output or efficiency.

When such situations occur, the supervisor should deal with them by speaking with employees as frequently as possible, trying to know them as individuals and improving communications with them. He should examine working conditions, review work assignments, be alert to staff relationships, and consider other possible causes of difficulty. Throughout this process, he should make maximum use of supervisory conferences.

Such conferences fall into several categories: (a) initial meetings with new employees; (b) individual conferences between supervisor and subordinate worker, which may be held at regular intervals or may be specially requested by either party; (c) group conferences, in which several employees meet with a supervisor to discuss staff progress and problems; and (d) evaluation conferences, which are held for the specific purpose of reviewing the worker's performance.

Such conferences should contain a number of important elements. They should be viewed as sessions in which the job itself, and the work setting, are examined in a constructive but analytical way. The employee should feel free to make suggestions in these sessions—or question why certain procedures or policies are followed—and to make alternative suggestions for other approaches. They should involve teaching, where appropriate, in the sense that the supervisor helps the subordinate employee review his own work and shows him how certain tasks can be accomplished more effectively. They should include personal counseling in areas of job attitudes, relations with other workers, or similar matters which are within the reasonable range of the supervisor's capability and judgment. Finally, the sessions should represent the opportunity for the supervisor to act as the "middle-management" employee mentioned earlier, in order to relay administrative concerns or directives to the employee, and to transmit the employee's views and suggestions to higher administrative levels.

At all times, in such conferences, the supervisor should attempt to be courteous, friendly, and cheerful, and to show respect for the individual employee and his opinions. He should seek to develop a spirit of shared concern and responsibility, a tension-free atmosphere, and a sense of confidence on the part of the employee that both the supervisor and the department he represents have confidence in the employee and want to work with him to help him become as effective and successful a worker as possible.

Only within such a framework can supervisors use conferences to their maximum benefit to improve employee performance and achieve departmental goals.

Guidelines for Supervisory Action

Summing up this chapter, the following guidelines represent a total approach to effective supervision. The successful supervisor observes the following guidelines:

1. Establishes high but attainable expectations for his staff in terms of work

standards and goals, and makes sure that these are designed to achieve the goals of the department itself.

2. Places staff members in job settings where their individual abilities are most likely to be fully utilized.

3. Recognizes the universal need for approval, and helps staff members meet this need by: (a) bestowing credit and praising accomplishments; (b) showing consideration toward staff members; and (c) acknowledging their share in the total enterprise, and their contribution in making it a success.

4. Seeks to help staff members become more effective, and removes obstacles to success by providing technical assistance and emotional support.

5. Avoids ego-threatening behavior, and uses the mistakes of subordinates as a basis for counseling and improving performance rather than as an opportunity for threats and punishment.

6. Clearly defines the responsibilities and accountability of staff members and makes clear that he has confidence in their ability to carry out these tasks.

7. Encourages staff members to participate in policy-planning, decision-making, and program development, not as a "token" gesture but with serious weight being given to their contributions.

8. Exercises leadership where necessary, asserting rank, making decisions, and exerting force to achieve department goals.

9. Is an effective link between management and leadership, communicating information helpful to their psychological well-being and morale, and to their awareness of total department developments.

10. Appraises employees on the basis of objective, measurable performance elements, taking into account differences in the qualities of individual workers, and different levels of task difficulty.

11. Does not play favorites but seeks to reward all workers equally, and to provide tangible rewards and status symbols, particularly for high-level performance.

12. Is friendly, sympathetic, and approachable, and yet also maintains a sense of his own dignity, based on the rank he has been assigned and the authority vested in him by the department.

SUPERVISORY SELF-MANAGEMENT

Finally, the effective supervisor must be able to manage himself in order to be as productive and well-organized on the job as possible. Most recreation and park supervisors are required to work on a number of different programs at the same time, coordinating the work of many employees with different types of job specialties, and cooperating with other municipal departments or community agencies. Clearly, this can be a difficult assignment, and it is not at all unusual for individuals who have been highly successful on the leadership level to discover that supervision poses many frustrations and problems for them.

In part, the problem is one of organizing one's own time, developing a workable set of immediate and long-range goals, and concentrating on major responsibilities rather than wasting effort and time on unimportant or extraneous tasks. The Boys' Clubs of America have published a set of guidelines for effective self-management that are intended to assist their professional employees.[16] The following suggestions are drawn from these guidelines. The guidelines recognize that many individuals on the supervisory level find difficulty in overcoming inertia and in using their time most profitably.

Twenty Ways to Get Things Done

1. *Make a list of things to do, and cross off each item as you do it.* Crossing off an item when you complete it shows that progress has been made, and also calls attention to tasks still to be done.

2. *Keep the work you have to do right in front of you.* This helps to eliminate competing distractions. Instead of having four projects on your desk at once, clear away everything except the one task that should be done first.

3. *Break tasks down into segments.* If a task is particularly long or laborious, break it down into segments and tackle them one at a time; that way, it can be handled by stages, and will not appear to be too overwhelming.

4. *Have an effective reminder system.* Develop a self-reminder system of events, deadlines, tasks to be accomplished, etc., and keep these notes in a place where they can be regularly checked.

5. *Be decisive.* Once you have all the facts on a given matter, take action on it. Don't bother to worry about whether or not your decision was the best possible one; move on to other tasks.

6. *Don't exaggerate a job's difficulties in advance.* Avoid building up all the problems in a given assignment beforehand, and you will find it easier to get at it, and to carry it out successfully.

7. *Don't overplan.* While it is necessary to plan carefully for each new project or task, excessive planning may be an excuse for not taking action. It is like the writer who keeps doing research, and avoids getting down to writing.

8. *Set specific time limits for tasks.* Be definite, rather than vague, about when projects should be undertaken and completed. If there are several activities to be done, put them in a time sequence based on their order of priority, their possible deadlines, and the degree and kinds of work it will take to carry them out.

9. *Don't be a perfectionist.* If you expect yourself to do everything perfectly, you may avoid new challenges for fear of failing. While your standards should be high, they should also be realistic, and should recognize that you, like others, have the right to make mistakes.

---

[16] Adapted from "20 Ways to Get Things Done," in *National Orientation Program Manual.* New York, Boys' Clubs of America, 1973.

10. *Strengthen your weak points.* Recognize your areas of weakness, or performance skills in which you lack confidence. Concentrate on improving your skills in these areas.

11. *Know when you work best.* Many people function differently at different times of the day. Analyze your own energy, alertness and "ups and downs" throughout the day, and plan your most demanding tasks for the times when you will be best able to meet them.

12. *Learn to say "No."* When you are able to make a choice, avoid taking on commitments that you would rather not have, or are not essential.

13. *Listen attentively.* Avoid errors, backtracking and repetition by getting pertinent information right the first time.

14. *Do it now.* Many people put off getting started by such devices as sharpening pencils, day-dreaming, or window gazing. Avoid procrastination—use your working time to the fullest.

15. *Seek short-cuts.* This does not mean to "skimp" on doing a job right, but rather looking for the most effective and efficient way to carry out an assignment, no matter how it was done in the past.

16. *Anticipate.* Look forward to the next day and make sure that all necessary arrangements have been made. Keep extra change, keys, eyeglasses and stamps in your office, and in other ways eliminate minor frustrations that waste time and energy.

17. *Make fullest use of time.* Use travel time and similar periods to think out problems, read reports, make plans or jot down ideas for future implementation.

18. *Vary your activities on the job.* Many jobs become tedious because of repetition. It is best to alternate tasks in order to fight off fatigue and keep mentally alert. Most supervisors do not have to worry about this; their jobs are seldom boring.

19. *Get an early start.* Many supervisors find that they can get a great deal of paper work and planning out of the way by starting early in the day, before distractions and other job demands begin.

20. *Gain a healthy respect for your own time.* Recognize that your time is an immensely valuable asset; use it as fruitfully as possible.

These guidelines would, of course, be helpful to administrative or management personnel in many types of job settings. They are particularly relevant to recreation and park supervisors who, at the same time they are responsible for the work of others, must also "police" themselves.

Suggested Examination Questions or Topics for Student Reports

1. Make a case for the argument that the supervisor represents the key level for delivery of service in recreation and parks—rather than the leader or administrator.

2. Select one type of supervisor from those presented in the text, and

prepare a detailed statement of functions and responsibilities, based on job descriptions, observations, and interviews.

3. It has been pointed out that personnel management is a major aspect of supervision today. Outline a detailed philosophy of modern supervision, with emphasis on such personnel-related concerns as freeing the will to work, management by objectives, improving communication, and counseling employees.

4. Develop a set of principles for effective direction of others or self-management, based on the ideas expressed in this chapter.

Suggested Action Assignments for Students

1. Interview a recreation supervisor, and do a detailed breakdown of his functions within a given season and throughout the year. Determine the areas in which he feels he is performing successfully, and those in which he is experiencing difficulty. Develop a set of recommendations to improve performance in the latter areas.

2. Although you are probably not a supervisor at the present time, do an analysis of your own "self-management" performance, based on the guidelines at the end of this chapter. Carry this on systematically for a week, and report your findings. How do you measure up? What can you do about it?

the recreation volunteer

Volunteers traditionally have been an important part of organized recreation and park programs. In part, this has been because so many people have skills in hobbies, sports, or the arts, which have lent themselves to program leadership. It also has been because volunteer leadership has played an important role in the American way of life, with many charitable and public-service organizations counting very heavily upon volunteers to assist their professional staff workers.

Volunteers, simply defined, are individuals who perform services without financial remuneration. They may, however, receive payment in other ways. Some volunteers give their time in order to receive public recognition and approval. Others volunteer to obtain early training for a career, often as part of college field work or internship. Great numbers of individuals volunteer because they are interested in supporting programs which serve members of their families, such as participants in Little League, or the Boy or Girl Scouts. Many volunteers work with special organizations which serve the disabled, because they themselves have family members or friends who have a particular type of disability.

Thus, the motivations for volunteering are varied. What are the types of roles which volunteers assume?

Roles of Volunteers

Generally, these are divided into three categories: (a) administrative or advisory volunteers; (b) program-oriented volunteers; and (c) service volunteers.

Administrative volunteers in recreation and parks generally tend to work closely with the professional executive staff in helping to determine policies, assisting in fund-raising or other fiscal matters, or advising on program or community relations problems. Often they are members of boards, commissions, or advisory councils. Other individuals, such as businessmen, architects, professors, planners, or psychologists, may also provide volunteer assistance to recreation and park administrators, although they may not be formal members of boards or commissions.

Program-oriented volunteers are those who accept responsibilities for helping to plan, carry out, or support direct program activities. Many coaches in such youth sports organizations as Little League, the Catholic Youth Organization, or Biddy Basketball, are volunteer leaders. In public or voluntary recreation agencies, volunteers may be used to provide transportation, chaperon social programs for teenagers, offer entertainment to nursing homes or hospitals, or in a variety of other ways essential to carrying out programs successfully.

Service volunteers are considered to be those who assist in clerical or other auxiliary functions. In some cases, professional persons who give direct guidance or help to staff members on a volunteer basis—such as newspaper men who help with public relations, or lawyers who provide sessions of advice on legal liability as part of in-service training—might also be considered service volunteers.

Values of Volunteer Leadership

Obviously, volunteer leaders hold a wide variety of responsibilities. Often they do routine, unchallenging, time-consuming tasks that offer little glamour or excitement—but that must be done. In some cases, however, they undertake difficult and extremely challenging tasks. In general, their values are considered to be:

1. Providing manpower in areas where it would be impossible to provide programs without a substantial corps of nonpaid workers.

2. Offering special skills, expertise, or leadership talents not possessed by regular professional staff members.

3. Providing an emotional ingredient—such as freshness of outlook, enthusiasm, and interest—that regular staff members, because of their length of service or heavy work load, often cannot match.

4. Serving as a special link between the community or neighborhood and the recreation department or agency. Volunteers can help professional staff members understand the needs and wishes of community residents and can help interpret department goals to local people.

These values of volunteer recreation leadership are well summed up in a section on "The Why's and Wherefore's of Volunteers," in the Recreation Manual of the Penetanguishene Mental Health Centre, in Ontario, Canada. This manual points out that the volunteer movement seeks to meet two important human needs—the needs of hospital patients for added, personalized human contact, and the needs of volunteers themselves for the opportunity to give altruistic service to the community. It suggests that volunteers are particularly able to help long-term patients in mental hospitals, because they do not accept the "dull, gray life" of the institution as the only reality, and because they are part of the outside world:

> Volunteers can give individual attention and personal contact. They can assist at different levels . . . They can help the staff to do the extra jobs for

which there is seldom time — reading, writing letters, tidying and sorting personal belongings, playing games, planning and organizing outings and excursions. They must be able to supply specialist help or instruction — in Braille, in languages, piano playing, etc. . . .

One of the important values of volunteer leadership is the fact that may individuals find leisure fulfillment themselves through community service. Since volunteers *do* accept unpaid positions very largely to meet their own psychological or social needs, it is important to recognize that they may pose a number of serious problems to recreation and park administrators who seek to use them.

While some volunteers have a high level of ability, others may volunteer for assignments which they are not equipped to handle satisfactorily. Some volunteers cannot be counted on, in terms of regular and responsible involvement. In some circumstances, volunteers may be in conflict with the basic goals or philosophy of an organization, or may be unwilling to abide by its leadership guidelines or principles. Since they are not regular employees, discipline or other forms of corrective action are difficult to apply.

Even those volunteers who carry out work assignments satisfactorily may pose special problems. They sometimes are resentful of the fact that regular employees are being paid for work which, in their judgment, they are performing more effectively — on an unpaid basis. Too often, the very reasons that may compel an individual to volunteer, such as need for approval or recognition, stem from the fact that they are basically lonely or insecure people. Thus, personality problems may prevent a volunteer from doing an effective job. It sometimes happens that volunteers demand so much of the professional recreation leader's time and attention that they represent a nonproductive drain upon the department rather than contribute to it.

Recognizing these possible difficulties, it is nonetheless true that volunteers have a great deal to offer, and that the recreation and park agency that is able to use them effectively should take full advantage of this potential resource. This requires a serious commitment to working with volunteers in the following areas: (a) recruitment; (b) selection and placement; (c) orientation and training; (d) supervision; (e) evaluation; and (f) recognition.

While these processes are similar to those used by supervisors with recreation leaders in general, a number of special factors must be considered in their application to working with volunteers.

Recruitment of Volunteers

First, it is necessary to determine the need for volunteers and the kinds of functions they may fulfill. Any agency that uses volunteers should define their potential roles and determine the kinds of individuals they need to carry out these unpaid assignments. It should then identify the possible sources for volunteers. Recruitment may use either the "rifle" or "shotgun" approach. That is, recruitment appeals may be directed to the public at large, or to special population groups or agencies. Examples of techniques for recruiting volunteers fall under the following categories:

1. General publicity addressed to the community at large, through such media as television, radio, newspapers, advertisements in subways or buses, and similar methods.

2. Appeals in the form of letters, invitations, or speakers who target such organizations as service clubs, Parent-Teacher Associations, hospital auxiliaries, or sports groups as potential sources of volunteers.

3. Emphasis on the need for volunteers in the bulletins, newsletters, or brochures published by a department as part of its overall public relations effort.

4. Development of special cooperative programs with appropriate organizations, such as a nursing home having a special arrangement with a community-based Senior Citizens' Club which furnishes volunteers on a regular basis.

5. Seeking direct volunteer assistance from those who have an important stake in the work of an agency — such as youth recreation programs obtaining parent volunteer help.

6. Development of continuing field work relationships with nearby colleges or universities, and particularly with their departments of recreation or social work.

7. Affiliation with a central recruitment and referral agency in the community that coordinates the assignment of volunteers to varied social agencies.

Customarily, many agencies begin with a generalized use of the media to reach the public at large, and then "zero-in" on more selective groups.

Much information has been gathered as to the types of motivations that affect the willingness of individuals to volunteer. For example, a recent conference of public and private agencies identified the following reasons for *not* being willing to volunteer: (a) timidity, shyness, or lack of confidence; (b) a fear of taking risks; (c) reluctance to associate with certain types of clients, such as the physically disabled, aged, or mentally retarded; (d) a feeling of not really being needed; (d) fear of being not sufficiently qualified; (e) laziness or lack of motivation; (f) the fact of not having been invited personally to volunteer; and (g) the view that the volunteer assignment would not be interesting enough.

On the other hand, it has been found that positive factors in recruitment included the following: (a) a feeling that the job to be done is an important one; (b) a sense of participating in community programs; (c) agreement with the basic objectives of an organization; (d) a feeling that volunteer work would contribute to one's self-development, and particularly to professional ambitions; (e) the wish to make a contribution to society or to other human beings in need; and (f) other psychosocial rewards, such as approval and recognition by others.

In view of these factors, it is clear that recruitment should not be carried out casually, and should in fact be made the responsibility of a knowledgeable and capable individual. Some organizations employ volunteer coordinators, usually on the supervisory level. The Volunteer Coordinator Guide, published by the Center for Leisure Study and Community Service of the University of Oregon, states of the volunteer coordinator:

> . . . he is responsible for developing and implementing the volunteer program within his organization. . . . He may recruit, interview, select, orient, train, place, supervise, motivate, recognize and evaluate volunteers. He may also be responsible for public relations, funding, budgeting, and record-keeping. . . .

Such individuals should be in close touch with community groups and organizations, and should be highly knowledgeable about the agencies they represent. They should be good "salesmen" in terms of being able to convince people to invest their time and energies in volunteer work. They should be able to work effectively with the groups that have traditionally provided the bulk of social service volunteers, as well as with others which have been relatively untapped but could be useful sources of volunteers, such as blue- or white-collar workers, teenagers, and retired citizens.

Selection and Placement of Volunteers

When individuals volunteer for nonpaid work with a recreation and park agency or department, it is important that they meet with the staff member responsible for coordinating volunteer services, so that their background and qualifications can be reviewed, and the wisest possible decision made about accepting their application and placing them in the agency. At this point, there should be a careful examination of the volunteer's background, experience, skills, motivation for volunteering, and similar information. A well-organized volunteer service will ask the candidate to fill out a detailed background form which systematically supplies the following kinds of information:

1. Personal information (name, address, telephone number, closest relatives).
2. Club or organization memberships.
3. Past experience in volunteer work.
4. Past experience or skills in dramatics, games, music, hobbies, or other recreational activities.
5. Educational background.
6. Clerical skills.
7. Schedule of availability (time preferred).
8. Occupation.
9. Transportation capability, including ability to transport others.

A

B

E. B. Mitchell

Administrative Leadership. Recreation and park administrators provide leadership on many levels. Here, leading administrators present awards to participants in Hollywood, Florida (*A*), and to staff members, in Orlando, Florida (*B*). In Mt. Vernon, New York, the recreation commissioner meets with his advisory board to plan and evaluate programs (*C*). The Vancouver, Canada, mayor joins with recreation administrators to dedicate a new adventure playground (*D*).

C

Paul Caramuto

D

10. Source of referral.

11. Additional relevant information, including personal references.

During a thorough personal interview, the volunteer coordinator should explore the individual's motivations and get a general picture of his personality. It is at this point that he makes a judgment as to whether the candidate would make a contribution to the department, or might pose problems. As an example of the qualities sought, the Penetanguishene Mental Health Centre seeks the following personal qualities or attitudes in volunteers:

1. Maturity and stability.

2. Positive work motivations, and self-directed manner.

3. Quality of being perceptive, but not rigidly judgmental.

4. Empathy, but not excessive sentimentality.

5. Willingness to learn.

6. Being a "doer," a normally busy and active person, and having a strong sense of identity.

At the same time, the volunteer should be given a thorough picture of the agency itself — its history, organization, goals, and philosophy — as well as a basic understanding of the kinds of persons it serves. This would be particularly important in the case of therapeutic agencies serving special populations, for which it would be desirable that the potential volunteer have a detailed understanding of the individuals with whom he would be working. A third element in such conferences would include review of the types of positions that the volunteer might hold, and areas in which he might be of service. These vary widely according to the type of agency or department.

For example, the Richmond, California, Department of Parks and Recreation makes use of volunteers in a variety of special roles and settings. The classifications of these volunteers and their duties include the following:

Equipment and Supplies Assistants: (a) keeping supply room in order; (b) keeping equipment in working order; (c) dispensing various types of tools or supplies; (d) dispensing and controlling suits and towels at swimming pools; and (e) keeping inventories and records of supplies and equipment.

Technicians in Performing Arts Programs: (a) movie projector operator; (b) phonograph operator in dance classes; (c) lighting or stage manager in drama productions; and (d) accompanist for musical activities.

Assistant Recreation Leaders: (a) helping club or special interest group leaders; (b) acting as monitor for large play areas such as playgrounds or gyms; (c) leading special activities, such as story-telling; (d) serving as officials or judges for contests or games; and (e) maintaining bulletin boards.

At the White Plains, New York, Center for Nursing Care, youth and adult volunteers assist in the following program areas:

art cart	religious services — assisting clergy
arts and crafts	sensory training sessions
book cart	serving refreshments
bulletin board posting	sewing circle
civic projects	escort service
current events discussion	flower arranging
driver corps	games and cards
newsletter assistance	hostessing
one-to-one visiting	strolling with patients
plant care	showing slides and movies
reading aloud	talking book machine

At the Penetanguishene Mental Health Centre, volunteers assist in both ward and outside activities. Examples include a wide variety of roles, such as:

On the Ward: answering telephone, clerical assistance, bathing patients, bedmaking, escorting patients, feeding patients, giving massage and exercise, library trolley, messenger service, providing entertainment, playing checkers and chess, organizing bingo, reading to patients, talking to lonely patients, and writing letters for patients.

Outside: assisting staff with patients on holidays or outings, helping in social club for discharged patients, inviting patients home, making survey of lodgings for discharged patients, providing transportation for outings and bringing family or friends to hospital, and visiting discharged patients.

At the same time that the possible roles are laid out, the Volunteer Coordinator should describe fully the regulations governing the use of volunteers, the expectation that the department or agency has of volunteers, and the possible benefits that may be provided, such as meals or other "fringe" items. It is at this initial meeting that the Volunteer coordinator should attempt to screen out those who appear to be unstable, who have unrealistic goals or expectations, or who seem to lack needed skills or personal qualities.

Orientation and Training of Volunteers

When a definite commitment has been made, the volunteer should receive a careful orientation to insure that he knows exactly what is expected of him, as well as the basic information about the department or agency he will be working in. Typically, the following areas should be covered in orientation meetings (to the extent that they were dealt with during the initial interview and selection process, it would not be necessary to repeat them):

1. Introducing the new volunteer to the physical layout of the department, agency, or facility where he will be working.

2. Having him meet the people he will be working with, and giving him an understanding of their functions and responsibilities.

3. Reviewing the basic philosophy and objectives of the organization, and making these as specific and factual as possible, in operational terms.

4. Outlining the specific tasks and functions of the volunteer in precise terms, including time schedule, individuals to whom he will be responsible, and how each task should be carried out.

5. Giving background information about the clientele he will be working with—their characteristics, background, limitations, needs, and other useful information.

6. Other regulations or legal limitations to the work of the volunteer, such as elements of safety, accident prevention, first aid, or rules relating to discipline or behavior control.

Following the orientation period, volunteers should receive continuing assistance in the form of in-service training programs, although it may not be feasible to involve them in the full range of staff development activities that are provided for regular paid workers. These activities are intended to strengthen their leadership skills and give them a fuller sense of involvement in the agency's work.

Supervision of Volunteers

Too often, volunteers are not given the same degree of conscientious supervision that professional workers receive. They should, however, be regularly observed and assisted by professional staff members. Such supervision will indicate to the volunteer that his contribution is being taken *seriously*—that he is not being ignored or treated in an off-hand manner simply because he is *giving* his time. His assignment must be a meaningful one and not just "busy work."

Supervisors should meet with volunteers at regular intervals to review their work, and to discuss problems that may have developed. When problems *do* occur, they frequently stem from the following causes: (a) poor communications; (b) lack of adequate job descriptions; (c) inadequate screening or inappropriate assigning of volunteers; (d) misconceptions held by the volunteer about the agency; and (e) conflict with other staff members.

The solution to such difficulties should be arrived at by the supervisor and volunteer meeting together, discussing the problem, and attempting to reach improved understandings that will solve it. In some cases, it may be necessary to give additional training or to give the volunteer different responsibilities. If he has been intelligently selected to begin with, it should not be necessary to ask him to leave the agency, although in some cases, personal reasons—such as health, family problems, or other job commitments—provide a valid basis for terminating the volunteer arrangement.

The key factor in the volunteer-agency relationship is *motivation*. If the volunteer is properly motivated, and if he has a sense of satisfaction in working at a significant job, as well as faith in the program to which he is assigned, it is usually possible to keep him enthusiastic and interested in the volunteer assignment.

Evaluation of Volunteers

An important element in the volunteer process is the evaluation procedure. Accurate records should be kept of the volunteer's work, including careful reports of his attendance and participation. The Volunteer Coordinator Guide, prepared by the Center for Leisure Study of the University of Oregon, provides an excellent volunteer evaluation form which covers many of the same points usually found in regular staff evaluation forms (see page 167).

Such evaluation forms and procedures are helpful in providing a concrete basis for counseling the volunteer and helping him improve his work. They also are useful in making out reference statements for individuals who do volunteer work with an agency and, years later, request that personal references be sent to a college or university, or to a potential employer.

Recognition of Volunteers

A final important guideline for the effective supervision of volunteers is that they must receive recognition and rewards for their contribution.

Rewards come in a number of ways. For example, some elements of the on-the-job experience may serve to encourage and motivate the volunteer from the very outset. These include such aspects as having a uniform (a practice in many hospitals or nursing homes); having benefits such as meals, a transportation pool, and insurance coverage; or gaining in professional skills through in-service training. Beyond the concrete advantage of volunteer work, nonpaid workers also may achieve personal satisfaction from the knowledge that they have done a worthwhile job, and have contributed significantly to the lives of others or to community well-being.

In addition, volunteers who have performed successfully should be given evidence of this in the form of concrete tokens of recognition. There are many ways in which an agency can make its appreciation known to volunteers, including:

1. Regular praise and encouragement, given by supervisors or other key professional workers.
2. Publicity, through mention of the volunteer's work in department newsletters, or releases to newspapers or other media.
3. Letters of commendation, or special mention of volunteer contributions at board or staff meetings, or at annual meetings of the organization.
4. Increased responsibilities, or change of title.
5. Award of pins, plaques, or special certificates of appreciation.

Some organizations have "volunteer recognition days" or other events at which they single out for praise all those who have provided assistance to their programs throughout the year. The American Hospital Association encourages such events, and some state Departments of Health, as in Connecticut, make available several different achievement certificates, based on length and type of service in health-related facilities. In one form or another, recognition is essential to the successful use of volunteers in recreation and park service.

Suggested Examination Questions or Topics for Student Reports

1. What are the major reasons why volunteers are so essential in many public and voluntary recreation programs? What unique benefits do they provide?
2. Identify and discuss some of the major problems involved in working with volunteers. How can these best be overcome?
3. Outline a careful, detailed process of selecting, training, and supervising volunteers, as it might be carried on within a specific community agency.
4. List and give examples of several of the best ways of providing recognition for volunteers.

Suggested Action Assignments for Students

1. Examine a specific agency, such as a hospital, nursing home, or community youth organization, with respect to its use of volunteers. Do a detailed report of its recruitment and assignment methods, and the level of supervision given to volunteers.
2. Prepare a detailed volunteer handbook for a specific organization or public recreation and park department. This would be a handbook given to volunteers to orient them to the agency and to their roles.

problem-solving in recreation and parks

Throughout this text, a number of guidelines have been presented for effective leadership and supervision in recreation and parks. These guidelines provide useful directions for handling most routine situations or responsibilities. However, it is probable that other situations will arise from time to time which call for special solutions. Situations of this type demand creative and intelligent decision-making and problem-solving.

These two terms are often treated synonymously in popular usage. Actually, they are not identical. *Decision-making* is often of a routine nature, involving the application of basic departmental policies and sound judgment to choosing between relatively equal alternatives.

In contrast, the term *problem-solving* implies that there are a number of barriers to an easy solution, or a series of actions which must be performed over a period of time before the matter can be successfully resolved.

THE PROBLEM-SOLVING PROCESS

Exactly how are problems dealt with in most public or voluntary organizations? Several basic approaches may be identified.

AUTHORITARIAN DECISION-MAKING. Here, the administrator, supervisor, or leader simply makes a decision on a unilateral basis, without consulting other subordinate employees or program participants.

GROUP-CENTERED PROBLEM-SOLVING. In direct contrast is the approach in which the members of the team become involved in a process of group discussion and analysis that examines alternatives and ultimately decides on an appropriate course of action. Such team-oriented approaches to problem-solving have become increasingly popular in recent years.

ANALYSIS BY PLANNING SPECIALISTS. In many recreation and park departments, problems of a special nature or of a high level of importance are assigned to special teams of planners or experts in systems analysis.

Such teams do a careful analysis of the problem and arrive at recommended solutions.

DECISIONS BY HIGHER AUTHORITIES.   One way of dealing with difficult problems is to automatically "pass the buck" by moving them up the chain of command. This may be done either because lower-level employees do not want to take the responsibility for handling more serious problems, or because administrators have made clear that they *wish* to be consulted on all such matters.

AVOIDANCE.   A final approach is simply to avoid the problem and hope it will go away. While there is some justification for letting difficulties work themselves out, and not making an emergency out of every momentary problem, this ostrich-like approach is obviously not a desirable course of action.

STAGES OF PROBLEM-SOLVING

There are six stages essentially involved in effective problem-solving. These are: (a) recognizing the problem; (b) assigning responsibility for it; (c) gathering relevant data; (d) identifying and analyzing alternative courses of action; (e) selecting an alternative; and (f) implementing the decision and following up on it.

Recognizing the Problem

As indicated earlier, there are many routine difficulties which can be solved by ordinary, day-by-day decision-making processes, through the automatic application of departmental policies or procedures. For example, in most recreation and park departments, drinking on the job would normally call for a warning, followed by suspension if it continued. However, unless the problem were very severe and touchy (if, for instance, the individual involved brought political pressure to bear to protect himself, or if it involved a large number of employees), it would not call for special problem-solving attention.

On the other hand, problems which are severe, of long duration, or concerned with controversial areas, call for a problem-solving approach. Examples of such problem areas follow:

1. Problems of staff functioning — either personality conflicts, consistently poor work records, serious insubordination, grievance cases, or matters affecting the unity of the group.

2. Problems with participants, such as low levels of attendance, unwillingness to accept rules dealing with such areas as fighting, drinking, or drug use, antagonism toward staff members, and so on.

3. Problems of co-worker relationships involving difficulties between peers, or between supervisors and subordinates, that are based on disagreements about responsibilities, conflicts between cliques of employees, or departmental policies.

4. Problems of interdepartmental relationships. Here, the conflict may involve a disagreement as to objectives or jurisdictional rights of a public recreation and park department and another municipal department, or it may occur between different departments in a single institution, such as activity therapies and nursing in a hospital.

5. Problems of community relations, such as complaints by parents, community councils, or local businessmen, or serious difficulties in obtaining public support, cooperation, or volunteer assistance.

In all such cases, it is essential first to recognize the severity of the problem, in order to determine if it requires special attention rather than routine decision-making procedures. Next, it is important to recognize the problem for what it is. This means that attention too often is paid only to the symptoms stemming from a problem rather than to the problem itself. This is like paying attention only to the small portion of an iceberg that is visible, and ignoring the much greater bulk beneath the waves. It is essential to recognize and to zero-in on the real difficulty, and not merely deal with the symptoms.

Assigning Responsibility

The second stage of problem-solving is to determine who should be responsible for tackling a particular difficulty. Usually, this depends on the level of concern that is involved. For example, if the matter involves a single playground or community center, or a small group of participants, it is likely that it would be assigned to a local recreation leader for solution. If the problem were a more persistent or widespread one, it would probably become the responsibility of a district supervisor. If it were more serious, it is probable that the departmental administrator would assume responsibility, or would ask one of his staff assistants to take over the task of investigation and problem-solving.

In general, it is best to handle such matters on the lowest possible level of staff operations, in order both to avoid overloading administrators with unnecessary responsibilities and to build a sense of authority at lower levels. However, since administrators will ultimately be held responsible for all staff decisions or actions taken to solve problems, it is usually wise to inform them of all such matters, and to consult them when controversial issues are involved. In any case, it is essential to make a clear assignment of responsibility for a particular problem. Making it "everyone's responsibility" in effect makes it "no one's responsibility."

Investigating the Problem

The third step is to investigate the problem thoroughly, gathering all relevant information. This should involve getting a precise picture of what has happened, who the concerned individuals are, the related circumstances, the possible causes of the difficulty, and appropriate solutions for it.

This may be done in a variety of ways: (a) by direct observation of the situation; (b) by discussing it with the individuals involved; (c) by examining case records; (d) by interviewing other individuals who are not directly involved but who are familiar with the situation; (e) by informal investigation, such as sending a group of "participants" to a community center who do not identify themselves; or (f) by a formal investigation. In some cases, it may be necessary to gather considerable amounts of statistics (as in the case of departmental efforts to reduce vandalism or accidents) and to analyze them through computer program methods. In other cases, observations and discussions will be sufficient to get the needed information.

Identifying Alternative Courses of Action

Occasionally there may be only one possible course of action to take in attempting to solve a problem. Once the background information has been gathered, the appropriate decision seems clear. However, such cases are rare. Instead, in most problems worthy of the name, several possible courses of action are likely to appear. For example, if the problem concerned extremely poor participation in recreation activities in a given area of a city, several possible courses of action intended to promote better participation might be:

1. Changing the program entirely by eliminating all existing activities and introducing an entirely new schedule of activities and events.

2. Building several new facilities to increase interest and attendance in appealing new programs.

3. Changing the leadership and supervisory staff, with the view that new faces and leadership approaches might attract large numbers of fresh participants.

4. Carrying out a comprehensive survey of community residents to gather their suggestions for improving and strengthening the program.

5. Eliminating all fees and charges, based on the possibility that these are discouraging large numbers of participants from attending program activities.

6. Mounting a large-scale publicity campaign to draw attention to the program and increase attendance.

Any or all of these alternative approaches *might* be helpful in solving the problem. Obviously, they are not all feasible or likely to be of equal value. The following questions must be asked in examining alternative solutions to a problem:

> Is a solution feasible, in the sense that it can be done within departmental limitations or funding, manpower, facilities, or other "cost" areas?

Does it seem to get at the heart of the problem rather than just the outward symptoms? Is it likely to be effective?

Is it an appropriate or desirable solution, in terms of basic departmental philosophy or policies?

What barriers stand in the way of each solution that must be overcome if it is to be successful?

Each alternative must be carefully scrutinized, in order to determine whether it is a logical and appropriate one. The probability of success must be balanced against the measurable cost and desirability of the proposed solution. Finally, a decision is made in favor of one of the alternatives.

Implementing the Decision

The final stage in problem-solving is to take action to carry out the approved alternative. Often, this cannot be done without careful preparation and briefing of all those concerned.

For example, a severe problem of low personnel morale might result in a plan to shift a number of individuals from one job to another, to promote some workers while demoting others, and to initiate a general realignment of staff responsibilities. Once the decision is made, to move ahead directly with these actions might result in even lower morale, lawsuits, a work stoppage, or similar reactions. Therefore, before this plan could be implemented, it would be advisable to hold a full-scale briefing of all individuals as to the actions being taken and the reasons for them. It would also be advisable to present and discuss the plan with the municipal personnel department, legal counsel, and the labor union involved. In some cases, these parties would have been involved in earlier discussion, and may have contributed their views as to the appropriate action to be taken.

Finally, each individual involved should be given the reassurance that the department is concerned with improving its overall functioning, and is interested in working with each employee from this point on to develop his career potential. If the problem-solving process has involved consultation with all staff members, with effective two-way communication throughout, this sort of preparation should make it possible to put the plan into effect. Once this has been done, it is obviously important to give it all the departmental support possible, to monitor it regularly, and evaluate its success.

THE GROUP-CENTERED APPROACH TO PROBLEM-SOLVING

Obviously, the manner in which a supervisor or administrator approaches the task of decision-making and problem-solving reflects his entire leadership style. Tannenbaum, Weschler and Massarik list a series of personal statements which reflect different administrative viewpoints on problem-solving:[1]

> "I put most problems into my group's hands and leave it to them to carry the ball from there. I serve merely as a catalyst, mirroring back the people's thoughts and feelings so that they can better understand them."

> "It's foolish to make decisions oneself on matters that affect people. I always talk things over with my subordinates, but I make it clear to them that I'm the one who has to have the final say."

> "Once I have decided on a course of action, I do my best to sell my ideas to my employees."

> "I'm being paid to lead. If I let a lot of other people make the decisions I should be making, then I'm not worth my salt."

> "I believe in getting things done. I can't waste time calling meetings. Someone has to call the shots around here, and I think it should be me."

These differences of opinion may be illustrated in a diagram which shows the range from one extreme of authoritarian, "boss-centered leadership" on the left, to the other extreme of "subordinate-centered leadership," on the right (see Figure 14–1).

Most authorities today agree that the group-centered approach to decision-making and problem-solving is a constructive and useful method. Generally, group problem-solving serves to bring a greater wealth of information and judgment to bear upon a problem. As pointed out earlier, it helps the morale of staff members to be consulted and drawn into a meaningful process of planning and decision-making. Shared decision-making is likely to result in a greater consensus in reaching the final solution — which should make it easier to develop support for its implementation.

There are a number of special techniques which may be used in group problem-solving. The first of these, and the most widely used, is the group discussion process. Other methods include sensitivity training, the use of encounter groups, "brainstorming," and role-playing. Each of these is discussed in the concluding section of this chapter.

Group Discussion

Group discussion relies on the orderly but informal interchange of ideas among a number of individuals. (There are usually 12 persons or less in the group situation.) As opposed to an arrangement in which a supervisor or administrator might stand before a group of subordinates who are sitting in rows facing him, the group discussion method works best when all members have equal status in the situation. A face-to-face arrangement is best achieved by having all participants place their chairs in a circle. There

---

[1] Robert Tannenbaum, Irving R. Weschler, and Fred Massarik: *Leadership and Organization: A Behavioral Science Approach.* New York, McGraw-Hill Book Co., 1961, p. 67.

Figure 14-1 Supervisory Behavior in Decision-Making[2]

| Boss-centered Leadership | | | | | | Subordinate-centered Leadership |

| Use of authority by the supervisor | | | | | | Area of freedom for subordinates |

| Superior makes decision and announces it. | Supervisor "sells" decision. | Supervisor presents ideas and invites questions. | Supervisor presents tentative decision, subject to change. | Supervisor presents problem, gets suggestions, makes decision. | Supervisor defines limits; asks group to make decision. | Supervisor permits subordinates to function within limits set by superior. |

are no special rules for group discussion beyond those of simple courtesy. Each member of the group is expected to contribute, when he has something to say, and to address his views to the entire group rather than to the leader. A conscious effort is made to get all members of the group to participate as fully as possible, and therefore group members should avoid dominating the discussion through overly long statements.

In most group situations, different members of the group tend to assume various roles that reflect their individual personalities, and which are needed to promote the effective functioning of the group. These roles are likely to include the following:

Initiator.   This is the person who gets things started. He is either the formal head of the work team who issues a formal request or order, or he is an informal member of the work team who, through his leadership role in the group, mobilizes others to begin to plan together.

Information Seekers and Opinion Seekers.   These individuals elicit fuller understanding of the situation through their questions. The information seeker is concerned chiefly with facts, while the opinion seeker asks others for their views and and values. Both tend to promote full communication within the group.

Elaborator.   This individual develops the meaning, explains the rationale, or gives examples which enrich the contributions that have already been made by others.

Coordinator.   The purpose of this role is to help orient the group to its goals and enable it to understand the direction in which it is heading in the

[2] Robert Tannenbaum and Warren H. Schmitt: "How to Choose a Leadership Pattern." *Harvard Business Review,* March–April, 1958, p. 96.

discussion. The coordinator also may evaluate the group's performance, or may help others do so.

Energizer.   This individual urges the group toward action, fuller involvement, or a higher quality of discussion and participation.

Procedural Technician.   This role involves routine tasks which assist group functioning, such as distributing writing materials, arranging chairs, blackboards, or other visual materials, or providing other needed resources for the group.

Recorder.   This individual keeps a record of the discussion, not in the sense of formal "minutes" (since group discussions do not rely on parliamentary procedure) but rather as a report of the major ideas covered, or suggestions made.

Other roles which are normally played in group discussions include the following: an *encourager,* who provides praise, agreement, and acceptance; a *critic* and a *discipliner,* who point out negative contributions or inappropriate behavior within the group; a *harmonizer,* who mediates conflicts among individuals; a *compromiser,* who reconciles different points of view; an *integrator,* who helps to build a common group-will and sense of unity; and an *expediter,* who moves the group toward action, or helps it arrive at a common decision.[3]

Within this framework, although democratic participation is the keynote, a skilled leader can help the group move more efficiently through the process of sharing views and achieving a consensus. Since they are usually vested with authority, in terms of their formal positions within the job hierarchy, supervisors and administrators are often called upon to provide such leadership. Although there are no precise guidelines for group discussion leadership in all situations, a number of general suggestions may be made. The discussion leader, or group chairman, should do the following:

Help group members define the limits of the problem they face.

Help group members define and select the elements of the problem area which are most important and real to them; as they move into the discussion, these may be extended.

Encourage all participants to share their information and views on the problem.

Keep the discussion focused on the problem the group is dealing with rather than on extraneous matters.

Help clarify the contributions to the discussion, and relate these to the short- and long-term goals of the organization.

Help maintain an atmosphere in which cooperation and maximum group productivity can be achieved. Is there freedom of expression and freedom from unhealthy anxiety or other pressures?

Help group members keep the line of discussion clear and moving from a general exploration of the problem toward practical planning and decision-making.

---

[3] See Frank P. Sherwood and Wallace H. Best: *Supervisory Methods in Municipal Administration.* Chicago, International City Managers' Association, 1958, pp. 62–65.

Make Use of all the experiences of group members, and special skills or resources they may have.

Strive to build a cohesive and productive team, not only to be more successful in this discussion, but in other work experiences and assignments.[4]

Obviously, such group discussions can be extremely helpful in defining the issues, exposing all relevant facts and information, identifying alternatives (and their strengths and weaknesses), and arriving at a decision which appears to have the fullest potential for success. In some cases, long-standing conflicts may exist among group members that prevent them from being able to share effectively in group discussions. Often, such conflicts, when they exist, are continuing sources of difficulty within an organization and hamper its overall functioning to a marked degree.

When fundamental disagreements of this type exist, it is necessary to deal with them before attempting to resolve other difficulties. Since the early 1960's, many organizations have made use of newly developed "sensitivity training" or "encounter group" methods to overcome such problems, and to build more positive and effective team relationships.

Sensitivity Training

This approach to developing more effective work groups stems from research done at the National Training laboratories at Bethel, Maine, during the 1950's and 1960's. The research involved promoting awareness of group processes and individual behavior through unstructured group experience. By means of a series of stages of development, in which detailed analysis is carried out concerning how individuals behave, how they relate to each other, and how they affect the overall functioning of the group, participants are helped to become much more aware of their own psycho-social needs, the meaning of their own behavior and the behavior of others, and how to operate most effectively — both as a person and as an individual within an organization or team.

In essence, the sensitivity training process is intended to help people become more aware, more alert, less defensive or aggressive, and better able to contribute meaningfully to group processes or on-going organizational tasks. As an extension of this approach, a variety of organizations, including the well-known Esalen Foundation on the West Coast, developed new group techniques for helping people achieve a state of openness, trust, and security with each other. Such "encounter" groups have made use of a wide variety of techniques, including many playlike or social experiences involving physical contact, creative expression, "marathon" sessions, and other similar techniques.

---

[4] Ken Herrold: *Group Problem Solving Manual.* New York, Teachers College, Columbia University, Center for Improving Group Procedures, pp. 1–2, n.d.

Both methods have been used in modified forms by many organizations to improve staff relationships and facilitate group problem-solving processes. To be carried out effectively, they usually require specially trained workshop leaders.

Role-Playing

Another technique which has been widely used in problem-solving situations — particularly those situations involving sharply opposed groups or cliques — is role-playing. This is a device or method which helps group members to explore the interpersonal dynamics of a problem situation. Typically, members of the group assume different roles, and act out specific scenes related to the problem as they understand it. Herrold describes some of the basic elements in role-playing, describing it as the "unrehearsed, free expression of individual and group personalities involved in a problem situation:"

> The *role-players* are participants on stage in the situation and are taken from the group in an unrehearsed sociodrama.
> The *director* starts, interrupts, resumes, and ends the drama proper; he adds or subtracts actors, shifts roles and situations.
> The *stage* is the locus of the situation, with or without appropriate properties.
> The *situation* is the topic or problem of vital interest; in defining this at the outset, time, place, roles, and relationships are included.
> The *audience* (observers) is comprised of participants off-stage who actively communicate their feelings and responses, and are dependent upon the situation.[5]

Essentially, there are two types of role-playing events: *psychodramas*, and *sociodramas*. Psychodramas are essentially concerned with problems in which single individuals or groups of individuals are privately involved. Sociodramas deal with problems in which the private relations of individuals are less important than collective or social factors. Either type may be presented on three levels: (a) totally spontaneous; (b) partially planned and prepared; and (c) totally planned and rehearsed presentations.

The major purpose of role-playing, as a tool in problem-solving, is to give participants — both those actually involved in the acting experience, and those who are observing — a fuller sense of involvement and a heightened awareness of the various points of view in a situation. Not infrequently, those taking part in a psychodrama or sociodrama may be asked to take roles which contrast sharply with their own identities. For example, a district recreation supervisor might be asked to play the role of a teenage boy who has been causing problems in his community center, or

---

[5] Ken Herrold: *Role Playing Manual.* New York, Teachers College, Columbia University, Center for Improving Group Procedures, pp. 1–2, n.d.

the departmental director of personnel might assume the identity of a labor union organizer.

Thus, participants are compelled to examine and express—as freely and spontaneously as possible—points of view that are different from their own. Ideally, role-playing helps to create a situation in which there is fuller understanding of the issues and acceptance of both sides of a dispute, and awareness of the motivations underlying the points of view of different protagonists. Often, both humor and more serious emotions are vividly expressed in psychodramas and sociodramas.

It should be clearly understood that role-playing does not provide solutions to problem situations by itself. Instead, it helps to develop a climate of understanding, a feeling of cooperation and sympathy, a greater readiness to develop acceptable solutions, and perhaps a fuller understanding of what the real issues are. Typically, a group might move from role-playing as an interlude or preliminary stage in its problem-solving process, to group discussion aimed at developing alternatives and making a decision for action.

Brainstorming

A final technique which is used to develop a large number of possible solutions to a problem in the most creative and spontaneous way possible is known as "brainstorming." It is based on a town-meeting type of session, in which participants throw rapid-fire suggestions for solving a problem into the hopper. As each idea is suggested, it is immediately written down on a large blackboard; to keep things moving at a fast pace, two recorders may alternately write down the suggestions. A tape recorder may also be used to record suggestions. Certain basic principles apply in brainstorming sessions, including:

1. All group members are encouraged to make whatever suggestions seem to them to have merit—no matter how far-fetched or unusual they are. They make one suggestion at a time, without long-winded justification or arguments.

2. No one may criticize or analyze previously made suggestions, since this might result in inhibiting new ideas or cutting off the flow of group creativity. Goble suggests a number of so-called "killer phrases" that are to be avoided:

   a. "We've never done it that way before."

   b. "It won't work."

   c. "We haven't the time . . . or the manpower."

   d. "It's not in the budget."

   e. "We've tried that before."

   f. "All right in theory but can you put it in practice?"

    g. "Too modern."

    h. "Too old-fashioned."[6]

3. Individuals may "piggy-back" on previous suggestions, by immediately throwing fresh ideas, based on preceding ones, into the session.

After a good number of ideas have been suggested (creativity becomes infectious, and it would not be unusual for a group to present 100 or more suggestions in a half-hour meeting), various procedures may be followed. Customarily, the majority of the group takes a "break" while a small committee goes over the list of ideas and places them into appropriate categories. In a second meeting of the entire group, participants review the suggestions and select those which appear to have the greatest merit. From these they develop actual alternatives for action, and arrive at a decision for solving the problem.

The obvious virtue of this process is that it serves to stimulate a wide variety of imaginative ideas, many of which may have rich possibilities.

It should be stressed that every problem, large or small, should not be regarded as requiring a fresh sequence of collecting information, analysis, and group decision-making. Instead, an intensive effort should be put into the formulation of policies that will deal with the bulk of possible problems and difficulties in a routine way. Group problem-solving should be reserved, as suggested earlier, for more serious, complex, or sustained problems which are not adequately covered by existing policies or procedures.

Suggested Examination Questions or Topics for Student Reports

1. What are the differences between decision-making and problem-solving, as outlined in this chapter, or based on your understanding of the two concepts? How do they relate to the development of departmental policies?

2. Outline the specific steps or stages of problem-solving. Show how each of these might be approached differently, according to whether one used the group-centered approach or a more authoritarian method.

3. Select one of the following techniques for problem-solving: "group discussion," "brainstorming," or "role-playing." Do additional research on this method, and then prepare a set of guidelines that will be useful in employing it in recreation situations.

4. When personality problems or conflicts underly staff difficulties, sensitivity training may be useful in developing more constructive attitudes and behavior. What are some of the key elements in this method, and what, in your opinion, are some of its limitations?

---

[6] Frank Goble: *Excellence in Leadership.* New York, American Management Association, 1972, p. 24.

Suggested Action Assignments for Students

1. Interview one or more recreation professionals (leader, therapist, supervisor, and so on), and identify the most common types of problems he must deal with. Then identify the problem-solving approaches that are most commonly used to deal with these situations.
2. As a class exercise, develop several hypothetical problem situations and use the various techniques outlined in this chapter to develop solutions for them. Evaluate the effectiveness of each method.

fifteen ◀◀◀

case studies in leadership and supervision

One of the most effective ways of developing one's understanding of leadership and supervision is to examine and analyze case studies based on actual problem situations. This method is often used in college courses in recreation leadership, supervision, or administration, as well as in departmental in-service training workshops.

This chapter presents 12 case studies which are based on real incidents or problem situations described by graduate students in courses at Teachers College, Columbia University, Herbert H. Lehman College, and the University of Oregon. The names of those involved have been changed, and the case records have been simplified and summarized. Basically, the cases are of four types: (a) those dealing with the relationship between leaders and participants; (b) those analyzing leader-supervisor problems; (c) those concerned with problems between lower-level personnel and administrators; and (d) those focusing on problems between recreation and park administrators and their boards, or with community groups.

In some cases, the problem situations have been "played out," in that they have been described fully, including the actions taken by those responsible, and the apparent outcomes.

In other situations, the cases are described fully, except that no final action has been taken; alternative solutions may or may not appear in the presentation of the problem.

In reading these case studies as class assignments, students may be asked to submit individual papers analyzing cases and responding to the questions that follow each one. Or, they may volunteer to take part in team problem-solving groups to report on and fully analyze some of the more complicated cases. If such assignments are undertaken, students may wish to make use of some of the problem-solving or decision-making methods described in the previous chapter, such as brainstorming, or role-playing.

Obviously, there is no single "best" solution to any of these problems, nor is it possible to present a set of universal guidelines for problem-solving. Different organizations have widely varying philosophies, and the unique differences among communities, as well as the variations among personalities, means that each case must be assessed on its own merits, and individual solutions developed. In general, the guidelines presented throughout this text that deal with group dynamics, the goals of recreation, and specific methods in various types of settings, should be useful in analyzing these cases.

Finally, whether the analysis is done by individuals or groups, it is essential to recognize that all problem situations have both *symptoms* and *causes*. It is not enough to deal with the most obvious aspect of problems — their symptoms. These can be attacked easily enough, but such action does not provide lasting solutions. Instead, it is essential to understand and deal with the fundamental causes of each problem situation.

Now — read and analyze the cases!

Case No. 1. Counselor at the Youth Home

Tom D. was employed as a youth counselor at Carter Village, a large home for disturbed and dependent youth situated on its own property of 150 acres, and located close to a large city. He was put in charge of a group of 10- to 12-year-old boys. By the time the first week of the summer had passed, Tom felt rather smug in the belief that he had struck it off very well with the boys and that few difficulties were likely to appear.

On Tuesday afternoon, he took the boys on a hike in a county park adjacent to Carter Village. While on the trail, several boys confided in Tom, telling him their personal feelings about the Village, discussing their problems with him, and generally showing their trust in him. Other than being aware of certain cliques within the group, Tom felt the situation was well in hand. That evening, after supper and general assembly, he took a final head-count of the group and walked with them toward their cottage. At this point, one of the boys, Freddy, came up to Tom and said, "Mr. D., you don't have to take the roster in to Mr. L. (the cottage parent). We're all here — why don't you let me take it in for you?" Without questioning the situation, and feeling in full command, Tom handed the roster slip over to Freddy and headed for his car.

While traveling home, Tom mused that this summer job was quite satisfying — both challenging and professionally rewarding — and a good assignment for a college physical education instructor with a special interest in youth work. At 9 o'clock that evening, however, he received a call from Carter Village's night supervisor, asking if he knew where the group had gone. Apparently, when he left the boys without escorting them directly into the cottage, Freddy and eight of the other boys had decided to take off for "greener pastures," and the cottage parent had not discovered immediately that they were missing.

It took the staff of Carter Village three days to round up the scattered group. Several of them returned to their old neighborhoods in the city, while others hung out in the woods near the Village, playing a game of cat-and-mouse with the searchers. At the expense of a deflated ego, Tom D. concluded that he would never again underestimate a child — normal, disturbed, or otherwise.

Questions for Discussion

What were the basic causes of this incident, in your judgment?

How might it have been avoided; i.e., what policies on the part of Carter Village's staff director might serve to prevent this or similar events from taking place again?

Case No. 2. Making Contact with Billy V.

Jeff. R., a white college student working as a summer counselor at Camp Stony Creek, a nonsectarian co-educational camp operated by the Federation of Neighborhood Houses, was placed in charge of eight boys ranging in age from 12 to 14 years. The boys were mixed in background. Five were white (three were Protestant and two were Jewish) and three were black. All were from low-income families.

During the first week of camp, most of the boys seemed to be getting along well with each other and with the counselor. However, Jeff soon realized that he would have trouble with one of the black boys, Billy V. Billy seemed to have no friends, and was constantly picking fights with other campers. Over a three-day period, Jeff tried several ways of controlling Billy's behavior. He punished him by ordering him to "police" the area, by having him do push-ups and, as a last resort, "docking" him by prohibiting him from attending an evening movie with the other boys.

That night, after the boys had gone to bed, Jeff and another counselor went into town, returning to camp about one o'clock in the morning. When Jeff returned to his tent, one of the other campers awoke and told him that Billy had urinated in Jeff's cot. Jeff was shocked. The thought of someone deliberately urinating in another person's cot was foreign to him. Furious, he aroused Billy and ordered him to strip his cot and to re-make it with fresh linen. Billy did so sullenly, cursing liberally as he yanked the wet sheets and blanket from the cot. However, since Jeff was much bigger and stronger, he obeyed him. When the cot was re-made, the counselor asked Billy why he had done this, but the boy refused to talk.

The following day, Billy had two more fights with other boys and had to be physically restrained each time. Jeff felt that he was reaching the end of his rope with Billy, and that he might have to recommend to the camp director that Billy be sent home.

After dinner, the boys decided to play Bombardment (a form of dodge ball). As a last resort, Jeff decided to try a different approach with Billy. He gave him his whistle and asked him to referee the game. At first Billy hesitated. But Jeff told him that he would be completely in charge, and announced to the other boys that whatever Billy said counted. What followed in the next few minutes struck Jeff as amazing. Billy went ahead to referee the game efficiently. He made the other boys follow the rules strictly, and tolerated no nonsense from any of them.

From that moment on, Billy became a self-appointed assistant counselor. He and Jeff got along very well and there was no friction between them for the remainder of the camp season.

Questions for Discussion

Without knowing the full background of Billy V.'s behavior problem, why do you think he urinated in his counselor's bed?

How do you regard Jeff's efforts at controlling Billy during the first few days of camp? What else might he have done? In your judgment, what assistance should be given to young camp counselors, in terms of understanding and working with such problems?

What was the key event that turned Billy's behavior around? How do you interpret the cause of this radical change? What principle might Jeff draw from it, for his own professional growth?

Case No. 3. Maria's Little Ritual

Nancy W., a nurse who had married and was no longer working, decided to do volunteer work as a recreation aide in a psychiatric hospital. She was accepted at Woods Island Hospital, a large state facility, where her responsibilities consisted chiefly of talking to patients, playing table games and sports with them, helping the occupational and recreational therapists, and assisting at parties. She had worked in a state hospital before, and was familiar with psychiatric patients.

The staff member responsible for supervising Nancy was a young man, Alex M., who was working for his doctorate in psychology. On the first day she reported for work, he took her, along with another volunteer, to see the ward where they would be assigned, and to meet the staff members and some of the patients. As they were leaving the ward after this meeting, they passed the lunchroom where the patients were eating. Alex said, "Wait, there's something I'd like you to see." He called to a woman patient, asking her to come out. When she did not rise, he went in to the lunchroom to bring her out.

Alex introduced her to Nancy by saying, "This is Maria S. She is a catatonic schizophrenic and displays all the classic symptoms of the disease."

He asked Maria to show them her little "ritual." When the patient did not respond, he took her hand, saying "Show us your hand ritual." He made a sudden spastic gesture with his hand, and she copied the movement. He commented that this was a very common gesture among catatonics, and they left the area.

Based on her past experience and personal philosophy of patient care, Nancy felt that this was inappropriate behavior on Alex's part. She asked him why he had done it. He replied that he did this sort of thing to "shock them out of it." Nancy replied that she felt that it was destructive to patients to put them up for show, and that she understood that it was customary hospital policy not to let psychiatric patients know their diagnosis, since they frequently misinterpreted the information, or were frightened by it.

Alex grew angry and said that if Nancy did not like his methods, she should resign as a volunteer. However, Nancy remained on the job. When she saw Alex again the following week, he said curtly that there was a universal law that one should never critize a staff member in front of another staff member. Nancy agreed that she could understand his becoming upset, because other staff members had observed the episode. She apologized and said she hoped they would be able to start over again, although she could not accept the principle of not criticizing another staff member as a "universal" law. Alex replied, "If you can't accept it, you should not be working here." Nancy felt that they were not getting anywhere, and merely stated that she wanted to continue to work as a volunteer in the hospital.

Although she did not have frequent contact with Alex, whenever she did, Nancy felt very uncomfortable. Although their relationship improved slightly, they were never able to really get along with each other.

Questions for Discussion

What is your reaction to Alex's asking Maria to show her little "ritual?" In your judgment, why did he become so upset when Nancy criticized him?

Although Nancy might have been justified in her criticism, in what way could she have behaved more constructively?

What recommendations could you make that might help to prevent this type of problem situation?

Case No. 4. Juan's Grand Strategy — The Fake Trip

Juan R. was recreation director in a center run by the Youth Aid League, a voluntary agency operating in a disadvantaged area of the city. One of his responsibilities was to work with a group of boys and girls who ranged in age from the early teens to about 18 or 19. There were about 40 participants in all. He was assisted by a woman leader, Luz S. Both Juan and Luz were in their mid-twenties, and neither was professionally trained for this work.

During the summer, most of the members of the group were not in school or working, and therefore spent most of their time at the Youth Aid League center. The program went fairly well. Most of the group members were cooperative, except for five older boys, all of whom were about 18 or 19 years old. They occasionally caused difficulty for Juan because they refused to obey center rules, particularly with respect to drinking. However, there were no serious incidents, and they took part satisfactorily in most activities. Because of their age and aggressive behavior, they were regarded by other group members as leaders.

Juan and Luz planned three bus trips to nearby resort areas, such as beaches and amusement parks, during the summer. They set out in the morning and returned to the city in the late evening. The first bus trip went well. However, on the second one, the five older boys brought some liquor with them, became drunk, and caused some difficulty on the beach by getting into a fight with local boys. Although Juan and Luz got them all back safely in the bus for the return to the city, Juan felt that the five older boys would have to be barred from making the last bus trip of the summer.

Plans were announced to the youth group that this trip would be made to Pine Shelter Beach, a popular resort area about 40 miles from the city — and that the clique of older boys would not be permitted to go with the group. However, one of the girls told Luz that the older boys were planning to follow them in a car to Pine Shelter Beach and disrupt the outing. In fact, she disclosed that some younger members of the group had lent them money, to help them with the expense of making the trip on their own.

Juan decided to outmaneuver the group. The day before the trip, he announced to several members of the group that he and Luz had changed their plans, and that the trip would be taken to Atlantic Knolls, another popular beach. As he had expected, the word of this "secret" plan quickly filtered through to the older boys. On the morning of the trip, Juan quietly gave the bus driver directions to take the group to Pine Shelter Beach, as originally planned. The older boys drove their car to Atlantic Knolls, and spent the day fruitlessly searching for the group. That night, when the bus returned, the older boys were waiting at the Youth Aid League center. They threatened and cursed Juan and Luz, and threw garbage on Juan's car, although they did not attack him directly.

Through that fall and winter, the older boys continued to be a problem. They took part in the activities of the youth group but frequently showed up drunk or stoned, were hostile, and often refused to cooperate. When two of their members joined the Army, the clique broke up and the older boys stopped attending the center.

Questions for Discussion

What do you feel were some of the basic causes of the problem Juan and Luz faced with respect to the older group?

Juan's strategy of changing the destination of the bus trip to send the older boys on a "wildgoose chase" avoided an immediate problem at the beach. How do you view it, as an example of long-range leadership tactics?

Do you see anything about the make-up of the group that might account for some of its difficulties? What fundamental recommendations could you make that might be helpful in working with a group such as this?

Case No. 5. The Youth Leadership Conference

Leona W., a physical education instructor at Miller College, volunteered to go along as one of the faculty members accompanying a large group of sophomore students to a special leadership training conference in the Pocono Mountains, about 100 miles from the college. In all, there were four men and four women faculty members, and about 120 students. A professor in the psychology department, John R., was coordinator of the conference.

The busses left on schedule, arriving in the late afternoon at the isolated motel facility where the conference was being held. Students were assigned to rooms – girls in one wing of the building and boys in another. (Note: this conference took place in the late 1960's, before many colleges shifted to co-ed dormitory arrangements). As Leona W. toured the girls' wing, she found that there were between two to five girls in each room.

Immediately after checking in, dinner was served. At dinner, Professor R. briefed the other faculty members on the plans he had developed for the conference. Later, the group assembled to hear a guest speaker lecture on leadership. It was necessary for the faculty advisors to patrol the room during the talk, since many students were noisy and inattentive. The remainder of the evening was devoted to having a dance in the motel lounge. Two men and two women faculty advisors were assigned to supervise this activity.

Leona W. was not involved, and played bridge until 3 o'clock in the morning with the other advisors. The dance was poorly attended, and many of the male students began wandering in and out of the girls' wing. Some of the girls complained that the boys were bothering them and would not leave; other rooms were completely quiet. Since their leadership function was not clearly defined, Leona and the other woman faculty member did not try to interfere with the activity, but made checks when there was excessive noise, and tried to keep the area quiet.

After breakfast, group meetings were set up and the conference progressed. During the morning, Leona W. went to Professor R. and asked him whether any action should be taken to control the nighttime activity in the girls' dorm area. It was apparent that several of the boys had spent the night in girls' rooms. Professor R. replied only that he hoped that no one would become pregnant.

However, at dinner that night, Professor R. announced that all students would have to be in their own dormitory areas by 12:30 a.m. When many students protested that this was unreasonable, he agreed that the lounge could be kept open all night.

Leona announced that she would be making a check of the girls' wing, to make sure that all male guests left by 12:30. Faculty and student leaders of the various workshop groups had a lengthy meeting that evening that ended at midnight. At 12:30, Leona and one of the male faculty members went off to clear the girls' wing. As they went from room to room, a large group of girls followed them. When doors opened, one by one, and boys came out (some in various stages of undress), the girls cheered. The boys went smilingly off to the lounge. Finally, when all the boys had left the girls' wing, the majority of girls took their pillows and blankets and stayed in the lounge with them. Only three remained in their rooms throughout the night.

The question of college policy regarding male-female relationships, or personal standards of sexual behavior, was not discussed by the conference, which ended the next day. Leona W. wondered whether she might have played a more effective role in this area.

Questions for Discussion

Could you analyze Professor R.'s role in organizing and directing this leadership conference, based on information you are given in the case study? How might the conference have been held more effectively?

Recognizing that this conference was held at a time when college policy toward the sexual involvement of students was less permissive than it is today, what steps might have been taken to anticipate and plan for the problem of who would be sleeping where? What else might Leona W. have done?

In general, what sort of guidelines would you suggest for planning a youth leadership training conference of this type?

Case No. 6. Hospital Security and Staff Morale

In a psychiatric unit of seriously disturbed patients in a large State Hospital, the supervisor of the activity therapy department, Tom L., emphasized at a staff meeting that it was essential to keep careful control of all keys for offices, equipment rooms, wards, and elevators. Although many halls and buildings were kept unlocked, it was necessary to lock others for security reasons. Tom then returned a set of keys to Alice M., a staff member who had misplaced them. Tom again warned those present of the dangers of misplacing or losing keys, and threatened to keep the keys the next time a staff member misplaced them.

The next week, another recreation therapist, Jean B., lost her keys. Tom found them and put them in his office. He told Jean that it was essential that she locate them, and she continued to search the building and question patients to see if they had taken her keys. Some of the patients began getting upset over this incident. Finally, another staff member who knew the facts told Jean that the activity therapy supervisor had taken the keys, because she had carelessly laid them down in a patient area.

Jean confronted Tom in front of several other staff members, crying and swearing at him. She then went to the Assistant Director of Rehabilitation to voice her complaint against Tom and to ask for a transfer. The Assistant Director of Rehabilitation called for a meeting of the entire activity staff assigned to the unit. The various incidents leading to the episode were reviewed. It became apparent that Jean felt she had been unfairly treated by Tom and other staff members. Racial prejudice was hinted at, in that Tom was black, and Jean was white. She also made clear her feeling that, because she had a masters degree in therapeutic recreation, she should not be supervised by him, since he had only a bachelor's degree (although he had several years of experience and had come up through the Civil Service career ladder). Other staff members supported Tom and indicated that they found Jean a difficult person to work with.

Tom's reaction at this meeting was to say nothing against Jean, or in his own defense. He apologized for hiding the keys, saying that he now realized that this was an inappropriate action.

However, Jean kept criticizing him and was unwilling to accept his apology. The final tone of the group appeared to be one of supporting Tom, and indicating disapproval of Jean. A week later, she was transferred to another unit of the hospital. After this episode, there seemed to be a stronger feeling of cohesion, and improved communication among the remaining staff members. Tom indicated that he would seek to avoid unilateral disciplinary action in working with staff problems, and would hold group meetings to deal with problems when they arose.

Questions for Discussion

What do you think of Tom's action in hiding Jean B.'s keys without telling her? How else might he have handled this situation?

In what way might the hostility between the recreation therapist and her supervisor have been improved? What did Tom apparently learn from the situation? How effective was the Assistant Director of Rehabilitation in dealing with the problem?

What general principles or guidelines regarding staff relationships can you draw from this case?

Case No. 7. The Leader Faces Herself

Dawn R., a college junior majoring in sociology, took a part-time job leading a group of 10- to 12-year-olds in a Girls' Club. The club was scheduled to meet three afternoons a week.

It appeared to Jane M., director of the club, that Dawn was uncertain about her leadership approach from the very beginning. On the first day she let the girls run wild and do whatever they wanted in the game room. The next time they met, she was extremely harsh, spending most of her time disciplining and scolding the members. At the third session, she again exerted strict controls and the group took part fairly well in craft activities. But, at the beginning of the next week, she was again highly permissive and the group members responded in a wild and uncontrolled manner.

Jane held a supervisory conference with Dawn to talk over her experiences thus far. The club director got the impression that Dawn was aware of the problem and extremely sensitive about it. She seemed to be defending herself by saying that she was a good leader, but was "stuck" with a group of uncooperative, immature girls.

Jane was concerned, in part because she wanted the girls in Dawn's group to have a better experience than they were having, and in part because she feared that this club's disruptive behavior might affect other groups in the Girls' Club. In dealing with the problem, from a sound human relations point of view, she felt that it was important for Dawn to realize that she was contributing to the problem — but that this would have to be done without scolding or lecturing her. In addition, Dawn would have to be involved in developing possible solutions to improve the situation.

The director met again with Dawn, and made it clear that she felt that Dawn's club was not functioning as well as it should. Without giving her views as to the cause of the difficulty, she again asked Dawn what she felt was the basic problem. No clear answer emerged. Jane then asked Dawn to observe a similar club which was directed by a more experienced leader, Phyllis D.

Dawn observed this club, which met on a day when her group did not. She recognized that Phyllis D. had structured the program, with a major part of the meeting devoted to games of low organization and craft activities, but with a good amount of time given to a members' planning session. All of the group members were active throughout the session. The leader was firm but fair with them, reminding the club members of certain basic rules of conduct at the beginning of the meeting, and repeating them when necessary, but allowing most of the discipline to emanate from the group members themselves.

Dawn met again with Jane. The director asked her what differences she saw between Phyllis' group and her own. Dawn commented that it was obvious that the program was more structured, and that the group members appeared to be more cooperative than the members of her own club were. Jane asked whether Phyllis' greater involvement with the group (she had taken part in the games with them) might have contributed to a better feeling of rapport. Dawn agreed that this was so. She also volunteered that the way Phyllis had quietly presented rules of conduct, reminding the group members of them when necessary, had apparently helped them gain a sense of responsibility for their own behavior, and to do their own "policing."

Jane then asked Dawn what changes she thought she might make in her own leadership. Dawn indicated that she would probably try to structure activities more carefully, and have a plan of activities made up in advance of each session. The club director suggested that it might be a good idea for her to meet with Phyllis to discuss her approach to planning the program. Later that day, the two club leaders met and discussed the problem. Phyllis suggested several activities that she had found useful. She also suggested that once the group had gotten successfully under way, the club members themselves might be involved in planning future sessions, as her girls did.

Dawn took careful notes on the meeting, and then outlined some plans for herself. She reported back to Jane and discussed the plans with her. Jane agreed that they seemed suitable, and suggested some additional ideas. She also asked Dawn whether she would mind being observed for the next two sessions. Dawn agreed, saying that she felt the director's presence would help her maintain better control, and that she would welcome Jane's comments and suggestions after the meetings. She seemed much more optimistic about her club than she had been before.

Questions for Discussion

Do you feel that Jane's approach to helping Dawn become a more effective leader was generally sound?

Isolate the specific concepts of supervision or methods of counseling that Jane used in helping Dawn understand the problem. Why was it logical for her to observe Phyllis and then meet with her?

What other approaches could you suggest that would be helpful to Dawn?

Case No. 8. The Coach Says "No!"

The Recreation Department in the town of Parksville obtained permission to use the local high school's gymnasium for an open sports program for teenage boys, to be held on Friday nights during the spring from 6:30

to 10:30 p.m. The two leaders placed in charge were Bill S. and Roy D., physical education teachers from the high school and junior high school. In this situation, they were hired and paid directly by the Recreation Department.

On the first evening of the program, over 70 boys from both school levels attended. They expressed an interest in forming a basketball league. They were assigned to teams, took part in practice, and league play was scheduled to begin on the following Friday. The operation would be quite informal: there would be no uniforms or outside officials, games would be played by "running time" rather than by a clock, and several parents agreed to serve as coaches.

There was considerable enthusiasm throughout the week, with the boys looking forward eagerly to playing. It appeared as if the Friday night open gym program would be a success.

However, late on Friday afternoon the varsity baseball coach of the high school arrived back at the school with his team, which had just played a league baseball game. When he saw many of his boys preparing to stay for evening basketball, he promptly announced that they would not be allowed to participate. When Bill asked him why, he indicated that he did not want any of the boys to sustain an injury that might prevent him from playing baseball. He added that boys on the junior varsity and freshman baseball teams also would not be allowed to play basketball.

It was clear to Bill and Roy that the baseball coach's decision posed a real problem. The evening basketball teams had been matched so that they were composed of players with roughly comparable age and ability. With many boys removed from play, the teams would be poorly balanced, and it would be necessary to set up the entire team structure again. This, however, was not the main point. The real question was whether a coach should be permitted to restrict players on his team from taking part in other wholesome sports activities during their leisure hours.

The baseball coach insisted that it was Roy's and Bill's responsibility, as school physical education teachers, to prevent any baseball players from taking part in the evening program. He made it clear that this was an order. The two leaders felt that this was unfair, because they were being employed in the Friday evening program by the Recreation Department, and not by the school district. They considered it to be their responsibility to allow as many youngsters to play as possible. While they respected the wish of the baseball coach to keep his team intact, they questioned his reasoning. Roy pointed out that it was just as likely that boys would get injured in pick-up basketball games on neighborhood playgrounds—which no one could prevent—as in an organized league game.

Further, if the baseball players were not allowed to take part in the open gym program, what would they be doing in their free time? Many Parksville teenagers sat in the woods near the high school on Friday and Saturday nights, drinking beer and wine or smoking "pot." Others drove hot-rods on the narrow, unlighted roads near the town. Was it really better

—and safer—for them to be doing these things than to be taking part in a basketball league on Friday nights?

When Roy and Bill presented these arguments to the baseball coach, he replied that he simply did not care. He did not want his players to take part in the basketball league and, if they were permitted to do so, he would report the two teachers to the chairman of the school's physical education department as having ignored his request. There was an hour to go before the games were scheduled to begin. Roy and Bill discussed their alternatives.

They could refuse to honor the order the baseball coach had given them.

They might accept it for the varsity baseball team but insist that the junior varsity and freshman players be permitted to take part.

They could telephone the department chairman, or even the school principal, for a ruling.

Or, they could take the position that they had no responsibility for telling the boys whether or not they could take part in the basketball games, and insist that if the coach wanted to restrict them, he would have to do it himself.

Questions for Discussion

What do you see as the fundamental issues in this disagreement?

From the point of view of what is best for the boys, do you feel that the coach or the recreation leaders are in the right?

Which of the possible alternatives do you see as the best course of action to take? Can you suggest any other solution for Bill and Roy? How might interjurisdictional problems like this be settled in the future?

Case No. 9. Volunteers in Trouble

The West Greenville Y.W.C.A. conducted an after-school sports and physical fitness program in the gymnasium of the Crawford Elementary School located in a nearby community. It was held once a week at the school, on Wednesday afternoons from 3 o'clock to 5 o'clock, and involved approximately 80 fifth- and sixth-grade girls. The program was free, since the Y.W.C.A. relied for leadership on three recreation majors from nearby Edgemont Collge, who participated in the program as part of a required field work assignment. These three young women were assigned by the Y's program director, Alice P., to the Crawford School, to organize an intramural sports program.

The program was held for the first time on February 3. Girls were organized into groups according to age, and they took part in volleyball, badminton, gymnastics and group games. A mother, who represented the Crawford Parent-Teachers Association, helped in the organization. Things seemed to be going fairly well that afternoon when Alice P. dropped by to see how the program was faring.

Two weeks later, however, a complaint report was submitted by the building custodian to the school principal. Entitled *Report of After-School Program,* and dated February 18, the complaint stated:

> On February 17, the Y.W.C.A. was in our building. When they left the gym was in a mess. These people leave the gym in a mess every time they are here. The girls are always running in the hallways. They spit water at each other in the halls. They also leave the gym mats thrown about. Mr. La Vena (physical education teacher) reported that two mats were ripped. On the same day, someone opened the gate that is across the hallway, left through the side door, and kicked a barrel of trash down the stairs into the basement. There is very poor supervision at this activity. The three people in charge cannot control the activity.

Immediately, Alice drove to the school and met with the principal and custodian to discuss the matter. She later met with the three volunteer leaders and the mother who assisted them. She concluded on the basis of these talks that the young women involved had never had experience with large groups of children before, and lacked the ability to carry on the program in an orderly manner. They did not exercise disciplinary control successfully, and spent a good deal of time chasing the less cooperative children through the hallways. When they did this, the sports activities began to fall apart, and all the children started to act up. The mother had been helpful in keeping the girls in line during the first two sessions. However, she had been late in arriving on February 17, and by the time she did arrive, things were well out of hand.

When Alice reviewed the situation with the Executive Director of the Y.W.C.A., the major causes of the problem appeared to be the following: first, there had been inadequate training or screening of the three field-work students from Edgemont College. It had been assumed that, because they were recreation majors, they would be able to handle the situation. The students had received only a brief orientation session before beginning the Wednesday program, and the mother had no preparation or training at all, Finally, the children had been recruited in a completely haphazard fashion, and no attempt had been made to determine their previously learned skills or interests. When they saw how informal and permissive the sports program was—compared with their carefully structured and supervised daytime physical education program—they began to challenge the leaders and misbehave whenever possible.

Because of the damage that had been done, and a lack of confidence in the ability of the three field-work students to carry on the program successfully, the program was terminated without meeting again.

Alice developed the following set of recommendations following this experience:

1. All volunteers for such programs should be carefully screened. Care should be taken to select individuals who have had experience in the appropriate activities, and in working with children.

2. Volunteers should be given a detailed orientation before beginning the activity. They should be given a written job description and a list of objectives to be accomplished. They should be informed that this is an important job, and that tardiness or absenteeism is not acceptable.

3. Appropriate disciplinary measures must be taken against those hindering the operation of the program, or who seek to destroy school property.

Questions for Discussion

Do you feel that blame for this unsuccessful program should be assigned primarily to the volunteer field-work students from Edgemont College, or should it rest primarily with the Y.W.C.A.?

How adequate were the recommendations developed by Alice P. to improve the use of volunteers in future programs?

Could you suggest other procedures that would assist volunteer programs of this type, which are situated in decentralized operations that are not in the Y.W.C.A. building itself, and that therefore are not easy to supervise regularly?

Case No. 10. Sharing the Load

At a meeting of about 40 recreation leaders and supervisors employed by the Allentown County Park and Recreation Commission, the bulk of the time was given to planning several special events due to occur during the fall season. The Recreation Division Director asked at the end of the meeting if there were any problems anyone wanted to bring up before it was adjourned. One of the leaders, Sharon S., stood up and presented the following problem:

As Sharon saw it, the workload of various recreation leaders throughout the county was not shared equally. Some leaders, she said, were assigned to do a greater amount of work than others, no matter what the season or program. Beside handling assignments on their own facilities, or in their own special programs, they were often assigned to be in charge of special county events, workshops, or competitions. Often, because of this increased workload, their own programs tended to suffer. The reason for this, Sharon said, was that these men and women were recognized as more productive and efficient than other leaders in the division. Supervisors tended to choose them for special assignments, since they were more likely to do a good job, and this would reflect on the supervisors and the Commission as a whole.

"What this means," Sharon concluded, "is that the reward for good work is more work. Conversely, if you want to get paid and do very little work, just do a poor job."

A heated discussion followed. Some leaders and supervisors agreed with Sharon. Others said that she had exaggerated the problem, and that, if some leaders were doing a poor job, all the department had to do was fire or suspend them. However, it was agreed that this was not easily done if the leaders lived up to the minimal requirements of the job (once they had passed their probationary periods), because the labor union contract and Civil Service procedures made it very difficult to take such action. In addition, it was agreed that the fact that some leaders got by with comparatively little effort hurt the morale of the more dedicated and capable leaders, and kept them from extending themselves. The frustration of seeing others work very little for the same salary tended to lead even competent and highly motivated leaders down the road to mediocrity.

Gradually, it was agreed that something had to be done to help less productive leaders work more effectively, if the entire department's program was to be carried on properly. Some leaders suggested that the most obvious method—that of promoting the best workers to supervisory positions—had limited potential, since within the Civil Service structure there were only a few supervisory positions, and these openings appeared very infrequently. The alternative of trying to fire the poorest leaders, as a drastic measure, also had its weakness, since a job freeze was in effect in county government, and it was unlikely that these individuals would be replaced. The question of concern was, "Is a warm body better than no body at all?"

The meeting finally adjourned without any conclusion being reached.

Questions for Discussion

Do you think that the kind of problem described by Sharon S. is a real one, particularly in large bureaucratic organizations? Have you seen examples of it in your own experience?

What steps would you take to bring about improve motivation and performance on the part of the weaker leaders in the Recreation Division, and to help them share the workload more equally? Be specific about the actions that might be taken.

Case No. 11. Swimming Pool Fees—Who Pays?

Frank M., Director of Recreation and Parks in the village of Dobbstown, held a meeting with his advisory board, which was composed of five elected members and two trustees appointed by the village mayor. The board reviewed his plans for the coming summer program, including schedule of activities, hiring plans, and budget, since it would be necessary shortly to send a brochure for the summer events to the printer. Frank described the swimming program, which involved busing children from various playgrounds to a nearby county swimming pool for instruction and free swimming. Since Dobbstown did not have its own swimming pool, this busing arrangement had been used for the past two years, and each family that wished to have its children take part in the program paid a special fee of $15.

Frank pointed out to the board that, although Dobbstown was a fairly comfortable community, a number of families were poor; some were on welfare. In the past, he had permitted children from these families to take part in the swimming program without paying the special fee. Would this policy be acceptable again this year?

Immediately, several of the trustees raised questions:

"Who or what determines if a family cannot afford the fee?"

"Do you just use your judgment, or is there a screening system to check financial ability?"

"Is this policy generally known in the community? Perhaps some families do not have their children take part in the swimming program, because they do not know that the fee might be waived."

A heated discussion followed. Various points of view were expressed. Some board members felt that any family or individual who could not afford to pay a fee for any fee-bearing activity offered by the department should be permitted to take part in it, without any formal screening action or application being necessary. In contrast, others took the position that, if some people were permitted to take part in activities without paying fees, many others would take advantage of it. In addition, they felt that waivers would pose a special problem in the winter program, when many activities were carried on in which the leader's fee was dependent on the amount of fees paid. However, it was agreed to confine the discussion to the summer swimming program, which was seen as vitally needed by all families in the village.

Gradually, the different points of view narrowed down to two positions: "idealist" and "modified realist." The attitudes of these groups were:

Idealist: Anyone who requested to have his or her child admitted to the swimming program should have the fee waived on the basis of a verbal request. There would be no investigation, and parents would not be asked to sign any type of paper. It was felt that: (a) people were basically honest and would not take advantage of this policy; and (b) to require them to sign a statement of financial need would be humiliating and might prevent some children from taking part in the program.

Modified Realist: Parents who wished their children to be admitted to the swimming program without charge should be asked to come to the recreation office to sign a statement to the effect that they could not afford to pay the fee. This policy would be printed in the Summer Program Bulletin, which was distributed to all families in the village.

Again, the argument boiled over. Some felt that families which really needed the aid would be too proud to accept it. It was feared that if the fee were eliminated without any formal request of waiver, it might cause a serious financial burden in the department. The argument was made that the policy should not be printed in the bulletin, since it might encourage too many families to apply, and all those in need would probably hear about it by word-of-mouth.

Throughout the discussion, Frank M. did not state his opinion, other than to answer questions raised by members of the board. Finally, he was asked directly to give his recommendations, based on his view of what would be most workable for the department and fairest to all the citizens of Dobbstown. He made the following suggestions:

1. The fee would be waived for any family requesting it. No screening system should be used, and there would be no need to sign any type of statement, or to prove financial need.

2. The policy would not be printed in the Summer Program Bulletin, but would appear in the minutes of the Commission, which were available to all residents at the Village Hall.

Questions for Discussion

What are some of the fundamental issues regarding the role of community recreation and parks programs that the Dobbstown advisory board was grappling with?

What do you think of Frank M.'s approach in presenting the problem but withholding his views until asked to give a recommendation at the end of the discussion?

Based on the arguments that have been summarized, do you believe that his proposal was a sensible one?

Case No. 12. A Parking Lot—or Trees?

The Yorktown Park District recently expanded its athletic facilities at Secor Woods Park by constructing a new ballfield and six additional tennis courts. When the volume of use of these facilities began to grow, it was apparent that there was a serious parking problem, particularly on summer and spring weekends. Often residents who wished to use the facilities were forced to park along Secor Road and adjacent residential streets, and sometimes they parked illegally along the entrance road into the park, creating a safety hazard.

The Yorktown Park Commission members reviewed the problem and determined that the best solution was to make use of an adjacent parcel of land, approximately 130 feet by 175 feet and situated under high-tension wires, which was owned by the local utilities company, United Electric. After considerable negotiation, United Electric gave its approval for the use of this property for overflow parking. The negotiations took a period of time to complete, and even after they were approved, engineering plans had to be drawn up. Meanwhile, a number of citizens began to protest against the use of this site for parking. It was quite a wild area, with considerable bird and animal life in the shrubbery, although there were no tall trees because of the high-tension wires. Several environmentalists wrote letters to the town newspaper, protesting the plan to blacktop the area.

When the specifications were completed and approved, the town highway department was assigned to do the job. On a Monday morning, they moved in with bulldozers to clean off and grade the site. That afternoon, several truckloads of crushed stone and gravel were dumped on the side of the property.

On Tuesday at noon, with the grading work half completed, the commissioner of the park district suddenly received an emergency call from his supervisor, the town manager, Bart F. Mr. F. indicated that a number of influential citizens had come to his office with a petition containing several hundred names, which demanded that work on the parking area be stopped. Students in the high school had held a protest meeting the day before, had circulated the petititons, and had aroused the concern of many adults. Bart was in a serious bind, as he explained to the Park Commissioner. As he saw it, there were three pressures being exerted on him.

First, there were the local residents in the Secor Woods area, who had been demanding action on the parking area for the past year because of the congestion the new facilities had caused in their neighborhood streets.

Second, there was the problem of public opinion. Bart did not want to have the label of "anti-environment" or "nature-spoiler" attached to him, and he assumed that the Park Commissioner did not want it either.

Third, it would be extremely difficult to stop work on the site, leaving it partially graded, particularly since he had been negotiating with United Electric for several months for a right-of-way into another town park that was to be developed. If the Secor Woods plan fell through, he was afraid that the other project would be jeopardized.

It was a difficult choice to make. The town manager turned to the Park Commissioner. "What do you think we ought to do?" he asked.

Questions for Discussion

What are the key issues in this controversy? What weight do you give to the arguments for and against clearing the land for the overflow parking area?

How might the Town Manager and Park Commissioner have avoided the difficult situation in which they found themselves?

What action should be taken in order to salvage the situation and make the wisest possible decision, both in terms of solving the parking problem at Secor Woods Park and maintaining effective community relations with town residents? In other words, what is *your* recommendation?

Suggested Examination Questions or Topics for Student Reports

1. Based both on your reading of the cases in this chapter and on your observation of actual programs, can you identify certain common factors or elements that cause difficulty in many recreation agencies? What are these, and how can they be prevented?
2. Select any case in this chapter that is primarily concerned with leaders and participants. Analyze it, and make recommendations geared to solving the problem situation immediately, and to preventing its recurrence in the future.
3. Select any case that is primarily concerned with supervisory or administrative problems, and deal with it as in Question 2.
4. Based on your own experience or observation, present a case study involving a leadership or supervision problem situation. Present alternative solutions to solving it, and describe their strengths and weaknesses.

Suggested Action Assignments for Students

1. Attempt to identify a real problem situation in a major public, voluntary, or therapeutic agency. This may be a current or past problem. Interview several of those involved on different levels, obtaining their perceptions of the problem, and their recommendations for solving it.
2. Based on the case studies in this chapter, develop a set of supervisory guidelines specifically designed to prevent or minimize problems commonly found in recreation leadership situations.

bibliography

GENERAL BOOKS ON RECREATION

Joseph J. Bannon: *Problem Solving in Recreation and Parks.* Englewood Cliffs, New Jersey, Prentice-Hall, 1972.

Charles K. Brightbill: *Man and Leisure, A Philosophy of Recreation.* Englewood Cliffs, New Jersey, Prentice-Hall, 1961.

Charles A. Bucher and Richard D. Bucher: *Recreation for Today's Society.* Englewood Cliffs, New Jersey, Prentice-Hall, 1973.

George D. Butler: *Introduction to Community Recreation.* New York, McGraw-Hill Book Co., 1967.

Reynold Carlson, Theodore Deppe, and Janet MacLean: *Recreation in American Life.* Belmont, California, Wadsworth Publishing Co., 1972.

Charles E. Doell and Louis F. Twardzik: *Elements of Park and Recreaiton Administration.* Minneapolis, Burgess Publishing Co., 1973.

David Gray and Donald Pelegrino: *Reflections on the Recreation and Park Movement.* Dubuque, Iowa, William C. Brown Co., 1973.

George Hjelte and Jay S. Shivers: *Public Administration of Recreational Services.* Philadelphia, Lea and Febiger, 1972.

Marion N. Hormachea and Carroll R. Hormachea (Eds.): *Recreation in Modern Society.* Boston, Holbrook Press, 1972.

Clayne R. Jensen: *Outdoor Recreation in America.* Minneapolis, Burgess Publishing Co., 1973.

Richard Kraus: *Recreation Today: Program Planning and Leadership.* New York, Appleton-Century-Crofts, 1966.

Richard Kraus: *Recreation and Leisure in Modern Society.* New York, Appleton-Century-Crofts, 1971.

Richard Kraus and Joseph Curtis: *Creative Administration in Recreation and Parks.* St. Louis, C. V. Mosby, 1973.

Sidney G. Lutzin and Edward H. Storey (Eds.): *Managing Municipal Leisure Services.* Washington, D.C., International City Management Association, 1973.

Harold D. Meyer, Charles K. Brightbill, and H. Douglas Sessoms: *Community Recreation: A Guide to Its Organization.* Englewood Cliffs, New Jersey, Prentice-Hall, 1969.

Susanna Millar: *The Psychology of Play.* Baltimore, Penguin Books, 1968.

Norman Miller and Duane Robinson: *The Leisure Age.* Belmont, California, Wadsworth Publishing Co., 1963.

James F. Murphy: *Concepts of Leisure: Philosophy and Implications.* Englewood Cliffs, New Jersey, Prentice-Hall, 1974.

James F. Murphy, John G. Williams, E. William Niepoth, and Paul D. Brown: *Leisure Service Delivery System: A Modern Perspective.* Philadelphia, Lea and Febiger, 1973.

Lynn S. Rodney: *Administration of Public Recreation.* New York, Ronald Press, 1964.

379

Allen V. Sapora and Elmer Mitchell: *The Theory of Play and Recreation.* New York, Ronald Press, 1961.

Jay S. Shivers: *Principles and Practices of Recreational Service.* New York, Macmillan Book Co., 1967.

Edwin J. Staley and Norman P. Miller (Eds.): *Leisure and the Quality of Life.* Washington, D.C.: American Association for Health, Physical Education and Recreation, 1972.

GROUP DYNAMICS, SUPERVISION, AND LEADERSHIP

Robert E. Bouton: *Effective Supervisory Practices.* Washington, D.C.: International City Management Association, 1971.

Dorwin Cartwright and Alvin Zander: *Group Dynamics: Research and Theory.* New York, Harper and Row, 1960.

H. Dan Corbin: *Recreation Leadership.* Englewood Cliffs, New Jersey, Prentice-Hall, 1970.

Howard Danford: *Creative Leadership in Recreation.* Boston, Allyn and Bacon, 1964.

Marshall E. Dimock and Gladys O. Dimock: *Public Administration.* New York, Holt, Rinehart and Winston, 1969.

Myrtle Edwards: *Recreation Leader's Guide.* Palo Alto, California, National Press, 1967.

Gerald B. Fitzgerald: *Leadership in Recreation.* New York, Ronald Press, 1951.

Frank Goble: *Excellence in Leadership.* New York, American Management Association, 1972.

A. Paul Hare: *Handbook of Small Group Research.* New York, Free Press, 1962.

Margaret E. Hartford: *Groups in Social Work.* New York, Columbia University Press, 1972.

Bernard L. Hinton and H. Joseph Reitz: *Groups and Organization.* Belmont, California, Wadsworth Publishing Co., 1971.

Gisela Konopka: *Social Group Work: A Helping Process.* Englewood Cliffs, New Jersey, Prentice-Hall, 1963.

Richard Kraus: *Recreation Leader's Handbook.* New York, McGraw-Hill Book Co., 1955.

Douglas McGregor: *The Human Side of Enterprise.* New York, McGraw-Hill Book Co., 1960.

Douglas McGregor: *The Professional Manager.* New York, McGraw-Hill Book Co., 1967.

Matthew Miles: *Learning to Work in Groups.* New York, Teachers College, Columbia, Bureau of Publications, 1959.

John M. Pfiffner and Marshall Fels: *The Supervision of Personnel: Human Relations in the Management of Men.* Englewood Cliffs, New Jersey, Prentice-Hall, 1965.

Marvin E. Shaw: *Group Dynamics: The Psychology of Small Group Behavior.* New York: McGraw-Hill Book Co., 1971.

Jay S. Shivers: *Leadership in Recreational Service.* New York, The Macmillan Co., 1963.

William R. Spriegel, Edward Schulz, and William B. Spriegel: *Elements of Supervision.* New York, John Wiley and Sons, 1957.

O. Glenn Stahl: *Public Personnel Administration.* New York, Harper and Row, 1962.

Ivan D. Steiner: *Group Process and Productivity.* New York and London, Academic Press, 1972.

Robert Tannenbaum, Irving R. Weschler, and Fred Massarik: *Leadership and Organization: A Behavioral Science Approach.* New York, McGraw-Hill Book Co., 1961.

Margaret Williamson: *Supervision: Principles and Methods.* New York, Woman's Press (National Board of the Young Women's Christian Association), 1950.

ACTIVITY LEADERSHIP METHODS, AND NEEDS OF
SPECIAL POPULATIONS

Ronald C. Adams: *Games, Sports and Exercise for the Physically Handicapped.* Philadelphia, Lea and Febiger, 1972.

David A. Armbruster, Robert H. Allen, and Hobert S. Billingsley: *Swimming and Diving.* St. Louis, C. V. Mosby, 1973.

Elliott M. Avedon: *Therapeutic Recreation Service: An Applied Behavioral Science Approach.* Englewood Cliffs, New Jersey, Prentice-Hall, 1974.

Elliott M. Avedon and Frances Arje: *Socio-Recreative Programing for the Retarded.* New York, Teachers College, Columbia University, Bureau of Publications, 1964.

Robert O. Bale: *Creative Nature Crafts.* Minneapolis, Burgess Publishing Co., 1959.

Edith L. Ball: *Hosteling: The New Program in Community Recreation.* New York, American Youth Hostels, 1971.

John Batcheller and Sally Monsour: *Music in Recreation and Leisure.* Dubuque, Iowa, C. Brown, 1972.

Gerald F. Brommer: *Wire Sculpture and Other Three-Dimensional Construction.* Worcester, Massachusetts, Davis, 1968.

Charles E. Buell: *Physical Education and Recreation for the Visually Handicapped.* Washington, D.C., American Association for Health, Physical Education and Recreation, 1973.

Bernice W. Carlson and David R. Ginglend: *Recreation for Retarded Teen-Agers and Young Adults.* Nashville, Tennessee, Abingdon Press, 1968.

Bernice W. Carlson: *Play a Part.* Nashville, Tennessee, Abingdon Press, 1970.

Donald R. Casaday: *Sports Activities for Men.* Riverside, New Jersey, The Macmillan Co., 1974.

Maurice Case: *Recreation for Blind Adults.* Springfield, Illinois, Charles C Thomas, 1966.

Alan R. Caskey: *Playground Operation Manual.* Cranbury, New Jersey, A. S. Barnes, 1972.

Frederick Chapman: *Recreation Activities for the Handicapped.* New York, Ronald Press, 1960.

Helen and Larry Eisenberg: *Omnibus of Fun.* New York, Association Press, 1956.

Helen and Larry Eisenberg: *The Handbook of Skits and Stunts.* New York, Association Press, 1953.

Phyllis M. Ford: *Your Camp and the Handicapped Child.* Bradford Woods, Indiana, American Camping Association,

Virginia Frye and Martha Peters: *Therapeutic Recreation: Its Theory, Philosophy and Practices.* Harrisburg, Pennsylvania, Stackpole Books, 1972.

Cecile Gilbert: *International Folk Dance at a Glance,* Minneapolis, Burgess Publishing Co., 1974.

Jane Harris, Anne Pittman, and Marlys Waller: *Dance a While.* Minneapolis, Burgess Publishing Co., 1968.

William Hillcourt: *New Field Book of Nature Activities and Hobbies.* New York, G. P. Putnam's Sons, 1971.

Darwin Hindman: *Handbook of Active Games.* Englewood Cliffs, New Jersey, Prentice-Hall, 1955.

Louis Hoover: *Art Activities for the Very Young.* Worcester, Massachusetts, Davis, 1961.

John Howkinson: *Collect, Print and Paint from Nature.* Racine, Wisconsin, Whitman, 1963.

Valerie Hunt: *Recreation for the Handicapped.* Englewood Cliffs, New Jersey, Prentice-Hall, 1955.

Marguerite Ickis: *Nature in Recreation.* New York, A. S. Barnes, 1965.

Mary Bee Jensen and Clayne R. Jensen: *Folk Dancing.* Provo, Utah, Brigham Young University Press, 1973.

Robert Kleemeir: *Aging and Leisure*. New York, Oxford University Press, 1961.

Richard Kraus: *Therapeutic Recreation Service: Principles and Practices*. Philadelphia, W. B. Saunders Co., 1973.

Richard Kraus: *Square Dances of Today*. New York, Ronald Press, 1950.

Richard Kraus: *Folk Dancing: A Guide for Schools, Colleges and Recreation Groups*. New York, The Macmillan Co., 1962.

Richard Kraus (Ed.): *Reader's Digest Book of 1000 Family Games*. New York, Reader's Digest, 1971.

Susan H. Kubie and Gertrude Landau: *Group Work with the Aged*. New York, International Universities Press, 1969.

Marjorie Latchaw and Jean Pyatt: *A Pocket Guide of Dance Activities*. Englewood Cliffs, New Jersey, Prentice-Hall, 1958.

John R. Lindbeck: *Basic Crafts*. Peoria, Illinois, Chas. A. Bennett Co., 1969.

Zaidee Lindsay: *Art and the Handicapped Child*. New York, Taplinger Publishing Co., 1972.

Betty Lowndes: *Movement and Creative Drama for Children*. Boston, Massachusetts, Plays, Inc., 1971.

Carol Lucas: *Recreational Activity Development for the Aging in Hospitals and Nursing Homes*. Springfield, Illinois, Charles C Thomas, 1962.

Bernard Mason and Elmer Mitchell: *Social Games for Recreation*. New York, Ronald Press, 1935.

Ralph Mayer: *Artist's Handbook of Materials and Techniques*. New York, Viking Press, 1970.

William McNeice and Kenneth Benson: *Crafts for the Retarded*. Bloomington, Illinois, McKnight Publishing Co., 1964.

Toni Merrill: *Activities for the Aged and Infirm*. Springfield, Illinois, Charles C Thomas, 1967.

W. K. Merrill: *All About Camping*. Harrisburg, Pennsylvania, Stackpole Books, 1970.

Anne C. Mosey: *Activities Therapy*. New York, Raven Press, 1973.

Margaret E. Mulac: *Games and Stunts*. New York, Harper and Row, 1964.

Virginia Musselman: *Learning About Nature Through Games*. Harrisburg, Pennsylvania, 1967.

Larry L. Neal: *Recreation's Role in the Rehabilitation of the Mentally Retarded*. Eugene, Oregon, University of Oregon Press, 1970.

Glenn C. Nelson: *Ceramics: A Potter's Handbook*. New York, Holt, Rinehart and Winston, 1971.

John A. Nesbitt, Paul D. Brown, and James F. Murphy: *Recreation and Leisure Service for the Disadvantaged*. Philadelphia, Lea and Febiger, 1970.

Gerald S. O'Morrow: *Administration of Activity Therapy*. Springfield, Illinois, Charles C Thomas, 1965.

Hally B. W. Poindexter and Carole Mushier: *Coaching Competitive Team Sports for Girls and Women*. Philadelphia, W. B. Saunders Co., 1973.

Janet Pomeroy: *Recreation for the Physically Handicapped*. New York, The Macmillan Co., 1964.

John Portmouth: *Creative Crafts for Today*. New York, Viking Press, 1970.

Public Health Service: *Activity Supervisor's Guide: A Handbook for Activities Supervisors in Long-Term Nursing Care Facilities*. Washington, D.C., Public Health Service, Department of Health, Education and Welfare, 1969.

Carl Reed and Joseph Orze; *Art from Scrap*. New York, Association Press, 1968.

Ferris Robins and Janet Robins: *Educational Rhythmics for Mentally and Physically Handicapped Children*. New York, Association Press, 1968.

Jay S. Shivers: *Camping: Administration, Counseling and Programming*. New York, Appleton-Century-Crofts, 1971.

Jay S. Shivers and Clarence R. Calder: *Recreational Crafts: Programming and Instructional Techniques.* New York, McGraw-Hill Book Co., 1971.

John Squires: *Fun Crafts for Children.* Englewood Cliffs, New Jersey, Prentice-Hall, 1964.

Thomas Stein and H. Douglas Sessoms: *Recreation and Special Populations.* Boston, Holbrook Press, 1973.

Maryhelen Vannier and Hally B. W. Poindexter: *Individual and Team Sports for Girls and Women.* Philadelphia, W. B. Saunders Co., 1968.

Marie Vick and Rosann McLaughlin Cox: *A Collection of Dances for Children.* Minneapolis, Burgess Publishing Co., 1970.

George S. Wells: *Guide to Family Camping.* Harrisburg, Pennsylvania, Stackpole Books, 1973.

Jean Young: *Woodstock Craftsman's Manual.* New York, Praeger, 1972.

Ruth Zechlin: *Complete Book of Handicrafts.* Newton Center, Massachusetts, Branford Press, 1968.

index